D1246940

JESUS AND JOHN WAYNE

ALSO BY KRISTIN KOBES DU MEZ

A New Gospel for Women:
Katharine Bushnell and the Challenge
of Christian Feminism

JESUS AND JOHN WAYNE

How White Evangelicals
Corrupted a Faith and
Fractured a Nation

Kristin Kobes Du Mez

LIVERIGHT PUBLISHING CORPORATION
A DIVISION OF W. W. NORTON & COMPANY
Independent Publishers Since 1923

For information about permission to reproduce selections from this book, write to Permissions, Liveright Publishing Corporation, a division of W. W. Norton & Company, Inc., 500 Fifth Avenue, New York, NY 10110

For information about special discounts for bulk purchases, please contact W. W. Norton Special Sales at specialsales@wwnorton.com or 800-233-4830

Book design by Lovedog Studio
Production manager: Anna Oler

Library of Congress Cataloging-in-Publication Data

Names: Du Mez, Kristin Kobes, author.
Title: Jesus and John Wayne : how white evangelicals corrupted a faith and fractured a nation / Kristin Kobes Du Mez.
Description: First edition. | New York, NY : Liveright Publishing Corporation, a division of W. W. Norton & Company, 2020. | Includes bibliographical references and index.
Identifiers: LCCN 2019059451 | ISBN 9781631495731 (hardcover) | ISBN 9781631495748 (epub)
Subjects: LCSH: United States—Church history—21st century. | Evangelicalism—United States. | Trump, Donald, 1946– | Christianity and culture—United States.
Classification: LCC BR526 .D85 2020 | DDC 277.308/3—dc23
LC record available at https://lccn.loc.gov/2019059451

Liveright Publishing Corporation, 500 Fifth Avenue, New York, N.Y. 10110
www.wwnorton.com

W. W. Norton & Company Ltd., 15 Carlisle Street, London W1D 3BS

This one is for Jack.

CONTENTS

JESUS AND JOHN WAYNE

INTRODUCTION

O N   A   B I T T E R L Y   C O L D   D A Y   I N   J A N U A R Y   2 0 1 6 , Donald Trump stood on the stage of an auditorium at a small Christian college in Iowa. He boasted of his poll numbers and his crowd sizes. He warned of the dangers posed by Muslims and undocumented immigrants, and he talked of building a border wall. He denigrated American politicians as stupid, weak, and pathetic. He claimed that Christianity was "under siege" and urged Christians to band together and assert their power. He promised to lead. He had no doubts about the loyalty of his followers: "I could stand in the middle of Fifth Avenue and shoot somebody and I wouldn't lose any voters," he claimed.[1]

That morning, the Rev. Robert Jeffress, pastor of First Baptist Dallas, introduced Trump. As a pastor Jeffress couldn't endorse a candidate, but he made clear that he wouldn't be there if he didn't think Trump "would make a great president." Jeffress wasn't alone. Already at that point, before the Iowa caucuses at the beginning of February, 42 percent of white evangelicals supported Trump—more than any other candidate. The reason was simple, Jeffress contended. Evangelicals were "sick and tired of the status quo." They were looking for the leader who would "reverse the downward death spiral of this nation that we love so dearly."[2]

I wasn't in Iowa at the time, but I watched this spectacle unfold as it streamed online. I knew the setting well. The college was Dordt

College, my alma mater. The town was Sioux Center, my hometown. I'd grown up a short walk from campus, on the other side of the old farmstead only recently converted back to native prairie. I'd attended the local Christian grade school, where my mom was my PE teacher. My dad, an ordained minister, taught theology at the college since before I was born. Every year as a child I'd attended Easter sunrise services in that auditorium, and as a college student I faithfully attended chapel services in that same space. Standing on the stage where Trump now stood, I had led prayers, performed in Christian "praise teams," and, during choir rehearsal, flirted with the man who would become my husband. We married in a church just down the road. Although I moved away after college, the space remained intimately familiar. But as I watched those in the overflow crowd waving signs, laughing at insults, and shouting back in affirmation, I wondered who these people were. I didn't recognize them.

Not everyone present that day shared in the enthusiasm for Trump. Some were there out of curiosity. Others came in protest. A small group of residents, including students from the college and the Christian grade school, stood bundled against the chill, holding handmade signs proclaiming "Love Your Neighbors" and "Perfect Love Casts Out Fear." But their numbers were dwarfed by Trump's supporters. Their numbers were again dwarfed on November 8, 2016, when 82 percent of Sioux County voters voted for Donald Trump—a proportion remarkably close to the 81 percent of white evangelical voters who backed Trump, according to national exit polls, and proved crucial to his victory over Hillary Clinton.[3]

Trump's confidence in the loyalty of his followers seemed like bluster at the time, but it soon took on a prophetic ring. His evangelical supporters stuck by his side even as he mocked opponents, incited violence at his rallies, and boasted of his "manhood" on national television. Then there were Trump's sexual indiscretions. Divorce was one thing, rumors of sexual escapades another, but the release of the *Access Hollywood* tape furnished irrefutable evidence of the candidate speaking in lewd terms about seducing and assaulting women.

How could "family values" conservatives support a man who flouted every value they insisted they held dear? How could the self-professed "Moral Majority" embrace a candidate who reveled in vulgarity? How could evangelicals who'd turned "WWJD" ("What Would Jesus Do?") into a national phenomenon justify their support for a man who seemed the very antithesis of the savior they claimed to emulate?

Pundits scrambled to explain. Evangelicals were holding their noses, choosing the lesser of two evils—and Hillary Clinton was the greatest evil. Evangelicals were thinking in purely transactional terms, as Trump himself is often said to do, voting for Trump because he promised to deliver Supreme Court appointments that would protect the unborn and secure their own "religious liberty." Or maybe the polls were misleading. By confusing "evangelicals-in-name-only" with good, church-attending, Bible-believing Christians, sloppy pollsters were giving evangelicalism a bad rap.

But evangelical support for Trump was no aberration, nor was it merely a pragmatic choice. It was, rather, the culmination of evangelicals' embrace of militant masculinity, an ideology that enshrines patriarchal authority and condones the callous display of power, at home and abroad. By the time Trump arrived proclaiming himself their savior, conservative white evangelicals had already traded a faith that privileges humility and elevates "the least of these" for one that derides gentleness as the province of wusses. Rather than turning the other cheek, they'd resolved to defend their faith and their nation, secure in the knowledge that the ends justify the means. Having replaced the Jesus of the Gospels with a vengeful warrior Christ, it's no wonder many came to think of Trump in the same way. In 2016, many observers were stunned at evangelicals' apparent betrayal of their own values. In reality, evangelicals did not cast their vote despite their beliefs, but because of them.

Donald Trump did not trigger this militant turn; his rise was symptomatic of a long-standing condition. Survey data reveal the stark contours of the contemporary evangelical worldview. More than any other religious demographic in America, white evangelical Protestants support preemptive war, condone the use of torture, and favor the death penalty. They are more likely than members of other faith groups to own a gun, to believe citizens should be allowed to carry guns in most places, and to feel safer with a firearm around. White evangelicals are more opposed to immigration reform and have more negative views of immigrants than any other religious demographic; two-thirds support Trump's border wall. Sixty-eight percent of white evangelical Protestants—more than any other demographic—do not think that the United States has a responsibility to accept refugees. More than half of white evangelical Protestants think a majority nonwhite US population would be a negative development. White evangelicals are considerably more likely than others to believe that Islam encourages violence, to refuse to see Islam as "part of mainstream American society," and to perceive "natural conflict between Islam and democracy." At the same time, white evangelicals believe that Christians in America face more discrimination than Muslims. White evangelicals are significantly more authoritarian than other religious groups, and they express confidence in their religious leaders at much higher rates than do members of other faiths.[4]

For evangelicals, domestic and foreign policy are two sides of the same coin. Christian nationalism—the belief that America is God's chosen nation and must be defended as such—serves as a powerful predictor of intolerance toward immigrants, racial minorities, and non-Christians. It is linked to opposition to gay rights and gun control, to support for harsher punishments for criminals, to justifications for the use of excessive force against black Americans in law enforcement situations, and to traditionalist gender ideology. White evangelicals have pieced together this patchwork of issues, and a nostalgic commitment to rugged, aggressive, militant white masculinity serves as the thread binding them together into a coherent whole. A father's rule in the home is inextricably linked to heroic leadership on the national stage, and the fate of the nation hinges on both.[5]

By November 2016, the affinities were clear. A substantial number of white evangelicals shared Trump's nationalism, Islamophobia, racism, and nativism. They condoned his "nasty politics": they agreed that injured protestors got what they deserved, that the country would be better off getting rid of "bad apples," and that people were "too sensitive" about what was said in politics. Drawn to his populist appeals, white evangelicals demonstrated a preference for rejecting political compromise, for strong, solitary leadership, and for breaking the rules when necessary. These dispositions held whether white evangelicals were defined by affiliation, self-identification, or belief and behavior.[6]

FOR THEIR PART, evangelicals prefer to define themselves not by their political beliefs but according to their theological convictions or, more precisely, according to four "evangelical distinctives." To be an evangelical, according to the National Association of Evangelicals, is to uphold the Bible as one's ultimate authority, to confess the centrality of Christ's atonement, to believe in a born-again conversion experience, and to actively work to spread this good news and reform society accordingly. When defined in this way, "evangelicalism" manifests as a racially diverse and global movement. Yet when it comes to delineating the contours of modern American evangelicalism, the primacy of these four distinctives is arguable.[7]

Evangelicals claim to uphold the Bible as the highest authority in the Christian life, but there are more than 31,000 verses in the Bible. Which ones are considered essential guides to faithful Christian practice, and which are readily ignored or explained away? In like manner, when evangelicals define themselves in terms of Christ's atonement or as disciples of a risen Christ, what sort of Jesus are they imagining? Is their savior a conquering warrior, a man's man who takes no prisoners and wages holy war? Or is he a sacrificial lamb who offers himself up for the restoration of all things? How one answers these questions will determine what it looks like to follow Jesus.

In truth, what it means to be an evangelical has always depended on the world beyond the faith. In recent years, evangelical leaders themselves have come to recognize (and frequently lament) that a "pop culture" definition has usurped "a proper historical and theological" one, such that today many people count themselves "evangelical" because they watch Fox News, consider themselves religious, and vote Republican. Frustrated with this confusion of "real" and "supposed" evangelicals, evangelical elites have taken pollsters and pundits to task for carelessly conflating the two. But the problem goes beyond sloppy categorization. Among evangelicals, high levels of theological illiteracy mean that many "evangelicals" hold views traditionally defined as heresy, calling into question the centrality of theology to evangelicalism generally. Moreover, many who do subscribe to these distinctives do not in fact identify as evangelical. This is the case especially when it comes to Christians of color: just 25 percent of African Americans who subscribe to all four distinctives identify as evangelical.[8]

This is not a simple misunderstanding. Black Christians have long resisted embracing the evangelical label because it is clear to them that there is more to evangelicalism than straightforward statements of belief. Survey data indicate that on nearly every social and political issue, black Protestants apply their faith in ways that run counter to white evangelicalism. The differences may be rooted not just in experience but in the faith itself; in practice, the seemingly neutral "evangelical distinctives" turn out to be culturally and racially specific. Although white evangelicals like to point to the existence of black "evangelicals" to distance their movement from allegations of racism and associations with conservative politics, black Christians themselves have attempted to draw attention to evangelicalism's "problem of whiteness," and to white evangelicals' inability or unwillingness to confront this problem. In the aftermath of the 2016 election, the chorus of those calling out evangelicalism's problem of whiteness became more difficult to ignore. To many black Christians, evangelicalism had become "a white religious brand."[9]

Although foundational to white evangelical identity, race rarely acts as an independent variable. For conservative white evangelicals, the "good news" of the Christian gospel has become inextricably linked to a staunch commitment to patriarchal authority, gender difference, and Christian nationalism, and all of these are intertwined with white racial identity. Many Americans who now identify as evangelicals are identifying with this operational theology—one that is Republican in its politics and traditionalist in its values. This God-and-country faith is championed by those who regularly attend evangelical churches, and by those who do not. It creates affinities across denominational, regional, and socioeconomic differences, even as it divides Americans— and American Christians—into those who embrace these values, and those who do not. In this way, conservative white evangelicalism has become a polarizing force in American politics and society.

White evangelicalism has such an expansive reach in large part because of the culture it has created, the culture that it sells. Over the past half century or so, evangelicals have produced and consumed a vast quantity of religious products: Christian books and magazines, CCM ("Christian contemporary music"), Christian radio and television, feature films, ministry conferences, blogs, T-shirts, and home decor. Many evangelicals who would be hard pressed to articulate even the most basic tenets of evangelical theology have nonetheless been immersed in this evangelical popular culture. They've raised children with the help of James Dobson's Focus on the Family radio programs or grown up watching *VeggieTales* cartoons. They rocked out to Amy Grant or the Newsboys or DC Talk. They learned about purity before they learned about sex, and they have a silver ring to prove it. They watched *The Passion of the Christ, Soul Surfer*, or the latest Kirk Cameron film with their youth group. They attended Promise Keepers with guys from church and read *Wild at Heart* in small groups. They've learned more from Pat Robertson, John Piper, Joyce Meyer, and The Gospel Coalition than they have from their pastor's Sunday sermons.

The diffusion of evangelical consumer culture extends far beyond the orbit of evangelical churches. Cultural evangelicalism has made deep inroads into mainline Christianity, to the point that distinguishing members of a denomination like the United Methodist Church from evangelicals obscures more than it reveals. (My own upbringing in the Christian Reformed Church, a small denomination founded by

Dutch immigrants, is a case in point; for generations, members defined themselves against American Christianity, but due to the onslaught of evangelical popular culture, large swaths of the denomination are now functionally evangelical in terms of affinity and belief.) Denominational boundaries are easily breached by the flow of religious merchandising. Indeed, one can participate in this religious culture without attending church at all.

Yet this cultural evangelicalism remains intertwined with "establishment evangelicalism." Denominational organizations and parachurch groups, pastors and theologians, colleges and seminaries, publishing houses and charities generate much of the religious content that is marketed to an immense congregation of consumers. Evangelical leaders bestow authority upon one another, blurbing each other's books, defending each other on social media, and determining which up-and-coming writers, pastors, and organizations are worthy of promotion—and which should be shunned. At times, evangelical popular culture can subvert the authority of the evangelical elite. During the Trump campaign, many pastors were surprised to find that they wielded little influence over people in the pews. What they didn't realize was that they were up against a more powerful system of authority—an evangelical popular culture that reflected and reinforced a compelling ideology and a coherent worldview. A few words preached on Sunday morning did little to disrupt the steady diet of religious products evangelicals consumed day in, day out.[10]

Rather than seeking to distinguish "real" from "supposed" evangelicals, then, it is more useful to think in terms of the degree to which individuals participate in this evangelical culture of consumption. There are those who rarely consume media produced outside of this world; when it comes to music, news sources, books, and radio, these individuals inhabit a separate and sanctified consumer space. There are also many who participate to lesser degrees—they may listen to "secular" music, catch the latest Hollywood blockbusters, and read occasional "non-Christian" books, even as they regularly tune in to Christian radio, sing along to "praise music," purchase books on

Christian child-rearing, and devour Christian romance novels. Still, by partaking in a common culture, individuals form bonds with other like-minded consumers, and these affinities form the basis of a shared cultural identity.

At any given time, numerous creeds have coexisted and competed for influence within evangelicalism. Even today, the evangelical tent includes Calvinists and Pentecostals, "social justice warriors" and prosperity gospel gurus. However, over the past several decades conservatives have consolidated their power within the broader movement. Offering certainty in times of social change, promising security in the face of global threats, and, perhaps most critically, affirming the righteousness of a white Christian America and, by extension, of white Christian Americans, conservative evangelicals succeeded in winning the hearts and minds of large numbers of American Christians. They achieved this dominance not only by crafting a compelling ideology but also by advancing their agenda through strategic organizations and political alliances, on occasion by way of ruthless displays of power, and, critically, by dominating the production and distribution of Christian consumer culture.

Like evangelicalism in general, evangelical popular culture encompasses a broad spectrum of religious and political commitments. The same store might stock books by conservative financial advisor Dave Ramsey and social justice activist Jim Wallis, Christian feminist manifestos penned by Rachel Held Evans and Sarah Bessey, and classic defenses of "traditional womanhood" by Elisabeth Elliot. Yet the power of conservative white evangelicalism is apparent in both the size of its market share and its influence over religious distribution channels. As a diffuse movement, evangelicalism lacks clear institutional authority structures, but the evangelical marketplace itself helps define who is inside and who is outside the fold. LifeWay Christian Stores, once the nation's largest Christian retail chain and an affiliate of the Southern Baptist Convention, has wielded that power overtly. When Rachel Held Evans and Jen Hatmaker ran afoul of conservative orthodoxies related to sexuality and gender, LifeWay stopped carrying their books. It did, however, stock Todd Starnes's *The Deplorables' Guide to Making America Great Again* ("Winning was just the beginning… change may start at the White House, but it finishes at *your* house") and R. C. Sproul and Abdul Saleeb's *The Dark Side of Islam.*

The products Christians consume shape the faith they inhabit. Today, what it means to be a "conservative evangelical" is as much about culture as it is about theology. This is readily apparent in the heroes they celebrate. Establishment evangelicals might count Jonathan Edwards and George Whitefield among their eminent forebearers, but evangelical popular culture is teeming with a different ensemble of heroes—men like William Wallace (as brought to life by Mel Gibson), Teddy Roosevelt, the mythic American cowboy, Generals Douglas MacArthur and George S. Patton, and the ordinary American soldier. And the actor John Wayne.

As the onscreen embodiment of the heroic cowboy and idealized American soldier, and also as an outspoken conservative activist in real life, John Wayne became an icon of rugged American manhood for generations of conservatives. Pat Buchanan parroted Wayne in his presidential bid. Newt Gingrich called Wayne's *Sands of Iwo Jima* "the formative movie of my life," and Oliver North echoed slogans from that film in his 1994 Senate campaign. In time, Wayne would also emerge as an icon of Christian masculinity. Evangelicals admired (and still admire) him for his toughness and his swagger; he protected the weak, and he wouldn't let anything get in the way of his pursuit of justice and order. Wayne was not an evangelical Christian, despite rumors to this effect regularly circulated by evangelicals themselves. He did not live a moral life by the standards of traditional Christian virtue. Yet for many evangelicals, Wayne would come to symbolize a different set of virtues—a nostalgic yearning for a mythical "Christian America," a return to "traditional" gender roles, and the reassertion of (white) patriarchal authority.[11]

Although Wayne occupies a prominent place in the pantheon of evangelical heroes, he is but one of many rugged and even ruthless

icons of masculinity that evangelicals imbued with religious significance. Like Wayne, the heroes who best embodied militant Christian masculinity were those unencumbered by traditional Christian
virtues. In this way, militant masculinity linked religious and secular conservatism, helping to secure an alliance with profound political ramifications. For many evangelicals, these militant heroes would
come to define not only Christian manhood but Christianity itself.

CONVENTIONAL WISDOM tells us that fundamentalists and
evangelicals retreated from public view and political engagement after
the Scopes Monkey Trial in 1925, or with the end of Prohibition in
1933, or out of a desire to focus on individual soul-saving, or due to
various combinations of the above, only to reappear on the national
stage in the 1970s, seemingly out of nowhere. But as we will see, the
roots of a militarized and politicized evangelical masculinity stretch
back to earlier in American history.

Antecedents can be found in nineteenth-century southern evangelicalism and in early-twentieth-century "muscular Christianity," but it
was in the 1940s and 1950s that a potent mix of patriarchal "gender
traditionalism," militarism, and Christian nationalism coalesced to
form the basis of a revitalized evangelical identity. With Billy Graham
at the vanguard, evangelicals believed that they had a special role to
play in keeping America Christian, American families strong, and the
nation secure. The assertion of masculine power would accomplish all
these goals.

By the 1960s, the civil rights movement, feminism, and the Vietnam
War led many Americans to question "traditional" values of all kinds.
Gender and sexual norms were in flux, America no longer appeared
to be a source of unalloyed good, and God did not in fact appear to
be on her side. Evangelicals, however, clung fiercely to the belief that
America was a Christian nation, that the military was a force for good,
and that the strength of the nation depended on a properly ordered,

patriarchal home. The evangelical political resurgence of the 1970s coalesced around a potent mix of "family values" politics, but family values were always intertwined with ideas about sex, power, race, and nation. Feminism posed a threat to traditional womanhood, and also to national security by removing from men their duty to provide and protect and opening the door to women in military combat. In similar fashion, Vietnam was not just a national security issue, but also a crisis of masculinity. Civil rights, too, dismantled time-honored traditions and destabilized the social order. Representing federal government overreach or even an insidious communist agenda, desegregation also heightened the long-standing imagined threat to white womanhood, and to the power of white men to police social and sexual boundaries. The reassertion of white patriarchy was central to the new "family values" politics, and by the end of the 1970s, the defense of patriarchal power had emerged as an evangelical distinctive.

The evangelical consumer marketplace was by then a force to be reckoned with, but this expansive media network functioned less as a traditional soul-saving enterprise and more as a means by which evangelicals created and maintained their own identity—an identity rooted in "family values" and infused with a sense of cultural embattlement. Christian publishing, radio, and television taught evangelicals how to raise children, how to have sex, and whom to fear. And Christian media promoted a distinctive vision of evangelical masculinity. Finding comfort and courage in symbols of a mythical past, evangelicals looked to a rugged, heroic masculinity embodied by cowboys, soldiers, and warriors to point the way forward. For decades to come, militant masculinity (and a sweet, submissive femininity) would remain entrenched in the evangelical imagination, shaping conceptions of what was good and true. By the 1980s, evangelicals were able to mobilize so effectively as a partisan political force because they already participated in a shared cultural identity.[12]

A militant evangelical masculinity went hand in hand with a culture of fear, but it wasn't always apparent which came first. During the Cold War, the communist menace seemed to require a militant response.

But when that threat had been vanquished, conservative evangelicals promptly declared a new war—a culture war—demanding a similar militancy. In 2001, when terrorists struck the United States, evangelicals again had an actual battle to fight. Yet even then, evangelical militancy was fueled by fraudulent tales of the Islamic threat, tales that were promoted by evangelicals themselves. Evangelical militancy cannot be seen simply as a response to fearful times; for conservative white evangelicals, a militant faith required an ever-present sense of threat.

In 2008, the election of Barack Obama ratcheted up evangelical fears. Initially, the culture wars appeared to be lost and the power of the Christian Right seemed to have reached an ignoble end. But conservative evangelicals had always thrived on a sense of embattlement, real or imagined, and this time would be no different. Donald Trump appeared at a moment when evangelicals felt increasingly beleaguered, even persecuted. From the Affordable Care Act's contraceptive mandate to transgender bathroom laws and the cultural sea change on gay marriage, gender was at the heart of this perceived vulnerability. On the foreign policy front, the threat of terrorism loomed large, American power wasn't what it used to be, and nearly two-thirds of white evangelicals harbored fears that a once-powerful nation had become "too soft and feminine."[13]

Evangelical fears were real. Yet these fears were not simply a natural response to changing times. For decades, evangelical leaders had worked to stoke them. Their own power depended on it. Men like James Dobson, Bill Gothard, Jerry Falwell, Tim LaHaye, Mark Driscoll, Franklin Graham, and countless lesser lights invoked a sense of peril in order to offer fearful followers their own brand of truth and protection. Generations of evangelicals learned to be afraid of communists, feminists, liberals, secular humanists, "the homosexuals," the United Nations, the government, Muslims, and immigrants—and they were primed to respond to those fears by looking to a strong man to rescue them from danger, a man who embodied a God-given, testosterone-driven masculinity. As Robert Jeffress so eloquently expressed in the months before the 2016 election, "I want the meanest, toughest, son-of-a-you-know-what I can find in that role, and I think that's where many evangelicals are."[14]

ACROSS TWO MILLENNIA of Christian history—and within the history of evangelicalism itself—there is ample precedent for sexism, racism, xenophobia, violence, and imperial designs. But there are also expressions of the Christian faith—and of evangelical Christianity— that have disrupted the status quo and challenged systems of privilege and power. The Christian Scriptures contain stories of a violent warrior God, and of a savior who summons followers to care for the "least of these." The Bible ends in a bloody battle, but it also entreats believers to act with love and peace, kindness, gentleness, and self-control. Contemporary white evangelicalism in America, then, is not the inevitable outworking of "biblical literalism," nor is it the only possible interpretation of the historic Christian faith; the history of American Christianity itself is filled with voices of resistance and signs of paths not taken. It is, rather, a historical and a cultural movement, forged over time by individuals and organizations with varied motivations—the desire to discern God's will, to bring order to uncertain times, and, for many, to extend their own power. The story that follows is one of world wars and presidential politics, of entrepreneurial preachers and theological innovation, of blockbuster movies, sex manuals, and self-help books. It does not begin with Donald Trump. Nor will it end with him.

Chapter 1

SADDLING
UP

THE PATH THAT ENDS WITH JOHN WAYNE AS AN icon of Christian masculinity is strewn with a colorful cast of characters, from the original cowboy president to a baseball-player-turned-preacher to a singing cowboy and a dashing young evangelist.

By the early twentieth century, Christians recognized that they had a masculinity problem. Unable to shake the sense that Christianity had a less than masculine feel, many blamed the faith itself, or at least the "feminization" of Victorian Christianity, which privileged gentility, restraint, and an emotive response to the gospel message. But American masculinity, too, had recently undergone dramatic changes, contributing to this sense of unease. Throughout much of the nineteenth century, when most men made a living by farming or otherwise working with their hands, or by owning small businesses, masculinity seemed more of a given. During this time, Christian manhood entailed hard work and thrift, and also the ability to exhibit a proper gentlemanly restraint. Self-denial, after all, was a useful virtue for entrepreneurial businessmen and industrious workers. But by the 1890s, this model of manly restraint had begun to falter.

A new corporate, consumer economy meant that more men were earning a living by punching the clock, and self-discipline no longer promised the same payoff. As men moved to cities, the work they did changed significantly. For men whose strength had become superfluous, who no longer identified as producers, their very manhood seemed in question. There were other disruptions, too. Immigrants from southern and eastern Europe began arriving at the nation's shores, and "new women" started going to college, entering the professions, riding bicycles, wearing bloomers, and having fewer babies. In response to all of these changes, old ideas of manhood seemed insufficient. In their place, white native-born Protestant men began to assert a new kind of masculinity—a rougher, tougher masculinity. Nothing less than the fate of the nation, even the future of white Christian "civilization" appeared to be at stake.[1]

No one advanced this new American masculinity with more gusto than Theodore Roosevelt. As a young man, Roosevelt had been ridiculed for his "high voice, tight pants, and fancy clothing" and derided as a "weakling" and "Punkin-Lily." But Roosevelt wanted power. Determined to reinvent himself, he went west, rechristening himself the "Cowboy of the Dakotas." It was on the frontier that a new masculinity would be forged, a place where (white) men brought order to savagery, where men served as armed protectors and providers, where violence achieved a greater good. If the Wild West could mold "the exquisite Mr. Roosevelt" into a rugged masculine specimen, perhaps it could do the same for American manhood generally, so the thinking went. But there was a flaw in this plan. Even as Roosevelt was honing his masculinity on the western frontier, the mythical West was fading away. Rugged American manhood would need to be forged elsewhere—on the new frontiers of empire. This shift to a global stage was perfectly encapsulated in Roosevelt's "Rough Riders," a volunteer cavalry who fought in the Spanish-American War—a war that Roosevelt himself helped bring about. In this way, the new American imperialism was framed as a conservative effort to restore American manhood.[2]

When Roosevelt became president in 1901, the embodiment of heroic American manhood became the undisputed leader of the American nation. By fashioning a violent, fantasized masculinity, and then injecting that sensibility into national politics, Roosevelt offered ordinary men the sense that they were participating in a larger cause.

Roosevelt's hypermasculinity appealed to men anxious about their own status, and the nation's. For many, these anxieties would become inseparable.[3]

FOR AMERICAN CHRISTIANS, the challenge was to reconcile this aggressive new masculinity with traditional Christian virtue. With its emphasis on gentility and restraint, Victorian Christianity suddenly seemed insufficiently masculine. Virile, aggressive men could hardly be expected to submit themselves to such an emasculating faith, and so in the 1910s, Christian men set out to "re-masculinize" American Christianity. Seeking to offset the "womanly virtues" that had come to dominate the faith, they insisted that Christianity was also "essentially masculine, militant, warlike." It was time for men to take back the church. There was precedent for such tinkering with Christian virtue. In the American South, white masculinity had long championed a sense of mastery over dependents—over women, children, and slaves. Southern men kept vigilant watch over these dependents and, by extension, over the larger social order. Initially, this southern culture of mastery and honor seemed to conflict with the egalitarian impulses of evangelical Christianity. (In Christ there was neither slave nor free, male nor female, according to the apostle Paul.) But southern evangelicals found a way to define Christian manhood in a manner that sanctified aggression; to maintain order and fulfill their role as protectors, there were times when Christian men must resort to violence. In the early twentieth century, then, a rugged American masculinity united northern and southern white men and transformed American Christianity.[4]

Former professional baseball player Billy Sunday preached this new "muscular Christianity" with unrivaled zeal. Wanting nothing to do with a sissy, lily-livered piety, Sunday preferred to pack his "old muzzle-loading Gospel gun with ipecac, buttermilk, rough on rats, rock salt, and whatever else came in handy," and let it fly. In the spring of 1917, with America's entry into the First World War, Sunday's militancy went beyond metaphor. He had no time for pacifists or draft dodgers ("God-forsaken mutts"), or apparently for nuance of any kind: "In these days all are patriots or traitors, to your country and the cause of Jesus Christ." An evangelist for war, Sunday was known to leap atop his pulpit waving the American flag.[5]

The Great War brought to a head mounting tensions within American Protestantism. On the one hand, a respectable, church-centered Protestantism had long located religious authority in the institutional church and ordained clergy. From time to time, however, evangelical revival movements would sweep across the nation. These revivals could disrupt the status quo and at times upend social hierarchies, before traditional denominational authority would once again reassert itself. But in the years after the Civil War, a new and enduring manifestation of evangelical revivalism took hold, one perfectly suited to the emerging consumer culture.

Borrowing from modern advertising techniques, evangelical innovators crafted a generic, nonsectarian faith that privileged individuals' "plain reading of the Bible" and championed a commitment to the pure, unadulterated "fundamentals" of the faith. Branding this innovative approach "old-time religion," they then marketed this faith directly to consumers. Through religious merchandising and with the help of celebrity pitchmen like Sunday himself, they effectively replaced traditional denominational authorities with the authority of the market and the power of consumer choice. "Fundamentalists" who embraced this market-driven revivalism included rabble-rousing populists and "respectable," middle-class professionals, and tensions and infighting between and among these factions would characterize the movement for the next century. It was only through the identification of common enemies that fundamentalists were able to fashion a powerful (if unstable) identity.[6]

Fortunately for them, enemies weren't hard to find. Religious "modernists," too, had wanted to make their faith relevant to the changing times, but they rejected fundamentalists' "plain reading" of the Bible. Accusing fundamentalists of substituting "propagandism" for a proper scholarly study of the Bible, they preferred to look to higher critical scholarship to parse the intricacies of the Scriptures. These liberal Protestants also tended to emphasize the social and environmental dimensions of Christianity, over against fundamentalists' more individualistic focus on personal sin and conversion. Fundamentalists, in turn, accused modernists of abandoning the historic Christian faith.[7]

Modernists and fundamentalists did, however, agree on the need to masculinize the faith. Liberal Protestants insisted that their own social activism exemplified a manly exercise of Christianity. Fundamentalists, meanwhile, asserted that a staunch defense of doctrine evinced masculine courage and conviction, and they derided liberal theology as an effeminate squandering of the virility of true Christianity.

During the First World War, these competing visions of muscular Christianity were caught up in a frenzied militarism. Liberal Protestants embraced the conflict as a war to end all wars, a means of extending democracy and Christianity across the globe. Among fundamentalists, the response was more complicated than Sunday's flag waving might suggest. For some, an unwillingness to characterize America as a "Christian nation" restrained their enthusiasm for the war. A Christian nation, according to editors at *The King's Business*, a monthly publication of the Bible Institute of Los Angeles, would be one that "has accepted Christ as its Saviour and as its Lord" in all aspects of governance—in politics, commerce, and international relations. But "such a nation does not exist on earth, and never has existed, and never will exist until our Lord comes again." For this reason, patriotism was no virtue; a Christian's loyalty belonged to God's kingdom, not to the nation. In a move that seems almost incomprehensible today, liberal Protestants pounced on this ambivalence, denouncing conservatives' "un-American" faith and labeling their lack of patriotism a threat to national security. Fundamentalists responded by pointing to the origins of liberals' higher-critical theology in German intellectual circles, and by shoring up their own patriotism.[8]

When the war came to a close, no amount of patriotism could obscure the fact that it had been fought at great cost, and with little apparent gain. Roosevelt's model of masculinity had been found wanting; the war, it seemed, had presented Americans with the horror of "having myths about blood and fire and mutilation and blindness come true." For liberal Protestant internationalists, the disillusionment was especially keen. Sherwood Eddy, a leading liberal Protestant proponent of the war, expressed dismay at his prowar activism: "I believed that it was a war to end war, to protect womanhood, to destroy militarism and autocracy and to make a new world 'fit for heroes to live in,'" he confessed. The carnage and horrors of warfare put an end to all that.[9]

In the wake of this disillusionment, the more militant model of Christian masculinity lost much of its luster. In its place, the ideal of the Christian businessman resurfaced as a prototype of Christian manhood. Bruce Barton's *The Man Nobody Knows* (1925) exemplified this shift. Barton, an advertising executive, depicted Jesus as "the world's greatest business executive," yet Barton's Jesus was no pushover. Not to be confused with the "pale young man with flabby forearms and a sad expression" depicted on Sunday school walls across the nation—the "physical weakling," the "sissified," "meek and lowly" man of sorrows—Barton's Jesus was a "winner," a strong, "magnetic" man, the kind who could "inspire great enthusiasm and build great organizations." Strength remained vital, but aggression and violence gave way to efficiency and magnetism.[10]

Yet many fundamentalists retained more than vestiges of the former militancy. As premillennialists, fundamentalists were less troubled by the horrors of war. They knew better than to expect a war to end all wars before Christ's return, and their penchant for apocalyptic prophecies gave them a framework for understanding the war's outcome without succumbing to disillusionment and despair. In fact, having shed much of their ambivalence, fundamentalists emerged from the war more patriotic, combative, and cantankerous than ever. And more convinced of their need to defend fundamental truths. Having attributed German wartime barbarism to the influence of liberal theology and evolutionary theory, they determined to secure American Christianity

and culture against those same hazards. On a more practical level, as
fundamentalists proved unable to seize or maintain control of major
denominations and seminaries in the postwar years, combativeness
seemed wholly appropriate—even a badge of honor.[11]

By asserting this militant masculinity in the postwar era, however, fundamentalists found themselves increasingly out of step with
mainstream American Christianity, and with American culture more
broadly. Authors like Sinclair Lewis and H. L. Mencken made a sport
of ridiculing the retrograde muscular Christianity of fundamentalists
as further evidence that they were hopeless relics of a time gone by.
Such cultural disdain only served to enhance fundamentalists' perception of themselves as an embattled, faithful remnant. Having failed in
their bid to gain control of existing denominational structures, fundamentalists struck off on their own, creating a vibrant array of Bible
schools, churches, mission organizations, publishing houses, and other
religious associations. But they chafed at their marginal status, and
by the 1940s they decided it was time to reengage on a national scale.
Rather than blundering about in isolated "squads or platoons," they
resolved to unite as "a mighty army."[12]

To launch the offensive, a group of fundamentalist leaders came
together in 1942 to form the National Association of Evangelicals
(NAE). Their choice of the word "evangelical" was strategic. Aware of
their image problem, fundamentalists knew they needed to rebrand
their movement. The fact that some of the more militant fundamentalists had started their own organization (the American Council
of Christian Churches, under the leadership of fundamentalist Carl
McIntire) helped with this project, enabling the NAE to distance
itself from more reactionary elements, and it was at this time that
"evangelical" came to connote a more forward-looking alternative to
the militant, separatist fundamentalism that had become an object of
ridicule. But evangelicals never entirely abandoned a combative posture, and even as evangelicals worked to bring a new respectability to
their "old-time religion," fundamentalists fought to define the contours

of that faith. The affinities ran deep, and it was not always possible to distinguish one from the other; eventually, fundamentalists would inject their militancy back into the broader evangelical movement.

In his opening address of the first meeting of the NAE in 1942, the Reverend Harold John Ockenga warned his fellow "lone wolves" of the ominous clouds looming on the horizon that "spell[ed] annihilation" unless they decided to "run in a pack." For decades, evangelicalism had "suffered nothing but a series of defeats," but the time had come to usher in "a new era in evangelical Christianity." As "children of the light," they could learn a thing or two from "the children of this world," from the Soviets and the Nazis. In matters of both church and state, defensive tactics had proven disastrous. Evangelicals must unite and take the offensive, before it was too late.[13]

Just how small was this remnant? When delegates came together the following year, news reports estimated that the NAE represented about two million members, based on denominational affiliation—a fraction of the 60 to 70 million Christians who were represented by the more liberal Federal Council of Churches. But the evangelical movement was never limited by denominational affiliation, and its influence was on the rise.[14]

The path forward was clear, and it would not be through denominational structures. To evangelize the nation, evangelicals needed magazines that could reach millions, and access to the airwaves for national radio broadcasts. They needed organizations for missions, and for evangelical colleges and Bible schools. They already possessed the resources and the brain power. What was missing was a network that would support and amplify these individual efforts.[15]

WHEN IT CAME TO evangelicals' rebranding efforts, it was a handsome young North Carolina minister who would play the starring role. More than anything else, Billy Graham's celebrity knit together the disconnected universe of American evangelicalism—so much so that historian George Marsden once quipped that the simplest definition of "evangelical" might well be "anyone who likes Billy Graham." A one-time Fuller Brush salesman, Graham became the face of the new evangelicalism—and that face was an attractive, masculine one, a fact that rarely went unnoticed. According to his biographer, "for the better part of sixty years, virtually every newspaper article about Graham commented on his appearance." Standing six feet two inches tall, he was the "All-American Male" with "Scottish genes and Nordic looks," a "craggy face, blue eyes, square jaw."[16]

Not leaving anything to chance, Graham took pains to bolster his masculine credentials. He jogged, lifted weights, and otherwise kept up a rigorous exercise regime; in preparation for his crusades, he trained "like a prizefighter." Before his conversion, Graham had "always thought of religion as being more or less 'sissy,'" something well suited for "old people and girls, but not for a real 'he man' with red blood in his veins." In his own conversion narrative, then, he drew on both athletic and military metaphors to make perfectly clear that his faith did not conflict with his masculinity. Jesus was no sissy—he was a "star athlete" who could "become your life's hero." The Christian life was "total war," and Jesus was "Our Great Commander." Graham's Jesus was "a man, every inch a man," the most physically powerful man who had ever lived.[17] In the interest of saving souls, and for the success of his own career, it was incumbent upon Graham to prove that Christianity was wholly compatible with red-blooded masculinity. The Second World War provided an ideal context in which to make this case.

Among fundamentalists and evangelicals, any lingering ambivalence toward war was swept away by the attack on Pearl Harbor. The new war was an indisputable battle between good and evil, and this time around they would give no reason to be tarred as unpatriotic. Among Americans more generally, the war rehabilitated a more militant—and militaristic—model of masculinity, and fundamentalists and newly branded evangelicals, many of whom had never entirely abandoned the older muscular Christianity, joined the fray.

Billy Graham speaking at a Youth for Christ rally in Grand
Rapids, Michigan, in September 1947. COURTESY OF THE BILLY
GRAHAM CENTER ARCHIVES, WHEATON COLLEGE, WHEATON, ILLINOIS.

Tellingly, when it came to the tactics of total war employed by the US
military, it was liberal Protestants—many still chastened by the First
World War—who expressed reservations. Ockenga, on the other hand,
defended the firebombing of German cities in the pages of the *New
York Times*. Evangelicals relished this role reversal, and their newfound
patriotism and militarism would help them overcome their reputation
as extremists and their marginal status.[18]

Even as they supported the war against totalitarianism, many evangelicals nonetheless harbored doubts about the US military. Through
the 1940s and into the 1950s, most evangelicals saw the military as
a place of moral corruption for young men. Contrary to later myths
about "the good war" and "the greatest generation," the military was
known as an institution where drunkenness, vulgarity, gambling, and

sexual disease abounded. (In 1945, when President Truman proposed universal military training for males over the age of eighteen, evangelical churches resisted, concerned about what would happen to men "removed from home and church influences" and "subjected to the temptations for which military training camps are notorious.")[19]

No font of virtue, the military became for evangelicals a mission field, ripe for harvest. Through organizations like the Navigators, the Officers' Christian Fellowship, the Overseas Christian Servicemen's Centers, and the Christian Military Fellowship, evangelicals stepped up to address the moral shortcomings of the nation's soldiers. The military, which had its own reasons to be concerned about the discipline and moral vitality of its forces, welcomed the work of evangelical organizations. It was the beginning of a long and mutually beneficial relationship.[20]

Graham cut his teeth as a revivalist during the Second World War. As the first paid evangelist for Youth for Christ, he worked both to evangelize the nation's youth and to craft heroic Christian citizens who could promote Christianity and democracy at home and abroad. YFC rallies featured patriotic hymns, color guards, and veterans' testimonies, and Graham preached a gospel of heroic Christian nationalism with unparalleled passion. By the end of the war, he had emerged as one of evangelicalism's rising stars.[21]

IN THE FALL OF 1949, however, Graham's future was uncertain. Harboring doubts about the authority of the Bible, he began to question whether God might be calling him to a different path. It was on a particularly dark night of the soul that Graham, open Bible before him, resolved to set his intellectual difficulties aside and surrender completely to the authority of God's Word. He later recalled waking up with a renewed sense of purpose as he prepared for his upcoming visit to Los Angeles, refreshed with a vision that "something unusual was going to happen" there. What happened next did seem nothing short of miraculous. Two factors contributed to the unprecedented success of Graham's LA crusade: the looming threat of nuclear annihilation and the conversion of a celebrity cowboy. The Lord worked in mysterious ways.[22]

Two days before the opening of Graham's revival, President Truman announced that Russia had successfully tested an atomic bomb. Imminent destruction suddenly seemed a very real possibility, which suited the revivalist's message just fine. With an urgent call for repentance, Graham brought the residents of Los Angeles to their knees: "Communism is a religion that is inspired, directed and motivated by the Devil himself who had declared war against Almighty God," he inveighed. In this war it was clear that America was on God's side, but it was time that Americans started acting like it. Their city was third on the list of Soviet targets, he warned, not because of its strategic significance but because of its reputation as a "city of wickedness and sin"—a city plagued by crime, drinking, rampant sexual immorality, and the dissolution of marriages. As an evangelist to America's youth, Graham hadn't shied away from addressing the younger generation's lax sexual morality, but in Cold War America the stakes suddenly seemed higher. With greatness thrust upon the nation, it was imperative that the nation's citizens also pursue goodness. A strong nation was a virtuous one; sexual morality was an issue of national significance.[23]

For Graham, the stability of the home was key to both morality and security: "A nation is only as strong as her homes." In the evangelical worldview, Satan and the communists were united in an effort to destroy the American home. And for Graham, a properly ordered family was a patriarchal one. Because Graham believed that God had cursed women to be under man's rule, he believed that wives must submit to husbands' authority. Graham acknowledged that this would come as a shock to certain "dictatorial wives," and he didn't hesitate to offer Christian housewives helpful tips: When a husband comes home from work, run out and kiss him. "Give him love at any cost. Cultivate modesty and the delicacy of youth. Be attractive." Keep a clean house and don't "nag and complain all the time." He had advice for men, too. A man was "God's representative"—the spiritual head of household, "the protector" and "provider of the home." Also, husbands should remember to give wives a box of candy from time to time, or an orchid. Or maybe roses.[24]

Not all evangelicals in Graham's day embraced such patriarchal teachings. Some believed Christ's atonement had nullified any "curse" placed on Eve in the Book of Genesis, opening the way to egalitarian gender roles; in the late nineteenth and early twentieth centuries, evangelicals in this tradition had been enthusiastic proponents of women's rights. Graham's patriarchal interpretation reflected the more reactionary tendencies of early-twentieth-century fundamentalism. He added a new twist, however, by wedding patriarchal gender roles to a rising Christian nationalism.

In the late 1940s, there was nothing altogether unique about Graham's instructions to husbands and wives. Many other Americans, too, celebrated "traditional" gender roles in Cold War America. The communist threat positioned women and men in distinct ways; men were to provide for their families and defend the nation, while women were deemed vulnerable and in need of protection. In this way, Cold War masculinity was intimately connected to militarism, to the point that they could seem inseparable. In the fall of 1949, then, Graham's message resonated within and beyond the evangelical fold. But it wasn't until the conversion of one of the city's most famous latter-day cowboys that Graham's revival would take hold in a way that would set the evangelist on course to become one of the most influential figures in the twentieth century.[25]

When Graham arrived in LA, the little-known thirty-three-year-old revivalist caught the eye of Stuart Hamblen, the hard-drinking "cowboy singer." One of Hamblen's biggest hits, "(I Won't Go Huntin', Jake) But I'll Go Chasin' Women," had released that year. The prodigal son of a Methodist minister, Hamblen was also a champion rodeo rider who dabbled in Westerns, often playing the heavy. Hamblen bonded with Graham over their shared southern upbringing and agreed to promote Graham's revival on his country music radio show.

After showing up at Graham's services, the celebrity cowboy got religion. Hamblen's conversion sparked a string of celebrity conversions, electrifying the city. As word spread, the national media keyed in on what was happening and in turn helped "puff Graham," giving his ministry celebrity coverage.[26]

That a celebrity cowboy in the heart of LA would help propel postwar evangelicalism as a religious and cultural movement is not as odd as it may sound. During the middle decades of the twentieth century, millions of southern evangelicals migrated to southern California and other Sunbelt locations. Lured by plentiful work in the burgeoning Cold War defense industry, they brought with them their distinctive faith—one shaped by a combative posture and an absolute certainty in the "inerrant" truths of the Bible, but also marked by an eagerness to experiment with new ways of communicating their uncompromising beliefs. All this unfolded in the shadow of Hollywood, the heartland of American celebrity culture and the crucible of American mythmaking.[27]

The myth of the American cowboy resonated powerfully with Sunbelt evangelicals. A model of rugged individualism that dovetailed with the individualism inherent within evangelicalism itself, the cowboy embodied a quintessentially American notion of frontier freedom coupled with an aura of righteous authority. Signifying an earlier era of American manhood, a time when heroic (white) men enforced order, protected the vulnerable, and wielded their power without apology, the myth of the American cowboy had been tinged with nostalgia from its inception. Half a century later, this nostalgia would be channeled into a powerful new religious and cultural identity, an identity harnessed for political ends.

As a born-again Christian, Hamblen put aside his drinking, smoking, and gambling, but not his career as a country-western singer. At the prompting of his friend and fellow celebrity cowboy John Wayne, he wrote a song about his conversion, "It Is No Secret (What God Can Do)," and he featured a mix of religious and country songs on his radio show, *The Cowboy Church of the Air*. Hamblen's religious songs focused on the darker side of the Christian story, especially God's wrath; the rugged, even reckless masculinity of his country-western ballads went hand in hand with his born-again Christianity. Blurring the line between sacred and secular, Hamblen was in many ways a harbinger of a new era of American evangelicalism.[28]

Hamblen wasn't alone in bridging the religious and mainstream entertainment industry. During the postwar years southern California became home to a vibrant local music scene where Southern Baptists and Pentecostals set aside denominational distinctions to sing along to the latest hits. Pat Boone was perhaps their greatest crossover celebrity; with roots in the Church of Christ and a lineage that could be traced back to Daniel Boone, he became one of pop music's all-time greats. Second only to Elvis Presley in his day, Pat Boone was the pride and joy of postwar evangelicals.[29]

Boone wasn't a revivalist, but he fit well with postwar evangelicals' efforts to expand their reach through modern media. In accord with Ockenga's plan—and with Graham as their lodestar—evangelicals began to fashion a vibrant media empire, along with a national network of institutions and parachurch organizations that flourished outside of denominational structures. Graham himself published two dozen books, and in 1956 he helped found *Christianity Today*, the flagship magazine of American evangelicalism. Nearly 700 stations carried his radio program across the nation and around the world. He helped evangelists Robert Schuller and James Robison get their start, and he lent his support to other evangelical organizations and institutions, including Wheaton College, Fuller Seminary, the National Religious Broadcasters, the NAE, Campus Crusade for Christ, Young Life, and Fellowship of Christian Athletes. All this was only a fraction of an emerging evangelical infrastructure that would come to support a vibrant religious consumer culture. Assisted by an expanding postwar economy, entrepreneurial evangelicals would bring Ockenga's vision to fruition.[30]

Evangelical books began to roll off the presses, ready to be distributed across the country through the newly organized Christian Booksellers Association (CBA). Earlier in the century, religious publishing houses had marketed their wares primarily to church leaders, a practice shaped largely by problems of distribution. For much of American history, bookstores were only profitable in larger urban centers; to reach other consumers, publishers worked through denominational distribution systems or resorted to door-to-door sales or mail order. All of this changed with the establishment of the CBA. In a booming economy buoyed by readily available credit, a loan and a CBA catalog were all that was needed to start a Christian bookstore. In 1950, when the CBA first organized, there were about 270 affiliated stores; by the mid-1960s there were 725, and by the end of the 1970s there were around 3000 scattered in small towns and cities across the country.[31]

The CBA solved the distribution problem, but it also changed the market—and the publishing industry feeding that market. With a broader Christian market replacing denominational distribution channels, authors and publishers needed to tone down theological distinctives and instead offer books pitched to a broadly evangelical readership. Books on "Christian living" achieved this goal without offending denominational sensibilities. Together with Christian music, radio, and television, the Christian publishing industry helped create an identity based around a more generic evangelical ethos. It was in this milieu that evangelical celebrities—singers, actors, and authors, popular pastors and revivalists—would play an outsized role in both reflecting and shaping the cultural values evangelicals would come to hold dear.[32]

IT'S NO SURPRISE that men like Graham, Hamblen, and Boone gained celebrity status within this burgeoning evangelical culture. What's more curious is the fact that John Wayne would, too. Unlike Hamblen, Wayne didn't have a born-again experience. Unlike Boone, Wayne could hardly be called the poster boy of "family values." Thrice married, twice divorced, Wayne also carried on several high-profile affairs. He was a chain-smoker and a hard drinker. Yet despite his

John Wayne and Joanne Dru on the set of *Red River*, circa 1948, in Los Angeles, California. GETTY IMAGES / MICHAEL OCHS ARCHIVES.

rough edges, Wayne would capture the hearts and imaginations of American evangelicals. The affinity was based not on theology, but rather on a shared masculine ideal.[33]

Wayne became one of Hollywood's biggest stars by embodying—defining, really—the heroic cowboy-soldier that captivated audiences in the early Cold War era. Wayne's breakout moment came in 1948, just as Cold War tensions eclipsed any sense of postwar peace. That year he starred in two Westerns: *Red River*, in which he played the role of a cattle rancher whose love interest was slaughtered by Indians, and *Fort Apache*, in which he played a Civil War captain who went on to subdue the Apache on the Western frontier. Reminiscent of the days of Theodore Roosevelt, Cold War Americans once again found themselves trading isolationism for a new imperialism—this time expanding the free market at home and abroad. Combining resurgent nationalism with moral exceptionalism, Americans divided the world into good guys and bad guys, and the Western offered a morality tale

Original film poster,
Sands of Iwo Jima,
1949. GETTY IMAGES /
LMPC.

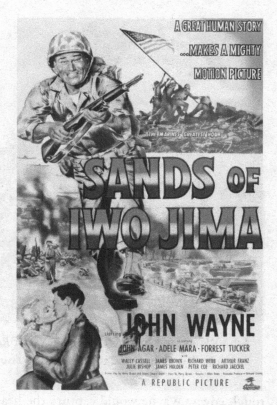

perfectly suited to the moment, one in which the rugged hero resorted to violence to save the day.[34]

The next year Wayne starred as Sergeant Stryker in *Sands of Iwo Jima*, a role modeled after the character he'd played in *Red River*. In this way, Wayne's Sergeant Stryker—and Wayne himself—combined the mythology of the American cowboy with that of the freedom-fighting soldier. Wayne never actually served in the military. When the Second World War broke out, he'd been reluctant to put his budding film career on hold to enlist. (As a minor film star he did undertake an OSS-sponsored "inspection tour" of the Pacific, but his contributions to the war effort were minimal.) Yet Wayne's Sergeant Stryker stood as a symbol of American toughness, and phrases Wayne uttered onscreen—"Saddle up!" and "Lock and load!"—entered the lexicon of American conservatism. In time, too, Wayne's embodiment of heroic masculinity would come to serve as the touchstone for authentic Christian manhood.[35]

Chapter 2

JOHN WAYNE WILL SAVE YOUR ASS

B ILLY GRAHAM WAS A LIFELONG REGISTERED
Democrat. This may come as a surprise, given the close alliance
between white evangelicals and the Republican Party that has come
to define the American political landscape in recent decades, but in
the middle of the twentieth century it would have been hard to find a
Southern Baptist from North Carolina who didn't identify as a Democrat. Contemporary evangelical partisanship can only be understood
in terms of a broader realignment that transformed partisan politics
from the 1950s to the 1980s, a realignment that evangelicals themselves helped bring about. At the heart of this realignment were attitudes toward civil rights, the war in Vietnam, and "family values."
For conservatives, a defense of white patriarchy emerged as a unify-
ing thread across this range of issues; for conservative evangelicals, a
defense of white patriarchy would move to the center of their coalescing cultural and political identity.

Graham's problems with the Democratic Party started early on.
Fresh off the success of his LA crusade, Graham decided to make the
most of his newly acquired celebrity status by requesting a meeting
with President Truman. This wasn't the first time he'd tried to secure
a meeting, but in the summer of 1950 he finally had enough clout.
By his own admission, he promptly made a fool of himself. Graham

thought part of the problem may have been his attire. Still in his flashy-dressing phase, Graham arrived at the White House wearing a "pistachio-green" suit, rust-colored socks, white buck shoes, and a hand-painted tie. But the more serious problem was Graham's comportment. He talked up his remarkable success in LA and at subsequent crusades, inelegantly quizzed the president on his "religious background and leanings," and then told Truman that his Golden Rule Christianity wasn't sufficient—what he needed was a personal faith in Christ and his death on the cross. The president informed him that his time was up. Graham insisted on closing with prayer, a prayer that extended several minutes past their allotted time. Graham's most egregious error, however, occurred as he left the Oval Office. Encountering the White House press corps, Graham blithely recounted the entirety of his conversation with the president, before reenacting his prayer by posing on one knee on the White House lawn. Truman never invited Graham back.[1]

But Graham's difficulties with Truman extended beyond this awkward encounter. Graham criticized the Truman administration's "cowardly" refusal to heed General MacArthur's advice in Korea and lamented that the country had settled for a "half-hearted war" when America's full military strength was needed. With Truman's term coming to an end, Graham began signaling to Republicans that they could woo the evangelical vote by aligning with evangelical views on morality and foreign policy. Eager to bring a new occupant to the White House, Graham took it upon himself to write a letter urging Dwight D. Eisenhower to enter the race. Eisenhower wasn't a particularly religious figure, but Graham was convinced that the war hero possessed the "honesty, integrity, and spiritual power" necessary to lead the nation. When Eisenhower decided to throw his hat in the ring, he called on Graham to help mobilize religious support. Graham delivered. Despite the Democratic loyalties of southern evangelicals, sixty percent of evangelicals nationally voted for Eisenhower, helping him achieve a decisive victory over Adlai Stevenson in 1952.[2]

As president, Eisenhower maintained a close relationship with Gra-

ham and his evangelical supporters. He asked Graham to help select
Bible verses for his inaugural address, and he kept an annotated red
leather Bible that Graham had given him on his bedside table. He
began opening cabinet meetings with prayer, and he appeared at the
first National Prayer Breakfast in 1953, an annual event organized with
Graham's assistance by members of "The Fellowship," a secretive group
that wielded tremendous power by connecting religious, political, and
business leaders to advance their mutual interests. In 1954, Congress
added the words "one nation under God" to the Pledge of Allegiance,
and the following year Eisenhower signed into law the addition of "In
God We Trust" to the nation's currency. For evangelicals who believed
that America was a Christian nation, the 1950s offered plenty of cir-
cumstantial evidence. More importantly, as the self-professed and
loudest defenders of Christian America, evangelicals enhanced their
own cultural and political power.[3]

Eisenhower and Graham were united in the conviction that Christianity could help America wage the Cold War. Early on, Eisenhower
recognized the religious nature of the conflict, and at a time when
American religiosity was higher than ever, he knew the religious angle
would be key to mobilizing support. By framing the Cold War as a
moral crisis, Graham made himself useful to Eisenhower—and to
subsequent Cold War presidents. Evangelicals weren't the only ones
with an interest in propping up Cold War politics; government officials, business leaders, educators, and the national media all played a
part. But evangelicals raised the stakes. Communism was "the greatest
enemy we have ever known," and only evangelical Christianity could
provide the spiritual resources to combat it.[4]

The defense of Christian America required more than spiritual
resources alone. Eisenhower presided over the vast expansion of America's military-industrial complex, and in his farewell address, he made
the connection explicit: a strong military would keep Americans free to
worship their God. At the same time, Eisenhower looked back on his
presidency with some trepidation, warning of the dangers of this mobilization. Few conservative evangelicals seemed to share his concern.

As late as 1952, the NAE had joined mainline groups in denouncing
the nation's peacetime militarization, but by the end of the decade,
the conflation of "God and country," and growing reliance on military
might to protect both, meant that Christian nationalism—and evangelicalism itself—would take on a decidedly militaristic bent.[5]

By that point, evangelicals had seen their own fortunes rise. By any
measure, they had succeeded in advancing the agenda Ockenga had
set before them, thanks to the auspicious Cold War consensus, an
expanding economy, and their own efforts to transform their scattered
endeavors into a powerful national movement. Within recent memory
they had been ostracized, relegated to the margins of American culture
and politics. But by the 1950s, the baby boom was in full swing and
the "traditional" family appeared to be flourishing. (The nuclear family
structured around a male breadwinner was in fact of recent invention,
arising in the 1920s and peaking in the 1950s and 1960s; before then,
multigenerational families relying on multiple contributors to the family economy had been the norm.) In the 1950s, too, Americans of all
sorts were reinvesting in religion. Churches were springing up in new
suburban neighborhoods across the country, and Sunday schools were
bursting at the seams. Cold War politics also united Americans across
party lines. To their delight, evangelicals found themselves securely
within the political and cultural mainstream. The formation of the
Religious Right was still two decades away, but the pieces were already
falling into place. By the end of the decade, evangelicals had become
active participants in national politics and had secured access to the
highest levels of power. And they had come to see a Republican president as an ally in their cause.[6]

Confident that God was on their side, evangelicals were at home in a
world defined by Cold War certainties. The next two decades, however,
would threaten to undermine evangelical hopes for the nation, and
their place in it. The civil rights movement, Vietnam, and feminism
would all challenge reigning dogmas, and for evangelicals who had
found a sense of security and significance in an America that affirmed
"traditional" gender roles, a strong national defense, and confidence

in American power, the sense of loss would be acute. But conservative evangelicals were not about to relinquish their newfound power. They would not go down without a fight.

In various ways, each of these disruptions challenged the authority of white men. In the 1960s and 1970s, then, conservative evangelicals would be drawn to a nostalgic, rugged masculinity as they looked to reestablish white patriarchal authority in its many guises. Over time, the defense of patriarchy and a growing embrace of militant masculinity would come to define both substance and symbol of evangelical cultural and political values.

TO WHITE AMERICANS who were willing to listen, the civil rights movement argued that America had never been a country of liberty and justice for all. Evangelicals' response to civil rights varied, particularly in the early stages of the movement. It is easily forgotten, but some evangelicals—especially those who would come to constitute the "evangelical Left"—were vocal supporters of civil rights. Others, primarily fundamentalists and southerners, were staunch opponents. In the aftermath of the Civil War, the Lost Cause of the Confederate South had blended with Christian theology to produce a distinctly southern variation of civil religion, one that upheld Robert E. Lee as its patron saint. In this tradition, fundamentalist pastors like W. A. Criswell of First Baptist Dallas (Robert Jeffress's future home) crusaded against integration as "a denial of all that we believe in." To such opponents, civil rights activism was a sign of disruption and disorder; many denounced Martin Luther King Jr. as a communist agitator.[7]

Most northern evangelicals were somewhere between these two positions. Like Graham, many were cautious supporters in the early years of the civil rights movement. In the early 1950s, Graham began to integrate his crusades, going so far as to personally remove ropes separating the seating between whites and blacks. In 1954, he praised the *Brown v. Board of Education* ruling to desegregate schools. In 1957, he invited King to pray at his New York City crusade. Yet Graham was wary about moving too fast, and he urged the Supreme Court to proceed with caution to quell "the extremists on both sides." This cautious support was reflected in institutional responses as well. In 1951, the NAE endorsed "equal opportunities" for people of all races. *Christianity Today*, too, published articles backing civil rights, although they also published articles suggesting that Christians were under no obligation to support integration.[8]

After the passage of the Civil Rights Act of 1964, these differences within the evangelical community began to diminish. Explicit support for segregation fell out of favor even among stalwart fundamentalists, as was the case for most segregationists more generally. At the same time, moderate proponents of civil rights began to cool in their support for further action. Graham, for example, withdrew his backing as activists began to engage in civil disobedience and to demand further government intervention. Many evangelicals followed his lead, concluding that it was not the role of government to interfere in issues of racial justice; only Jesus could change human hearts. Many evangelicals, too, found it hard to accept that the sin of racism ran deep through the nation's history. To concede this seemed unpatriotic. Having embraced the idea of America as a "Christian nation," it was hard to accept a critique of the nation as fundamental as that advanced by the civil rights movement.[9]

Understanding this ambivalence toward civil rights within white evangelicalism is key to understanding the role that race would play within evangelical politics more generally. By backing away from their support for civil rights, evangelicals like Graham ended up giving cover to more extremist sentiments within the insurgent Religious Right. Today some historians place race at the very heart of evangelical politics, pointing to the fact that evangelical opposition to government-mandated integration predated anti-abortion activism by several years. Others, however—including the vast majority of evangelicals themselves—prefer to point instead to the significance of moral and "family values." But in many ways, this is a false dichotomy. For evangelicals, family values politics were deeply intertwined with racial politics, and both were connected to evangelicals' understanding of the nation and its role on the global stage.[10]

In the wake of *Brown*, for example, many southerners turned to private Christian academies to maintain segregation, and when the tax-exempt status of these "segregation academies" was revoked in 1970, evangelicals defended their right to whites-only schools by arguing for the authority of parents to make decisions about their children's education, free from governmental "overreach." Later, "forced busing" would offend these same sensibilities, in the North as well as the South. Although blatant defenses of segregation and racial inequality would be rare, many southern evangelicals and fundamentalists who persisted in their unreconstructed views of race would find common cause with more "tolerant" evangelicals on issues like social welfare policy and "law and order" politics that would carry clear racial undertones.[11]

In this way, the evangelicalism that gained respectability and prominence in Cold War America cannot be separated from its southern roots. Ideals of evangelical masculinity that manifested during this period reflect this formative influence. Some proponents of Christian masculinity praised Confederate generals and defended the institution of slavery, but for many, the racial subtext was more subtle. Invariably, however, the heroic Christian man was a white man, and not infrequently a white man who defended against the threat of nonwhite men and foreigners.

THE CONNECTION BETWEEN white masculine power, family values politics, and a militant defense of Christian America was on clear display in the early 1960s in southern California, the center of the evangelical political resurgence. In 1961, Pepperdine College, a hotbed of Sunbelt evangelicalism popular with conservative donors and Christian celebrities alike, hosted a "freedom forum." With the recent election of the Catholic Democrat John F. Kennedy, the mood was more urgent than triumphalist. Kennedy's Catholicism was cause for serious concern among fundamentalists in particular, and the contention that Kennedy was soft on communism—this despite the fact that Kennedy had increased military spending by 14 percent during his first nine months in office—was also a matter of concern. At the forum, fifteen hundred businessmen and educators discussed ideas such as outlawing the Communist Party, refusing to seat Red China in the UN, disbanding President Kennedy's Peace Corps, and commending the extremist John Birch Society. The highlight of the event was a televised luncheon with Barry Goldwater.[12]

Goldwater seemed the perfect antidote to Kennedy, and conservative evangelicals were drawn to his hard-edged, bombastic style, and to the "cowboy conservatism" he embodied. For his 1958 Senate campaign poster he'd stood, rifle in hand, in a buckskin jacket and cowboy hat, and in public appearances he liked to conjure the aura of the heroic cowboy, standing alone against all odds, refusing to compromise. As the freedom forum's featured speaker, Goldwater invoked his own hero, Theodore Roosevelt—"America's ultimate cowboy president." Like Roosevelt, Goldwater warned against "peace at any price," and called instead for a strong defense and courageous citizenry. Goldwater wasn't known for his religious beliefs, but that wasn't really the point. He was bringing a message Sunbelt evangelicals wanted to hear.[13]

Four months later, the region's evangelicals came together again, this time in Anaheim. The occasion was an event organized by the Southern California School of Anti-Communism, a "citizen's training program" headed by Fred Schwarz. Schwarz, an Australian physician who founded the Christian Anti-Communism Crusade, had recently set up shop in southern California. At the close of the five-day event, sixteen thousand young people and their parents sang the "Star-Spangled Banner," pledged their allegiance to the flag, and listened to celebrity speakers. First up was Marion Miller, a housewife who had gained fame crusading for anticommunist education in public schools, and for infiltrating the Los Angeles Left as an FBI informant. Next up was Ronald Reagan. Still a Democrat at the time, Reagan warned of communists' devious plans to target teenagers' "rebellious

Voices of Strong Men...

this is the
SOUND of
FREEDOM...

HON. BARRY M. GOLDWATER
featured Speaker at
California Freedom Forum III

Program cover for Barry Goldwater's Pepperdine Freedom Forum
luncheon, 1961. FROM THE PEPPERDINE COLLEGE FREEDOM FORUM
COLLECTION, PEPPERDINE UNIVERSITY SPECIAL COLLECTIONS AND
UNIVERSITY ARCHIVES.

nature," fooling them into thinking that their "patriotism is hollow."
Roy Rogers, Dale Evans, and John Wayne then followed suit. But it
was pop star Pat Boone who stole the show that night, closing with
an impromptu address that Reagan would recall years later: "I would
rather see my four girls shot and die as little girls who have faith in God
than leave them to die some years later as godless, faithless, soulless
Communists," Boone asserted. His audience was thrilled, even if his
wife was not.[14]

That same year, fundamentalist pastors were among those who
rebuffed President Kennedy when he challenged the Soviet Union "not
to an arms race, but to a peace race." And they came to the defense of
men like General Edwin Walker, who had been admonished by the
Department of Defense for his attempts to indoctrinate troops with
right-wing anticommunist materials supplied by fundamentalist evangelist Billy James Hargis. Walker resigned his post so that he would no
longer be subject to "the power of little men," as he put it, but Goldwater joined Senator Strom Thurmond and other Republicans to call
for Senate hearings on the "muzzling" of the military. In the fallout
of these events, Kennedy gave a speech at the Hollywood Palladium
in November 1961, reproaching "those on the fringes of our society"

who were easily wooed by "an appealing slogan or a convenient scape-goat" and warning against "the discordant voices of extremism"—against those who called "for a 'man on horseback' because they do not trust the people." Thurmond responded by denouncing "pussyfooting diplomats."[15]

General Walker may have resigned, but he did not go quietly. He was later arrested for "inciting rebellion" among segregationists as federal marshals attempted to desegregate Ole Miss, and in 1963 he took up with Hargis to lead anticommunist "crisis crusades," persisting in his charge that the government was soft on communism and hamstringing the military. Pastor Bob Wells of Los Angeles's Central Baptist Church hosted many of these crusades. Wells thought it crucial that Americans "not be deceived about all of this talk about peace and safety"; disarmament would imperil both American sovereignty and Christianity. For the many members of Wells's congregation whose livelihood was wrapped up in the defense industry, disarmament was problematic for other reasons as well.[16]

Wells was a key figure in the southern California evangelical community. To counter the perceived failures of public schools, he established a Christian elementary school and Orange County's first Christian high school, Heritage High. Dedicated to teaching "Christian Americanism," the school board screened textbooks to ensure that God and Christianity were well represented in American history. (They chafed at the lack of attention one popular textbook gave to General Douglas MacArthur—a paltry 26 words.) The school's drama department staged musicals celebrating the values of patriotism and frontier democracy in which boys acted as the nation's "valiant protectors." One drama, *God of Our Fathers*, contained inspirational words from Abraham Lincoln, Robert E. Lee, and General MacArthur. From the Patriot's football team to school floats adorned with students dressed as Union, Confederate, and WWII soldiers all raising the flag at Iwo Jima, the school was steeped in a mythical, militant past.[17]

When Goldwater ran for president in 1964, Wells set up a table promoting Goldwater's campaign on the church's front lawn. Before the

California primary, members of his church traveled together to Knott's Berry Farm to attend a Goldwater rally featuring John Wayne, Ronald Reagan, and Goldwater himself. Owned by conservative businessman Walter Knott, the amusement park was the perfect venue—with a Wild West ghost town, a patriotic tour celebrating the Founding Fathers, and a Freedom Center stocked with pamphlets on free enterprise, it was a fantasy world that they hoped to make a reality.[18]

Goldwater's truculent style and aggressive foreign policy went hand in hand with his cowboy mystique. Here was a man who was not afraid to shoot first. Goldwater had recommended withdrawing from the UN and appeared open to provoking nuclear war. Opponents tarred him a warmonger and an extremist, to which Goldwater famously retorted: "Extremism in the defense of liberty is no vice. And . . . moderation in the pursuit of justice is no virtue!" Just days before the election, Reagan, who had only recently switched to the Republican Party, gave a televised address on Goldwater's behalf. Linked by their ardent anticommunism and cowboy conservatism, Reagan defended Goldwater's promise of peace through strength and denounced those who sought a utopian peace without victory, proponents of "appeasement" who thought the enemy might "forget his evil ways and learn to love us." Americans had "a rendezvous with destiny." Either they would preserve for their children "the last best hope of man on earth," meaning the American nation, or they would step into "a thousand years of darkness."[19]

Reagan's endorsement wasn't nearly enough; Goldwater won only Arizona and five southern states, losing to Lyndon Johnson in one of the biggest landslides in American presidential history. Although fundamentalists and Sunbelt evangelicals were drawn to Goldwater's politics, most northern evangelicals ended up voting for Johnson, even if they did so without much enthusiasm. Johnson knew that the evangelical vote was in play, and he worked hard to keep Billy Graham on his side. The two had struck up a friendship, and Graham supported Johnson's Vietnam policy and his approach to civil rights legislation, even though he had declined to endorse the 1964 Civil Rights Act. Yet Graham's support was muted. He had in fact briefly toyed with running for president himself. In the end, most evangelicals outside the Sunbelt deemed Goldwater too radical. Goldwater's defeat, however, masked a political realignment already under way. Although Graham refrained from supporting Goldwater in 1964, he claimed to have received "over one million telegrams" urging him to do so. Four years later, the choice would be easier.[20]

In 1968, Richard Nixon knew that conservative evangelicals could hold the key to his victory. A lapsed Quaker, Nixon wasn't a particularly religious man, but he understood that anticommunism abroad and "moral values" and "law and order" politics at home could woo this coalescing voting bloc. And he knew that one man—Billy Graham— could help him win over this crucial component of his "great silent majority." When Nixon had run against Kennedy in 1960, Graham had come close to endorsing him. He'd submitted an article to *Life* magazine praising Nixon, but after having second thoughts he requested that it not be published. When Nixon lost the election, Graham was tortured by this decision. This time around, Graham was ready to abandon the guise of neutrality.[21]

"There is no American that I admire more than Richard Nixon," Graham proclaimed at one of his crusades that year. Although some rural Southern Baptists and Methodists were drawn to segregationist third-party candidate George Wallace, most evangelicals preferred Nixon, the more viable and respectable choice. By the late 1960s, even fundamentalist leaders like Billy James Hargis and John R. Rice thought it best to distance themselves from the overt racism of a man like Wallace, and Nixon's "Southern strategy" helped draw former segregationists into the Republican Party. With Democratic administrations overseeing federally mandated desegregation efforts, and with Johnson signing the Civil Rights Act into law, the Republican Party's defense of "states' rights" appealed to southern whites. An increasingly militant civil rights movement (and the 1965 Watts riot that erupted in the backyard of southern California evangelicals) enhanced the allure of "law and order" politics across the nation, as did the growing disruptions caused by the antiwar movement and the emergence of an unruly counterculture. Nixon won by appealing to his so-called Silent Majority, capitalizing on the political realignment signaled by Goldwater that would come to shape the next half century of American politics. White evangelicals were a significant part of his majority; 69 percent cast their vote for Nixon.[22]

With Graham's assistance, Nixon had worked to identify himself with born-again Christianity. Nixon's faith was shaped by a western strand of Quakerism that bore some similarities to fundamentalism and was not to be confused with the pacifist Quakerism of the East, but there remained a distance to be bridged. Already in the 1950s, Graham had coached Nixon on how to appeal to evangelicals, drafting a speech for Nixon to give to Christian audiences referring to the "new birth" teachings of Quakerism and recounting a childhood marked by Bible reading and prayer. In a 1962 article in Graham's *Decision* magazine, written at Graham's prompting, Nixon described making a personal commitment "to Christ and Christian service" at a revival led by Chicago evangelist Paul Rader. Once in the White House, Nixon continued to solidify this strategic alliance. He instituted Sunday morning church services in the East Room and placed Special Counsel Charles Colson in charge of handpicking politically advantageous guests. Nixon knew how to speak the language of evangelicals and how to appeal to their values through symbol and spectacle. This "ceremonial politics" was on full display at "Honor America Day" on July 4, 1970, an event organized with Graham's help and staged on the steps of the Lincoln Memorial, with the aim of bolstering Nixon's agenda. Pat Boone was master of ceremonies. Clad in red, white, and blue, Boone lamented that patriotism had become a bad word. The country wasn't bad, he insisted: "We've had some problems, but we're beginning to come together under God." Graham concurred. It was time to wave the flag with pride.[23]

Connections between the Nixon White House and conservative Christians went beyond ceremony and spectacle. When Nixon came under fire for his secret bombing of Cambodia, Colson tapped

Billy Graham and Richard Nixon at Graham's East Tennessee
Crusade in Knoxville, May 29, 1970. GETTY IMAGES / BETTMANN.

the Southern Baptist Convention to pass a resolution endorsing the
president's foreign policy. Graham, too, worked to promote the president's foreign policy agenda—including the escalation of the war in
Vietnam—with talk of patriotism and unity. Nixon's reelection campaign prompted Graham to step up his support.[24]

Nixon's opponent, George McGovern, was a former ministry student, son of an evangelical minister, and a deeply religious candidate.
Despite having served as a fighter pilot in the Second World War, however, he opposed the war in Vietnam and proposed large cuts in military spending and amnesty for draft dodgers. In his acceptance speech,
McGovern issued a prophetic critique of the nation and its culture of
militarism. He promised to end bombing in Indochina on Inauguration Day, and within ninety days to bring every American soldier
home: "There will be no more Asian children running ablaze from
bombed-out schools" and no more Americans sent to die "trying to
prop up a corrupt military dictatorship abroad." He called on Americans to live with more faith and less fear. Countering those who said

"America—love it or leave it," he instead urged Americans to work to change their nation for the better, "so we may love it the more." A small group of Evangelicals for McGovern rallied around the Democratic candidate, but they were a tiny minority. Powerful evangelicals like Graham and Ockenga publicly endorsed Nixon, and when McGovern spoke at Wheaton College, he was greeted with resounding boos.[25]

Evangelical support for Nixon was manifest at Campus Crusade's Explo '72. With an eye toward reelection, Nixon had been looking for ways to reach evangelical youth. At Graham's urging, Nixon aide (and ordained Southern Baptist minister) Wallace Henley reached out to Bill Bright, head of Campus Crusade, to convince him to join in a media strategy to advance the conservative cause. By "media strategy," Henley meant "doing things like syndicated news columns, developing evangelical-oriented radio and television spots, undertaking a specific effort to land some of the big names on Christian talk shows." The possibilities were vast.[26]

Timed to the run-up to the election, Explo '72 attracted 80,000 evangelical young people to Dallas's Cotton Bowl. At a time when hippies were taking to the streets to protest the war, young evangelicals were celebrating Flag Day by applauding more than 5000 parading military personnel, saluting the Stars and Stripes, and cheering the South Vietnamese flag. Such overt displays of patriotism troubled some evangelicals; Jim Wallis and other members of the People's Christian Coalition unfurled a banner lamenting the "300 GIs killed this week in Vietnam." African American evangelist Tom Skinner said he didn't have a problem with Flag Day, "but to associate God with that is bad news." But most in attendance shared the organizers' conservative values. They favored Nixon over McGovern by more than five to one; they also supported stronger penalties for marijuana possession and felt that American attitudes toward sex were "too permissive." The event closed with an eight-hour Christian music festival, a "Christian Woodstock" attended by between 100,000 and 200,000 students, featuring "Righteous Rocker" Larry Norman, recent convert Johnny Cash, Kris Kristofferson, and other Christian musicians. Evangelicals had long rejected rock 'n' roll, which they associated with drug culture and youthful rebellion, but by offering a Christian version of popular music, Explo '72 helped pave the way for what would become a thriving Christian contemporary music industry. As Henley's strategy suggested, the expanding world of evangelical popular culture would offer an ideal conduit for the dispersal and reinforcement of conservative politics.[27]

Nixon won reelection handily, capturing 84 percent of the evangelical vote. The alliance between the Republican Party and evangelical Christians seemed secure. But things didn't turn out exactly as planned. It would later be revealed that Explo '72 took place during the week of the Watergate break-in. When news of the scandal broke and the extent of Nixon's corruption (and Colson's role in the cover-up) was revealed, Graham came to regret his unabashed foray into partisan politics. It was a lesson that most other evangelicals refused to abide.[28]

THE ANTIWAR LEFT, though often disparaged by evangelicals, was in fact animated in part by religious faith. Mainline clergy vociferously condemned American war crimes and called into question the morality of the war and that of American soldiers. They expressed outrage over the use of napalm, indiscriminate bombing, search-and-destroy operations, and the scale of civilian casualties, and they didn't hesitate to expose the brutality of American soldiers and violations of international rules of warfare. They criticized military chaplains, too, for failing in their prophetic roles, for preaching a "military religion," and for essentially serving as "an indoctrination agent in behalf of the military."[29]

Conservative evangelicals saw things differently. Most not only supported the war in Vietnam but also held the military itself in high (and often uncritical) esteem. Having spent two decades working to inculcate moral and religious values in the armed forces, they often had nothing but praise for American troops. For instance, Graham, who had visited troops in Korea and in Vietnam, spoke admiringly of the "tough, rugged men" he encountered, men who shed manly tears when they came forward to receive Christ. Fundamentalists were among the most enthusiastic supporters of the war—a war to prevent "godless communism with its murder and torture and persecution from taking over other lands which ask our help." According to fundamentalist leader Carl McIntire, "the infallible Bible . . . gives men the right to participate in such conflicts" and the knowledge that God was on their side; believers felled in battle would be "received into the highest Heaven." McIntire castigated calls "to cringe and retreat" and denounced America's " 'no-win' policy" as "a sin against righteousness, the heritage of our nation, the mothers and wives of boys who have sacrificed for political expediency."[30]

When word of American atrocities began to filter back to the home front, conservative evangelicals minimized the violence and advanced moral equivalencies. In a 1967 *Christianity Today* editorial supporting intensified bombing in North Vietnam, Carl Henry employed sanitized language dismissing any "civilian damage" as "regrettable," adding that it paled in comparison to the damage inflicted by the communists. To Baptist pastor Jerry Falwell, the US soldier in Vietnam remained "a living testimony" to Christianity, and to "old fashioned patriotism." A defender of "Americanism," the American soldier was "a champion for Christ."[31]

When confronted with undeniable evidence of American brutality, evangelicals could always fall back on the concept of human depravity. With sin lurking in every human heart, violence was inevitable, and only Jesus was the answer. When the young army lieutenant William Calley faced trial for his role in the murder of some five hundred Vietnamese men, women, and children in what came to be known as the My Lai massacre, Billy Graham remarked that he had "never heard of a war where innocent people are not killed." He told, too, of "horrible stories" he'd heard from missionaries of "sadistic murders by the Vietcong," and he reminded Americans that Vietnamese women and children had planted booby traps that mutilated American soldiers. His moral reflection in the pages of the *New York Times* was remarkably banal: "We have all had our Mylais in one way or another, perhaps not with guns, but we have hurt others with a thoughtless word, an arrogant act or a selfish deed."[32]

In 1969, Graham sent a thirteen-page letter to President Nixon—a letter only declassified twenty years later—offering an array of policy scenarios, some of which clearly abandoned Christian just-war theory and the Geneva Conventions. It is unclear what effect Graham's letter had on Nixon's strategy, but Graham's was certainly not a voice of restraint. Even as Graham became increasingly ambivalent about the war, he remained unwavering in his support for Nixon. Meanwhile, conservative evangelicals continued to celebrate American servicemen, and looked to returning soldiers to provide leadership on the home front as well. At a time when evangelical churches needed to take a stand, who better to lead a nation—and its churches—than men who had "carried those concerns through the jungles of Viet Nam"?[33]

The Vietnam War was pivotal to the formation of an emerging evangelical identity. For many Americans who came of age in the 1960s and 1970s, Vietnam demolished myths of American greatness and goodness. American power came to be viewed with suspicion, if not revulsion, and a pervasive antimilitarism took hold. Evangelicals, however, drew the opposite lesson: it was the absence of American power that led to catastrophe. Evangelical support for the war seemed to grow in direct relation to escalating doubts among the rest of the public. After the Tet Offensive in the summer of 1968, a poll revealed support for continued bombing and an increase in US military intervention "among 97 percent of Southern Baptists, 91 percent of independent fundamentalists, and 70 percent of Missouri Synod Lutherans; only 2 percent of Southern Baptists and 3 percent of fundamentalists favored a negotiated withdrawal." Aware of their outlier status, many evangelicals understood themselves to be a faithful remnant, America's last great hope. With the fate of the nation hanging in the balance, conservative evangelicals "assumed the role of church militant."[34]

The war was a watershed moment for American Christians overall. As the established power of the Protestant mainline eroded in step with their critique of government policy, evangelicals enhanced their own influence by backing the policies of Johnson and Nixon. Moreover, by affirming the war and the men who fought it, evangelicals gained favor and status within the military. This partnership was acknowledged ceremonially in 1972, when West Point conferred its Sylvanus Thayer Award—an award for a citizen who exhibits the ideals of "Duty, Honor, Country"—upon Billy Graham.[35]

Still, there remained within evangelicalism a small contingent of outspoken critics, including national figures like Senator Mark Hatfield, who, together with McGovern, had called for a complete withdrawal of US troops in Vietnam. In 1973, progressive evangelical leaders issued the Chicago Declaration of Evangelical Social Concern. Like members of the emerging Religious Right, they saw politics as an expression of their faith, but on nearly every issue they parted ways with their conservative brethren. They denounced racism and called for Christians to defend the rights of the poor and oppressed. Confessing that Christians had "encouraged men to prideful domination and women to irresponsible passivity," they called instead for "mutual submission and active discipleship." And they challenged "the misplaced trust of the nation in economic and military might—a proud trust that promotes a national pathology of war and violence which victimizes our neighbors at home and abroad." The evangelical Left, however, failed to convince most fellow evangelicals that their faith required a critique of patriarchy and American power, rather than the assertion of both, and they would remain a relatively marginal group within the larger movement.[36]

The evangelical Left and the Christian Right would pursue divergent trajectories, building their own networks and alliances. A common evangelical heritage and shared theological commitments diminished in significance as Christian nationalism, militarism, and gender "traditionalism" came to define conservative evangelical identity and dictate ideological allies. Conservative evangelicals would find they had more in common with conservative Catholics, Mormons, and with other members of the Silent Majority who were not particularly religious. Elements of class conflict also helped define these emerging coalitions. As children of blue-collar workers gave their lives in Vietnam, children of the elite protested the war on college campuses across the nation. In the early decades of the twentieth century, conservative Protestants had tended to lag behind other white Americans economically, but thanks to a thriving postwar economy, growing numbers of evangelicals were moving into the middle class. Still, many were only one generation removed from humbler circumstances, and in the 1960s and 1970s, as patriotism took on a populist dimension, conservative evangelicals were drawn to the values of the white working class. For these new allies, nostalgic celebrations of rugged masculinity would come to symbolize a shared identity, and a political agenda.[37]

THE VIETNAM WAR was a foreign policy crisis, and a domestic one. Young men dodged the draft, shirking their duty to protect American interests in the face of global communism. Antiwar protesters shunned authority, advising their generation to make love, not war. Sporting long hair and flowered shirts, the young men and women of this generation seemed nearly indistinguishable, at least according to conservative critics. The failure of American soldiers to defeat a ragtag enemy testified to serious problems of American manhood, and no group felt this crisis more keenly than American evangelicals.[38]

For evangelicals, the problem of American manhood was at its heart a religious one, properly addressed within the Christian family. Fundamentalist megachurch pastor Jack Hyles made this case in his 1972 book *How to Rear Children*. The son of a distant, alcoholic father, Hyles had grown up in Texas, served in the 82nd Airborne Division in the Second World War, and later turned to ministry. In 1959, the "skinny, charismatic Bible thumper with a Southern-fried drawl and a couple of cheap suits" showed up in Hammond, Indiana, and took charge of its First Baptist Church. He quickly built the church into one of the largest Independent Fundamental Baptist churches in the nation, boasting an attendance of over 20,000 and housing "the world's largest Sunday School."[39]

Hyles's book included a section on "How to Make a Man Out of a Boy." Boys needed to be taught to be winners: "This is how we get our General MacArthurs. This is how Billy Sundays are made." Teaching boys how to be good losers left you with a generation of young men who didn't want to fight for their country and were instead "willing to let the strongest nation on earth bow down in shame before a little nation like North Vietnam." It was up to Christian parents to rear a new generation of men, and to this end they should make boys "play with boys and with boys' toys and games," with "guns, cars, baseballs, basketballs, and footballs." Boys who engaged in "feminine activities," he warned, often ended up as "homosexuals." A boy must be taught to fight, to "be rugged enough" to defend his home and those he loved. Hyles bought his own son a pair of boxing gloves when he was five, an air rifle at thirteen, and a .22 at fifteen. When a neighbor boy insulted Hyles's daughter, he encouraged his son to "let him have it" and walked away as his son beat the boy bloody. Such violence was sanctified: "God pity this weak-kneed generation which stands for nothing, fights for nothing, and dies for nothing."[40]

Hyles prefigured a style of militant masculinity that other evangelical pastors would perfect. Known for angry outbursts and a nasty temper, Hyles had "a penchant for ironfisted control" over his growing religious empire. He instituted a dress code—men wore jackets and ties and close-cropped hair, and women skirts below the knee—and he commanded women to "be in complete and total submission to their husbands and to male leadership." Whereas boys must be trained to be leaders, girls should be trained to submit. They "must obey immediately, without question, and without argument." By enforcing submission, parents would be doing a future son-in-law "a big favor." Hyles also advocated corporal punishment of children, even infants. (Spankings should last "at least ten or fifteen minutes" and should "leave stripes," as necessary.) Parents in his church took his advice to heart; one woman recalled receiving more than three hundred lashes from a leather belt, and Hyles advised the girl's parents how to avoid arrest after authorities were notified. "Our natural man" might rebel at such punishment, Hyles explained, but children must learn obedience or end up in hell.[41]

As religious leaders like Hyles championed a militant application of patriarchal authority, other conservatives, too, embraced a nostalgic vision of aggressive, even violent masculinity. In this way, militant masculinity linked religious and secular conservatism. In time, the two would become difficult to distinguish. As red-blooded American manhood became infused with God-and-country virtues, otherwise secular models would come to exemplify an ideal Christian manhood. This conflation of religious and secular can be seen in the cultlike status John Wayne enjoyed among American conservatives in the 1960s and 1970s.

If an evangelical could be defined as anyone who liked Billy Graham, by the 1970s a conservative might well be defined as anyone who loved John Wayne. Wayne was more than just a movie star. As far back as the 1940s, Wayne's masculinity had been intertwined with his conservative activism. In 1944, he'd helped create the anticommunist Motion Picture Alliance for the Preservation of American Ideals (MPA), and in 1949 he became its president. He was a vocal supporter of the House Un-American Activities Committee, and in 1952 he made and starred in *Big Jim McLain*, a propaganda piece in which he played a HUAC investigator. In 1960 he supported Nixon and took jabs at Kennedy, and in 1964 he voiced a campaign ad for Goldwater deriding appeasement and celebrating the "high morals" of a "free America." In 1968 he gave a rousing, patriotic address at the Republican National Convention. When Nixon wanted to explain his own views on "law and order," he pointed to Wayne's *Chisum* as a model, a bloody tale of frontier justice in which Wayne achieved order—and revenge—through violence.[42]

Many of Wayne's films were politically charged, none more so, unsurprisingly, than the two films he directed. *The Alamo* (1960) was inspired by Wayne's Cold War activism in the late 1940s; Davy Crockett's sacrifice for the cause of liberty offered a heroic model for Cold War America. But *The Green Berets* (1968)—the only major

John Wayne starring as Colonel Mike Kirby in *The Green
Berets*, 1968. TCD / PROD.DB / ALAMY STOCK PHOTO.

motion picture in support of the Vietnam War filmed during the war
years—was Wayne's most direct contribution to Cold War militarism.
A commercial success, *The Green Berets* offered fans a make-believe
substitute for the actual war, one that perpetuated the myth of American greatness. To conservatives, the fact that both films were "viciously
panned and vilified, dismissed as rightest message films and artistic
duds," was another point in their favor, even more confirmation that
cultural elites disdained heroic masculinity. Like the heroes Wayne
played onscreen, conservatives' sense of embattlement only heightened
their resolve.[43]

The mythical wars Wayne fabricated had very real repercussions. As
one working-class Vietnam veteran later recalled, he went to Vietnam
to "kill a Commie for Jesus Christ and John Wayne." It was *Sands of
Iwo Jima* that inspired Ron Kovic to volunteer for the marines during
the Vietnam War, a war that would cost him the use of his legs and lead
to a disenchantment with war that he chronicled in his memoir, *Born
on the Fourth of July*. Offscreen, too, Wayne worked to recruit young

men to the war effort, ridiculing as "soft" those who didn't enlist. One critic labeled Wayne "the most important man in America," given the role his films played in driving American engagement in Vietnam.[44]

However, the war heroes Wayne played left recruits ill-prepared for the realities of war. Onscreen, good triumphed over evil, and the lines between the two were clearly drawn. War was a place where boys became men and men became heroes, where America was a force for good, and where American ends justified any means. Shipped overseas, new recruits soon learned that real war fell far short of this ideal. Reared on a false narrative of wartime heroism, many men were haunted by the sense that they somehow failed to measure up. As for making boys into men, Kovic reflected bitterly that the war robbed him of his manhood: "I gave my dead dick for John Wayne." Wayne himself had secured a deferment in order to avoid serving in a war with a far more clear-cut division between good and evil.[45]

For veterans like Kovic, the disconnect between expectation and reality led to disillusionment. Many conservatives, however, continued to cling fiercely to the role of the military in defining American manhood and preserving American greatness. Those inspired by Wayne's bravado came to see all of life as a war, and toughness as a virtue. This had repercussions on a personal level, and on a global one. Indeed, critics characterized American foreign policy in the 1960s and 1970s as afflicted with a "John Wayne syndrome."[46]

Through his films and his politics, Wayne established himself as the embodiment of rugged, all-American masculinity. Understanding the man and the myth—and it was not clear where one left off and the other began—is key to understanding his enduring legacy. To begin with, Wayne's masculinity was unapologetically imperialist. All of Wayne's greatest hits involved valiant white men battling (and usually subduing) nonwhite populations—the Japanese, Native Americans, or Mexicans. Like Teddy Roosevelt, Wayne's rugged masculinity was realized through violence, and it was a distinctly white male ideal. This was not lost on his fans. In 1977, on the occasion of Wayne's seventieth birthday, an article in the conservative journal *Human Events* attempted to explain Wayne's allure, and the racialized portrait of Wayne is revealing: Wayne was a "basic American breed," a "tall Celt" of "pioneer Scots, Irish and English stock." In films like *The Searchers*, Wayne plays unapologetically racist characters; in others, the racial politics are more subtle. His own views on race were conventional among conservatives, but still appalling. In a 1971 interview in *Playboy*, Wayne was particularly harsh in his assessment of "the blacks"—"or colored, or whatever they want to call themselves: they certainly aren't Caucasian":

> With a lot of blacks, there's quite a bit of resentment along with their dissent, and possibly rightly so. But we can't all of a sudden get down on our knees and turn everything over to the leadership of the blacks. I believe in white supremacy until the blacks are educated to a point of responsibility. I don't believe in giving authority and positions of leadership and judgment to irresponsible people.

As far as African American representation in his own films, Wayne asserted that he'd given "the blacks their proper position"—he had "a black slave in *The Alamo*," and he had "a correct number of blacks in *The Green Berets*." His views on Native Americans were no more enlightened: "I don't feel we did wrong in taking this great country away from [the Native Americans]. . . . Our so-called stealing of this country from them was just a matter of survival." People needed land "and the Indians were selfishly trying to keep it for themselves."[47]

Nor did Wayne feel a need to apologize for America's actions overseas. He downplayed "the so-called My Lai massacre" and instead highlighted atrocities committed against "our people" by the Vietcong. With all the terrible things happening all over the world, he saw no reason "one little incident in the United States Army" should cause such uproar. And he took great pride in the inspiration servicemen drew from his portrayal of Sergeant Stryker in *Sands of Iwo Jima*. General MacArthur himself told Wayne that he represented "the American Serviceman better than the American Serviceman himself."[48]

Onscreen and off, Wayne epitomized an old-fashioned, retrograde masculinity, and one increasingly understood in politicized terms. A staunch proponent of "law and order," Wayne had no time for "cowards who spit in the faces of the police," for "judicial sob sisters," for people who advocated for criminals without thought for the innocent victim. He was similarly dismissive of student protestors. "There doesn't seem to be respect for authority anymore," he opined. As the *Human Events* chronicler put it, "As a man he is loathed and demeaned by sanctimonious 'liberals' and a whole mess of bugout-on-America hypocrites," but the Duke was "top shelf with freedom fans, who thrill to the big guy's charge."[49]

Wayne's crassness was part of his appeal, if not the key to it—and this would become a pattern among evangelical heroes, religious and secular. He defended his use of profanity and his dramatization of violence onscreen ("All our fairy tales have some kind of violence—the good knight riding to kill the dragon, etc."). There was a place, too, for sex in films, but only heterosexual sex. He had no use for *Midnight Cowboy*, "a story about two fags," but "as far as a man and a woman is concerned," he was "awfully happy there is a thing called sex"—it was "an extra something God gave us" and he didn't see why it shouldn't be portrayed in film, in a "beautifully risqué" way. "Healthy, lusty sex" was a wonderful thing.[50]

To many conservatives, including evangelicals, Wayne personified "a tone of life" that needed to be recovered if the country was to reverse course "from the masochistic tailspin of this prideless age." He modeled a heroic American manhood that rallied the good against evil; took pride in the red, white, and blue; and wasn't afraid of getting his hands dirty. That Wayne never fought for his country, that he left behind a string of broken marriages and allegations of abuse—none of this seemed to matter. Wayne might come up short in terms of traditional virtue, but he excelled at embodying a different set of virtues. At a time of social upheaval, Wayne modeled masculine strength, aggression, and redemptive violence.[51]

FEAR HAD BEEN AT THE HEART of evangelical postwar politics—a fear of godless communism and a fear that immorality would leave Americans defenseless. What changed by the 1960s was evangelicals' sense of their own power. Between the end of the Second World War and the beginning of the 1960s, evangelicals had become more and more confident that they had a providential role to play in strengthening American defenses and upholding American faithfulness. The events of the 1960s, however, and the realization that the larger culture seemed to scorn what they had to offer, undercut their newfound confidence. Among evangelicals, a rhetoric of fear would persist, though it would be aimed at internal threats as much as external ones. Instrumental to their efforts to reclaim power, this rhetoric of fear would continue to bolster the role of the heroic masculine protector. There might be a place for the softer virtues, but the perilous times necessitated ruthless power. In the words of Baptist scholar Alan Bean, "The unspoken mantra of post-war evangelicalism was simple: Jesus can save your soul; but John Wayne will save your ass."[52]

Chapter 3

GOD'S GIFT
TO MAN

BY 1970, MARABEL MORGAN'S MARRIAGE WAS ON the rocks. By her own account she had turned into "a nag and a shrew" and her marriage had devolved into "a cold war"—until she devised a strategy to achieve détente. The source of women's marital woes, she discovered, wasn't male chauvinism, inequality of the sexes, or women's untapped potential. The problem was women's sullen resistance to their designated role. To achieve marital bliss, a wife needed to devote herself wholly to her husband and give him the honor he was due. Morgan began to share her solution with other women in a series of "Total Woman" courses. Fifteen dollars bought you four two-hour sessions and the tools to turn your marriage around. Demand was high. In 1973 she published her advice in a book, *The Total Woman*. Popular evangelical publisher Fleming Revell printed an initial run of 5000 copies, but by the end of the first year over 500,000 copies had sold, and it would become the best-selling nonfiction book of 1974. Eventually America's housewives would consume more than ten million copies. Morgan achieved celebrity status in American evangelicalism, and her book became an iconic expression of conservative evangelical femininity.[1]

Morgan offered practical tips to help women "become the sunshine" in their homes, advice that included time management, more efficient meal planning (prepare your dinner salads right after breakfast), and weight loss. Most importantly, women just needed to stop nagging

Marabel Morgan
with her book
The Total Woman.

their husbands. If the examples Morgan cites in *The Total Woman* were in any way a reflection of the state of American marriages, things were in a sorry state indeed. Women and men lived in silent and simmering resentment. Marriage was drudgery and sex perfunctory, or nonexistent. Stay-at-home wives lived in constant fear of their husbands taking up with secretaries, and really, who could blame men for doing so? Morgan's solution was simple: treat your husband like a king, revere him, and cater to his every need. This was especially important for working women, because a man's "masculinity may be threatened by your paycheck." A wife needed to let her husband know that he was her hero, and it was her job to put her husband's "tattered ego" back together at the end of each day by admiring his masculine qualities—his muscles, or whiskers.[2]

Morgan's advice had a religious foundation: "The biblical remedy for marital conflict" was the submission of wives to husbands. It was God's plan for women to be under a husband's rule. But Morgan mostly drew on her own experience, particularly when it came to questions of intimacy, a topic about which she had much to say. To begin with, it was important for women to keep up their "curb appeal," to "look and smell delicious," to be "feminine, soft, and touchable," not "dumpy, stringy, or exhausted"—at least if they wanted husbands to come home to them. But that was just the beginning. To keep a husband's interest, Morgan was a strong believer in the power of costumes in the bedroom (or kitchen, living room, or backyard hammock), so that when a husband opened the front door each night it was like "opening a surprise package." One day a "smoldering sexpot," another "an all-American fresh beauty," a pixie, a pirate, "a cow-girl or a show girl." (Contrary to popular belief, Morgan never recommended that women clothe themselves in nothing but Saran Wrap. She wasn't sure where that rumor got its start, though she conceded it was "a great idea.")[3]

Most of Morgan's "homework assignments" for readers and seminar attendees involved sex. A wife was to love her husband "unconditionally," and that meant making herself sexually available to him. The Bible, after all, said not to "cheat each other of normal sexual intercourse," and to "let her breasts satisfy thee at all times." God understood women, and "He knew they would probably use the prized possession of sex to manipulate men." That's why he warned against rationing it out. Morgan assigned women the task of making themselves available to their husbands for seven nights in a row: "Be the seducer, rather than the seduced." She offered numerous and very specific tips to help wives spice up their sex lives, and also a word of caution. When meeting one's husband at the door wearing a risqué costume, be absolutely sure that the person at the door was in fact one's husband. (One Fort Lauderdale housewife wearing a "gypsy costume" consisting of "beads, bangles, and bare skin" found herself standing face to face with a rather startled meter reader.) Morgan's Total Woman wasn't "just a good housekeeper," she was "a warm, loving homemaker." She was "not merely a submissive sex partner," she was "a sizzling lover." Did this disempower or demean women? Morgan didn't think so. In fact, she promised women a sizable return on their investment: "If you're stingy in bed, he'll be stingy with you." Give him what he wants, and he'll give back to you. And by that she meant tangible gifts, like a new refrigerator, a whole new wardrobe, or a cruise to the Bahamas![4]

By giving husbands what they wanted, women could transform marriage from "an endurance contest" into something enjoyable. And they could keep men at home, which was good for women, and good for their kids—especially their boys. If a father was absent, a boy might start to identify too much with his mother "and begin to develop certain feminine qualities on a subconscious level," opening the door to homosexuality. Morgan's good friend Anita Bryant was one of the first women to participate in a Total Woman course. Bryant, a popular singer, beauty pageant winner, and, for a time, Florida orange juice spokeswoman, based her own book *Bless This House* on Morgan's teachings. She then went on to become the spokeswoman for evangelical antigay activism. Within evangelicalism itself, this activism is often depicted as an expression of long-standing opposition to same-sex relationships triggered by the gay rights movement of the 1960s and 1970s, but the virulence with which conservative Christians opposed gay rights was rooted in the cultural and political significance they placed on the reassertion of distinct gender roles during those decades. Same-sex relationships challenged the most basic assumptions of the evangelical worldview.[5]

Morgan became a national phenomenon even before the publication of her book. In 1972, twelve wives of Miami Dolphin football players attended one of her Total Woman classes. The next season the Dolphins won every game, the first undefeated team in NFL history. Not that Morgan took credit for their winning streak, but just in case, several other teams asked for classes for their players' wives. When Morgan's book *The Total Woman* is remembered today, it is often dismissed as a rather fringe and altogether laughable example of the conservative backlash against feminism. But within (and beyond) evangelical circles, it wasn't all that fringe. Morgan's message reached a large audience in part because she was able to take advantage of the new distribution network within the Christian publishing industry. Sold through the

Christian Booksellers Association, her book found its way into Christian bookstores across the country. *The Total Woman* sold millions of copies because it spoke to the needs and desires of middle-class, conservative Christian women, and also because it was available to them.[6]

The Total Woman offered Christians a model of femininity, but it also presented, along the way, a model of masculinity. To be a man was to have a fragile ego and a vigorous libido. Men were entitled to lead, to rule, and to have their needs met—all their needs, on their terms. Morgan's version of femininity hinges on this view of masculinity. It's not difficult to see what part of this equation appealed to men, but Morgan's primary audience was women. What attracted millions of women to *The Total Woman*?

Morgan's message appealed to women invested in defending "traditional womanhood" against the feminist challenge. In 1963, Betty Friedan's *The Feminine Mystique* had invited a generation of women to examine "the problem that has no name," prompting many housewives to reconsider their circumscribed lives. But for many women stuck in unsatisfying marriages and leading unfulfilling lives, the Total Woman curriculum offered a more viable paradigm of hope and change. It wasn't an easy solution, by any means. For a wife stewing with resentment, the demands imposed by Morgan's program were high. Making yourself sexually available to your husband seven nights in a row, praising his whiskers, calling him at work to tell him you craved his body—none of this came easy for many women. But thousands if not millions deemed it an easier path than the one offered by women's "liberation." For many housewives, the new opportunities feminism promised were not opportunities at all. To those who had few employable skills and no means or desire to escape the confines of their homes, feminism seemed to denigrate their very identity and threaten their already precarious existence. It was better to play the cards they were dealt.

Women who chose "traditional womanhood" didn't always do so because they wanted an easier path, however; many believed it to be the *better* path. Consider Elisabeth Elliot, the widow of Jim Elliot—one of five missionaries speared to death in 1956 while trying to make contact with the Huaorani tribe in Ecuador. Elisabeth Elliot had become a popular figure in American evangelicalism after publishing a book on the missionary martyrs and returning to serve for two years among the Huaorani. In 1976, she published *Let Me Be a Woman*, a book of advice to her daughter upon her engagement. Elliot's maternal voice stands in contrast to Morgan's livelier prose, but their messages were compatible.

God created male and female as complementary opposites, Elliot explained: "The woman is totally other, totally different, totally God's gift to man." God gave husbands their "rank" and a "virile drive for domination" necessary to fulfill their duty to rule. Self-denial, meanwhile, was at the heart of Christian womanhood; marriage and motherhood required "self-giving, sacrifice, suffering." Yet men were required to love their wives, and this was the biblical basis for chivalry; love and submission were intimately intertwined.[7]

The very notion of hierarchy came from the Bible, Elliot contended. In short, equality was "not a Christian ideal." A hierarchical order of submission and rule descended "from the nature of God Himself." God the Father exercised "just and legitimate authority"; the Son exhibited "willing and joyful submission." Within the trinitarian God, then, existed "the elements of rule, submission, and union." Due to a hatred of authority, however, "the blueprint has been lost."[8]

No man would fulfill his role perfectly, Elliot reminded her daughter: "You marry a sinner," and "you love, accept and forgive that sinner." A woman should also accept the fact that she marries a *man*: "He is likely to be bigger and louder and tougher and hungrier and dirtier" than expected. But Elliot assured her daughter that real women wanted real men, and real men wanted real women: "The more womanly you are, the more manly your husband will want to be."[9]

Like Morgan, Elliot became a celebrity within the evangelical subculture. Although it's unlikely that the millions of women who read their work did so explicitly as a political act, many evangelical women would develop their own fierce partisan allegiances in alignment with the gender identities they advanced. Motivated to defend "traditional" femininity and masculinity, evangelical women would play a critical role in the grassroots activism that launched the Religious Right.

THE PERSON WHO WOULD most clearly turn the personal political for evangelical women wasn't an evangelical at all. Phyllis Schlafly was Catholic, but her popularity among evangelical women reflected new alliances forming among conservative women, alliances she herself helped cement. A petite woman who never failed to exhibit remarkable poise, Schlafly established herself as "the sweetheart of the Silent Majority." Her very appearance evoked a nostalgic past; her upswept hair, feminine suits, and string of pearls remained virtually unchanged over her half century in the public eye.[10]

Although Schlafly gained notoriety for championing "traditional" womanhood, her own life could hardly be described as traditional. After earning a master's degree in political science from Radcliffe, she worked for a time at the American Enterprise Association, forerunner of the American Enterprise Institute. She then returned to St. Louis to run the campaign of a Republican candidate for Congress, embarking on what she would refer to as her "lifetime hobby" of politics. Her primary vocation, she liked to insist, was as wife to wealthy St. Louis lawyer Fred Schlafly and mother to their six children. In 1952, Schlafly ran for Congress herself. Campaigning with the slogan "A Woman's Place Is in the House," she won the Republican primary but lost in the general election. Undaunted, she worked her way up the party's ranks, and in 1962 she began hosting a fifteen-minute radio show on national security. An ardent anticommunist, she had ties to the far Right; Robert Welch, founder of the John Birch Society, once called her "one of our most loyal members," although Schlafly always denied membership in the organization. In 1964, Schlafly burst onto the national stage with the publication of *A Choice Not an Echo*, a small book promoting Goldwater's campaign. Goldwater, she insisted, was the leader America yearned for. He would solve problems at home and beat the communists abroad. The book was a sensation, selling an estimated 3.5 million copies and helping Goldwater secure the nomination.[11]

Over the next decade Schlafly continued to write on foreign policy, and she began a monthly newsletter, *The Phyllis Schlafly Report*. Initially, Schlafly focused on opposing communism, maintaining the strength of America's nuclear arsenal, and defending states' rights and laissez-faire economics. In 1970, she launched another failed bid for Congress. For Schlafly, the highlight of that campaign was the radio ad that John Wayne recorded on her behalf. Two years later, a friend asked her to speak on the Equal Rights Amendment, but she wasn't interested. The amendment didn't concern Schlafly; she considered it somewhere "between innocuous and mildly helpful." Originally proposed in the 1920s, the text of the amendment was simple: "Equality of rights under the law shall not be denied or abridged by the United States or by any State on account of sex." With the resurgence of feminism in the 1960s, interest in the amendment revived, and in 1972 it was approved by both houses of Congress and sent to states for ratification. When Schlafly came across conservative critiques of the amendment's potential implications, however, she quickly changed her mind.[12]

In her February 1972 newsletter, Schlafly outlined her issues with the ERA. To begin with, she insisted that the very notion of women's oppression was ludicrous. Of all people who had ever lived, no one had enjoyed more privilege than the American woman. Beyond that, no legislation could erase the fact that men and women were different: women had babies and men didn't. Those who didn't like this fact should take up their complaint with God himself. In light of this God-given difference, "Judeo-Christian" society had developed laws and customs requiring men to carry out their duties to protect and provide for women. Women's rights, then—their rights to have babies and to be protected—were achieved through the family structure and ensured through men's chivalry. Tragically, " 'equal rights' fanatics" threatened to undo all this. All of a sudden, "aggressive females" were everywhere "yapping" about how mistreated they were, equating marriage to slavery, suggesting that housework was "menial and degrading, and—

perish the thought—that women are discriminated against." This was "the fraud of the century."[13]

Don't be fooled, Schlafly warned her readers. Employment opportunities, equal pay for equal work—all of this was "only a sweet syrup which covers the deadly poison masquerading as 'women's lib.'" Women's libbers were radicals waging war on marriage, children, and the family—they promoted free sex, "Federal 'day-care centers' for babies instead of homes," and "abortions instead of families." What feminists failed to understand, she argued, was that women *liked* to be housewives and homemakers. Besides, women's employment in offices and on assembly lines was hardly something to strive for: "Most women would rather cuddle a baby than a typewriter or a factory machine." Her message resonated not only with religious women but also with many working-class women for whom the labor market offered unfulfilling work and low pay.[14]

Though late to the ERA, Schlafly was already concerned about abortion in 1972, the year before *Roe v. Wade*, in part because she was Catholic. Catholics had a long history of condemning abortion, even when women's lives were at stake. Some fundamentalist pastors agreed, though they weren't eager to cooperate with Catholics on the issue. But most evangelicals were far less certain. The Bible didn't offer specific advice on the topic. Many evangelicals disapproved of "abortion-on-demand," but not in the case of rape or incest, where fetal abnormalities were present, or when a woman's life was at risk. In 1968, *Christianity Today* considered the question of therapeutic abortion—was it a blessing, or murder? They gave no definitive answer. As late as 1971, the Southern Baptist Convention passed a resolution urging states to expand access to abortion. But with the liberalization of abortion laws, and as abortion proponents began to frame the issue in terms of women controlling their reproduction, evangelicals started to reconsider their position. In 1973, *Roe v. Wade*—and the rising popularity of abortion in its wake—helped force the issue, but even then, evangelical mobilization was not immediate. Only in time, as abortion became more closely linked to feminism and the sexual revolution, did evangelicals begin to frame it not as a difficult moral choice, but rather as an assault on women's God-given role, on the family, and on Christian America itself.[15]

Like Billy Graham and other evangelical lodestars, Schlafly moved fluidly between family matters and national security. She linked gender equality to communism (in Russia, a woman was *"obliged* to put her baby in a state-operated nursery or kindergarten" and abortions were "available for the asking") and fretted that the ERA would force women into military service. She couldn't imagine "why any woman would support such a ridiculous and un-American proposal as this."[16]

Schlafly also argued that the ERA would make women more vulnerable to sexual exploitation. This argument baffled feminists. After all, *they* were the ones who had worked to criminalize violence against women. But Schlafly helped convince conservative women that it was feminists who were violating them, forcing them into roles they didn't want and exposing them to danger by depriving them—and their daughters—of masculine protection.

For its opponents, the ERA took on a symbolic quality, encompassing a larger moral and existential threat to women, and to the nation. Any careful rebuttals or explanations that the ERA's proponents offered fell flat among antiratificationists, leading feminists to deride conservative women's "hysterical apocalypticism." But their opponents were drawing on a coherent worldview, one carefully crafted by activists like Schlafly. Conservative women across the nation rose up to defend their place in the world, to protect a way of life that depended on gender difference—on the provision and protection God had ordained for them.[17]

In 1977, Schlafly published *The Power of the Positive Woman*. (The book was republished four years later as *The Power of the Christian Woman* to appeal to the growing Christian market segment; the text was virtually unchanged, except "Christian" was intermittently substituted for "Positive," and the occasional Bible verse added.) Women didn't need the intrusion of the federal government to flourish, Schlafly asserted: "The Positive Woman starts with the assumption that the world is her oyster. . . . She understands that men and women are different, and that those very differences provide the key to her success as a person and fulfillment as a woman."[18]

What is striking is just how much of Schlafly's best-selling book is devoted to an explicit political agenda. Given Schlafly's "lifelong hobby," this isn't entirely surprising, but it reveals that conservative Christian anti-feminism in the 1970s was intimately connected to a larger set of political issues—to anticommunism, Christian nationalism, and militarism, among others. For example, Schlafly concluded her book with her "Vision for America." First and foremost, "The Positive Woman starts with the knowledge that America is the greatest country in the world and that it is her task to do her part to keep it that way." She must oppose bureaucratic government and creeping socialism (with its "destructive goal of equality") in order to protect the American family and the greatness of private enterprise. She was a patriot and defender of "Judeo-Christian civilization," and she supported legislators who did the same. Finally, the Positive Woman must work to keep the military strong. Women shouldn't think that the problems of military defense were too complex or controversial to engage with. It was up to women to help save their country—*God's* country.[19]

Schlafly didn't have much to say about race, at least not explicitly. But at a time when racial politics found expression in an array of adjacent issues, her views came through clearly. Needless to say, they were frequently at odds with those of civil rights activists. She defended private schooling and sought to keep the federal government from interfering with parental choice. That she meant white parents went without saying. (She would later oppose immigration and promote English-only schools.) In an era when race was increasingly discussed through coded language, her ideas were embraced by the same communities who opposed civil rights. In fact, the ERA was the first issue conservatives rallied around after they lost the legal battle for segregation. As one politician noted at the time, conservatives didn't talk about desegregation and busing all the time, but they were "seething inside," and that anger could erupt in the form of impassioned opposition to the "equality of rights" ensconced in the ERA.[20]

The very language that critics of the ERA employed mirrored that used by segregationists. They spoke not of "forced" busing but of "forced" women, and they coined the term "desexegration." Racial anxieties also surfaced in their rhetoric around "the potty issue." Schools and public facilities had recently been integrated, and now the ERA threatened to turn public restrooms into unisex spaces. This was intolerable. One white woman in North Carolina wrote to her state senator to explain what was at stake: "We will have to use the same restrooms as the men both black and white." A state legislator, too, made the connection plainly: "I ain't going to have my wife be in the bathroom with some big, black buck!"[21]

This blending of racism and the perceived sexual vulnerability of white women had a long history in the South, even if historical evidence irrefutably demonstrates that it was black women who had reason to fear white men's sexual aggression, not the other way around. But with the civil rights movement ending legal separation by race, white fears of imagined black male aggression reached a fevered pitch. That anti-ERA rhetoric focusing on the vulnerability of women found expression in racist terms is not altogether surprising. White men had long positioned themselves as protectors of white womanhood—a tradition that cultivated male bravado, and one that could easily spill over into racial aggression. Opponents' fixation on unisex bathrooms caught many feminists off guard, but it pointed to deeper social anxieties that this new movement for "equal rights" was tapping into. It also prefigured the furor on the Right, and the evangelical Right in particular, over transgender people and bathrooms in our own time.[22]

A WITTY, BRILLIANT WOMAN, Schlafly infuriated feminists. When she spoke in public, she liked to thank her husband for allowing her to do so just to get a rise out of any "women's libbers" who might be

Phyllis Schlafly poses with a five-month-old baby at the Illinois
State Capitol in Springfield on May 14, 1980, before the House
was expected to vote on the ERA. AP PHOTO.

present. Betty Friedan derided her as an "Aunt Tom," a "traitor to her
sex." Feminists burned her in effigy. But Schlafly was unflappable. (She
once received a death threat while dining in a Houston restaurant;
in response she merely smiled and asked for milk in her coffee.) She
chalked up feminists' frustration to the weakness of their arguments:
"They're losing, so they're irrational and mad." Her opponents thought
she was the irrational one, but she had developed a neatly packaged
ideology that seemed impervious to critique. When her adversaries
accused her of hypocrisy—she was, after all, hardly the "traditional
woman"—she turned that criticism on its head. Look at her! She was
proof that women were already free to do what they wanted, without
the help of the ERA.[23]

Almost singlehandedly, Schlafly sabotaged the ratification of the
ERA. In doing so, she also helped put gender at the center of an emerging evangelical political identity. To Schlafly's supporters, the ERA was
a religious issue. As one of her STOP ERA state workers explained,

"Phyllis is a religious leader—perhaps the most powerful in the country today. Because it's women who generally keep the family's faith and it's women who support Phyllis." STOP ERA was "a religious war," and that's why they were winning. As women like Marabel Morgan and Elisabeth Elliot helped unify white Christian women around a shared domestic identity, Schlafly converted these women into political activists. Speaking directly to ordinary housewives across the nation, she endowed their quotidian lives with religious and national significance, uniting Catholic, evangelical, and Mormon women, women in the white middle and working classes—the women of the Silent Majority—in a common cause.[24]

It's hard to overstate Schlafly's significance in marshalling the forces of the Religious Right. Years before James Dobson or Jerry Falwell entered the political fray, Phyllis Schlafly helped unify white Christians around a rigid and deeply conservative vision of family and nation. Although her star faded by the end of the century, it wasn't because her influence had waned. By that time, her ideas had come to define the Republican Party, and much of American evangelicalism. If she seemed superfluous, it was only because what she was saying had become the lingua franca among American conservatives.[25]

Chapter 4

DISCIPLINE
AND COMMAND

POSTWAR EVANGELICALISM CONSISTED OF A collection of diverse traditions and overlapping markets. Celebrities like Billy Graham, Marabel Morgan, and Anita Bryant represented the more outwardly focused, culturally engaged brand of modern evangelicalism, but within the larger movement there existed a more reclusive fundamentalist strand that remained largely invisible to the broader public. On questions of masculine authority, however, the two strands would find significant common ground. In the 1970s, this convergence was illustrated by two figures. One would become a widely recognized evangelical leader who would wield significant power at the national level for nearly half a century. The other would remain unknown outside of evangelicalism. Together, they would facilitate the alliance of separatist and "respectable" evangelicals around the assertion of patriarchal power, an alliance that would form the basis of a common cultural and political identity.

BILL GOTHARD IS A NAME unfamiliar to those outside of conservative evangelical circles, and within those circles his name is likely to provoke conflicting reactions, including not a few straight-up denunciations. Gothard got his start in 1961 by founding Campus Teams, an organization that aimed to address the problems of "wayward youth." Inspired by research he had conducted for his master's thesis in Christian education at Wheaton College, Gothard sought to apply Christian principles to solving conflicts between parents and teens. He later changed the name of the organization to the Institute in Basic Youth Conflicts to reflect this focus. (He would later change the name again to the more general Institute in Basic Life Principles, or IBLP.) The advice Gothard offered to Christian parents navigating the difficult adolescent years, a task made even more challenging by the cultural upheaval of the 1960s, centered on the proper administration of divinely ordained authority.

In this way, Gothard's philosophy built on the Christian Reconstructionist teachings of Rousas John Rushdoony. A somewhat shadowy but influential figure in conservative evangelicalism, Rushdoony gained prominence in the 1960s and 1970s by advocating a strict adherence to the authority of "biblical law." By any measure, Rushdoony was an extremist. He believed that America was founded as a Christian nation, but also that Enlightenment notions of equality were dangerous and wrong and that democracy was antithetical to God-ordained governing structures. The Civil War wasn't a battle over slavery, he insisted, but rather a religious war in which the South was defending Christian civilization. In his view, slavery had been voluntary, and beneficial to slaves. He opposed interracial marriage, looked unfavorably on the education of African Americans and women, and disapproved of women's suffrage and of women speaking in public. Some of his writings bordered on anti-Semitism. Rushdoony believed that the disorder of modern society could be remedied with the institution of Old Testament law, and at the heart of this project was the assertion of hierarchical authority. For Rushdoony and his devotees, freedom was found not in individual autonomy, but in proper submission to authority, and he believed that God-ordained authorities in each sphere of life—family, church, and government—should function without outside interference. Churches must be free from government interference, and the family, under the authority of the patriarch, must also be protected from state intrusion. Public schools, too, posed a direct threat to the authority of the family by usurping parents' role in inculcating values. For this reason, Rushdoony and his followers promoted Christian schools and, even more preferable, homeschooling.[1]

Like Rushdoony, Gothard believed that most problems could be solved by submitting to the proper authorities in each domain of life. To this end, he advanced the idea of a divinely ordained "chain of command" similar to that of the military. In the family, the father was the ultimate authority. A wife owed her husband total submission, requiring approval for even the smallest household decisions, and children owed parents absolute obedience in both action and attitude. The church was also part of the proper functioning of society, and church leaders were to wield absolute, God-given authority over members. Government, too, administered divinely sanctioned authority, with national leaders exercising authority over local officials, who in turn exercised authority over citizens. Proper authority structured business as well; the employer wielded God-given authority over employees. In this way, proponents of "biblical law" married "traditional" gender roles to unrestrained, free-market capitalism. It was a match made in heaven.

For Gothard, those in authority were stand-ins for God and were owed absolute obedience. In his moral universe, the notion of personal rights interfered with the hierarchical structure of authority, contradicting God's design and provoking only anger and resentment. The meek would inherit the earth; the solution for the aggrieved was not in changing their circumstances, but rather in wholesale submission to the authorities placed over them. For both Gothard and Rushdoony, this order found expression in the authoritarian rule of men. Men who forsook their duty to impose order abdicated their masculinity, allowing women to usurp their power, and Rushdoony eagerly awaited the day when "once independent and feministic women" would be humbled and "seek the protection and safety of a man."[2]

To help families navigate conflicts, Gothard offered extensive and inflexible rules. Dating was forbidden, and instead courtship was arranged and supervised by fathers. Girls were ordered to avoid "eye-traps"—anything that would draw attention to their bodies, such as necklines that dropped lower than the collarbone and skirts that fell above the ankle. Domesticity was upheld as women's highest calling, and higher education for girls was discouraged. When family conflicts proved irresolvable, IBLP offered to institutionalize children until their attitudes and behaviors were rectified. In submission to Gothard's authority, parents entrusted their problem children to IBLP institutions, sometimes for months at a time.[3]

The draconian measures of surveillance and discipline Gothard introduced at IBLP, the closed system of authority, and the enforced submission of women and children created a climate ripe for abuse. In 1980, news broke that Gothard's brother and vice president of the institute had been involved in affairs with seven of the institute's secretaries. The scandal eventually grew to include fifteen people, and it became clear that Gothard had known of the improprieties for years but had silenced witnesses and covered up the abuse. In 1976, in fact, he had introduced a new teaching based on Matthew 18, requiring staff to promise that they would never "give an evil report but only say good things about other people." Only later would the full extent of the abuse be revealed.[4]

Gothard was not without detractors within conservative evangelicalism. Critics charged that his "chain of command" replaced the role of Christ with human mediators. They critiqued his legalistic and authoritarian tendencies, and noted that he failed to put himself under any authority. Some accused him of being a cult leader. Yet to his followers, such criticism only revealed an unwillingness to submit to proper authorities. Many evangelicals were sympathetic to his cause; Gothard and his followers, it seemed, were trying to live faithfully in an increasingly hostile, secular age. He could be forgiven for perhaps taking things a bit too far.

Although Gothard remained little known outside of evangelicalism, within conservative circles he exerted significant influence. In 1968 around 2000 people attended his seminars; by 1973 that number had grown to over 200,000. As the author of a popular homeschooling curriculum, he inculcated generations of children in his teachings of biblical law and patriarchal authority. As homeschooling increased in popularity in the 1980s, many families who would not have identified as Christian Reconstructionists nevertheless came to embrace the tradition's core precepts. In this way, authoritarian teachings infused Christian homes, churches, and the wider evangelical subculture.[5]

Gothard didn't engage directly in politics, but others influenced by the ideas he and Rushdoony advanced did. Howard Phillips, a convert to evangelicalism and a key behind-the-scenes operative, came across Rushdoony's ideas in the mid-1970s, and soon joined forces with Rushdoony to combat "the 'IRS assault' on Christian schools." Phillips's son, Doug Phillips, would later emerge alongside Gothard as a leading figure in the Christian homeschool movement. Pat Robertson and D. James Kennedy hosted Rushdoony on their broadcasts, helping to meld charismatic and prosperity gospel traditions with Reconstructionist-inspired teachings, and Rushdoony's work was cited by law school faculty at Oral Roberts University, at Pat Robertson's CBN/Regent University, and at Jerry Falwell's Liberty University. Francis Schaeffer, John W. (Wayne) Whitehead, and Tim LaHaye were also among those influenced by Reconstructionism. Rushdoony is often seen as the "crazy uncle" of the Religious Right, and Gothard himself was not viewed much differently. Yet a generation later, ideas once considered extreme would resonate widely, advanced by young culture warriors in positions of power.[6]

IN 1970, AN AS-OF-YET LITTLE-KNOWN child psychologist named James Dobson published a small book, *Dare to Discipline*. Its subject matter was deceptively mundane: how to discipline children. Dobson decided to write the book after seeing too many troubled children of the 1960s come through the doors of his clinic. Believing that their problems could be traced to the breakdown of the social order— the sexual revolution, divorce, and the disintegration of the family— Dobson began dispensing old-fashioned parenting advice based on

"Judeo-Christian values" to church and PTA groups, advice he then published in his book. Repudiating the permissive approach to child-rearing championed by the recently retired and widely celebrated Dr. Benjamin Spock, Dobson encouraged parents to reassert authority over unruly children. Spanking was a good way to accomplish this, and Dobson offered detailed instructions. He advised using a belt or a switch and keeping the implement in plain sight to remind children that insubordination brought consequences. He made clear that it wasn't necessary "to beat the child into submission." A little pain went a long way.[7]

Dobson's authority rested on his training as a psychologist, but his evangelical faith informed his ideas about child-rearing. Whereas Dr. Spock promoted a nurturing approach to parenthood, advising parents to trust their instincts and treat their children with affection and leniency, Dobson saw children as naturally sinful creatures, inclined toward defiance and rebellion. He may also have been inspired by his own childhood to believe that seemingly innocent children required stern discipline to keep them on the straight and narrow.[8]

The son of three generations of ministers in the evangelical Church of the Nazarene, "Jimmy" was a difficult child. Born in Louisiana, he spent much of his early childhood staying with relatives in Oklahoma, Texas, and Arkansas, while his parents traveled as itinerant evangelists. When he was seven, his mother decided her wayward son needed a proper home. Setting up house outside Oklahoma City, she doted on her only child. "She would always let him say whatever he wanted to say," asking questions but never giving her own opinion, Dobson's wife later recalled. Her son would become an expert at doling out opinions.[9]

During his teenage years, Jimmy again entered a rebellious phase, causing his father to cancel four years of scheduled revival services to come home to his family. His sacrifice seemed to pay off; through sports, hunting, and working in the garage, father and son developed a close bond. When the time came for college, Dobson enrolled in Pasadena College, a small Nazarene school in southern California. There he met his future wife, Shirley. For their first date, the witty, charismatic tennis captain—the "big man on campus"—took the beautiful, brown-haired homecoming queen to Sunday-evening services. Instead of going into the family business of soul-winning, Dobson grew fascinated with the discipline of psychology, and after graduating in 1958 he went on to pursue a PhD in psychology at USC. Hoping to avoid the draft, he hurried to join the National Guard. He served six months, followed by five years of reserve duty. After finishing his degree, he joined the staff at Children's Hospital of Los Angeles, and before long he became a professor of pediatrics at the USC School of Medicine. It was then that he began to diagnose the problems of the younger generation. At the root of these problems was a rejection of authority.[10]

Dare to Discipline was not an overtly political book, but it did address the political moment. Discipline was necessary in order to counteract the "slowly deteriorating 'youth scene,'" to assert authority over a generation of "young revolutionaries who want to burn and destroy the holdings of the establishment." These "young militants" underestimated "the vital function of authority in a civilization," Dobson contended. "Respect for leadership is the glue that holds social organization together. Without it there is chaos, violence, and insecurity for everyone." Parental permissiveness was the last thing children needed in such tumultuous times. If more evidence was needed, one could have looked at Dr. Spock himself; upon retirement he'd turned from dispensing child-rearing advice to political activism, and in 1967, and again in 1968, he was arrested for protesting the war and for aiding and abetting draft resisters.[11]

Dare to Discipline wasn't just a guide to child-rearing. Owing to the social upheaval of the 1960s, the behavior of America's youth had risen to a level of national concern. The reassertion of an authoritarian family structure would preserve order, discipline, and security—not only of the family but of the nation. To a generation of parents bewildered by how drastically things had changed since their own childhoods, the book offered definitive answers. It quickly sold over two million copies, establishing Dobson as a trusted voice in the emerging evangelical subculture.[12]

In 1973, Dobson resigned from the American Psychological Association after it removed homosexuality from its list of mental disorders. Three years later, he took a sabbatical from USC and Children's Hospital, and he never went back. He turned to radio to spread his ideas. His first show, a fifteen-minute program that aired on weekends, was funded by a Christian publisher that had distributed his early writings. Meanwhile, his "Focus on the Family" seminars were drawing thousands of attendees, and he began speaking across the nation. With two children of his own, however, Dobson feared making the mistakes of his own absentee father, and so he decided to retire from the speaking circuit—but not before agreeing to record one of his final talks. Produced by a Christian publisher and marketed to evangelical churches, his seven-part video series was compatible with the first VCRs. One segment of the series addressing distant fathers was packaged separately as a one-hour television special, *Where's Dad?*, and Dobson sent a representative around the country to solicit donations from evangelical businessmen to fund its airing in local markets. This distribution model worked spectacularly well. By the early 1980s an estimated one hundred million people around the world had viewed the special. Dobson founded Focus on the Family in 1977, a parachurch organization dedicated to defending the institution of the family, and by the mid-1980s his half-hour daily show was playing on nearly 800 stations across the nation.[13]

Dare to Discipline had little to say about gender roles, but Dobson's subsequent books made up for that omission. As the decade wore on, it became clear to Dobson that preserving distinct gender roles was critical to turning back the tide of social chaos. Dobson's focus on gender can be explained in part by larger trends undermining "traditional" gender roles in the 1970s. The postwar years had been marked by economic gains that made it possible for many men to serve as sole breadwinners for their families. The global economic restructuring beginning in the 1970s, however, resulted in a decline of American manufacturing jobs and stagnation of male wages. The breadwinner economy had always been as much myth as reality, but by the 1970s, this aspirational ideal was becoming increasingly difficult to attain, even among members of the white middle class. In 1950, 37 percent of women worked for pay, but that number began to rise significantly in the 1970s. Linked in part to women's growing economic independence, rates of divorce began to increase dramatically in the 1970s as well. All of this amounted to a "crisis" of the family, and for evangelicals, gender and authority, not global economic patterns, were at the heart of this crisis.[14]

In addition to larger economic challenges, a number of developments at the national level appeared to threaten the stability of a God-given gender order. In 1971, Congress passed the bipartisan Comprehensive Child Development Bill with the purpose of establishing a national day-care system to help working parents. It was only thanks to Pat Buchanan, a conservative Catholic White House aide who denounced the plan as one that would bring about "the Sovietization of American children," that Nixon vetoed the bill. Conservatives saw the legislation both as a socialist scheme to replace parents with the federal government and as an attack on American motherhood. In 1972, the same year Congress overwhelmingly approved the ERA, they also passed Title IX as part of the Education Amendments Act, prohibiting sex discrimination in federally funded schools. In 1973, the Supreme Court established women's constitutional right to an abortion in *Roe v. Wade*. Together with the growing power of the feminist movement, this series of events appeared to evangelicals to be a coordinated assault on traditional, God-ordained gender roles.[15]

In 1975, Dobson took it upon himself to articulate the "critical difference" between men and women. "Males and females differ biochemically, anatomically, and emotionally," he asserted. "In truth, they are unique in every cell of their bodies." He portrayed the distinction in stark terms: Men liked to "hunt and fish and hike in the wilderness" while women preferred to "stay at home and wait for them." Men played sports as women watched, "yawning on the sidelines." But per-haps the most profound difference between men and women, accord-ing to Dobson, was their source of self-esteem: "Men derive self-esteem by being *respected*; women feel worthy when they are *loved*." Five years later, in his book *Straight Talk to Men and Their Wives*, he expanded on this theme. Echoing Marabel Morgan, he explained that because of a man's fragile ego and "enormous need to be respected," together with a woman's vulnerability and need to be loved, it was "a mistake to tam-per with the time-honored relationship of husband as loving protector and wife as recipient of that protection."[16]

Dobson championed distinct gender roles and identities for the sake of marriages, but also for the sake of the nation. "We *must* not aban-don the Biblical concept of masculinity and femininity at this delicate stage of our national history," Dobson implored. Writing in 1975, he had asserted that the future of the nation depended without question on "how it sees its women." He denounced the "feminist propaganda" behind media depictions of women as tough (albeit gorgeous) figures who "could dismantle any man alive with her karate chops and flying kicks to the teeth," who could shoot with deadly accuracy and play tennis, or even football, like a pro. "Oh, yeah! This baby has come a *long, long* way, no doubt about that," he wrote with thinly veiled revul-sion. But by the end of the 1970s, Dobson had turned his attention to men. He blamed feminists for calling into question "everything tradi-tionally masculine" and for tampering with the "time-honored roles of protector and protected." Most perniciously, they had denigrated masculine leadership as "macho," leaving men in confusion and the nation in peril. The media, too, had colluded with feminists to portray "the macho man" as an anachronism. The demeaning portrayal of men in popular sitcoms was part of a "concerted attack on 'maleness.'" All this left men in a state of confusion over their role: "Will he march off to defend his homeland in times of war, or will his wife be the one to fight on foreign soil? Should he wear jewelry and satin shoes or carry a purse? Alas, is there anything that marks him as different from his female counterpart?"[17]

Drawing on the work of the economist George Gilder, Dobson described what was at stake when society abandoned "the beauty of the divine plan." A man was supposed to fall in love with a woman and then protect and support her. When millions of families followed this plan, the nation remained strong and stable. If men failed to follow this course, "ruination" was inevitable. When men didn't "harness their energies in support of the home, then drug abuse, alcoholism, sexual intrigue, job instability, and aggressive behavior can be expected to be unchecked throughout the culture." What was needed was "a call to arms," a return to "the traditional masculine role as prescribed in the Good Book." Dobson knew he was out of step with prevailing trends, but he was unapologetic: "If this be macho, sexist, chauvinist, and stereotypical, then I'm guilty as charged." With evident pleasure, he added: "Please address all hate mail to my secretary, who has a special file prepared for it."[18]

Dobson would play a critical role in mustering the forces of the Religious Right. But he was able to mobilize American evangelicals so effectively precisely because he did not appear to be doing so, at least not initially. His folksy style stood in stark contrast to the fire-and-brimstone approach of preachers who dominated the religious airwaves. Even his appearance suggested a friendly, harmless demeanor. With his blond hair, blue eyes, gentle smile, and lanky figure—and his California address—Dobson coated his patriarchal teachings with a modern veneer. Early on, Dobson took great pains to appear apolitical. He knew that his authority was as a dispenser of domestic advice, and he was careful not to alienate listeners with strident political messaging, particularly the housewives who tuned in for practical child-rearing tips. He was merely offering help to uncertain parents— and what parents haven't faced uncertainty when it comes to raising children?[19]

Dobson was careful, too, not to appear to usurp the role of local churches. Instead, he worked alongside them, offering weekly bulletin inserts, video series, and other resources for churches to distribute to their members. Pastors and elders, rural and suburban housewives, all became part of the larger Focus family. Fine doctrinal differences that may have separated Nazarene from Southern Baptist, evangelical from fundamentalist, made little difference when it came to Dobson's growing empire. The organization avoided divisive theological issues, and tuning in required no conversion experience, statement of faith, or claims of exclusivity. Evangelicals of all stripes turned to Dobson for advice, as did mainline Protestants and Catholics. (For Catholics looking for practical advice on Christian parenting, celibate priests only had so much to offer.) Dobson also reached nonchurchgoers, including "believers but not belongers" who eschewed formal institutional affiliation. For those who believed that Christianity meant being in relationship with Jesus, church attendance wasn't necessarily the primary marker of religious devotion. Incorporating one's beliefs into one's daily activities could be a more authentic expression of one's faith. For all its religious diversity, however, Dobson's audience remained predominantly white.[20]

Through books, newsletters, and especially radio, Dobson became a fixture in the homes and lives of tens of millions of Americans. As one faithful listener described: "[Focus on the Family] was so knitted into the fabric of my thinking and beliefs that it's hard to pick it out now. Because it has become so much a part of us." By the 1980s Dobson was receiving hundreds of thousands of letters a year, the vast majority from women. Attentive to his "constituents'" needs, Dobson assembled a team of staffers who offered tailored advice and recommended various Focus on the Family publications. His organization dispensed this advice without charge, asking only for "suggested donations." In this way, Dobson amassed a loyal following, a community united by the consumption of his freely given advice. The money followed. By 1987, Focus on the Family had developed into "a full-blown evangelical media empire" with a budget of around $34 million; by 1995 the budget surpassed $100 million.[21]

Within a decade of the publication of *Dare to Discipline*, Dobson had established himself as an evangelical power broker. By the 2000s, Dobson's radio show aired on around two thousand stations, reaching six to ten million weekly listeners. He had amassed a mailing list of over two million addresses, and his organization had launched its own publishing house, capitalizing on its efficient distribution system. By that time, the Southern Baptist Convention's Richard Land would label Dobson "the most influential evangelical leader in America.... The closest thing to his influence is what Billy Graham had in the sixties and seventies." That a child psychologist, not a pastor or evangelist, would in Land's opinion surpass Graham's influence testifies to changes within evangelicalism itself. As gender and "family values" moved to the center of evangelical identity, a man who dispensed advice on kids' chores, potty training, and teenage sex ed could achieve celebrity status formerly reserved for pastors and evangelists.[22]

DOBSON INITIALLY DENIED the political nature of his work, but his teachings had clear political implications. When he did begin to engage directly in politics in the early 1980s, he brought his enormous and devoted following with him. In 1988, a survey found that 92 percent of Focus on the Family respondents voted in the presidential election, 79 percent had signed or circulated a petition, and 45 percent had boycotted a company or product. Even after he began to engage in activism, the vast majority of his organization's resources remained devoted to its "family ministries," yet Dobson's domestic advice was always linked to a larger political vision. Cognitive linguist George Lakoff has proposed that competing metaphors of the family constitute a key divide in modern society. Morality is imagined through metaphor, and family metaphors reside at the core of contemporary political worldviews; whereas liberals favor a nurturing parent model, conservatives embrace a strict father metaphor. At the center of Dobson's worldview—and that of many conservative evangelicals—was the strict enforcement of patriarchal authority.[23]

For both Dobson and Gothard, the problems of the modern family, and of society writ large, could be traced to the erosion of patriarchal power. Within both separatist and "respectable" wings of modern evangelicalism, then, a shared defense of patriarchy contributed to an emerging cultural identity, and to a growing commitment to political activism. Over time, this alliance would begin to dictate the boundaries of evangelicalism itself.

Chapter 5

SLAVES AND SOLDIERS

A S EVANGELICALS BEGAN TO MOBILIZE AS A
partisan political force, they did so by rallying to defend "family values." But family values politics was never about protecting the well-being of families generally. Fundamentally, evangelical "family values" entailed the reassertion of patriarchal authority. At its most basic level, family values politics was about sex and power.

Inspired by men like James Dobson and Bill Gothard, evangelicals propped up patriarchal authority in ways that were both personal and political. In the home, fathers disciplined children and husbands exercised authority over wives; in the case of husbands and wives, this authority could be administered in the most intimate of ways. Beyond the home, the power of the patriarch ensured the security of the nation. In the aftermath of Vietnam, this required a renewed commitment to militarism. Family values politics, then, involved the enforcement of women's sexual and social subordination in the domestic realm and the promotion of American militarism on the national stage.

Phyllis Schlafly had helped piece together this interlocking set of priorities, but by the 1970s, evangelicals themselves came to play a critical role in defining family values politics. By the early 1980s, Tim LaHaye, Beverly LaHaye, and Jerry Falwell had established themselves as architects of the Religious Right. Together, they ensured that the enforcement of patriarchal authority, in all its facets, would occupy the heart of evangelical politics for decades to come.

TIM LAHAYE IS BEST KNOWN today as the coauthor of the *Left Behind* books, a fictional series based on the rapture, a premillennialist end-times scenario in which believers are taken up into heaven before an apocalyptic series of events unfolds on earth. LaHaye's novels are rife with paragons of rugged masculinity and redemptive violence. The hero is a man by the name of Rayford Steele, husband to faithful wife Irene, whose work for Richard DeVos's Amway testifies to her charitable character. But Rayford's libido draws him to a "drop-dead gorgeous" flight attendant; when his wife is raptured, he and the flight attendant are not. The series ends in a violent bloodbath ushered in by Christ himself. The conquering Christ brings peace through the sword, slaying tens of thousands of opposition soldiers who fall dead, "splayed and filleted," blood bursting "from skin and veins," entrails gushing to the ground. In acts of unprecedented violence, Christ's enemies get what they had coming. LaHaye's *Left Behind* books have sold more than sixty-five million copies; one survey estimates that one in five Americans has read at least one of the books. It was, however, a rapture of a different sort that inspired LaHaye's earlier writing.[1]

In 1968, LaHaye published a guide to marriage with the curious but telling title *How to Be Happy Though Married*. The book promoted "male headship," the notion based on New Testament teachings that the husband was "the head of the wife," that he had authority over her and was responsible for her; for LaHaye, this was particularly relevant in matters of finances. In addition to other more mundane topics, LaHaye included a chapter on "Physical Joys" that contained a helpful glossary of terms ("clitoris," "vulva area," "glans penis," "areas of sexual sensitivity") and two detailed charts of male and female sexual anatomy. This book was published by the evangelical Tyndale House Publishers two years before the feminist classic *Our Bodies, Ourselves*, and by 1973 it was already in its sixteenth printing, with more than 300,000 copies in print.[2]

LaHaye's marital sex guide came at a time when evangelicals were increasingly concerned about sex in general. In 1960, the FDA approved the first birth control pill. In 1962, Helen Gurley Brown published *Sex and the Single Girl*, and two years later *Newsweek* heralded a "new morality" that required only a "meaningful relationship" to legitimate sexual intimacy. To conservative evangelicals, there was nothing remotely moral about this new morality, and as the morality gap grew, so, too, did evangelicals' worry over what was being taught about sex in public schools. With no more consensus over moral values, which values would be conveyed to their children?[3]

This was not a question to take lightly, and Billy James Hargis—the fundamentalist pastor who helped spearhead Christian anticommunism in the 1950s and 1960s—took it upon himself to safeguard the sexual purity of America's children. When Hargis turned his attention to sex in the mid-1960s, he didn't do so at the expense of his anticommunism. Like Graham, Hargis considered sexual morality critical to the nation's defense against communism. Others soon joined his new crusade. With none-too-subtle pamphlets like *Is the School House the Proper Place to Teach Raw Sex?* conservative Christian leaders sounded the alarm, and battles over sex ed soon broke out in nearly half of all school districts across the nation. Many of the citizens who waged this battle were the same ones who were fighting against gun control and unsettled by the prospects of interracial dating at desegregated schools. Organizations like the John Birch Society and the Ku Klux Klan teamed up with Hargis. Hargis's career would be cut short in 1976, when *Time* magazine published an exposé of the crusader's sexual improprieties. The allegations came to light after a student at Hargis's college revealed to his bride on their honeymoon that he'd had sex with Hargis, only to discover that she had, too. But others took up Hargis's crusade where he left off.[4]

The year of Hargis's downfall, LaHaye and his wife Beverly coauthored a more detailed Christian sex manual, *The Act of Marriage*. The

LaHayes were also deeply concerned about changing sexual mores, but like Marabel Morgan, they were not anti-sex. Instead, they offered a different model of sexual liberation—the liberation of heterosexual couples to freely enjoy sex within the confines of patriarchal marriage. Inspired in part by Morgan's *The Total Woman*, the LaHayes also advised women to "clean up, paint up, fix up" before "hubby" returned from work, as the sight of a "bedraggled wife" rarely inspired love.[5] But the LaHayes took Morgan's advice a step further by situating sex more fully within the framework of patriarchal authority. "God designed man to be the aggressor, provider, and leader of his family," they explained, and these roles were directly tied to a man's sex drive. You couldn't have a man's "aggressive leadership" without his aggressive sex drive, and women who resented the latter had better come to terms with this fact. In satisfying their husbands sexually, wives played a critical role in propping up men's egos, which in turn bolstered them for leadership. If a husband lacked confidence, his wife should "make aggressive love to him ... dress provocatively and use her feminine charm to seduce him" to help him "bounce back." A woman's failure in the bedroom, the LaHayes made clear, had consequences: "Few men accept bedroom failure without being carnal, nasty, and insulting." In other words, if a man didn't enjoy his wife's lovemaking, he would find ways to make his disapproval known. This was simply the way things worked.[6]

The problem was that many Christian wives *were* failures in the bedroom. And here the LaHayes confronted a conundrum. What happens when you believe that men have voracious sexual appetites, that their very ability to lead their families and their nation is linked to the satisfaction of those appetites, but wives have been taught from childhood that their sexuality must be restrained, controlled, suppressed? What happens when good Christian wives have little sexual knowledge and little apparent desire? When they are filled with guilt and an overbearing sense of modesty? Obviously, this led to conflict in the bedroom, and the LaHayes offered a solution.

They worked to convince modest Christian women that it was not sinful to let their husbands see them naked, that they should learn to talk about sex without embarrassment and educate themselves about how to have sex in a way they and their husbands enjoyed. In *The Act of Marriage* they offered a vastly expanded treatise on sex. The book was a nearly 300-page how-to guide that answered virtually every imaginable question, often in graphic detail: *How can a man delay orgasm long enough for his wife to get aroused? What about oral manipulation of breasts? Is a woman's clitoris always the spot she desires her husband to touch to arouse her sexual tensions? Are some women born frigid? Is it right for a Christian woman to have silicone injected into her breasts? Can a homosexual or lesbian ever be cured? Is it right for Christians to practice birth control?* Charting a course between an unhealthy repression of sexuality on the one hand, and the excesses of the sexual revolution on the other, the LaHayes offered a vision of sexuality securely confined within the structures of patriarchal authority. Men could have unrestrained libidos—they simply needed to satisfy themselves within marriage. Women needed to restrain themselves until marriage, at which point it was their duty to satisfy their husbands' demands.[7]

For the LaHayes, women's subordination was theological, social, and sexual: "The very nature of the act of marriage involves feminine surrender." In language that would resurface in countless subsequent books on evangelical masculinity, the LaHayes assured men that women desired their heroic masculine leadership, in the bedroom and beyond: "Lurking in the heart of every girl (even when she is grown up) is the image of prince charming on his white horse coming to wake up the beautiful princess with her first kiss of love."[8]

Beverly and Tim would each play strategic roles in the emerging Christian Right. The two had met as students at Bob Jones University in the 1940s, a school that would be at the center of debates over segregation and private Christian education throughout the 1970s and 1980s. (BJU did not admit African American students until 1971, and then only with strict rules against interracial dating and marriage that remained on the books until 2000.) Tim had served as a machine gunner on a bomber in the Second World War, and after college he earned a doctorate in literature from Liberty University. In the 1950s, the LaHayes joined in the evangelical migration to southern California, and there they would knit together the new set of issues that would come to define modern American evangelicalism.

Deeply influenced by Phyllis Schlafly, Beverly emerged as an influential leader in her own right. In 1976 she published *The Spirit-Controlled Woman*, a book that would sell over 800,000 copies, and in 1979 she founded Concerned Women for America (CWA), an evangelical organization devoted to carrying forward the pro-family, anti-feminist cause. Within only a few years, CWA surpassed Schlafly's Eagle Forum in terms of membership and influence within American evangelicalism. Even more than Dobson, Beverly LaHaye motivated her followers to engage with politics; 98 percent of CWA members voted in the 1988 presidential election, 93 percent had signed or circulated a petition, 77 percent had boycotted a company or product, 74 percent had contacted a public official, and nearly half had written a letter to the editor.[9]

Tim LaHaye was a pastor and speaker (including for the John Birch Society in the 1960s and 1970s), and the author of more than 85 books. A sampling of his nonfiction titles reveals the contours of his worldview: *The Unhappy Gays: What Everyone Should Know about Homosexuality* (1978), *The Battle for the Mind* (1980), *The Battle for the Family* (1981), *The Battle for the Public Schools* (1982), *Faith in Our Founding Fathers* (1987), and *Raising Sexually Pure Kids* (1993). In these writings LaHaye denounced "abortion-on-demand, legalization of homosexual rights . . . the size and power of big government, elimination of capital punishment, national disarmament, increased taxes, women in combat, passage of ERA, unnecessary busing." For LaHaye, these were all facets of the same project.[10]

LaHaye strove to arouse Christians' sense of embattlement. He warned of the "liberal, humanist" media corrupting the nation, evident in "the pornographic indoctrination now masquerading as TV entertainment"—in "anti-moral" programs like *Three's Company*, *Dallas*, and *Saturday Night Live*—but also in television and print news. Most pointedly, he blamed American news stations for their biased coverage of the Vietnam War, for constantly "twisting" news reports "to make America appear the aggressor," causing a generation to become disillusioned with their own country. *Time* and *Newsweek* were also not to be trusted; he recommended magazines like *Human Events* and *Conservative Digest* as alternatives. But what was really needed was a fourth television news network "committed to rendering a conservative view of the news," along with a conservative wire service and a chain of newspapers, news sources that would defend "traditional moral values, the church of Jesus Christ, a strong national defense," and other conservative values.[11]

Like many other leaders in the Religious Right, LaHaye was inspired by Christian Reconstructionism. Citing Rushdoony and those influenced by Rushdoony, he argued that America was founded as a Christian nation, and he advocated for biblical authority in the realm of family, church, and government. Yet LaHaye's embrace of Christian Reconstructionism is in some ways curious. Like most fundamentalists, LaHaye was a premillennialist. Premillennialists tended to see America, like any other nation, as doomed to destruction. Reconstructionists, on the other hand, were postmillennialists who believed Christians needed to establish the Kingdom of God on earth by bringing all things under the authority or dominion of Christ before Christ returned. LaHaye's embrace of Reconstructionism demonstrates how theological contradictions could be smoothed over in practice. In adopting Reconstructionist teachings piecemeal, premillennialists patched over a long-standing division within conservative Protestantism. Such quibbles apparently paled in comparison to what they held in common—a desire to reclaim the culture for Christ by reasserting patriarchal authority and waging battle against encroaching secular humanism, in all its guises.[12]

In addition to helping construct the philosophy of the Religious Right, LaHaye was also instrumental in building its organizational scaffolding. In 1981, LaHaye founded the Council for National Policy, an influential and secretive organization that served as a conservative policy incubator and helped nudge the Republican Party to the Right, and he would have a hand in creating a number of other conservative organizations in the 1980s as well. By generating ideas and networks, LaHaye established himself as one of the most influential evangelicals of the late twentieth century, a status he shared with another key player in the rise of the Christian Right, the Reverend Jerry Falwell.[13]

JERRY FALWELL ECHOED and amplified themes articulated by Schlafly, Dobson, and the LaHayes. These leaders had connected Christian manhood to a strong national defense and championed a return to "macho" masculinity, but it was Falwell who most clearly represented the shift toward a more brazen militancy—and militarism.

Like Dobson, Falwell had a troubled relationship with his own father, an alcoholic who succumbed to cirrhosis of the liver when Falwell was a teenager. Falwell grew up in Lynchburg, Virginia, a town that had never recovered from the economic challenges that beset the region in the wake of the Civil War. His mother sought to raise him as a proper Baptist, taking him to church and having him listen to Charles Fuller's Old Fashioned Revival Hour each week on the radio. (A purveyor of modern evangelicalism, Fuller was neither old-fashioned nor Baptist.) Falwell was a standout athlete, the captain of his high school football team, but he was also a math whiz and class valedictorian. After "getting saved" in high school, he decided to attend a Baptist Bible college to train for the ministry. Upon returning to Lynchburg in 1956, he started his own fundamentalist Baptist church. By that time, thanks to the nascent military-industrial complex, new factories were springing up in the region. Falwell had already imbibed anticommunism in his fundamentalist Baptist circles, but now the business interests of his town—and his new church—were directly linked to Cold War capitalism.

Among the people streaming into Falwell's Thomas Road Baptist Church were large numbers of Appalachian transplants. Having left rural America for new opportunities, these blue-collar migrants were searching for new forms of community and identity. They brought with them a culture of militarism (and perhaps also a suspicion of "outsiders") that some historians trace back to the rough-and-tumble Scotch-Irish borderlands from which their families originally hailed. Falwell fashioned a Christianity that was well suited to this local context—one that was anticommunist, pro-segregationist, and infused throughout with a militant masculinity. Building a religious empire in Lynchburg, Falwell then exported this politicized faith across the nation through his radio and television ministries.[14]

In 1979, at the nudging of Goldwater campaign veterans Howard Phillips, Paul Weyrich, and Richard Viguerie, Falwell launched the Moral Majority, a political organization with the purpose of training, mobilizing, and "electrifying" the Religious Right, but he had been championing Christian nationalism throughout the 1970s. In 1976, the year of America's bicentennial, he had organized a series of "I Love America" rallies, elaborately choreographed performances staged on the steps of state capitals across the nation. The next year he supported Anita Bryant and Phyllis Schlafly in their "pro-family" campaigns, and then he initiated his own "Clean Up America" campaign. At the end of the decade he returned to his "I Love America" rallies, possibly because he had leftover Bicentennial Bibles to dispense with. Falwell loved patriotic pageantry. One of his musical groups, the Sounds of Liberty, was composed of women wearing "Charlie's Angels hairdos" who seemed "to snuggle up against their virile-looking male counterparts."[15]

In 1980, Falwell published *Listen, America!*, a primer on the politics of the Religious Right. His audience was the sixty million people Gallup had recently identified as "born-again Christians," in addition to another sixty million "religious promoralists"—all told, his "Moral Majority." With numbers on their side, the time had come to reclaim the country from "a vocal minority of ungodly men and women" who had brought America to "the brink of death." However, the first pages of *Listen, America!* aren't about America at all. Instead, Falwell opened with graphic details of atrocities committed by the Russia-backed "Vietnamese Communists" and the "Red China"–backed Khmer

Rouge in Cambodia. Such slaughter would soon be upon America, he warned, if they didn't hold communism at bay and fight the "moral decay" destroying American freedoms. Signs of this decay abounded: "welfarism," "income-transfer programs," divorce, abortion, homosexuality, "secular humanism" in public schools, federally funded day care, and the Domestic Violence Prevention and Treatment Act. The Domestic Violence Act was especially insidious, for it would do away with "physical punishment as a mode of childrearing" and "eliminate the husband as 'head of the family.'" Another bill pending in the Senate (S. 1722) at that time would enable women to sue husbands for rape, he claimed. The Department of Health, Education, and Welfare was a particular target of conservative ire. Created in 1953, the department oversaw school integration, public-school curriculum revision, and welfare expenditures, money that conservatives felt could better be spent on national defense.[16]

Falwell offered solutions to the grim situation the country found itself in: free enterprise (as "clearly outlined in the Book of Proverbs"), patriotism, turning to God instead of government, and taking a firm stand against the ERA, feminism, and "the homosexual revolution." Defending the family was the linchpin of Falwell's ideology. God had created families for a purpose: families were central to procreation, and, properly structured around patriarchal authority, families were also God's mechanism for controlling and "containing" the earth. But the family was in peril. Protecting the family required moral revival, but even more importantly, a revitalized military. As Falwell explained, "the most notable example of government malfeasance in its family obligations is in the area of defense." Due to the government's "unilateral disarmament, mutually assured destruction, and the acceptance of Soviet military superiority," America was failing to protect its families.[17]

Christian citizens must rectify this situation. Lest Americans be misled by traditions of Christian pacifism, Falwell insisted that Christianity sanctioned military aggression. The Book of Romans stated plainly that God granted government officials "the right to bear the sword." Moreover, "a political leader, as a minister of God, is a revenger to execute wrath upon those who do evil." The US government, then, had every right "to use its armaments to bring wrath upon those who would do evil by hurting other people." Good citizens submit to their governments and honor those in authority over them; in turn, government officials—"ministers of God"—ensure the safety of their citizens by "being a terror to evildoers within and without the nation." Ultimately, American security depended on its men: "We need in America today powerful, dynamic, and godly leadership."[18]

Falwell's overt political activism in the 1970s and 1980s marked a dramatic personal reversal. In the 1960s, he had preached *against* Christian political engagement. Christians had only one task: to preach God's word of salvation through Christ. "We are not told to wage war against bootleggers, liquor stores, gamblers, murderers, prostitutes, racketeers, prejudiced persons or institutions, or any other existing evil as such," he had argued. Christian ministry was one of transformation, not reformation: "The gospel does not clean up the outside but rather regenerates the inside." A Christian's civic duty was to pay taxes, vote, and obey the laws of the land. Any political activity beyond this would distract Christians from their sole purpose, "to know Christ and to make Him known."[19]

If this apolitical rhetoric seems odd coming from the founder of the Moral Majority, consider that Falwell addressed his earlier denouncement of Christian political activism to "Ministers and Marchers"—in other words, to Christian pastors active in the civil rights movement. A child of the South, Falwell was a segregationist. Rather than fearing that American racism would discredit the country globally, Falwell insisted that civil rights agitation was inspired by communist sympathizers. He saw Marxism at the root of the movement, not a Christian social justice tradition. Falwell helped lead local efforts to resist school integration, even when that meant defying the Eisenhower administration, both national parties, and Lynchburg's own business leaders. He opened his own private Christian academy in 1967, the same year his state mandated the immediate desegregation of public schools. Falwell

only changed his tune on political engagement when he deemed it necessary to preserve the rights of segregationists and fend off a secularist
assault. By 1980, Falwell had repudiated his earlier teaching as "false
prophecy." In fact, by that time he was advocating civil disobedience—
were Congress to begin drafting women into military service.[20]

As Falwell battled for the rights of (white) families and in defense of
the nation, he employed explicitly militaristic language. In 1981, journalist Frances FitzGerald introduced Falwell to the American public
in a lengthy *New Yorker* profile. Falwell was "fighting a holy war," a
war to resist feminism, abortion on demand, government intervention
in the family, the abandonment of Taiwan, IRS interference in Christian schools, children's rights, and "rampant homosexuality"—the very
things that had corrupted the nation's morals and blunted its ability to
resist communism. According to Falwell, this war was between those
who loved Jesus and those who hated him, and those who loved Jesus
should expect to be reviled by others.[21]

Military metaphors structured Falwell's understanding of Christianity. The church was an "army equipped for battle," Sunday school
an "attacking squad," Christian radio "the artillery." Christians, "like
slaves and soldiers," ask no questions. As an occupation force, they
needed to advance "with bayonet in hand" to bring the enemy under
submission to the gospel of Christ. The enemy here was a human one,
according to FitzGerald: anyone who didn't subscribe to Falwell's
brand of fundamentalism. Falwell's militarism gave shape to the gospel he preached, and to the savior at the heart of that gospel. Falwell
couldn't stomach "effeminate" depictions of Christ as a delicate man
with "long hair and flowing robes." Jesus "was a man with muscles. . . .
Christ was a he-man!"[22]

Falwell's rhetoric was reminiscent of earlier fundamentalist militancy, but he combined it with Cold War militarism and a rigid reassertion of patriarchal gender roles; for Falwell, each would define and
reinforce the other. Falwell's rhetoric resonated with members of his
congregation. The region surrounding Lynchburg had a strong military
heritage, and at Thomas Road Baptist Church, military service was

"probably the rule rather than the exception." For members who had relocated from Appalachia, Falwell's militaristic brand of Christianity dovetailed nicely with long-held traditions of masculine honor and violence. Falwell's militancy promised protection, from enemies within and without. In this way, Falwell's authority depended on maintaining a sense of vulnerability among his followers. This was achieved through the continual fabrication of new enemies. Danger, discrimination, and disparagement lurked around every corner. Malevolent forces aligned against true believers. Outsiders were likely to be enemies. Threats of a spiritual and cultural nature required a militant Christianity; threats to the nation required unrestrained militarism.[23]

IN THE SUMMER OF 1980, a pivotal event brought together Falwell, the LaHayes, and other architects of the Religious Right in dramatic fashion. Conservatives, it turns out, hadn't been the only ones concerned with the fate of American families. Feminists, liberals, progressive churches, African American and Chicana activists, doctors, teachers, academics and professionals—even the National Gay Task Force—were all invested in strengthening and protecting families in the 1970s. Thinking that conservatives and liberals might come together in a common cause, President Carter organized a White House Conference on Families. Things didn't go as planned.

Well before the conference, the fault lines were impossible to ignore. Who got to define "family"? Conservatives championed the "traditional" model: an archetypal family headed by a white, heterosexual male breadwinner. Liberals proposed a more adaptive family model, one that allowed for single parents and gay men and women. Liberals looked to government to support families. Conservatives opposed government "interference" and sought instead to protect families from moral erosion.[24]

When it came to marshaling grassroots forces, conservatives had the upper hand. They'd been building networks and refining policy positions for over a decade, and they knew what they were up against. Nationally funded childcare, the ERA, *Roe v. Wade*, the Domestic Violence Prevention and Treatment Act, feminism, and gay rights—each of these flashpoints had mobilized a "pro-family" movement and fine-tuned conservative Christian talking points. But grassroots activism had its limits; after organizers had selected participants—more than 100,000 citizens engaged in various stages of the process—conservatives began to complain that they were not properly represented. Despite his later protestations that Focus on the Family was not a political organization, Dobson's overt political engagement can be traced to his urging listeners to write to the White House to request his inclusion in the conference. They didn't disappoint; 80,000 letters were delivered to the White House. Even then, Dobson only received an invitation to address a preconference event.[25]

Frustrated, conservatives denounced what they saw as a liberal scheme to hijack the conversation. Fuming that conference organizers had excluded conservatives' issues—including banning abortion, defending school prayer, and opposing gay rights—from their final recommendations, conservative delegates walked out of the official conference in protest. The next month, they organized their own counter-conference in Long Beach, California, an event that united the forces of the pro-family Religious Right. Dobson, Schlafly, Falwell, and the LaHayes all spoke, rallying the troops. The timing was strategic. With the 1980 election weeks away, they were united in their efforts to unseat Carter.

To evangelicals, Carter had been a disappointment on all counts. They denounced the Carter administration for siding with feminists and for "wooing the homosexual vote." To make matters worse, Carter had overseen what conservatives perceived to be the stunning decline of American strength. On his first day in office he had pardoned draft evaders. He agreed to hand over the Panama Canal and signed a nuclear arms control agreement. He'd allowed the Sandinistas to gain control of Nicaragua and enabled the overthrow of the Shah of Iran. The kidnapping of 52 American hostages at the US embassy in Tehran was an especially humiliating blow. Meanwhile, the president was mired in a "crisis of confidence," and seemed unable to lead America out of the mess he'd made. On top of all this, he wore cardigans and he smiled too much. Even the national media proclaimed Carter a "wimp," and the label stuck.[26]

For American evangelicals who had placed patriarchal power at the heart of their cultural and political identity, Carter's wimp factor was particularly infuriating, and their sense of betrayal acute. After all, Carter was supposed to be one of them—he was a born-again evangelical, a southerner, a Sunday school teacher—and they had helped elect him in order to restore the nation's firm moral footing in the aftermath of Watergate. He had even served a stint as a naval submariner. Yet it was clear that he was *not* one of them on the issues that mattered most. For the strong, masculine leadership the country so urgently required, they would need to look elsewhere.

Chapter 6

GOING FOR
THE JUGULAR

IN AUGUST 1980, ONLY A MONTH AFTER THE LONG
Beach Pro-Family Conference, conservative Christian leaders gathered again, this time in Dallas at the national meeting of the Religious Roundtable. With American flags waving and shouts of "Hallelujah!" ringing, speakers warned of the nation's moral decline and diminishing military might. Masterminded by televangelist James Robison, the event brought together Falwell, Schlafly, and the LaHayes, along with Pat Robertson, D. James Kennedy, and prominent conservatives including Republican senator Jesse Helms, Amway cofounder Richard DeVos, and Dallas Cowboys coach Tom Landry.[1]

An evangelist, Robison was there to convert his audience to politics. "Not voting is a sin against Almighty God!" he pronounced. "I'm sick and tired of hearing about all the radicals and the perverts and the liberals and the leftists and the Communists coming out of the closet! It's time for God's people to come out of the closet, out of the churches, and change America!" Robison wasn't just calling for political participation; he was calling for partisan activism. Political salvation could be found in the Republican Party. After Robison had riled up the crowd, the guest of honor took his place behind the lectern: "I know that you can't endorse me," the Republican nominee for president quipped. "But I want you to know that I endorse you, and your program." In Ronald Reagan, the Religious Right had found their leader.[2]

True, Reagan's religious credentials left something to be desired.

Although raised Presbyterian, his church attendance was sporadic. There was also the matter of his divorce. "Reagan was not the best Christian who ever walked the face of the earth," acknowledged one leader of the Christian Right, "but we really didn't have a choice." His record as governor of California was also mixed. He had supported the ERA, legalized therapeutic abortion, and refused to support an anti-gay-rights referendum. But by 1980 he had become proficient in conservative talking points. He supported prayer and the teaching of creationism in public schools, came out against abortion, and reversed course on the ERA, deciding that it denigrated stay-at-home mothers and would force women into combat. (He placed Beverly LaHaye on his campaign's family policy advisor board.) What had drawn Reagan to the Republican Party were the same things that had drawn evangelicals: a mix of anticommunism, Christian nationalism, and nostalgia for a mythical American past. By the time he took the stage in Dallas, Reagan was fluent in the language of the Christian Right. Echoing Goldwater years earlier, he promised peace through strength. Rejecting Carter's "despair and pessimism," he declared that America could still become that "shining city upon a hill."[3]

Reagan didn't just speak the language of the Right, he looked the part. In contrast to Carter, Reagan emanated a firm, masculine strength. Fresh off his California ranch, he looked to be a real cowboy—and, thanks to his films, a war hero. With his ruddy face, easy manner, and staunch conservatism, he was perfectly cast for his role as hero of the Religious Right.[4]

THE NIGHT BEFORE THE 1980 ELECTION, Reagan made one last pitch to voters on national television. He drew a dim picture of the era, speaking of "riots and assassinations," of Vietnam, and of the "drift and disaster in Washington." It was time for Americans to choose a path forward. Some might want to give up on the American dream, but he offered a vision modeled on his friend John Wayne, "a symbol of our country itself." Wayne had died the year before, and headlines had eulogized him as "The Last American Hero." But Reagan rejected the epitaph. He knew Wayne well, "and no one would have been angrier at being called the 'last American hero,' " Reagan asserted. "Duke Wayne did not believe that our country was ready for the dust bin of history," and neither did he. The next day, Americans chose heroism. Wayne didn't live to see his old friend elected president, but even in death he had played a role.[5]

Reagan was never a movie star of Wayne's caliber, but the two were similar in many ways. Onscreen and off, both blended myth and reality. Both had played the war hero, and among admirers this fiction was often confused for fact. Both, too, symbolized an old-school rejection of the social upheaval of the 1960s and 1970s. A writer in *American Cowboy* magazine described Wayne as "emblematic of strong, silent manhood, of courage and honor in a world of timidity and moral indifference." In a society "racing toward permissiveness," Wayne stood for authority. In a 1971 interview with *Playboy*, Wayne had denounced this culture of permissiveness in no uncertain terms, and by permissiveness, Wayne made clear that he meant "simply following Dr. Spock's system of raising children." After fifteen or twenty years, the consequences of this "anything goes" attitude were everywhere apparent, not least in the behavior of a generation of "hippie dropouts." Reagan agreed.[6]

Reagan specialized in playing the role of the stern, authoritarian father. Only a month before the Kent State shootings in the spring of 1970, his response to student unrest was blunt: "If it takes a bloodbath, let's get it over with. No more appeasement." He ran as a tough-on-crime candidate, and for conservatives, "tough on crime" generally connoted only certain types of crime: "street crime," or the threat of black men. Domestic violence, sexual assault, and child abuse didn't register. Domestic tranquility could be established through the imposition of law and order. It should come as no surprise that a country that embraced Wayne as its favorite movie star (he held the top spot as late as 1995) would also elect a man like Reagan president. White men in particular admired their swagger, their old-school masculine confidence, and their apparent willingness to exercise authority even if it required violence.[7]

To conservative evangelicals, Reagan was a godsend. In the face of Carter's "wimp factor," Reagan projected the rugged, masculine leadership they believed the country so desperately needed. (It was much easier to chalk up Carter's failures to deficient masculinity than to blame US policy stretching back decades.) Reagan's irrefutable masculinity also reassured conservatives unsettled by the gay rights movement. It wasn't lost on conservative Christians that Carter's own masculinity seemed lacking, even as "the homosexual movement reached its maximum level of influence" under his watch.[8]

In 1980, the election widely hailed as the moment the Christian Right came into its own, evangelical voters bypassed the candidate who shared their faith tradition in favor of the one whose image and rhetoric more closely aligned with their values and aspirations. Guided by preachers like Robison, Falwell, and LaHaye, 67 percent of white evangelical voters chose Reagan over Carter; just four years earlier, Carter had received 49 percent of the evangelical vote and 56 percent of the white Baptist vote. Although white evangelicals supported Reagan at higher rates than white nonevangelicals, they probably weren't the deciding factor in the election; Carter's widespread unpopularity, a stagnant economy, and the drama of the Iran hostage crisis likely would have ensured Reagan's victory even without the mobilization of evangelical pastors and grassroots activists. The Christian Right may not have swung the election to Reagan, but it did succeed in securing the loyalty of evangelicals to the Republican Party. From Reagan on, no Democrat would again win the majority of white evangelical support, or threaten the same. Evangelicals' loyalty to the Republican Party would continue to strengthen, and they would use their electoral clout to help define the Republican agenda for the generation to come.[9]

Reagan benefited from the southern strategy that his Republican predecessors had pursued. Since the 1950s, white southerners had been abandoning the Democratic Party, and Johnson's signing of the Civil Rights Acts accelerated this process. Like Nixon, Reagan was adept at using racially coded rhetoric like states' rights, "law and order," and "forced busing" to appeal to white voters. Indeed, Reagan had launched his campaign at the Neshoba County Fair, praising states' rights just a few miles down the road from Philadelphia, Mississippi, where three civil rights workers had been murdered in 1964, and he campaigned at Bob Jones University at a time when the school was a flashpoint for private Christian schools fighting against desegregation mandates. By the 1980s, then, the Democratic Party had become the party of liberals, African Americans, and feminists, and the Republican Party the party of conservatives, traditionalists, and segregationists.[10]

White evangelicals didn't just participate in this realignment, they helped instigate it. Billy Graham aided and abetted the southern strategy, advising Republicans on how to make inroads with southern evangelicals who, like him, were birthright Democrats. Southern Baptist pastors, too, switched to the Republican Party earlier than white southerners generally. The Southern Baptist shift to the Republican Party coincided with a "conservative resurgence" within the denomination. Traditionally, Baptists had supported a separation of church and state and advocated a civil libertarianism when it came to social issues. Their power secure in the South, Southern Baptists had largely avoided the challenges of modernism in the 1920s, and the reactionary response modernism provoked; in the 1940s, they'd seen no reason to join the NAE. Having devoted less energy to delineating doctrinal boundaries, Southern Baptists allowed for a relatively wide range of views on theological and social issues. Thus the SBC was home to Billy Graham, W. A. Criswell, Jimmy Carter, and Bill Clinton, among others.[11]

To be sure, many Southern Baptists backed the status quo, including both patriarchy and white supremacy. By the end of the 1960s, when explicit white supremacy was no longer tenable, gender became even more significant. Until that time, Southern Baptists held varying views on gender roles. Some believed the Bible prohibited women from preaching and teaching, while others supported women's religious leadership. Beginning in the 1960s, however, fundamentalists began to battle for control of the SBC, and gender was at the heart of the struggle.[12]

By 1979, conservative Southern Baptists' sense of cultural crisis was acute, and they set out to take over the denomination. Paige Patterson, Paul Pressler, W. A. Criswell, and other like-minded pastors and laymen had hatched a plan that involved electing conservatives to the presidency of the SBC and controlling strategic committee appointments. That year, through carefully orchestrated designs, they succeeded in electing one of their own as president of the Houston convention. Moderates cried foul—political machinations of this sort were not the Baptist way—but conservatives were unapologetic; they were "going for the jugular." One by one, conservatives gained control of the denomination's seminaries, purging faculties of moderate voices. Moderates denounced this "power-crazed authoritarianism, a win-at-any-cost ethic and a total disregard for personal values and religious freedom," but to little avail.[13]

Accounts of the battles over the SBC commonly focus on the question of biblical inerrancy, but the battle over inerrancy was in part a proxy fight over gender. Conservatives were alarmed by women's liberation, abortion, and changing views on sexuality generally, but they also had concerns specific to the SBC. "Evangelical feminism" had been making inroads in Southern Baptist circles, and growing numbers of Baptist women had begun challenging male headship and claiming leadership positions; between 1975 and 1985, the number of women ordained in the SBC increased significantly. These women insisted on interpreting biblical texts contextually, attentive to the settings in which they were produced. Conservatives, however, insisted on a "populist hermeneutic," a method privileging "the simplest, most direct interpretations of scripture." For conservatives, this wasn't just the right method, it was also the masculine one. They depicted biblical authors like Paul as uncowed by political correctness. Paul wasn't afraid to prohibit female authority, and masculine men should do likewise. They accused liberals and moderates of waffling, of introducing needless complexity while they stood firm in their quick grasp of the obvious, literal truth of the Scriptures.[14]

The issue of inerrancy did rally conservatives, but when it turned out that large numbers of Southern Baptists—even denominational officials—lacked any real theological prowess and were in fact functionally atheological, concerns over inerrancy gave way to a newly politicized commitment to female submission and to related culture wars issues. It wasn't just Baptist men who helped accomplish this shift. Influenced by Elisabeth Elliot's writings and by their participation in Phyllis Schlafly's Eagle Forum and Beverly LaHaye's Concerned Women for America, Baptist women themselves advanced conservative gender roles within the SBC.[15]

Al Mohler, who oversaw the purging of moderates from Southern Baptist Theological Seminary, offered a revealing glimpse into this process: "Mr. and Mrs. Baptist may not be able to understand or adjudicate the issue of biblical inerrancy when it comes down to nuances, and language, and terminology," he acknowledged. "But if you believe abortion should be legal, that's all they need to know. . . ." The same went for "homosexual marriage." Inerrancy mattered because of its connection to cultural and political issues. It was in their efforts to bolster patriarchal authority that Southern Baptists united with evangelicals across the nation, and the alliances drew them into the larger evangelical world. Within a generation, Southern Baptists began to place their "evangelical" identity over their identity as Southern Baptists. Patriarchy was at the heart of this new sense of themselves.[16]

EVEN IF EVANGELICALS were not the decisive factor in Reagan's victory, they believed they were, as did many pundits. Through extensive networks and public pageantry, evangelical leaders had rallied supporters behind Reagan and the Republican Party. Some, like Pat Boone and Jerry Falwell, had traveled the country stumping for Reagan. When Reagan won in a landslide, evangelicals were euphoric. Falwell effused that Reagan's election was "the greatest day for the cause of conservatism and morality in my adult life." And they were quick to claim credit: "The people who put Jimmy in, put Jimmy out," declared Robison, with apparent glee. These were celebratory words, but also cautionary ones. With Reagan in the White House, they expected a return on their investment.[17]

At first, things looked promising. At his inauguration, Reagan paid homage to his evangelical supporters. His Bel Air pastor opened with prayer, and Reagan himself quoted the biblical passage Falwell had invoked while stumping for him. It was the same passage Eisenhower had quoted at his swearing-in: "If my people, which are called by my name, shall humble themselves, and pray, and seek my face, and turn from their wicked ways; then I will hear from heaven, and will forgive their sin and will heal their land." The message was clear: a new era of civil religion was nigh.[18]

Once in office, however, Reagan's loyalty to the Religious Right wasn't what its members had hoped for. They'd expected Reagan to do away with abortion, bring back prayer in schools, and usher in a spiritual and moral renewal. They also expected some plum assignments in the new administration. On all these counts they were disappointed. Reagan did not prioritize the domestic family values agenda he had championed during the campaign, abortion rights remained the law of the land, and there was little evidence of moral revival. When Reagan failed to back Bob Jones University in the IRS's civil rights case against them, Bob Jones III denounced him as a "traitor to God's people." Falwell, too, was disenchanted. A year in, he griped that he had expected more "with one of our 'own' in the White House."[19]

On issues of foreign policy, however, evangelicals would not be disappointed, and it was Reagan's "repayment" on the military front that kept evangelicals from feeling they'd been had. To their delight, Reagan brought his cowboy conservatism to the global stage. Here his rugged masculinity appeared to serve him well. After all, as evangelicals saw it, the Cold War wasn't really all that different from the Wild

West. Violence, or the threat of violence, secured order. Rules might have to be broken, but the ends justified the means. What was needed was a strong leader, a man who could assert masculine power in the international arena.[20]

Reagan didn't merely project an image of toughness. As president, he translated that image into foreign policy achievements. His clear-eyed characterization of America's enemies resonated with evangelicals' conception of what was at stake in the Cold War, and his efforts to bolster American military power aligned with their yearning to restore American greatness in the post-Vietnam era. In the late 1970s and early 1980s, a number of evangelical books made this case. In *Listen, America!* Falwell had lamented that the United States was "no longer the military might of the world," no longer "committed to victory," no longer "committed to greatness"; for the first time in two centuries, Americans' survival as a free people was in doubt. In *America at the Crossroads*, John Price, too, had mourned the decline of US military power. In forgetting God, the nation had let its strength ebb away, and only when America "comes to its senses" and "repents of its sins and turns to God" would its military position be restored. Perhaps the most influential evangelical book on military rearmament was Hal Lindsey's *The 1980's: Countdown to Armageddon*, a sequel to his best-selling *The Late Great Planet Earth* that was timed to the 1980 election. For Lindsey, rearmament was not simply a pragmatic decision; it was a religious requirement. The Bible was telling the United States to build a powerful military force, to "become strong again." The book spent twenty-one weeks on the *New York Times* Best Sellers list.[21]

In this respect, evangelicals found they had an ally in the White House. Not content to sit on the sidelines, evangelical leaders worked to muster support for Reagan's foreign policy agenda. Falwell and other televangelists were happy to expose the folly of détente, disarmament, and pacifism. During the election they had derided Carter's agenda as "a blatant compromise with Communism," and they were tired of what Falwell characterized as a "no fight and no win policy" stretching back decades. Reagan appreciated the televangelists' support, and in 1983 he invited Falwell to the White House to strategize on how to counteract the domestic nuclear freeze movement.[22]

In the early 1980s, a campaign to halt the production of nuclear weapons had been gaining momentum, and by 1982 it had become a leading issue for the political Left. Many Christians supported the idea of a nuclear freeze, including some evangelicals. Surprising many, Billy Graham had come out in the late 1970s in favor of SALT II, an agreement to limit the development of missile programs, fearing that the destructive power of nuclear weapons contradicted the Christian faith. *Christianity Today*, too, endorsed Mark Hatfield's plan for "a complete freeze on the development, testing, and deployment of strategic missile systems." Many leaders of the Christian Right, however, thought otherwise. Falwell promised Reagan he would help get his message out, "in laymen's language," and he did so by taking out full-page ads in major newspapers deriding "freezeniks," "ultralibs," and "unilateral disarmers" who were undermining Reagan's efforts to rebuild the nation's military strength. "We cannot afford to be number two in defense!" he warned.[23]

Televangelists also came to Reagan's aid in selling the Strategic Defense Initiative, popularly known as Star Wars, as a moral imperative. Two weeks after Reagan called for the space-based nuclear defense system, he appeared before the National Association of Evangelicals. Again he left no doubt that he was on their side, rattling off a list of conservative talking points and reciting a popular but spurious Tocqueville quote: "If America ever ceases to be good, America will cease to be great." Evangelicals, he added, were the ones "keeping America great by keeping her good." But it was Reagan's discussion of foreign policy that made this speech memorable. He spoke of the Soviet Union as "an evil empire," and cautioned against reducing the arms race to "a giant misunderstanding," thereby ignoring the very real struggle between good and evil. Quoting C. S. Lewis, he warned of "quiet men with white collars and cut fingernails and smooth-shaven cheeks who do not need to raise their voice," men who spoke "in soothing tones

of brotherhood and peace." History had revealed that "wishful thinking about our adversaries is folly." Reagan then urged evangelicals "to
speak out against those who would place the United States in a position of military and moral inferiority."[24]

Although evangelicals remained divided over whether to pass a resolution on the nuclear freeze, the NAE was receptive to Reagan's larger
call, and they instituted a "Peace, Freedom, and Security Studies"
program to counter the influence of mainline churches. Evangelicals
found many reasons to support American military might. On a pragmatic level, they believed a strong military would ward off a godless
communist takeover. When it came to risks of nuclear annihilation,
evangelical theology's emphasis on eternal life for the faithful helped
mitigate such earthly terrors. In end-times scenarios they believed
God would protect them; a nuclear holocaust might even be part of
God's plan. But a strong military and an aggressive foreign policy also
aligned with evangelicals' view of masculine power. Representatives of
the Christian Right were not above insinuating a deficit of manliness
among those who opposed the president's policies. "Freezeniks" were
sissies who lacked the courage to stand up to the communist threat.[25]

PERHAPS NO EPISODE better reveals the connections between the
Reagan administration and the leadership of the Christian Right than
the Nicaraguan Contra War. In the summer of 1979, the Sandinistas,
a revolutionary leftist group, had overthrown the dictatorial Somoza
regime. The United States suspected the Sandinistas were supported
by the Soviets and the Cubans, and as president, Reagan promised military aid to the counterrevolutionary Contras. From 1981 until 1988,
the war between the Sandinistas and US-backed Contras devastated
the Central American country. Both sides committed brutal atrocities,
and tens of thousands of Nicaraguans died. The war was not primarily
a religious war, but in the United States it was framed as such.

In Nicaragua, evangelical Protestants and Catholics alike were
divided. Some evangelicals supported the Sandinistas, though not

uncritically; like Catholics who embraced liberation theology, they saw socialism as a biblical response to poverty and oppression. But many others feared communist encroachment and opposed the Sandinistas' revolutionary efforts. Many of these conservatives joined together in the National Council of Evangelical Pastors of Nicaragua (CNPEN), an organization that developed close ties with conservative evangelical groups in the United States, including the NAE.[26]

In America, conservative Christian organizations mobilized on behalf of the Contras. Framing the conflict as a matter of religious liberty and the global persecution of Christians, organizations like the Institute for Religion and Democracy accused the Sandinistas of committing atrocities against conservative evangelicals and Catholics. Supporters of the Sandinistas had their own Christian allies in America, with progressive evangelicals and Catholics blaming the conflict not on Soviet interference, but on "poverty, oppression and injustice." After a trip to Nicaragua, Jim Wallis, the most prominent spokesperson for the evangelical Left, wrote a scathing report in *Sojourners* accusing the Contras of horrific acts of violence.[27]

Such opposition proved inconvenient when it came to the Reagan administration's attempt to secure congressional support to intervene on the Contras' behalf. When Congress refused to comply, instead prohibiting the use of any funds "for the purpose of overthrowing the government of Nicaragua," Reagan turned to his evangelical allies for help in winning over the public. Inviting religious groups to special White House foreign policy seminars, administration officials peddled stories of the horrors perpetrated by Marxist guerrillas, framing the conflict as one between revolutionaries and Christians and urging religious organizations to assist them through lobbying and letter writing. In 1983, the Office of Public Liaison started holding weekly briefings on US–Central American relations and invited religious leaders to attend, and they prepared a series of White House Digests on the topic and sent out mailings to religious groups. Conservative evangelical organizations were only too happy to assist, offering their burgeoning media networks to promote the administration's agenda. The NAE advocated on behalf of the administration, and Christian news services that focused on global religious persecution provided regular updates on the oppression of evangelicals who opposed the Sandinistas.[28]

Religious disagreement intensified the congressional debates over Nicaragua. In 1985 and in 1986, the Reagan administration again requested funding. To shore up support, The White House invited figures including Falwell, Robertson, and LaHaye to receive special briefings from Oliver North, a highly decorated marine and a convert to evangelicalism who served as the NSC's deputy director for political-military affairs. Only later would it be revealed that this was not the only action North was taking on behalf of the Contras.

After finally succeeding in securing congressional approval to provide humanitarian aid to the Contras, the administration stepped up lobbying efforts to secure military funding as well. In early 1986, the White House provided the Trinity Broadcasting Network, Robertson's Christian Broadcasting Network, Falwell's own television ministry, and other Christian television outlets with a five-minute video of Reagan arguing for support for the Contras. Reagan made his case in stark terms. This was an urgent battle for democracy, and it was "nothing less than a sin to see Central America fall to darkness." Reagan also recorded an audio message distributed to more than 1500 Christian radio stations that included a number for listeners to call for information on contacting their elected representatives. The administration's efforts succeeded; Congress approved a $100 million spending measure in support of the Contras.[29]

Even as the White House was tapping evangelical networks to drum up support for a military intervention in Nicaragua, some members of the administration were pursuing more clandestine avenues as well. In 1984, Iran had secretly requested weapons from the United States to use in its war with Iraq. Despite an arms embargo, Reagan was desperate to secure the release of seven American hostages held by Iranian terrorists in Lebanon. With Reagan's support, the administration arranged for the shipment of more than 1500 missiles to Iran. Three hostages were released (but three more taken), and a portion of the

Lt. Col. Oliver North testifying before the House Select
Committee, July 7, 1987. AP PHOTO / SCOTT APPLEWHITE.

payment for the arms sales was then diverted to support the Contras in
Nicaragua. The NSC staff member responsible for this transaction was
Oliver North. Thanks in part to an improperly entered bank account
number, the entire scheme came to light, and in May 1987 North was
called to testify before Congress.

In six days of televised testimony, North affirmed that he had acted
to advance the president's foreign policy, but he refused to implicate
Reagan directly. "This is a dangerous world," North attested, and
covert operations were necessary to protect the country. He confessed
to lying to Congress and shredding documents, but this was all for the
greater good. Moreover, as a good lieutenant colonel, he was "not in the
habit" of questioning his superiors, least of all his commander in chief:

> This lieutenant colonel is not going to challenge a decision of the
> Commander in Chief for whom I still work, and I am proud to
> work for that Commander in Chief, and if the Commander in
> Chief tells this lieutenant colonel to go stand in the corner and

sit on his head, I will do so. And if the Commander in Chief decides to dismiss me from the NSC staff, this lieutenant colonel will proudly salute and say "thank you for the opportunity to have served," and go, and I am not going to criticize his decision no matter how he relieves me, sir.

North knew how to submit to his proper authorities. More importantly, he believed that he had the highest authority on his side.[30]

OLIVER NORTH ENDED UP being indicted on sixteen felony counts, including lying to Congress and destroying documents. Found guilty on three counts, he received a three-year suspended sentence. As commander in chief, Reagan was never directly implicated in the arms-for-hostages deal, and he emerged from the scandal relatively unscathed.

In 1990, North's convictions were reversed on a technicality. The following year, North was a featured speaker at the Southern Baptist Convention, the first where moderates were not expected to challenge the conservative majority. Oliver North had become a hero of the Christian Right. The affinities were clear. Conservatives in the SBC had skirted conventions and eschewed niceties in order to wrest control of the denomination, just as North had skirted the rule of law in order to pursue a greater good. For both, the ends justified the means. But it wasn't just tactics that united fellow renegades. Like North, conservative evangelicals defined the greater good in terms of Christian nationalism. It was this conflation of God and country that heroic Christian men would advance zealously, and by any means necessary, with their resurgent religious and political power.

Chapter 7

THE GREATEST
AMERICAN
HERO

AT THE TIME OF THE IRAN-CONTRA HEARINGS, A certain subset of Americans had been gripped by "Olliemania." A T-shirt store in Albany, New York, sold a shirt emblazoned with an American flag, boasting "God, guns, guts and Ollie made this country." A restaurant near Buffalo added an "Oliver North Sandwich" to their menu. Made with "red-blooded American beef" and topped with shredded lettuce, the sandwich was served up on a hero roll. But North's moment in the spotlight soon came and went. Retailers had a hard time moving Barbie and Ken-like dolls modeled on North and his wife, and only about half of the 775,000 copies of Pocket Books' paperback edition of North's testimony transcript were expected to sell. Before long, a pork barbecue sandwich replaced the Oliver North on the menu in the Buffalo restaurant.[1]

Even as he faded from view among the general public, North's stature only increased among conservative Christians who were hungry for a hero of their own. Jerry Falwell led the way in lionizing North. In the spring of 1988, he had started a national petition drive to pardon North, and in May of that year he welcomed North to Liberty University as the school's commencement speaker. When North arrived on campus, just one day after retiring from the military, Falwell compared him to Jesus. Reminding his audience that "we serve a savior who was indicted and convicted and crucified," Falwell christened North "a true American hero."[2]

Outside the event, North's hero status was up for debate. Around sixty protestors had gathered, carrying signs declaring "Real Heroes Don't Lie" and passing out flyers objecting to Falwell spending "millions of dollars to paint Ollie North as a national hero who needs and deserves special treatment before the law." But they were in the minority. Shouts of "Ollie, we love you!" could be heard from those vying for pictures. "They don't understand," remarked one graduate's parent. "He is a national hero."[3]

Months later, Falwell was distributing $25 audio tapes of North's commencement address, his "Freedom Message." In a fundraising letter sent to supporters, Falwell framed what was at issue: "In my judgment, petty partisan politics have made Ollie North, his family and the very lives of the Nicaraguan freedom fighters pawns in a liberal campaign to humiliate President Reagan." Critics accused leaders like Falwell of exploiting North in order to reap a "financial bonanza" in their direct-mail campaigns. Falwell's spokesperson refused to say how much his campaign had brought in, but he wasn't the only one cashing in on North. Beverly LaHaye's Concerned Women for America offered a "beautiful full-color picture" of North being sworn in at the Iran-Contra hearings for a mere $20 contribution. Other conservative evangelical organizations also participated in the "Olliemania." For American evangelicals, Ollie North was the perfect hero at the perfect time.[4]

TO EVANGELICALS, it was clear that North did what he did "for the love of God and for the love of country." By all accounts, North was a true believer. He had grown up in a patriotic Catholic household in upstate New York. His father had served under General Patton in the Second World War, and as a boy he had briefly attended a Catholic military school. One year into college, he enlisted in a marine corps officer's training program at Camp Lejeune, where he was smitten with the mystique of the marines, whom he saw as "the toughest, the bravest and the best." Before long he secured a transfer to the United States Naval Academy in Annapolis.[5]

North entered the academy in August 1964, the week of the Gulf of Tonkin incident. He was in his final year in 1968 when the Tet Offensive occurred. Vietnam was a constant presence at the academy, but among the American public the perception of the war changed dramatically during the years North was a cadet. While North and his fellow midshipmen were observing strict discipline, their high school classmates were smoking pot, growing out their hair, and communing at Haight-Ashbury. When he and other cadets ventured beyond the walls of the academy, local college students taunted them as villains, not heroes. In April 1968, the assassination of Martin Luther King Jr. had shocked the nation and sparked rioting across the country. Opposition to the war continued to mount. In June, on the morning of North's graduation, news broke of Robert Kennedy's assassination. North's commissioning ceremony was interrupted by protestors jeering that they were "cannon fodder." But North could not wait to get to Vietnam.[6]

North's commission had been in jeopardy because of injuries he had sustained in a car accident. Taking matters into his own hands, he snuck into the administration building during his final year to alter his records. When caught, he expressed no remorse. He "considered the higher ideal of serving our country worth the risk," and "as long as he was doing it for our country, it couldn't be wrong." North's wish was granted. Skipping the traditional sixty-day postgraduation leave, he assumed command of a platoon stationed along the DMZ. Conditions in Vietnam were grim—over 16,000 American service members died in 1968, the deadliest year of the war—but North was in his element, and he served with distinction. As the war began to wind down, he took up a position as instructor at Quantico. His subject: How to kill the enemy. North was a popular instructor, but he wasn't without critics. One colleague disapproved of the role North seemed to revel in:

You can just see Ollie there with his camouflage utilities with his bush hat . . . camo on his face as if it had been put on in Holly-wood, two bandoliers of ammo strapped across and three pouches, four weapons and three knives. . . . Ollie was popular with the studs because he was their image of what the Marine Corps was about. . . . He invented Rambo before Rambo made the movie. He was the creator of his own myth.[7]

A soldier's soldier, North grew increasingly frustrated with Americans who didn't buy into this myth, and he didn't just mean antiwar protestors. He also blamed the media. In the summer of 1971, just months after William Calley was convicted on twenty-two counts of murder in the My Lai massacre, North and two other marine captains addressed a letter to the three major television networks, and to conservative columnist William F. Buckley Jr., criticizing reporting on "alleged" atrocities and war crimes and rejecting any implication of broader complicity. "None of us have ever witnessed, participated in, or been cognizant of, a single instance wherein any Vietnamese noncombatant, North or South, was treated in anything less than a humane fashion," they attested. American soldiers were the good guys, and the public needed to know this. The networks ignored the letter, but Buckley invited the authors to join him on his show on Public Broadcasting, *Firing Line*. North was eager to have his say. Families shouldn't be made to feel that sons and husbands were coming home as war criminals. Marines had in fact shown remarkable restraint. North "believed in America and the sanctity of its commitments," and he was furious that politicians and peaceniks were getting in the way of the military doing what needed to be done.[8]

In 1978, North experienced a personal religious transformation. His commanding officer at the time, Lt. Col. John S. Grinalds, was a born-again Christian, and he convinced North to leave behind the Catholicism of his youth and embrace charismatic Protestantism. (The fact that North's priest was a leading proponent of disarmament might have played into this decision.) This wasn't North's first exposure to evangelical Protestantism. In the mid-1970s, his wife Betsy, "tired of living with a headstrong military leader" who was absent as a husband and father, had asked for a divorce. The two agreed to marital counseling, and while waiting in the lobby for their first appointment, North picked up a book: James Dobson's *Dare to Discipline*. He credited it with saving his marriage. After his conversion, North joined a predominantly white, charismatic congregation of the Episcopal church that seamlessly blended patriotism and Christianity. An American flag graced the front of the sanctuary, and from the pulpit North was instructed, "Wherever we are, the Lord has put us there to make the difference for Him." It was all part of God's plan. By that time, North was a member of the Reagan administration.[9]

In his role at the NSC, North had led the hunt for the perpetrators of the 1983 Beirut barracks bombing and had helped plan the invasion of Grenada and the bombing of Libya. Through all of this, he wore his faith on his sleeve. His conversation was seasoned with religious expressions and he drove a station wagon with a bumper sticker boasting "GOD IS PRO-LIFIC." As one of his friends explained, "To Ollie, religion, flag and family are all part of the same makeup." He prayed privately with President Reagan; he participated in Bible studies, prayer groups, and Christian retreats; and he and his wife were active members of the Officers' Christian Fellowship. As he worked to drum up support for aid to the Contras, he collaborated closely with leaders of the Christian Right who shared his God-and-country faith, even assisting the Gospel Crusade in producing *Studies in Faith and Freedom*, a documentary in support of the Contras. To evangelical leaders, "Ollie was a shining example of American righteousness."[10]

North had put his faith in God and country on full display during the Iran-Contra hearings, to the delight of supporters. Republican Representative William Broomfield spoke for many when he expressed his affirmation: "I don't want to see you go to jail because I think you're a great patriotic American, and I'm proud of what you've tried to do." President Reagan, even as he claimed ignorance of North's actions, heralded him as "an American hero." But not everyone agreed. Democratic Senator George Mitchell, a devout Catholic with his own military pedigree, rebuffed North's patriotic platitudes:

> . . . you asked that Congress not cut off aid to the contras, for the love of God and for the love of country. . . .
>
> Please remember that others share that devotion and recognize that it is possible for an American to disagree with you on aid to the contras and still love God and still love this country just as much as you do.
>
> Although he's regularly asked to do so, God does not take sides in American politics. And in America, disagreement with the policies of the Government is not evidence of lack of patriotism.[11]

For conservative evangelicals, there were no two sides. When North spoke at the 1991 Southern Baptist Convention, Richard Lee, president of the SBC Pastors' Conference, explained: "To some he's controversial. But to the vast majority of us he's an American patriot." Standing before a 40-foot by 60-foot flag, North urged the more than 15,000 Southern Baptists in attendance to become politically active in order to counter "a veritable Sodom and Gomorrah on the banks of the Potomac." One man in the audience described his appeal: "There is a commitment to country and to God," he explained. "I think Oliver North represents a commitment to God."[12]

That same year North published *Under Fire* with Zondervan, a Christian publisher recently acquired by Harper and Row. The memoir sold 650,000 copies and ended up on both the *New York Times* and the Christian bestseller lists, and the royalties helped cover North's considerable legal fees. He gave frequent talks at evangelical churches, too, speaking (for undisclosed fees) about his devout faith and criticizing the media; he joked that he read the "Washington Post/Washington Compost" and the Bible—because he "wanted to see what both sides were up to." North also appealed directly to conservative "armchair activists" to raise money, both for legal expenses and to fund his failed congressional campaign. With the help of direct-mail strategist Richard Viguerie, who provided him with select lists of conservative voters, North targeted key demographics: "anti–gun control, pro-life, school prayer, strong defense, anti-gay, and the like." All told, North brought in around $16 million in a single year through direct mail alone, an unprecedented haul.[13]

Conservative political operative Ralph Reed described North's appeal in this way: "Part of politics is having the right friends, but an important part of politics is having the right enemies." Conservative Christians loved him for the enemies he'd made. His strategist and pollster explained his appeal in the words of country singer Garth Brooks: North appealed to the "hard-hat, gun rack, achin'-back, over-taxed, flag-waving, fun-lovin' crowd." With his God-and-country heroism, North tapped a populist vein in American politics. Critics, however, warned of his authoritarian tendencies, and of his disrespect for the truth. But for his supporters there was "what's right" and "what's legal," and the two were not always the same. If North lied, "it must have been necessary." There was no doubt "he was a good soldier."[14]

OLLIE NORTH WAS A PERFECT HERO for evangelicals eager to defend God and country. He also came at the perfect time. To understand why evangelicals were so desperate to enshrine a hero like North, it helps to start with pastor Edwin Louis Cole, a man widely considered to be the "father of the Christian men's movement."

Born in Dallas in 1922, Cole moved to Los Angeles as a child where he was soon playing trumpet in Aimee Semple McPherson's street-corner evangelistic teams. After serving in the United States Coast Guard in the Second World War, he began his career in radio and television ministry. In 1979, he founded the Christian Men's Network, and not long after he diagnosed a catastrophic condition plaguing the nation. An "anti-hero syndrome" had "eliminated our heroes and left us bereft of role models as patriotic examples." His 1982 book on the topic, *Maximized Manhood*, would sell more than one million copies.[15]

Cole couched his call for Christian manhood in the language of the prosperity gospel. By following God's plan, men would "enjoy Canaan land" in every part of their lives—their marriages and families, their professional and financial lives. They would "live the life of maximized manhood." Cole believed men had three purposes: to guide, guard, and govern, and to fulfill these roles men needed to be "both tender *and* tough." Jesus was a perfect balance of the two; the same man who drew little children to himself "gripped that scourge of cords and drove the money-changers out of the temple." Cole had no use for "sissified" portraits of Jesus that failed to reveal his true character. "*Christlikeness and manhood are synonymous*," he insisted, and to be Christlike, to be a man, required "a certain ruthlessness."[16]

When Cole appeared on Pat Robertson's *700 Club* to argue that masculine leadership in the home required toughness, the female cohost balked. But Cole didn't back down, and he couldn't resist noting that his interlocutor seemed to be usurping properly masculine leadership on the program. He assured his readers that women were in fact begging for men to lead, and when men did lead, women loved them more. Cole took pains to distinguish "toughness" from a "macho" conception of manhood, which to him connoted a childlike immaturity, lack of character, and promiscuous sexuality, but even as Cole's understanding of masculinity retained a place for tenderness, measured tenderness should never be confused with effeminacy. "I like a man's man," Cole made plain. "I don't like the pussyfooting pipsqueaks who tippy toe through the tulips." At one time people might have overemphasized toughness, Cole acknowledged, "but today it is the softness that is killing us." Women, children, churches, and nations all needed masculine decision makers; America was great only when its men were great. Tragically, however, a pernicious anti-hero syndrome plagued the nation.[17]

This syndrome was evident in television dramas that had created and destroyed images of manhood, "with dangerous results." A generation traumatized by foolish male authority figures like Archie Bunker had stamped on their minds an image of manhood that invited "resentment, derision, anarchy, and mockery." These children then rejected authority figures in their own lives, and the effects extended to the nation as a whole. In recent decades, "a philosophical and emotional sickness" had been allowed to fester in the life of the nation, all because the idea of America "as a 'virtuous' nation, a benefactor to the entire world, a savior from enslaving dictatorships," had been undercut by a malignant media.[18]

For Cole, the cure for the anti-hero syndrome could be found in Christian broadcasting. Christian media could offer godly heroes for popular consumption. "Sick and tired of the world system creating the ungodly as heroes, making the bad good, and the good bad," Cole created and chaired a Committee for International Good Will with the purpose of making "the godly of the land our heroes." The group offered annual awards to exemplary men such as Pat Robertson. However, if Christian broadcasting offered means of instilling the heroic masculine ideal in the hearts and minds of Americans, evangelicals had cause for concern. At that critical moment, Christian media figures weren't entirely up to the task.[19]

DURING THE 1980s, a series of televangelist sex scandals felled a number of popular Christian preachers and rattled evangelicals who thought they had a corner on moral values. The first to fall was Marvin Gorman, a charismatic Assemblies of God pastor in New Orleans. In 1986, Jimmy Swaggart, a rival televangelist located upriver in Baton Rouge, accused Gorman of committing adultery with several woman—including the wife of another preacher, a woman Gorman had been providing with "biblical counseling." Gorman eventually confessed to "one act of adultery," though he claimed it was the pastor's wife who had started grabbing and kissing him. Defrocked and ostracized, Gorman declared bankruptcy in 1987.[20]

Remarkably, Gorman wasn't the only rival televangelist Swaggart accused of adultery that year. He also took aim at Jim Bakker, host of *The PTL Club*. Bakker and his wife Tammy Faye had dropped out of college to become Pentecostal evangelists in the early 1960s, and in 1965 they joined Robertson's Christian Broadcasting Network (CBN). It was the popularity of their variety show that helped launch Robertson's *700 Club*, and by 1980, CBN was pulling in over $50 million. CBN didn't air exclusively religious programming; in the late 1970s and early 1980s it expanded its "secular" offerings to include traditional family programming like reruns of Westerns and shows like *Leave It to Beaver* and *The Brady Bunch*. In 1974, the Bakkers established their own PTL (Praise the Lord) network, and within a dozen years PTL had acquired a private satellite network, amassed annual revenues of $129 million, employed 2500 people, and created a popular theme park, Heritage USA. A "Christian Disneyland," Heritage USA contained a hodgepodge of colonial, Victorian, and imaginary southern architecture, a waterslide, a "Heavenly Fudge Factory," and gift stores selling an impressive assortment of knickknacks, jewelry, and toys. At its peak in 1986, the park attracted six million visitors, making it the third most popular amusement park in the nation. Then, Swaggart accused Bakker of a "15-minute tryst" with church secretary Jessica Hahn.[21]

Bakker had initially arranged for $279,000 in hush money to be paid to Hahn, but when Swaggart got wind of this, Bakker resigned and asked Jerry Falwell to take the helm of his ministry. As an independent Baptist, Falwell didn't share the Bakkers' Pentecostal faith, but he knew an opportunity when he saw one and swooped in. It is worth noting, however, that Hahn's version of events differed on key points. For Hahn, this was no "tryst"; what happened to her was premeditated rape. She told of attempting to resist Bakker's advances, of being plied with wine and possibly drugs, and of Bakker complaining that his wife couldn't satisfy him sexually. As he put it, "When you help the shepherd, you're helping the sheep." Looking back, Hahn acknowledged her naivete. She watched Bakker every day on television: "It's like 'Oh my God, this is like God walked into the room.'" She initially kept quiet after the assault. The church was her world, and she feared that "millions of people" would be affected if she told her story.

In Hahn's telling, beneath the scandal and sensationalism was an act of violence, the manipulation and rape of a young woman, a preacher's abuse of power, and the betrayal of a faith community. Bakker's lawyer, meanwhile, claimed he was the victim.[22]

In 1988, Swaggart himself was caught cavorting with a prostitute by none other than Marvin Gorman, who enjoyed a sweet revenge when Swaggart, too, was defrocked. A few years later, Swaggart would again be caught with a prostitute, but rather than confessing, he would tell his congregation, "The Lord told me it's flat none of your business."[23]

The televangelist soap operas of the 1980s were catnip for a national media that seemed to delight in the hypocrisy of conservative Christians. Sex, church secretaries, fraud, intrigue, prostitution, conspicuous consumption of the most tawdry sort—the revelations tarnished the image of evangelicalism generally, revealing the dark side of a religious movement driven by celebrity. Evangelicals had long framed sexual immorality as a worldly sin, the product of secularism, liberalism, feminism—that is, as something that happened *outside* the Christian fold. Yet the televangelist sex scandals revealed that their own religious heroes had feet of clay. If Christians needed manly heroes, Christian broadcasting was coming up short.

The canonization of Oliver North can be understood against this backdrop. Robert Grant, head of both the Christian Voice and the American Freedom Coalition, acknowledged that rallying around North had "provided a financial shot in the arm to organizations that had seen contributions plunge in the wake of the televangelist sex-and-money scandals." He declined to assign North's impact a dollar figure but conceded that "we've made it work very much for us." North helped evangelicals change the narrative and refill their coffers. Viguerie, too, acknowledged that there hadn't been much to galvanize the Religious Right, but then along came North: "Ollie is a certified five-star hero in a movement that is particularly short on heroes at this time."[24]

Evangelicals revered North in part because he seemed so exceptional, a throwback to an earlier era when things were right with the world, an antidote to unscrupulous celebrities who were perhaps the inevitable products of a consumer-driven faith. Here was a Vietnam veteran who battled communists and chased terrorists around the globe, a man who would do whatever it took to serve God and country. At a time when religious leaders lacked the heroism that was so urgently needed, evangelicals found that heroism in a place where virtue and discipline still prevailed: the United States military.

DURING THE VIETNAM WAR, evangelicals had come to admire the military as a bulwark against the erosion of authority and as a holdout for traditional values amid a hostile, secularizing, and emasculating culture. During the 1980s, they worked to forge closer connections with the military in order to strengthen this last bastion of American greatness. Not surprisingly, Falwell assisted in this effort. Working at the Reagan administration's behest to point out the follies of détente, he frequently called on retired military men to help him make his case. But it was James Dobson who would play the most critical role in cementing ties between evangelicals and the military.

In 1983, army chief of staff General John A. Wickham Jr. tapped Dobson—who had just been named the NAE's "Layman of the Year" for his work in "saving the family"—to spearhead a campaign to inculcate evangelical "family values" within the military. Wickham, "a man of great faith," had recommitted to faith and family in a foxhole in Vietnam, and as chief of staff he made it his priority to strengthen moral values throughout the army. He had learned of Dobson from two Republican congressmen, Indiana's Dan Coats and Virginia's Frank Wolf. Two years earlier, Coats and Wolf had attended a screening of Dobson's *Where's Dad?* They promoted the film and other Focus on the Family materials to fellow members of Congress and their families, and they thought Dobson's film could be used to strengthen military families, too. Wickham agreed to bring Dobson on board. The two first met at a Pentagon fellowship breakfast, and Dobson told Wickham that he felt "a definite sense of camaraderie and Christian brotherhood with you and the other military leaders." The

two men began to work closely together with the purpose of strengthening "family values" among those serving in the military. The next
year, Wickham invited Dobson to the Spring Commanders' Conference at the Pentagon, where Dobson gave a talk on "the importance of
traditional home-life values" for officers and their wives. The following year, Wickham arranged for the distribution of Dobson's *Where's
Dad?* video throughout the army; all 780,000 active-duty soldiers were
expected to view the film, and it served as the "building block" for the
army's entire "Family Action Plan."[25]

The military scrubbed all overtly religious language from the video,
but the family values ideology remained intact. Dobson believed that
the fate of the family, and the nation, depended on men taking up
proper leadership roles: "Folks, if America is going to survive, it will be
because husbands and fathers begin to put their families at the highest level of priorities and reserve something of their time, effort and
energy for leadership within their own homes." Wickham concurred.
"The readiness of our Army is directly related to the strength of our
families," he attested. "The stronger the family, the stronger the Army,
because strong families improve our combat readiness."[26]

Their partnership paid dividends for both men. Dobson was able
to expand his influence throughout the military and tap new distribution networks (neither the army nor Dobson's publisher would disclose
how much the army paid for *Where's Dad?*), all while enhancing his
own image by playing up his military ties. In turn, Dobson helped bur-
nish the image of the military. In 1984, *Focus on the Family* magazine
published a cover story on Dobson's work with the army and brought
Wickham and other military leaders on Dobson's daily radio program.
The next year the magazine ran another article praising Wickham's
pro-family stance; Dobson made sure to send Wickham a copy, noting that it had been distributed to 650,000 people on their mailing
list. Reaching millions of regular listeners, Dobson helped rehabili-
tate Americans' view of the military in the post-Vietnam era: "We've
been led to believe that military generals and admirals are egocentric
maniacs who are itching to blow up the world," he wrote in a Focus on

the Family newsletter, but "nothing could be further from the truth."
Commanders like Wickham were "dedicated patriots who have sacrificed dearly for their country." The military was a noble institution.[27]

Wickham wasn't the only military leader to promote evangelical
teachings. In 1985 the Officers' Christian Fellowship magazine *Command* published a special issue, "The Christian Commander," urging
officers to use their positions of influence for evangelistic purposes.
None other than marine colonel John Grinalds—Oliver North's
supervising officer in 1978—wrote an article detailing his longstanding practice of "evangelism in command." Grinalds thought commanders ought "to present Christ" to those in their command, and he
believed this to be mandated both by the Bible and by military regulations. Commanders, after all, were supposed to look after the spiritual welfare of their troops. Grinalds openly shared his faith, inviting
marines to attend worship services on Sunday and encouraging the
Navigators—an evangelical Christian ministry—to witness to marines
in his command. He kept New Testaments in his desk drawer for distribution and regularly sought to turn one-on-one conversations to "a
discussion about Christ." The results of his evangelistic efforts could
be quantified; during his twelve-month command he "saw the S-3, S-4,
Communications Officer, Motor Transport Officer, two Company
Commanders and the Assault Amphibian Platoon Commander commit their lives to Christ," in addition to many others who recommitted
and were baptized.[28]

HAVING EMBRACED THE MILITARY, evangelicals would find
it difficult to articulate a critique of militarism. If the military was a
source of virtue, war, too, attained a moral bearing—even preemptive
war. In the 1987 book *One Nation Under God*, Christian Reconstructionist Rus Walton offered a robust defense of preventive war. Suppose
a "thug," a barbarian, a "depraved maniac," threatened your wife or
daughter. "What would you do? When would you move to protect her?
Before the attacker made his advance? . . . When he began ripping the

clothes from her body?" Yes, Jesus might have instructed his followers to love their enemies, but not *His* enemies. Christians must steel
themselves: "Let others seek to remove that great old hymn 'Onward
Christian Soldiers' from their hymnals. Let us go forth, the Cross of
Jesus going on before." Christians were called to fight the Lord's battle,
at home and abroad, and seek dominion in His name. The paperback
edition of Walton's book boasted 150,000 copies in print, and Walton
became a frequent speaker at D. James Kennedy's annual Reclaiming
America for Christ conferences.[29]

By promoting preemptive war, Walton contributed to a "crusade
theory of warfare." In wars of Christian conquest, "righteous states"
were justified in taking the offensive against their enemies. Crusade
warfare made sense in the context of Cold War politics, where neutrality was not an option. But in the summer of 1987, in the midst
of the Iran-Contra hearings, President Reagan had stood in front of
the Brandenburg Gate in West Berlin, ordering Mikhail Gorbachev to
"tear down this wall." Two years later, the wall came down. Although
conservative evangelicals had been discomfited by Reagan's pursuit of
disarmament during his second term in office, in the end, it was his
aggressive posture on the world stage, his penchant to "talk tough and
carry a big stick," that seemed to have produced indisputable results.
The dominoes would soon begin to fall, but not in the direction conservative evangelicals had long feared.[30]

For decades, anticommunism had been a linchpin in the evangelical
worldview, justifying militarism abroad and a militant pursuit of moral
purity at home. The victory of the free world was something to celebrate, but it was also disorienting. Without a common enemy, it would
be more difficult to sustain militant expressions of the faith. Yet even
as the Cold War came to an anticlimactic end, the crusade theory of
warfare endured. A flexible guide to combat, it could be employed to
justify aggression against threats both foreign and domestic. Among
Christian nationalists, it could effectively sanctify any engagement
where the United States resorted to force. On the home front, it could

validate questionable or even ruthless tactics wielded in defense of Christian America. In heroic pursuits of a higher good, the ends would justify the means. Conservative evangelicals knew they were called to fight the Lord's battle. It just wasn't entirely clear what that battle would be.

Chapter 8

WAR FOR
THE SOUL

F OR EVANGELICALS, THE 1980s HAD TURNED OUT TO
be a mixed blessing. On the one hand, evangelicals relished
their newfound political power and worked to make the most of it.
In addition to their public advocacy and presidential photo ops, they
extended their influence behind the scenes. In the wake of the 1980
White House Conference, James Dobson had established the Family Research Council, a conservative policy research organization to
support "pro-family" policies. With Reagan in the White House,
Dobson became a "regular consultant" to the president. (Dobson even
recorded one of his Focus on the Family radio broadcasts with Reagan
in the Oval Office, and Reagan had appointed him cochair of Citizens for Tax Reform and to the National Advisory Committee to the
Office of Juvenile Justice and Delinquency Prevention.) In 1980, Tim
LaHaye had set aside his pastoral ministry for a full-time career in
political activism. The next year he founded his secretive Council for
National Policy. Leaked membership directories reveal the thicken-
ing web of conservative alliances: James Dobson, Jerry Falwell, Phyl-
lis Schlafly, Beverly LaHaye, R. J. Rushdoony, Howard Phillips, Gary
North, Pat Robertson, D. James Kennedy, Tony Perkins, Bill Bright,
Ken Starr, Michael Farris, Jesse Helms, John Ashcroft, Trent Lott,
Richard DeVos, Elsa Prince, Erik Prince, Wayne LaPierre, Richard
Viguerie, Grover Norquist, Gary Bauer, Paul Weyrich, and Oliver
North. LaHaye also established the American Coalition for Tradi-

tional Values, organizing hundreds of conservative Christian pastors and churches for the promotion of patriotism and moral values, and the Coalition for Religious Freedom to lobby for religious rights. In 1986, Falwell, LaHaye, Kennedy, Jimmy Swaggart, Jim Bakker, and Bill Bright joined with other leaders of the Christian Right to form the Religious Coalition for a Moral Defense Policy.[1]

On the other hand, in some ways evangelicals' political success threatened to undo them. In 1984, Reagan was reelected in a landslide, winning 60 percent of the popular vote. (At the 1984 Republican National Convention, a video recounting Reagan's first-term achievements opened with a series of clips from John Wayne films, lest anyone forget what Reagan represented.) Around 75 percent of white evangelicals voted for Reagan, but thanks to a rebounding economy, their support wasn't critical to his reelection. In some ways, Reagan's decisive victory took the wind out of evangelical sails. Conservative evangelicals had learned to trade on a sense of embattlement. When liberals, communists, feminists, or secular humanists seemed to be winning, supporters dug deep into their pockets. With Reagan in the White House, the sense of urgency diminished. Together with the tarnished image wrought by the televangelist sex scandals, this led to a precipitous decline in donations, notwithstanding the temporary boost North provided.[2]

In response, leaders of the Religious Right began to sound increasingly shrill. Falwell sparked controversy by characterizing AIDS as "the wrath of God upon homosexuals" and recommending that those with AIDS be quarantined. He also forged connections with some of Reagan's most controversial overseas allies, including South Africa's apartheid regime, Ferdinand and Imelda Marcos in the Philippines, and the brutal right-wing dictatorship in El Salvador. LaHaye, meanwhile, tried to claim credit for Reagan's reelection, but his victory lap was derailed when it was revealed that Sun Myung Moon's Unification Church, a South Korean cult whose followers were popularly called Moonies, was one of LaHaye's largest donors. After the 1986 midterms, LaHaye closed down his American Coalition for Traditional

Values. Falwell's Moral Majority disbanded in 1989. By the end of Reagan's second term, in the absence of a common enemy, the power of the Christian Right appeared to be ebbing away.[3]

THE MOST URGENT ORDER OF BUSINESS was to elect a new president, but there was no clear heir apparent, despite the fact that one of their own had thrown his hat into the ring. Sometime in the mid-1980s, God had told Pat Robertson to run for president, according to Pat Robertson. In 1987 he announced his candidacy, but his campaign got off to a rough start when journalists uncovered the fact that he had been lying about his wedding date to disguise the fact that his wife had been seven months pregnant when they tied the knot. The media also discovered that, contrary to his claims, he'd never seen combat—his father, a United States senator, had apparently pulled strings to keep him out of harm's way. These two significant issues aside, Robertson seemed to check all the boxes.[4]

Campaigning to "Restore the Greatness of America Through Moral Strength," Robertson placed foreign policy front and center. He opposed arms control, denounced "Godless communism," called for "the defeat of Marxist regimes in the Third World," and vowed to "never negotiate with Communists or terrorists." Robertson didn't just talk the talk when it came to foreign policy. During the Reagan administration, he had expanded his evangelistic empire into Central America, and he came to support brutal right-wing regimes in El Salvador and Guatemala; CBN also became "the largest private donor to the Nicaraguan contra camps in Honduras" and a powerful advocate for aid to the Contras in Washington. On the campaign trail Robertson extolled the virtues of Christian America and railed against what he saw as an assault on Christian faith and values.[5]

Robertson's CBN had an estimated annual viewership of 16 million and collected $2.4 million in contributions in 1986, and he hoped to translate this into political support, into an "invisible army." Due to the improbability of his campaign, opponents and journalists used the

term derisively, but Robertson embraced it. His army consisted primarily of charismatics, Pentecostals, and "spirit-filled" Christians, a subset
of white evangelicalism, but he failed to win the support of most evangelicals. Falwell, LaHaye, Kennedy, Robison, and Dobson all declined
to endorse him. This may have been due in part to professional rival-
ries, but it had also never seemed that Robertson had much of a chance
of winning. For those who wanted access to the Oval Office for the
next four years, backing the establishment candidate seemed a safer
bet. But there was also the fact that Robertson's occupation as a cler-
gyman was seen by some as a detriment. It wasn't just that he was a
televangelist launching a campaign amid a slew of televangelist sex
scandals, but many Christians themselves didn't seem entirely confident that a pastor could provide the robust leadership necessary on the
national stage. Certainly, Robertson paled in comparison to Reagan.
Most evangelicals ended up backing George H. W. Bush, who, sensing
which way the winds were blowing, had slowly aligned himself with
religious conservatives.[6]

Evangelical support for Bush was tepid, and the feeling was mutual.
Bush, too, lacked the rugged masculinity of his predecessor, but fortunately for him, he was running against Michael Dukakis. Republicans
wasted no time in impugning Dukakis's patriotism and sabotaging
his masculinity—and in their view the two were closely connected.
At least since 1972, Republicans had been arguing that Democrats
lacked the strength to defend the nation. In the fall of 1988, evangelicals remained loyal to the Republican Party; 70 percent voted for Bush,
and Bush easily beat his Democratic rival.[7]

The second year of Bush's presidency, in the summer of 1990, Iraq
invaded Kuwait. In response, the United States forged an international
coalition to end the Iraqi occupation. Unlike Catholic bishops and
Protestant mainline clergy, most evangelicals enthusiastically supported Operation Desert Storm. In this first major military engagement since America's humiliating defeat in Vietnam, it wasn't initially
apparent how things would unfold, but once the ground assault
against Saddam Hussein's forces commenced, the answer became clear.

This was no Vietnam. It was a stunning display of American military superiority. Granted, cleanup operations were a little messy. Oil wells burned, and Hussein remained in power. But for a time, the taste of renewed American power was exhilarating.[8]

In 1991, the Cold War officially came to an end. For more than four decades, evangelicals had mobilized against an imminent communist threat. With American power restored and their enemy vanquished, the need for evangelical militarism was no longer self-evident.

Nothing if not creative, Pat Robertson led the way in identifying the requisite crisis. Having failed in his presidential bid, Robertson used the millions of names on his campaign mailing list to found the Christian Coalition. In 1991, Robertson published *The New World Order*, arguing that President Bush was being duped into thinking the threat of communism was over. In his view, totalitarianism had returned to the former Soviet bloc in a more "deceptive and dangerous form." He also accused Bush of launching the Iraq War as a devious plot to cede American sovereignty to the United Nations. Inspired by their interpretation of biblical prophecies in the Book of Revelation, conservative Protestants had long feared a "one-world" government that would be ruled over by the Antichrist. In the early twentieth century these fears had attached to the League of Nations, and during the Cold War these fears were often channeled into a virulent anticommunism—though Hal Lindsey's best-selling *The Late Great Planet Earth* (1970) had warned of a European Community that would usher in the reign of the devil. With the fall of the Soviet Union, suspicions fell squarely on the UN. And, in the case of Robertson, on the Illuminati, on wealthy Jewish bankers, and on conspiratorial corporate internationalists. The *Wall Street Journal* dismissed Robertson's book as "a predictable compendium of the lunatic fringe's greatest hits," written in an "energetically crackpot style." Meanwhile, it climbed to number four on the *New York Times* Best Sellers list, selling half a million copies. Under the leadership of Ralph Reed, Robertson's Christian Coalition quickly grew into the most powerful grassroots organization of the Religious

Right, building networks in all fifty states and claiming more than one million members by 1994.[9]

At the end of the Gulf War, President Bush's approval rating stood at 89 percent. But with the recession of 1990–91, and with his reneging on his "no new taxes" pledge, his popularity soon plummeted. Sensing the president's vulnerability, Pat Buchanan—a standard-bearer for the Religious Right who had worked for Nixon, Ford, and Reagan—decided to challenge Bush in the 1992 primaries. Concerned about Buchanan's level of support, Bush reached out to the National Association of Evangelicals and the Southern Baptist Convention and began to more openly champion conservative social values. In this way, Bush ushered in what Reed termed "the most conservative and the most pro-family platform in the history of the party." It called for a ban on abortion, opposed LGBT rights, and defended school prayer and homeschool rights. Buchanan didn't unseat Bush, but he did shift the Republican Party farther to the Right. The Cold War might have ended, but at the opening night of the Republican National Convention, Buchanan declared that a different sort of war had begun: "There is a religious war going on in this country . . . a cultural war as critical to the kind of nation we shall be as the Cold War itself. This war is for the soul of America."[10]

The Religious Right, however, promptly lost the first battle of Buchanan's war. In a three-way race, Bill Clinton emerged victorious over Bush and Ross Perot. If Bush had been a disappointment for American evangelicals, Bill Clinton appeared to be a disaster.

DESPITE HIS SOUTHERN and Baptist credentials, Clinton was anathema to the Religious Right. A draft dodger, a marijuana smoker, and a Democrat, he represented everything they despised about the 1960s. And then there was his wife. She had advocated for civil rights and children's rights and had campaigned for the antiwar liberal George McGovern and the masculinity-challenged Jimmy Carter.

Even worse, as a feminist and a career woman, Hillary Rodham had provoked the ire of religious conservatives when she refused to take her husband's name. (She later changed her name in an attempt to appease critics and smooth her husband's path forward.) On the campaign trail in 1992, her feminism became a point of contention when, in response to the insinuation that her law firm had received favors from her husband when he was governor, she retorted: "I suppose I could have stayed home, baked cookies and had teas." The backlash was swift, and brutal. "If I ever entertained the idea of voting for Bill Clinton," one woman wrote in a letter to *Time* magazine, "the smug bitchiness of his wife's comment has nipped that notion in the bud." She spoke for many. Since the 1970s, the identity of housewives had become highly politicized, and Hillary Rodham Clinton triggered fear, resentment, and disdain among many conservative women, some of whom felt devalued by her very existence. Of course, many women had been read-ing books and listening to sermons for a good two decades to prepare them to respond in this way. It made no difference that Hillary liked to bake cookies, or that her recipe for chocolate chip cookies took home the top prize in the *Family Circle* presidential cookie bake-off. When it came to Hillary Clinton, conservative evangelicals were not about to forgive and forget.[11]

With the Clintons occupying the White House, prospects looked bleak for religious conservatives. On the bright side, the Religious Right had always thrived on a sense of embattlement, and with Clin-ton's election, the Christian Coalition and other conservative organi-zations saw a significant uptick in membership and fundraising. The Clinton White House provided fresh fodder for conservative outrage on a daily basis. In addition to the constant din of corruption allega-tions, of more immediate concern was the First Lady's ill-fated attempt to reform American health care. Not only did this smack of socialism as far as conservatives were concerned, but the Christian Coalition insisted that health-care reform concealed a "radical social agenda," ostensibly by promoting abortion, gay rights, and sex education. But this was just the tip of the iceberg.[12]

"The New World Order Wants Your Children," Phillis Schlafly warned. When Hillary Clinton published *It Takes a Village*, a book describing how forces beyond the immediate family impacted the well-being of the nation's children, Schlafly and other conservatives were adamant that it did *not* take a village to raise a child. They saw failed efforts to secure federal day-care legislation and the work of the Children's Defense Fund and the UN Convention on the Rights of the Child as thinly veiled attempts to infringe on parental rights. Parents didn't want a village "butting in." If you allow the village to "usurp your parental authority, you can be sure that the village will teach your children behaviors you don't want them to learn." Schlafly envisioned a future where parents no longer had the right to discipline their children, where children could demand to watch television, refuse to attend their parents' church, even join a cult. By advancing the absurdity of "children's rights," the Clinton administration, and the UN, threatened parental authority, an orderly society, and American sovereignty.[13]

Failing to protect national sovereignty wasn't the only way Clinton was undermining the nation's security. The Gulf War had briefly reinvigorated narratives of a heroic military and American power, but for conservatives this confidence diminished quickly as Clinton took the helm as commander in chief. On the military front, Clinton's sins were legion. Early in his presidency he announced his intention to open the armed forces to people regardless of their sexual orientation. Facing immediate backlash, he settled for a "Don't ask, don't tell" policy. Opposition came from within the military itself and from American evangelicals, and by this point, to be sure, the two groups were not mutually exclusive. Evangelicals in the military used materials supplied by the Family Research Council, Concerned Women for America, Focus on the Family, and Exodus International to oppose opening the military to gay service members. In turn, Dobson hosted Colonel Ronald D. Ray on his radio show, and Ray warned listeners that "military leaders were real naive about the widespread agenda" homosexuals were advancing.[14]

Evangelicals weren't just concerned about "gays in the military." They feared the "feminization" of the military as a whole under Clinton's watch. In 1994, Clinton signed an order allowing women to serve on combat ships and fighter planes, a move that raised the ire of religious conservatives. This not only went against God-ordained gender difference, but by putting women where they didn't belong it exposed them to the threat of sexual assault. During the 1990s, a series of sex scandals rattled the military. From the Tailhook incident in 1991 to the adultery of air force pilot Kelly Flinn, it was clear to conservatives that the military was no place for women. Women belonged on a pedestal, not on the field of battle. Making matters worse, Clinton further emasculated the military by sending troops on an array of UN peacekeeping missions. As Schlafly put it, Clinton and "overpaid bureaucrats" seemed intent on establishing the UN as "a world government with its own police force and its own taxing authority," but she reminded readers that "no man can serve two masters." Sending US soldiers as "UN mercenaries . . . on phony 'peacekeeping' expeditions" to places like Somalia, Haiti, and Rwanda was unconstitutional and un-American. And unmanly.[15]

Schlafly was right to sense that peacekeeping forces differed from traditional militaries. Decoupled from nationalist agendas, the UN stood as a model of post–Cold War, nonimperialist military force, one that appeared to eschew traditional militarism and patriarchal masculinity. Some members of the military also found this change unsettling. In the aftermath of the Cold War and the Gulf War, marine fighter pilots reported that they were losing confidence in themselves. Two years after their decisive victory in Iraq, without a clear mission, they didn't even feel "like real marines."[16]

IF CONSERVATIVE EVANGELICALS needed one more thing not to like about the Clintons, there was the Lewinsky affair. As word leaked out about the president's "inappropriate relationship" with the former White House intern in January 1998, Schlafly lashed out:

"At stake is whether the White House will become a public relations vehicle for lying and polling, akin to a television show, or will remain a platform for the principled articulation of policies and values that Americans respect." Clinton had "converted the once-serious offense of lying to the American public into a daily rite," extinguishing all reverence for the presidency. The issue wasn't really "what Bill Clinton did or didn't do with Paula or Gennifer or Monica," but "whether we are going to allow the president to get by with flouting the law and lying about it on television, while hiding behind his popularity in the polls." If this precedent prevailed, Schlafly prophesied, "Americans can look forward to a succession of TV charlatans and professional liars occupying the White House."[17]

James Dobson, too, issued a lengthy letter to his followers expressing shock and dismay at the humiliation of the president, his family, and the nation. Like Schlafly, Dobson was appalled by his fellow citizens' willingness to excuse the president's behavior as "just a private affair—something between himself and Hillary." Reminding readers that military officials were being held accountable for sexual misconduct, Dobson found it "profoundly disturbing" that the rules seemed to be rewritten for Clinton. What's more, Clinton's dishonesty was part of a long history of immorality and untruthfulness. He'd lied about Gennifer Flowers and about dodging the draft. He'd "visited the Soviet Union and other hostile countries during the Vietnam War, claiming that he was only an 'observer.'" He'd organized and participated in antiwar rallies, and evaded questions about his marijuana use. "Character DOES matter," Dobson opined. "You can't run a family, let alone a country, without it."[18]

Pat Robertson weighed in as well. Clinton had "debauched, debased and defamed" the presidency, turning the White House into a "playpen for the sexual freedom of the poster child of the 1960s," he told 3000 members of the Christian Coalition, bringing his audience to their feet. Ralph Reed, too, insisted that character mattered: "We care about the conduct of our leaders, and we will not rest until we have leaders of good moral character." Meanwhile, Jerry Falwell sent a special edition of his weekly report to more than 160,000 evangelical pastors, urging them to call undecided House members to vote for Clinton's impeachment. The Christian Coalition collected more than 250,000 signatures on petitions calling for the same. Dobson's Family Research Council ran television ads calling for Clinton's resignation due to his "virtue deficit." Evangelical theologian Wayne Grudem signed a public letter criticizing Clinton for his "ill use of women" and his "manipulation of truth," and SBC leaders Paige Patterson, Al Mohler, and Richard Land signed a letter taking Clinton to task.[19]

The unfaithful, draft-dodging, morally deficient president embodied all that was wrong with America. Yet, to evangelicals' consternation, Clinton's sexual misconduct seemed to enhance his standing in the eyes of many Americans. Since the 1970s, conservatives had been tarring liberal men as wimps, deficient in masculine leadership qualities. As the details of the Lewinsky scandal came to light, "Bill Clinton's image went from that of the neutered househusband of an emasculating harridan to that of a swaggering stud-muffin whose untrammeled lust for sexual conquest imperiled all females in his orbit," according to clinical psychologist Stephen Ducat. Perhaps, "behind the tongue-clucking disapprobation of some male commentators" there lurked "a thinly disguised envy." Clinton's job rating received a significant boost as the scandal unfolded—"the formerly feminized president had been resurrected as a phallic leader."[20]

Among Clinton's evangelical critics, it appears that their concern with Clinton's predatory behavior was more about Clinton than about predatory behavior. Within their own circles, evangelicals didn't have a strong record when it came to defending women against harassment and abuse. In the 1980s, for example, Dobson had recommended a healthy skepticism toward certain allegations of domestic violence. In *Love Must Be Tough* (1983), he warned of women who "deliberately 'baited'" their husbands into hitting them, "verbally antagoniz[ing]" them until they got "the prize" they sought: a bruise they could parade before "neighbors, friends, and the law" to gain a "moral advantage," and perhaps also justify an otherwise unbiblical escape from marriage through divorce. This argument remained unchanged in his 1996 edition of the book.[21]

In 1991, President Bush's nomination of Clarence Thomas to the United States Supreme Court provided occasion for evangelicals to reflect further on questions of harassment and abuse. Upon Thomas's nomination, Anita Hill—herself a devout Christian who had served on the law faculty of Oral Roberts University—reluctantly came forward with her account of Thomas's persistent sexual harassment. According to Hill, Thomas liked to detail various scenes he'd viewed in pornographic films and boast of his "sexual prowess." Both Hill and Thomas were black, and the contentious hearings split the African American community. Among white evangelicals there was little dissent; they saw Hill as representative of the corrupt and conniving influence of modern feminism, and they stood behind Thomas.[22]

In the pages of *Christianity Today*, Charles Colson argued that the Thomas hearings were the result of feminism run amuck. Feminists insisted that women should be sexually liberated ("read promiscuous"), use explicit language ("read obscene"), and freed from "the burden of childbearing" (to compete in the workplace), yet now they complained when men used explicit language when talking to women in the workplace. "The very people who deliberately tore down older codes of chivalry and deference to women now want the protection they offer," he groused. It wasn't just the family that was under attack, but something even more fundamental: "the very notion of what it means to be a man, what it means to be a woman." What Americans were seeing was the result of confusion sowed by militant feminists, and since God was "not the author of confusion," something diabolical must be at work.[23]

Phyllis Schlafly scoffed at the very idea that Hill could be a victim of sexual harassment, or, as she put it, "some bad words in the workplace." Hill was an EEOC lawyer, after all, and would know how to deal with sexual harassment if any such thing had occurred. Schlafly slandered Hill as the epitome of the "phony pose" feminists adopted when they wanted to grab power: "'poor little me,' the injured ingenue, the damsel in distress who cries for Big Brother Federal Government to defend her from the wolves in the workplace—not merely from what they might do, but even from what they might say." Schlafly wasn't buying it. Hill was smart, tough, and "perfectly capable of telling a man to button his lip, keep his hands off, get lost, bug off or just plain 'no.'" To Schlafly, the whole thing was just a "last-minute smear" orchestrated by a "feminist mob" trying to lynch Thomas.[24]

Though few matched Schlafly's expressiveness, other leading figures of the Christian Right, including Paul Weyrich, Pat Robertson, Ralph Reed, and Gary Bauer, came to Thomas's defense as well. This can be explained in part by the greater good evangelicals hoped to accomplish with the ascension of another conservative justice to the Supreme Court. Yet long after Thomas was safely ensconced on the highest court, conservatives continued to mobilize against measures to address sexual harassment and abuse. They opposed the Violence Against Women Act, signed into law by President Clinton in 1994, on many counts. As Schlafly explained, the VAWA was just one more example of "the federal government's insatiable demand for more power." Schlafly also accused feminists of inflating rates of harassment and abuse, and she suggested that most of the exceedingly rare instances of actual harassment could be blamed on feminists themselves. Before the feminists burst on the scene in the 1970s, there had been all sorts of laws protecting and advantaging women, Schlafly contended, but feminists had dismantled these protections in their quest for equality. Now, playing the victim, they busied themselves with inventing new infractions. Adding to the absurdity, feminists wanted to criminalize "all heterosexual sex" as rape "unless an affirmative, sober, explicit verbal consent can be proved." Apparently jokes, too, were no longer allowed, because feminists didn't have a sense of humor. Finally, concerns about domestic violence could be linked to a global feminist agenda; when Hillary Clinton represented the United States at the 1995 World Conference on Women in Beijing, giving her highly lauded speech "Women's Rights Are Human Rights," it only confirmed the nefarious link between globalism, feminism, and the Clinton administration. All the pieces fit together in an intricate plot to undermine the sovereignty of the United States, and the authority of the family patriarch.[25]

RELIGIOUS LEADERS WERE NOT the Clinton administration's only, or even its loudest, critics. The 1987 repeal of the FCC's Fairness Doctrine, which had mandated honest and equitable on-air treatment of controversial issues, ushered in an era of talk radio that would change the tenor of American political conversation. Rush Limbaugh's bombastic style set the tone. Each day, listeners could tune in to a world where white men still reigned supreme in the public and private spheres. Limbaugh was known for his sexist and misogynistic comments about women. Hillary Clinton was a favorite target, as were various "feminazis" and female journalists, whom he referred to as "infobabes" and "anchorettes." An enthusiastic supporter of the military, Limbaugh loved to deride Clinton as a draft dodger, even though he himself had secured a deferment to avoid serving in Vietnam. He also liked to talk football and smoke expensive cigars while ridiculing liberal men as the "new castrati." Millions listened in, often on a daily basis. Blurring the line between news and entertainment, Limbaugh's popularity was clear, but his influence was difficult to discern. A 1995 *Time* cover story, at least, warned that his "electronic populism" threatened to short-circuit representative democracy."[26]

In 1996, Bill O'Reilly joined Limbaugh in the right-wing media universe. Hired by Roger Ailes to host *The O'Reilly Factor* at the start-up Fox News Channel, O'Reilly channeled masculine rage in a similar manner, tapping into the anger and resentment brewing among conservative white men sensing their cultural displacement. O'Reilly, too, framed politics, and especially foreign policy, in terms of masculine power. Fox News quickly became a mouthpiece for American conservatism. With bombastic male commentators sharing the screen with women whose qualifications apparently included a sexualized hyper-femininity, throwback masculinity was at the heart of the network's appeal.[27]

Neither Limbaugh nor O'Reilly made their name as Christian broadcasters, but many conservative evangelicals were attracted to their masculine brand. In the 1980s, Tim LaHaye had called for a Christian news network. Fox News didn't frame itself in religious terms, but it more than fit the bill. The fit wasn't a theological one, at least not in terms of traditional doctrine; it was cultural and political. Fox News hawked a nostalgic vision where white men still dominated, where feminists and other liberals were demonized, and where a militant masculinity and sexualized femininity offered a vision for the way things ought to be. White evangelicals were drawn to the network, and the network, in turn, shaped evangelicalism. But this is not a case of politics hijacking religion; the affinities between Fox News and conservative evangelicalism ran deep. Long before O'Reilly invented the "War on Christmas," evangelicals knew he was on their side. Within two decades, the influence of Fox News on conservative evangelicalism would be so profound that journalists and scholars alike would find it difficult to separate the two.[28]

IN THE ABSENCE of a clear, external threat, culture warriors like Robertson, Dobson, Schlafly, and Buchanan identified a new battle, a war on which the soul of the nation depended. Thanks to the steady barrage of scandal, actual and imagined, issuing from the Clinton White House, they were often successful in stoking the fires of evangelical militancy. But during the 1990s, other, and in some cases opposing movements signaled potential new directions for post–Cold War evangelicalism. No longer preoccupied with defending against the spread of communism, many evangelicals began to embrace a more expansive foreign policy agenda as they turned their attention to global poverty, human trafficking, the global AIDS epidemic, and the persecution of Christians around the world. In 1996, the NAE issued a "Statement of Conscience" that elevated religious persecution and human rights as chief foreign policy concerns. As Richard Cizik, the NAE's vice president for governmental affairs, explained, in the post–Cold War era evangelicals had become "more interested in making a difference than in making a statement." For a time, it seemed evangelicals' "knee-jerk bellicosity" might be waning as they began to embrace a more diffuse set of commitments.[29]

The NAE represented a more moderate establishment evangelical-ism, but even within the Christian Right some sought to broaden the coalition by softening the message. As head of the Christian Coali-tion, Ralph Reed advised members to "avoid hostile and intemperate rhetoric" and to instead embrace a more tolerant posture, emphasizing inclusion. "We have allowed ourselves to be ghettoized by a narrow band of issues like abortion, homosexual rights and prayer in school," he warned, and it was time for a new direction. Not all members of the Christian Coalition were on board. By 1996 a rift had opened between Reed and members of the old guard unwilling to compro-mise on deeply held values, men like Falwell, Dobson, Gary Bauer, and many of the organization's rank and file.[30]

Tensions between militant and more forward-looking expressions that characterized evangelicalism in the 1990s found expression in evangelical discussions of Christian manhood as well. Here, too, old certainties did not necessarily hold sway. Without the threat of godless communism to justify militant Christian masculinity, many evangel-ical men began to express uncertainty about what manhood in fact required. Times had changed, it seemed. Perhaps masculinity needed to change as well.

Chapter 9

TENDER
WARRIORS

I N THE SUMMER OF 1997, AROUND 700,000 CHRISTIAN
men streamed into the nation's capital to "stand in the gap," to step
up as men of God, to keep their promises to honor and obey God, protect their families, pursue virtue, and influence their world. Six years
earlier, 4200 men had attended the first Promise Keepers rally, the
brainchild of Bill McCartney, then head football coach at the University of Colorado. McCartney had experienced a personal and religious
crisis after his daughter had given birth to a child fathered by one of his
players. Realizing that he had failed to prioritize his family, he ended
up leaving his Catholic church for the evangelical Vineyard Christian
Fellowship. Thinking he wasn't alone in his struggles, he decided to
issue a call for the renewal of Christian manhood. The next year, James
Dobson promoted Promise Keepers on his radio program, helping to
ignite a national movement. By 1994, 278,000 men were attending PK
events held in stadiums around the country. The next year 700,000
participated, and the year after that an estimated 1.2 million. By 1997,
the evangelical men's movement had become impossible to ignore.[1]

Many observers were alarmed by the throng of Christian men on
the National Mall. Patricia Ireland, president of the National Organization for Women, saw the movement as a threat to women's rights:
"The Promise Keepers seem to think women will be so thrilled that
men are promising to take 'responsibility' in their families that we
will take a back seat in this and every other area of our lives." Though

Promise Keepers billed itself as an apolitical organization, Ireland was skeptical; when she saw the men gathered in Washington, DC, she saw "hundreds and thousands of names on direct mail lists." To Ireland, evangelical men's ministries were nothing more than "stealth political cells." Though she conceded that many of the men gathering in stadiums across the country had little awareness of the group's larger political agenda, she identified a "religious right pantheon behind Promise Keepers," and to suggest they were "all about Godly male bonding and not about political organizing" was simply indefensible. To critics like Ireland, Promise Keepers was the next iteration of the Religious Right, more dangerous than the Moral Majority or the Christian Coalition precisely because of their outwardly apolitical stance.[2]

Ireland had a point. Dobson's Focus on the Family provided critical ongoing support for the organization, and Bill Bright's Campus Crusade for Christ lent Promise Keepers eighty-five full-time employees. Bright's book *The Coming Revival*, in which he railed against abortion, divorce, race riots, sexual promiscuity, the removal of God from public schools, the teaching of evolution, and the "homosexual 'explosion,'" was sold at all PK rallies. Mark DeMoss, the organization's national spokesperson, had worked for Jerry Falwell and had served on Pat Buchanan's presidential campaign. Frequent speakers included Ed Cole, author of *Maximized Manhood*, and Charles Colson, the disgraced Nixon aide who, after converting to evangelicalism, had gone on to found Prison Fellowship Ministries and establish himself as a power broker in the Religious Right. Beverly LaHaye's Concerned Women for America heartily endorsed the organization, and McCartney himself was a member of Colorado for Family Values and an advocate for Amendment 2, the effort to prohibit granting "special rights" to homosexuals. Promise Keepers avoided taking positions on theological issues in order to maintain their "big-tent" coalition, but they did declare their pro-life stance on the issue of abortion, and they issued a statement asserting that "the Bible clearly teaches that homosexuality violates God's creative design for a husband and a wife and that it is a sin"—though they also addressed "homosexuals" as "recipients of God's mercy, grace, and forgiveness," and invited them to be "included and welcomed" at all PK events.[3]

However, Promise Keepers was not merely the Christian Coalition in disguise. Organizers instituted policies against lobbying and political endorsements and focused instead on reaching across religious and denominational divides, bringing together charismatics and Pentecostals with Southern Baptists, Methodists, and the growing contingent of nondenominational evangelicals, along with Catholics, liberal Protestants, and Mormons. Many liberal critics failed to realize that Promise Keepers had vocal critics on the Right as well as the Left. Some conservatives felt the movement was too ecumenical, and a threat to the authority of the institutional church, while others worried that it was influenced by "new age" teachings, wasn't "conservative enough," or didn't adequately promote biblical literalism.[4]

Reflecting the unsettled times, no singular notion of masculinity dominated the evangelical men's movement of the 1990s. Following Ed Cole's lead, many evangelicals sought a middle path between an outmoded "macho" masculinity and the "softer" modern one they found lacking. They found the answer in "soft patriarchy." Yet many other Promise Keepers speakers and writers hewed toward a more expressive and sometimes even egalitarian model. This is most clearly seen in Gary Oliver's *Real Men Have Feelings Too* (1993), sold by the PK organization and championed by McCartney. Unlike Cole, Oliver rejected stark gender difference. He argued that traditional "masculine" traits ("bravery, strength, stoicism, an insatiable sex drive, a preoccupation with achievement") were nothing more than "myths of masculinity." Likewise, "gentleness, compassion, tenderness, meekness, sensitivity" were not essentially feminine characteristics, but rather healthy human ones—traits modeled by Jesus Christ himself. Oliver urged men to get in touch with their emotions and he rejected the patriarchal chain of command, instead endorsing egalitarian marriage.[5]

Both Cole and Oliver were popular writers and speakers within the movement, suggesting that Promise Keepers encompassed varied and even contradictory models of manhood. Cole, for example, favored masculine "toughness," but he also critiqued men who wielded their domestic authority in unbending or abusive ways, and he gave a nod to female equality by suggesting that women were "joint heirs" in the home. Oliver, meanwhile, hedged on his egalitarianism by calling out the "'lunacy' and 'ridiculous assumption[s]' of those who have 'jumped on the gender-same bandwagon.'" In this way, men could find within Promise Keepers both a justification for traditional masculine authority and a defense of an emotive, egalitarian, reconstructed Christian manhood.[6]

For a time, both coexisted in creative tension, thanks in part to the idea of "servant leadership." Less abrasive than "male headship," servant leadership framed male authority as obligation, sacrifice, and service. Men were urged to accept their responsibilities, to work hard, to serve their wives and families, to eschew alcohol, gambling, and pornography, to step up around the home, and to be present in their children's lives. The notion of "servant leadership" had originated in the business world. With the decline of production in the 1970s and 1980s, service work took over a larger share of the labor market, and servant leadership helped redefine masculine authority in a way that didn't conflict with men's role in a service economy. No longer producers in a traditional sense, men could still be leaders. Within Christian circles, the concept of servant leadership similarly enabled men to maintain their authority in the home even as they no longer maintained breadwinner status. By the 1990s, the male breadwinner economy was largely a thing of the past. Since the 1960s, male blue-collar work such as construction, manufacturing, and agriculture had been in decline, shrinking from approximately half of the workforce to less than 30 percent at the end of the 1990s. Over that same period, sectors that employed pink- and white-collar women—areas such as health care, retail, education, finance, and food service—expanded to well over half of the workforce; by 1994, 75 percent of working-age women worked for pay. Despite their rhetoric, evangelicals were not immune to these economic trends; among conservative Protestants, rates of dual-income households began to approach the national aver-

age. Nevertheless, women who worked outside the home still shoul-
dered the burden of housework, and for some of these women, "servant
leadership" appeared to offer a way to incentivize men to reinvest on
the home front.[7]

For women who found this patriarchal bargain attractive, the harsh
critique leveled by feminists was alienating and confusing. Here was
a group of men confessing their shortcomings, promising to be better husbands, to be more attentive to their families, more respectful
of women. What could be wrong with that? Although studies show
that conservative Protestant men did less household labor than men
in nonevangelical homes, they were more likely to express affection for
their wives and appreciation for the housework women did. They also
spent more time than other men with their kids, even if they tended
to administer harsher discipline. Moreover, depending on where any
given man was coming from, "soft patriarchy" and "servant leadership" might be a significant improvement over harsher authoritarian
tendencies, whether religious or secular in origin. In some families,
these concepts functioned in a way that could "reform machismo" by
reattaching men to their families.[8]

Despite talk of sacrifice, tenderness, and servanthood, however, it
was hard to ignore language like that of Tony Evans in *Seven Promises
of a Promise Keeper*, the organization's best-selling book. Men shouldn't
ask for their leadership role back, Evans insisted, they needed to *take it
back*: "There can be no compromise here." Men must lead for the sake
of families, "and the survival of our culture." (On the very rare occasion
when a woman was invited to address a Promise Keepers event, Holly
Phillips, wife of president Randy Phillips, asked men to forgive women
for their lack of respect, for "the demeaning and belittling words we
have uttered," and "for the ways we have coddled and smothered you
with our protectiveness, thereby emasculating you.") To critics, Promise Keepers simply marketed "male supremacy with a beatific smile." In
their view, servant leadership helped salvage a patriarchal order even as
men no longer maintained their role as providers. By promising inti-

Promise Keepers praying at the Seattle Kingdome in May 1997.
AP PHOTO / LOREN CALLAHAN.

macy in exchange for power, servant leadership passed off authority as humility, ensuring that patriarchal authority would endure even in the midst of changing times. As far as critics were concerned, this was more insidious than a straightforward power grab.[9]

Militaristic rhetoric surfaced at times in PK literature, and despite the organization's apolitical posture, this rhetoric inevitably found expression in a conservative political agenda. McCartney, for example, rallied the "men of the nation" to "go to war," reminding them that they had "divine power" as their weapon: "We will not compromise. Whatever truth is at risk, in the schools or legislature, we are going to contend for it. We will win." For the most part, however, PK speakers preferred sports metaphors to military ones. Rallies invariably took place in sports stadiums, and athletes often took center stage. The role of sports in fashioning Christian masculinity was nothing new. The apostle Paul, after all, urged disciples of Christ to run the race before them, and following in the tradition of Billy Sunday, twentieth-

century religious leaders had frequently melded sport with Christianity in order to render the faith more masculine—and, ideally, bring
men to Christ. In 1954, evangelicals founded the Fellowship of Christian Athletes, an organization that sought to leverage the popularity of
sports for evangelistic purposes. (If sports celebrities could sell shaving
cream and cigarettes, why couldn't they sell Christianity?) In the Cold
War era, sports had seemed an ideal domain in which to instill Christian values in young men.[10]

At a time when evangelicals were striving for greater respectability and relevance, mixing religion with sports made sense. Few had
excelled in this endeavor more than Jerry Falwell. At Falwell's Thomas
Road Baptist Church, sports served both as training ground and as
metaphor for the spiritual life. While talk of sports was ubiquitous, for
Falwell and his followers it wasn't about how you played the game. It
was about winning. Upon visiting Thomas Road, Frances FitzGerald
remarked that "sports, the oldest of Anglo-Saxon prescriptions for the
sublimation of male violence and male sexual energies, might stand as
a metaphor for the whole social enterprise of the church." In Falwell's
words, "God wants you to be a champion."[11]

In the 1970s and 1980s, Falwell used military and sports analogies
interchangeably. By the 1990s, however, as some evangelicals began to
back away from militaristic rhetoric, sports offered a more palatable
alternative. In 1996, for instance, Ralph Reed sent a memo instruct-
ing grassroots leaders of the Christian Coalition to "avoid military
rhetoric and to use sports metaphors instead." Still, sports and military metaphors could function in similar ways, critics pointed out. In
a world destabilized by modern feminism, sports offered disaffected
men a masculine haven. Like military metaphors, sports called to mind
a world in which men, by virtue of their superior physical strength, still
dominated. Both sports and the military, too, reinforced a dualistic
view of the world. In athletics, as in battle, there were winners and losers. In this way, sports-infused rhetoric and pageantry allowed Promise
Keepers to address male anxieties while maintaining the semblance of
benevolent patriarchy.[12]

It was when the evangelical men's movement elevated sports as the preferred metaphor for Christian manhood that "racial reconciliation" emerged as a guiding purpose. Under McCartney's leadership, Promise Keepers was one of the few white Christian organizations in the country willing to take on racism. Critics viewed Promise Keepers' focus on racial reconciliation with skepticism. Some accused leaders of "jumping on the racial reconciliation bandwagon, in part because it allows them to sound supportive of people of color, without actually having to support any of the political and social policies that would benefit people of color." Framing racism as a personal failing, at times even as a mutual problem, PK speakers routinely failed to address structural inequalities. In this way, the pursuit of racial reconciliation could end up serving as a ritual of self-redemption, absolving white men of complicity and justifying the continuation of white patriarchy in the home and the nation. Several African American pastors critiqued this unwillingness to address deeper structural questions and called out the organization for racial tokenism. Yet, far more than other evangelical organizations, Promise Keepers provided a platform for African American voices. Black pastors like Tony Evans, Wellington Boone, and E. V. Hill, and sports stars like Reggie White frequently appeared at PK rallies.[13]

Promise Keepers' pursuit of racial reconciliation did amount to more than mere posturing. Its 1996 book *Go the Distance: The Making of a Promise Keeper* (published by Focus on the Family) included chapters by Charles Colson, Bill McCartney, Stu Weber, and other white evangelicals, but it also included an unsparing critique of white Christianity penned by African American pastor and civil rights activist John Perkins. How much this commitment to racial reconciliation trickled down to the rank and file is difficult to gauge. The movement remained overwhelmingly white; a 1998 questionnaire revealed that whites made up 90 percent of its membership. Moreover, some observers link the decline of the Promise Keepers movement to its pursuit of racial reconciliation. McCartney himself conceded that the focus on race was "a major factor in the significant fall-off" in attendance—it was "simply a hard teaching for many." In 1996, for instance, 40 percent of complaints registered by conference participants were negative responses to the theme of racial reconciliation. The falloff in attendance caused a significant decline in revenue, and in the summer of 1997 Promise Keepers laid off more than one hundred employees; the next two years witnessed successive waves of restructuring and downsizing.[14]

Other factors also contributed to the organization's decline. The high attendance at the Stand in the Gap rally in Washington, DC, probably meant men were less likely to spend money to attend local and regional gatherings. The novelty was also wearing off; without new content it was harder to entice men to attend conferences. But there was also a shift within evangelicalism that would begin to render the "soft patriarchy" that Promise Keepers espoused less appealing. By the end of the decade, the emotional timbre of the events had started to feel too "soft."[15]

Promise Keepers as a movement began to wane, but by spawning dozens of smaller denominational ministries and parachurch groups, its influence persisted. The Southern Baptist Convention entered cooperative agreements with Promise Keepers and developed its own men's ministry. The Assemblies of God appointed a "men's ministries secretary" to work with Promise Keepers, and the Presbyterian Church (USA) developed its own men's Bible study series. Catholics, too, organized two new men's ministries, the Saint Joseph's Covenant Keepers and a Ministry to Black Catholic Men.[16]

The proliferation of men's groups sparked "a minor revolution in the Christian publishing and retailing industry." At PK events one could find "a virtual messianic mini-mall, hawking books, T-shirts," souvenirs and baseball caps. Christian retailers, too, began stocking shelves with men's products. As the president of the Christian Booksellers Association explained, more men started shopping in Christian bookstores because there was more there for them to buy; in 1996, nearly one-quarter of customers were men, up from one in six fifteen years earlier. The most lasting influence of the Promise Keepers movement may well have been the market it spawned.[17]

THANKS TO THE EVANGELICAL men's movement, books on Christian masculinity began to roll off the presses. Drawing on charismatic and therapeutic traditions, prosperity teachings, Christian Reconstructionism, conservative Southern Baptist theology, and neo-Calvinism, authors ended up crafting visions of Christian masculinity that looked remarkably similar. In the 1990s, the most popular "blueprint for Christian manhood" to emerge was that of the "tender warrior."

Setting the stage for the genre was Gordon Dalbey's *Healing the Masculine Soul*. It was published in 1988, but Dalbey had been struggling to come to terms with masculinity since the 1970s. In 1983, he had come across a newspaper article by Robert Bly. Influenced by Carl Jung, Bly was concerned that fathers no longer initiated sons into proper manhood; drawing on fairy tales and myths, he pointed to the role of a heroic quest in preparing young men to assume roles as productive members of society. Lacking this proper male development, society would be left with "soft males" unable to fulfill their roles. Dalbey also read Leanne Payne's 1986 *Crisis in Masculinity*. Payne, a Christian psychologist, identified the roots of this "crisis" in men's failure to separate themselves from their mothers' femininity. Only a father could affirm a son's masculinity and a daughter's femininity, according to Payne, but with absent or overly authoritarian fathers (and overbearing mothers), a generation of men had become separated from their own masculinity. The results were devastating: "homosexual neurosis," addiction to pornography, the proliferation of androgynous gender roles, widespread confusion and despair. Dalbey found inspiration in both Payne's and Bly's "explorations on the frontiers of masculinity," but wondered why "a secular man and a Christian woman" should be paving the way. "Was there no Christian man to pioneer the journey?"[18]

Dalbey took up the challenge, but securing a publisher was no easy task. In 1987, when he was shopping his manuscript, "the unique needs of men had not yet appeared on the church's radar screen." Editors at Word Publishing were intrigued enough to bring him to Dallas so that he could explain in person why men would be interested in such a book, and Dalbey succeeded in convincing them to take a gamble on the project. Initially spreading through word of mouth, the book eventually ended up in the hands of Shirley Dobson, who brought it to her husband James, who then invited Dalbey on his Focus on the Family radio show. His 1991 appearance sparked a listener response that ranked in the top 10 percent of the program's history, Dalbey later recalled. By then, evangelical men across the country were awakening to the problem of masculinity.[19]

In *Healing the Masculine Soul*, Dalbey introduced themes that would animate what soon became a cottage industry of books on Christian masculinity. First and foremost, Dalbey looked to the Vietnam War as the source of masculine identity. The son of a naval officer, Dalbey described how the image of the war hero served as his blueprint for manhood. He'd grown up playing "sandlot soldier" in his white suburban neighborhood, and he'd learned to march in military drills and fire a rifle in his Boy Scout "patrol." Fascinated with John Wayne's WWII movies, he imagined war "only as a glorious adventure in manhood." As he got older, he "passed beyond simply admiring the war hero to desiring a war" in which to demonstrate his manhood.[20]

By the time he came of age, however, he'd become sidetracked. Instead of demonstrating his manhood on the battlefields of Vietnam, he became "part of a generation of men who actively rejected our childhood macho image of manhood—which seemed to us the cornerstone of racism, sexism, and militarism." Exhorted to make love, not war, he became "an enthusiastic supporter of civil rights, women's liberation, and the antiwar movement," and he joined the Peace Corps in Africa. But in opting out of the military he would discover that "something required of manhood seemed to have been bypassed, overlooked, even dodged." Left "confused and frustrated," Dalbey eventually conceded that "manhood requires the warrior."[21]

Dalbey agreed with Bly that an unbalanced masculinity had led to the nation's "unbalanced pursuit" of the Vietnam War, but an over-correction had resulted in a different problem: Having rejected war making as a model of masculine strength, men had essentially abdicated that strength to women. As far as Dalbey was concerned, the 1970s offered no viable model of manhood to supplant "the boyhood image in our hearts," and his generation had ended up rejecting manhood itself. If the warrior spirit was indeed intrinsic to males, then attempts to eliminate the warrior image were "intrinsically emasculating." Women were "crying out" for men to recover their manly strength, Dalbey insisted. They were begging men to toughen up and take charge, longing for a prince who was strong and bold enough to restore their "authentic femininity."[22]

Unfortunately, the church was part of the problem. Failing to present the true Jesus, it instead depicted him "as a meek and gentle milk-toast character"—a man who never could have inspired "brawny fishermen like Peter to follow him." It was time to replace this "Sunday school Jesus" with a warrior Jesus. Citing "significant parallels" between serving Christ and serving in the military, Dalbey suggested that a "redeemed image of the warrior" could reinvigorate the church's ministry to men: "What if we told men up front that to join the church of Jesus Christ is ... to enlist in God's army and to place their lives on the line? This approach would be based on the warrior spirit in every man, and so would offer the greatest hope for restoring authentic Christian manhood to the Body of Christ." Writing before the Gulf War had restored faith in American power and the strength of the military, Dalbey's preoccupation with Vietnam is understandable, yet the pattern he established would endure long after an easy victory in the latter conflict supposedly brought an end to "Vietnam syndrome." American evangelicals would continue to be haunted by Vietnam.[23]

There was one point on which Dalbey was more perceptive than many of his later imitators, and that was social class. The occasion that prompted this reflection was a midlife crisis of sorts that manifested in a failed attempt to buy a pair of cowboy boots. Finding himself too ashamed to admit to the salesman that he didn't drive a truck or work in construction (he was a minister, a writer!), Dalbey left the store empty-handed. But he recognized that he wasn't alone in his feeling of inadequacy. Only a generation or two removed from "the so-called 'working class,'" professional men of his generation found themselves "caught between an image of our physically hardworking grandfathers in farms and factories, and the white-collar professionals in antiseptic office buildings." Despite pressure for men to achieve higher socioeconomic status, and despite the nascent popularity of "servant leadership," American culture still associated masculinity with working-class jobs. Times were confusing, indeed.[24]

Reaching more than 250,000 copies in print, Dalbey's book clearly struck a chord. It was soon joined by two other best-selling books that would refine and further popularize Christian warrior masculinity: Steve Farrar's *Point Man: How a Man Can Lead His Family* (1990) and Stu Weber's *Tender Warrior: God's Intention for a Man* (1993). Farrar and Weber both addressed the "confusion" Christian men experienced in discerning God's will for men, and both sought to navigate a course between an overly "macho" masculinity on the one hand and a disturbingly "effeminate" one on the other. Significantly, both also opened with Vietnam combat stories.

Farrar never fought in Vietnam, but he talked to men who had. He asked readers to imagine being elected "point man"—the leader of a combat patrol. He then described a bloody ambush in vivid detail. It was up to the point man to lead his men out of the jungle and back to safety: "If your plan works, you may get out alive with half your men. If it doesn't, they'll be lucky to find your dogtags...." Farrar then abruptly transitioned to a different scenario. The reader was still a point man, but now he was leading his family: a tearful little girl, brave little boy, and a wife, who was caring for a baby. There was nothing imaginary about this scenario: "If you are a husband/father, then you are in a war. War has been declared upon the family, on your family and mine. *Leading a family through the chaos of American culture is like leading a small patrol through enemy-occupied territory.* And the casualties in this war are as real as the names etched on the Vietnam Memorial." Farrar provided a litany of evidence: divorce, single mothers, prostitution, drug addiction, out-of-wedlock pregnancies, abortion, suicide, homosexuality, sexual abuse, and "social awkwardness." If a man was going to keep his children off the casualty list, he would need to prepare them "to defend themselves against the snipers, ambushes, and booby traps of this silent war."[25]

For Farrar, gender confusion was at the root of the war on families. In stressing equality, people had minimized the differences between women and men, and this was taking a tremendous toll on the younger generation. It was up to fathers to help boys "find the correct path to masculinity," and for this reason the father's role was "more critical now than at any time in history." In this respect, Farrar agreed with Dobson that "our very survival as a people will depend upon the presence or absence of masculine leadership in millions of homes," but in the decade since Dobson had characterized the Western world as standing at a "great crossroads in its history," things hadn't improved. If anything, they'd gotten worse. As "point man," the father needed to protect sons from feminization. Boys, he explained, were naturally aggressive due to their higher levels of testosterone; aggression was "part of being male." Little boys were prone to doing reckless things like jumping off slides and swinging like Tarzan, splitting their heads open on occasion. But this was just part of being a boy. "They will survive the scars and broken bones of boyhood," Farrar wrote, "but they cannot survive being feminized." Boys who were overprotected, particularly by mothers, were in danger of having their masculinity "warped." Homosexuals, Farrar believed, were made, not born. Satan's strategy in the war against the family was to "neutralize the man," but the solution was clear: "God made boys to be aggressive. We are to accept it and channel it." Farrar's *Point Man* was a training manual for culture warriors.[26]

Stu Weber, too, opened his *Tender Warrior* in the "heat and terror" of Vietnam, but he wrote from personal experience. A 1967 graduate of Wheaton College, Weber had strayed from his spiritual roots during "the social and intellectual turmoil of the sixties," but as a Green Beret in Vietnam he had come face to face with death, drawing him back to his faith. His was a book about manliness, "real, God-made, down-in-the-bedrock masculinity," something that men were "scrambling to understand." The confusion was everywhere evident. Were men tender or tough? Strong or sensitive? All this confusion left men frustrated, but also determined: "Determined to discover our manhood and live it to the hilt."[27]

Weber, too, believed that "a gender war" was being waged, and it was necessary to look culture's confusion "straight in the eye." Channeling Dobson and Elisabeth Elliot, Weber insisted that men and women were profoundly different. Here Weber turned to the ancient Hebrew word for man, *Ish*, which means "piercer," and the Hebrew word for woman, *Isha*, or "pierced one," insisting that the distinction went beyond the obvious "anatomical or sexual elements." In this case, the physical was "a parable of the spiritual." Man, at his core, was tough and strong, a risk taker, "an initiator—a piercer, one who penetrates, moves forward, advances toward the horizon, leads." Women, on the other hand, preferred security and order; they were gentle responders, tender companions, "aloneness fighters." These differences were woven through all of Scripture, and nothing was more pitiful "than a man forfeiting his masculinity or a woman her femininity by transgressing the created order."[28]

For models of masculinity Weber looked to the Western, and, like Dalbey, to the mythopoetic men's movement pioneered by men like Robert Bly, author of the popular *Iron John* (1990). Weber thought Bly had journeyed far in his search for manhood, but not far enough. Instead, Weber directed men to the "Genesis spring," to the biblical source of masculinity. In Scripture, one learned that man was given dominion to rule "with all power and authority," to defend, guard, and protect. A man's most critical function was that of warrior. According to Weber, "warrior tendencies" were evident even in little boys: "It doesn't matter if you never give your little guy a gun; he'll use his finger." As for its "unmistakable" presence in Scripture, no one could debate the warrior imagery of the Old Testament, but Weber insisted that God was the warrior of both testaments. The apostle Paul, after all, was an "ancient warrior," a "never-say-die kind of guy" who withstood "imprisonment, torture, betrayal, and beatings that left him an inch from death." Rambo had nothing on him, and he "would have done Louis L'Amour proud." And then there was Jesus, the "ultimate man," the "complete Hero." Tragically, images of Jesus had been grossly disfigured by "a media that either hates and distorts Him or vastly misunderstands Him." Too many men had become victims of a "demasculinized" portrait of Christ, making it difficult for them to follow Jesus and leaving them looking elsewhere for models of manhood. In the final chapter of the Bible, Weber reminded readers, Jesus "closes the Book on a white war horse, in a blood-spattered robe, with a sword in His mouth and a rod of iron in His hand." The Bible ended in a roar, not a whimper.[29]

At the same time, a true warrior had a tender heart. For Weber, the "tender warrior" was the perfect solution for navigating a path between an outmoded "macho" masculinity and an unacceptable, effeminate one. Here, even John Wayne as masculine icon came up short. It was hard to imagine John Wayne diapering a baby, and that's because Hollywood didn't understand the tender warrior. Better to look to a real-life hero like General Norman Schwarzkopf, the "conquering commander of Desert Storm," who wasn't afraid to get a little misty-eyed on occasion. "Now don't get me wrong," Weber quickly clarified. "There is a difference between 'tender' and *soft*." Weber wanted *tender warriors*, not *soft males*. Weber's tender warrior motif was perfectly suited to the soft patriarchy of the evangelical men's movement, and Weber was a popular speaker at Promise Keepers events and a regular contributor to PK publications.[30] Like the larger Promise Keepers movement, Weber emphasized male companionship: "every fighter pilot needs a wing man." Here, again, John Wayne's model of masculinity needed tweaking. "As much as we love John Wayne," Weber acknowledged, "all you ever saw was the steel." John Wayne left the impression that real men stand alone, and they do, when necessary. But it was important to realize that real men also stand together.[31]

Within the evangelical men's movement, men did stand together, citing each other—sometimes even bordering on plagiarism—sharing platforms, and promoting each other's work. The pursuit of warrior masculinity helped forge a larger community across the evangelical subculture. Books on evangelical masculinity were marketed to suburban megachurch men's groups, denominational and nondenominational men's ministries, and homeschool networks, binding disparate strands of American evangelicalism together in a shared cultural identity. At first glance, these books didn't appear to be about politics; they were merely helpful handbooks on family and child-rearing. Yet they were both subtly and profoundly political. Farrar liked to cite the bogus Tocqueville line that had appealed to Reagan, too: "America is great because she is good, and if America ceases to be good, America will cease to be great." They were, after all, in the midst of a war for the soul of America. For America to be good—and great—the warrior must be awakened.[32]

WITH ITS MASSIVE PUBLIC RALLIES and the enthusiastic participation of men across the nation, Promise Keepers captured the attention of the larger public. Yet, within evangelicalism two parallel movements would also play key roles in shaping understandings of Christian masculinity. One was the "complementarian" theology espoused by the Council on Biblical Manhood and Womanhood (CBMW). The other was the sexual purity movement.

Whereas the popular arm of the evangelical men's movement often rested on somewhat shaky theological footing, CBMW marshaled the power of conservative theologians to fashion a scriptural defense of patriarchy. With close ties to the Southern Baptist Convention,

CBMW helped ensure that gender would remain firmly embedded at the center of evangelical identity.

In 1986, in an address before the Evangelical Theological Society, theologian Wayne Grudem had called for a new organization to uphold biblical manhood and womanhood. The next year an informal group gathered to discuss the rise of "unbiblical teaching" about women and men, and in December of that year they convened more formally, this time in Danvers, Massachusetts. There, under the leadership of Grudem and fellow Reformed evangelical John Piper, they crafted a statement affirming what would come to be known as "complementarianism": God created men and women "equal before God" yet "distinct in their manhood and womanhood." The statement attested that God had established male headship as part of the order of creation and closed the door to women in church leadership. In 1989, CBMW published this "Danvers Statement" in a full-page advertisement in *Christianity Today*, drawing "a huge response."[33]

The Danvers Statement was a response both to an alleged "gender confusion" ushered in by the 1960s and to the "evangelical feminism" that had emerged in the 1970s. It was not, however, a call to an aggressive, militant masculinity. It dictated that a husband's headship be humble and loving rather than domineering, and it stipulated that "husbands should forsake harsh or selfish leadership and grow in love and care for their wives." Yet in asserting female submission as the will of God, it foregrounded a biblical defense of patriarchy and gender difference that would come to serve as the bedrock of a militaristic Christian masculinity.[34]

In 1991, Piper and Grudem published the 500-page *Recovering Biblical Manhood and Womanhood*, a manifesto in defense of God-given gender difference. "Mature masculinity" convicted a man of his responsibility "to accept danger to protect women," and a mature woman accepted this protection: "She is glad when he is not passive. She feels herself enhanced and honored and freed by his caring strength and servant-leadership." Unfortunately, the "devastating sin" of men's failure to lead at home and in the church had destabilized this God-given order. By spreading the idea that male leadership was "born of pride and fallenness," Satan had achieved a major tactical victory. In fact, pride was precisely what prevented spiritual leadership. *Recovering Biblical Manhood and Womanhood* was *Christianity Today*'s "Book of the Year" in 1992.[35]

CBMW was concerned with church and home but also with the fate of the nation. In 1996, in response to what it saw as President Clinton's meddling with the military, CBMW promoted a "Resolution on women in combat," which they recommended "to all interested denominations." Alarmed that "Biblical norms for the exclusively male vocation of warfare" were being ignored, CBMW noted that the whole purpose of combat was "to kill, slay and destroy," a purpose and essence that aligned with masculinity, not femininity. Moreover, the moral justification for war involved the protection of vital national interests, most essentially the security and welfare of families. In other words, moral justification for combat was derived from and thus linked to self-sacrificial male headship. On a practical level, integrating women into combat weakened unit cohesion and threatened military order by "escalating sexual tensions," straining the marital fidelity of "male warriors," and subjecting "female warriors" to rape and abuse when taken as POWs. In short, it threatened national security and fundamentally controverted the will of God.[36]

Together with conservatives in the SBC, CBMW worked to promote patriarchal authority as a nonnegotiable requirement of the orthodox Christian faith. Functioning as theological think tanks, CBMW and SBC seminaries provided resources for denominations, organizations, and local churches, helping to build a network of evangelicals committed to advancing a patriarchal version of Christianity. They worked in close cooperation; in the mid-1990s CBMW took up residence at the SBC's Southern Seminary, and the council endorsed the seminary's resolution to hire only faculty members who were opposed to the ordination of women—over the opposition of students and faculty. Meanwhile, the conservative takeover of the SBC continued apace. The fact that Bill Clinton was a moderate Southern Baptist only furthered the aims of conservatives. The SBC became increasingly political during his administration, endorsing capital punishment and affirming Americans' right to bear arms.[37]

In 1998, conservative Southern Baptists revised their Baptist Faith and Message, for the first time since 1963, to add a section calling men "to provide for, to protect, and to lead" their families, and wives to submit themselves "graciously to the servant leadership of her husband." Paige Patterson's wife Dorothy helped author the amendment, which was closely based, in many cases word for word, on the Danvers Statement. Like the Danvers Statement, this new position rooted the submission of women in the pre-Fall creation, not as a result of the Fall—overturning previous characterizations of submission issued in 1984. When moderates proposed a motion to replace "women's submission" with "mutual submission," it quickly went down in defeat, and the original proposal passed to a chorus of "amens" and thunderous applause.[38]

A CBMW conference in Dallas in the spring of 2000 illustrated the expanding complementarian network. Participants included Grudem, Piper, and SBC president Paige Patterson; Richard Land, president of the SBC Ethics & Religious Liberty Commission; Randy Stinson, newly appointed executive director of CBMW; and Al Mohler, president of the Southern Seminary and member of the council. Among complementarians, other doctrinal commitments seemed to pale in comparison to beliefs about gender, and ideas about male authority and the subordination of women increasingly came to distinguish "true evangelicals from pseudo evangelicals." The already mature market for resources on Christian masculinity meant that distribution channels were in place to disseminate conservative teachings on "biblical manhood" far and wide, works that would further orient American evangelicalism around the gender divide.[39]

IN TANDEM WITH EFFORTS to promote "biblical manhood and womanhood," an elaborate "purity culture" was taking hold across

American evangelicalism. Purity culture emerged as a cohesive movement in the 1990s, but it drew on teachings long championed by conservative evangelicals accustomed to upholding stringent standards of
female sexual "purity" while assigning men the responsibility of "protecting" women and their chastity. Female modesty was a key component of purity culture. If men were created with nearly irrepressible,
God-given sex drives, it was up to women to rein in men's libidos.
Wives were tasked with meeting husbands' every sexual need, but it
was the responsibility of women and girls to avoid leading men who
were not their husbands into temptation.

What counted as appropriate modesty depended on one's location
in the evangelical subculture. In certain homeschool circles, women
wore dresses that fell below the knee and fashioned their hair in long,
unadorned styles. Other evangelicals defined modesty more liberally.
But wherever evangelicals drew the line, women were judged for their
failure to uphold the ideal. Evangelicals had far less to say about male
modesty. Instead, they emphasized the rewards that awaited boys who
waited. A message of delayed gratification was at the heart of purity
teachings for adolescent boys. Since wives served to gratify male desire,
men only needed to wait until marriage to be rewarded with "mind-
blowing" sex. Such promises were the stock-in-trade of evangelical
youth pastors in the 1990s. In the words of purity evangelist Josh
McDowell, God was not a "cosmic killjoy." After all, God created sex.[40]

McDowell, an evangelical pseudo-intellectual who first made a
name for himself writing popular books on Christian apologetics,
helped launch the purity movement. In 1987 he published *Why Wait?
What You Need to Know about the Teen Sexuality Crisis*, and he followed this purity primer with a VHS video series. In the early 1990s he
joined with Christian rock band Petra to promote his purity message.
It was an odd pairing, the middle-aged father figure who appeared
onstage at rock concerts mixing in dad jokes with frank talk of sex
and venereal disease. But it all made sense within the larger evangelical
culture.[41]

A decade after McDowell's book appeared, Josh Harris helped

transform the purity message into something cool for the younger set. Harris was the son of pioneering Christian homeschoolers—his parents helped establish the Christian homeschooling movement, and his father's 1988 book, *The Christian Home School*, was a Christian Booksellers Association bestseller. Harris got his start as a teenager publishing a magazine for fellow homeschoolers, and in 1997, at age twenty-one, he published his magnum opus, *I Kissed Dating Goodbye*. Influenced by the writings of Elisabeth Elliot, Harris introduced a generation of young Christians to "biblical courtship," the idea that fathers were charged with ensuring their daughters' purity until their wedding day, at which point they handed unsullied daughters over to husbands who assumed the burden of protection, provision, and supervision. The book became the bible of the purity movement, selling more than one million copies.

The purity movement received strong support from evangelical institutions and organizations. The Christian homeschool community helped fuel its popularity, and the Southern Baptist Convention was home to True Love Waits, one of the most influential purity organizations. (Three years before Promise Keepers rallied at the National Mall, 20,000 evangelical teenagers showed up to pledge their sexual purity as part of the True Love Waits campaign.) Countless local churches promoted purity teachings, and purity culture found expression in an array of consumer products. Families purchased silver "purity rings" to provide girls with a constant reminder of the value of their virginity, and of their obligation to guard it vigilantly. "Purity balls" started popping up across the country, offering families opportunities to enact their commitment to sexual purity through public ceremony. At these events, fathers provided a model of masculine headship by "dating" their daughters, and girls pledged their sexual purity before their families and communities. Like "servant leadership" and complementarian theology, the purity movement enabled evangelicals to reassert patriarchal authority in the face of economic, political, and social change. The widespread popularity of the purity movement was fueled in part by an injection of federal funds. As early as 1981, President Reagan began directing government funding to abstinence-only sex education, and this funding continued through the 1990s, reaching its peak under the George W. Bush administration; by 2005, more than 100 abstinence-based groups would receive more than $104 million in federal funding. Here was a case of government intrusion into the most intimate of matters, yet evangelicals didn't seem to mind.[42]

THE EVANGELICAL MEN'S MOVEMENT of the 1990s was marked by experimentation and laden with contradictions. "Soft patriarchy" papered over tensions between a harsher, authoritarian masculinity and a more egalitarian posture; the motif of the tender warrior reconciled militancy with a kinder, gentler, more emotive bearing. Inconsistencies within the evangelical men's movement reflected those within evangelicalism as a whole in the post–Cold War years. Earlier in the decade, it might have appeared that the more egalitarian and emotive impulses had the upper hand. It was a new era for America, and for American evangelicals. Rhetoric of culture wars persisted, but evangelicals' interests had expanded to include a broader array of issues, including racial reconciliation, antitrafficking activism, and addressing the persecution of the global church. At the end of the decade, however, the more militant movement would begin to reassert itself. When it did, this resurgent militancy would become intertwined both with the sexual purity movement and with the assertion of complementarianism within evangelical circles. In time it would become clear that the combination of all three could produce toxic outcomes.

Chapter 10

NO MORE
CHRISTIAN
NICE GUY

JOHN ELDREDGE DIDN'T LIKE OFFICE WORK. IT wasn't good for his masculinity or his spirituality. Spiritual life was meant to be "frontier," untamed. If evangelical men wanted to experience true Christianity, they'd need to get out of "their La-Z-Boys and climate-controlled shopping malls and into God's wild creation." Eldredge's 2001 book, *Wild at Heart: Discovering the Secret of a Man's Soul*, set the tone for a new evangelical militancy in the new millennium. Eldredge's God was a warrior God, and men were made in his image. Aggression, not tenderness, was part of the masculine design. *Wild at Heart* would sell more than four million copies in the United States alone, becoming a ubiquitous presence in megachurch men's groups, college dorm rooms, Christian bookstores, and church libraries. Spawning dozens of copycat books that borrowed copiously from Eldredge's formula, it would frame evangelical explorations of masculinity for years to come.[1]

For Eldredge, masculinity was thoroughly militaristic. Little boys loved to play with capes and swords, bandannas and six-shooters. Yearning to know they were powerful and dangerous, someone to be reckoned with, they specialized in inventing games "where bloodshed is a prerequisite for having fun." God made men to be dangerous, Eldredge explained. Women didn't start wars or commit many violent crimes. But the very strength that made men dangerous also made them heroes. If a neighborhood was safe, it was because of the strength of its men. Men, not women, brought an end to slavery, apartheid, and the Nazis. Men gave up their seats on the *Titanic*'s lifeboats. And, crucially, "it was a Man who let himself be nailed to Calvary's cross."[2]

According to Eldredge, God created all men to long for "a battle to fight, an adventure to live, and a beauty to rescue." But society offered confusing messages. For thirty years people had been redefining masculinity into something "sensitive, safe, manageable and, well, feminine," yet now they berated men for not being men. The church bore a large share of the blame. A "crisis in masculinity" pervaded both church and society because a warrior culture no longer existed, but men needed a place where they could learn "to fight like men." Eldredge dismissed the charge that Jesus instructed his followers to turn the other cheek: "You cannot teach a boy to use his strength *by stripping him of it*." Eldredge's Jesus more closely resembled William Wallace than either Mother Teresa or Mister Rogers. Attempts to pacify men only emasculated them. "If you want a safer, quieter animal, there's an easy solution: castrate him." Sadly, "clingy mothers"—and the public-school system—effectively did just that.[3]

Eldredge opened his book with a portion of Matthew 11:12: "The kingdom of heaven suffers violence, and violent men take it by force." Much of his inspiration, however, came from popular culture. It wasn't women, after all, who made *Braveheart* one of the best-selling movies that decade. Mel Gibson's William Wallace was one of Eldredge's favorite heroes, but the American cowboy also occupied a special place in Eldredge's vision of masculinity. The cowboy embodied a yearning every man felt, the desire "to 'go West,'" to be "wild, dangerous, unfettered and free." Eldredge also showcased the heroic masculinity of Teddy Roosevelt, tenacious American soldiers, Indiana Jones, James Bond, and Bruce Willis in *Die Hard*.[4]

It was from popular culture that Eldredge discovered the underlying truth that it was not enough for a man to be a hero; he must be the hero to the woman he loves. James Bond, Indiana Jones, young soldiers going off to war—every man required his own beauty to rescue. Women, too, possessed something "wild at heart," but it was "feminine to the core, more *seductive* than fierce." They yearned to be *fought for*, to be wanted, to share a man's adventure. According to Eldredge, a woman sinned when she tried to control her world, when she was grasping rather than vulnerable, when she sought to control her own adventure rather than share in the adventure of a man. Echoing Tim and Beverly LaHaye, Eldredge believed that God had written on little girls' hearts a fairy-tale dream of Prince Charming coming to their rescue. (This theme was then picked up by Christian singer Rebecca St. James, whose 2002 *Wait for Me*, a book promoting purity culture, sold over 100,000 copies.) Women wanted to be pursued, delighted in, fought for; the "deep cry of a little girl's heart is *am I lovely*?" Rather than "brutalizing" femininity, Eldredge warned, we should take these princess dreams seriously. For Eldredge, gender difference resided at the level of the soul.[5]

Eldredge's fans were legion, but he was not without critics within evangelicalism. Randy Stinson, executive director of CBMW, took issue with Eldredge's theology. Stinson alleged that Eldredge neglected the reality of sin, and he accused Eldredge of promulgating "an unbiblical view of God" by depicting God as a "risk-taker," thereby implying that God did not have full knowledge of the future. Theological quibbles aside, Stinson praised Eldredge for rightly identifying several key problems: the feminization of men by our culture and churches, the emasculation of our boys, and the truth that "every man needs a battle for which he can live and die." In other words, Eldredge based his conclusions on a faulty theological foundation, but those conclusions were nevertheless largely sound. A decade later, Stinson would follow in Eldredge's footsteps, coauthoring his own book on "biblical manhood."[6]

Calvin College professors Mark Mulder and James K. A. Smith also called out Eldredge's failure to reckon with the reality of sin, but they considered it a more fundamental flaw. While Eldredge claimed to root his notion of masculinity in a theology of creation, in the God-given "essence" of men and women, Smith and Mulder insisted that "what Eldredge attributes to creation, biblical Christianity ascribes to the Fall!" War, conflict, and enmity resulted from humanity's sinfulness, not from God's good creation; thus "it cannot be the case that being a warrior is essential to being a man." The Bible promised a coming kingdom of peace; endorsing this "warrior-ideal" would foster "sinfulness, not redemption," they warned. Mulder and Smith, however, were in the minority, certainly if book sales were any measure.[7]

ELDREDGE'S BOOK was the most popular book on evangelical masculinity published in 2001, but it wasn't the only one. Other writers, too, had tired of tenderness. The time had come to toughen up American manhood, starting with boys. In January of that year, James Dobson published *Bringing Up Boys*. The key to understanding boys, according to Dobson, was testosterone. The hormone made boys "competitive, aggressive, assertive, and lovers of cars, trucks, guns, and balls." A "masculine will to power" was evident in little boys who dressed up as superheroes, cowboys, and Tarzan. It was why boys fought, climbed, wrestled, and strutted around. Feminists and liberals seemed to think that testosterone was "one of God's great mistakes." They preferred to make boys more like girls, and men more like women—"feminized, emasculated, and wimpified." But "reprogramming" men and boys interfered with God's careful design.[8]

Men's competitive nature was evidenced in their proclivity for risk and adventure, as well as in their greater political and economic achievements—these despite feminist affirmative action campaigns—and the wars they had prosecuted throughout history. From his office at Focus on the Family, Dobson could peer across the valley at the United States Air Force Academy. Watching cadets train to be pilots and officers, he pondered how men's competitive nature explained "the bloody military campaigns that have raged through the ages," yet how "this masculine thirst for conquest" had also produced "daring and adventuresome feats that benefited humanity." General MacArthur, "one of the greatest military leaders of all time," was one of Dobson's heroes.[9]

In his book about boys, Dobson found occasion to denounce Hillary Clinton, "bra burners," political correctness, and the "small but noisy band of feminists" who attacked "the very essence of masculinity." He praised Phyllis Schlafly and recommended homeschooling as "a means of coping with a hostile culture." He advised girls not to call boys on the telephone (to do so would usurp the role of initiator) and encouraged fathers to engage in rough-and-tumble games with their sons. He lamented that films presenting moral strength and heroism had given way to "man-hating diatribes" like *Thelma & Louise* and *9 to 5*, and that "lovely, feminine ladies" on the small screen had been replaced by "aggressive and masculine women" like those in *Charlie's Angels*. Mel Gibson's *The Patriot*, a tale in which Gibson starred as a Revolutionary militia leader who ruthlessly avenged his son's death, proved the exception to the rule.[10]

Dobson's *Bringing Up Boys* found a receptive audience. Its sales would eventually top two million copies. By that time Dobson had amassed a considerable following; his radio program was reportedly carried on over 4200 stations around the world and heard daily by over 200 million people. Charles Colson boasted that "All people, Christian and non-Christian alike" should read the book: "It just could save America."[11]

Less than five months after Dobson's book appeared, Douglas Wilson published *Future Men: Raising Boys to Fight Giants*. The son of an evangelist who settled in Moscow, Idaho, Wilson had helped found "a Baptist-leaning, 'hippie, Jesus People church.'" He had little formal theological training, and his church was, in his words, a "Baptist-Presbyterian 'mutt.'" After encountering the teachings of Rushdoony, he inculcated Reconstructionist-inspired values within his faith community. Due to his hybrid theology, and no doubt also to his cantankerous personality, no established Reformed denomination would claim him. Undaunted, Wilson started his own denomination. In 1981, he founded the Logos School, a classical Christian academy,

and he became a leader in the classical Christian education movement, establishing the Association of Classical and Christian Schools
in 1994, and that same year founding New Saint Andrews College, a
four-year classical Christian college with the motto: "For the faithful,
wars shall never cease."[12]

Wilson's *Future Men* was a perfectly timed primer on militant masculinity that reached far beyond his enclave. Looking to Theodore
Roosevelt as a model of Christian masculinity, Wilson asserted that as
future men, boys were "future warriors." Consistent with Reconstructionist thought, the concept of dominion was central to Wilson's definition of masculinity; like Adam in the Garden of Eden, all men were
made to exercise dominion. Boys had an innate drive to conquer and
subdue, and they should be trained to be adventurous and visionary,
to become "lords in the earth." For this task, it was essential for young
boys to play with toy swords and guns, and for older boys to be trained
in the use of real firearms. Indeed, Wilson called for a "theology of fist
fighting" to instruct boys when, where, and how to fight. Lest there be
any doubt, Wilson clarified that Christianity was in no way pacifistic.
True, Old Testament prophets foretold a time of peace, or an "escha-
tological pacifism," but the peace Christ brings was purchased with
blood. Until that time men and boys must study war; to do otherwise
would leave men "fighting the dragon with a pruning hook."[13]

Like other writers, Wilson defined masculinity in terms of initiation. As he explained in his earlier writings on marriage, "a man
penetrates, conquers, colonizes, plants. A woman receives, surrenders,
accepts." Although egalitarians might rebel against the concept of
authority, Wilson believed that the submission of wives to husbands,
when occurring "in countless families," would bring about "a larger
patriarchal society" and a greater social good. According to Wilson,
marriage had three purposes: companionship, producing godly children, and the avoidance of sexual immorality. With regard to the latter,
God offered very practical help for Christians struggling with temptation: sexual activity. Like Marabel Morgan and the LaHayes, Wilson believed that sexual relations within marriage should be frequent.

God intended for women to meet their husbands' (considerable) sexual needs; it was woman's duty "to submit to the will of God and gladly bear children for her husband." Moreover, marriage could not be "spiritually consummated" if the husband acted as a "spiritual eunuch," as one "impotent in his masculinity." Women must understand that they were "led by a *lord*." To this end, young suitors should be "disruptively masculine," cheerfully interfering with a future wife's plans. Woman was made for man, not the other way around. Young women should be instructed to be homemakers; women became "increasingly beautiful" when they cultivated "a gentle and quiet spirit." Not surprisingly, Wilson thought women had no place in combat; they were a sexual distraction to male soldiers, they could get pregnant, they distorted "covenantal lines of authority," and they were not as good as men in "the important work of violence."[14]

Wilson understood that some readers might recoil at his use of the word *dominance* to describe the husband's role, but in his view such a response testified to the extent to which the church had been influenced by feminism, "whether the man-hating secular variety or the sanitized, 'evangelical' kind." The real problem was "the wimping out" of Christian men. By wandering from biblical teaching, Christians had replaced "the hardness of masculinity with the tenderness of women," and the results had been disastrous. Wilson was no fan of Promise Keepers. In 1999 he critiqued the movement for promoting "a quiet adoption of feminism" rather than a masculine approach to godliness. As Wilson put it, "Contrary to popular teaching on the Christian home, a man's duty is not to be a real sweet guy." With characteristic bluntness, Wilson denounced much of the Christian men's movement as "nothing more than a discipleship program for weenies."[15]

THE BOOKS BY Wilson, Dobson, and Eldredge appeared in the months before September 11, 2001. When terrorists struck the United States, their call for "manly" heroes acquired a deep and widespread resonance among evangelicals. A very real, not merely rhetorical, "bat-

tle to fight" had suddenly materialized for American men. The success
of these books, and their cultural impact, can be understood in light
of the renewed sense of crisis.

The new millennium had ushered in a new era for American evangelicals. The Clintons were out of the White House and a cowboy president was back in the saddle. Of course, George W. Bush had bought
his Crawford Ranch just before announcing his candidacy; it made for
good photo ops. Still, Bush's evangelical faith was authentic. Reflecting
the less militant strand of 1990s evangelicalism, Bush had campaigned
on a message of "compassionate conservatism." The terror attacks, however, would transform him into a crusader.[16]

The moral certainties of the War on Terror—framed as they were
by an evangelical president—put an end to any post–Cold War uncertainty among evangelicals. Not since the height of the Cold War had
foreign affairs so clearly connected to domestic concerns. In fact, in
the days and weeks following the attacks, many Americans turned to
Cold War rhetoric and thinking as they grappled with how to respond
to this new threat. Once again, America needed strong, heroic men
to defend the country at home and abroad. Evangelicalism had never
completely abandoned its Cold War militarism, and those who had
become unsettled by the "soft patriarchy" of the 1990s men's movement were primed for this moment. The very existence of the nation
again depended on the toughness of American men, and raising young
boys into strong men became elevated to a matter of national security.
Instructional books already lined the shelves of Christian bookstores.

The actual events of September 11 had called for all the manly
strength men could muster. As Phyllis Schlafly put it, one of the unintended consequences of the attack on the World Trade Center was
"the dashing of feminist hopes to make America a gender-neutral or
androgynous society." When the firemen charged up the stairs of the
burning towers, the death tally was: "men 343, women 0." Clearly this
was no place for affirmative-action women. Fighting the Taliban, too,
was a job for "real men." Fortunately, a "warrior culture" had survived
thirty years of feminist assaults, so there were still some men "macho

enough to relish the opportunity to engage and kill the bad guys of the world." Watching the war unfold on television, Schlafly almost expected to see "John Wayne riding across the plains." America needed manly heroes.[17]

In 2005, Steve Farrar echoed this renewed urgency in his first book published after 9/11, *King Me*: "When those two planes hit the Twin Towers on September 11, what we suddenly needed were masculine men. Feminized men don't walk into burning buildings. But masculine men do. That's why God created men to be masculine." Like his *Point Man*, Farrar's *King Me* illustrated the versatility of evangelical notions of militant masculinity; masculine men were needed to save the nation from terrorists *and* defend against cultural forces that threatened America from within. But such men were hard to come by because the media, the public-school system, and the academic elite colluded in the emasculation of boys. The church wasn't helping matters; by emphasizing "feminine traits" like tenderness, compassion, and gentleness, churches had neglected the equally spiritual but masculine traits of aggressiveness, courage, and standing on the truth. Again Farrar castigated the church for feminizing Jesus. Songs about Christ's "beauty" were especially galling. As he wrote, "If you went up to John Wayne and said he was beautiful, he would separate several of your molars and bicuspids into a new world order." Mel Gibson's film *The Passion* offered a good antidote to the image of a wimpy Christ, but more needed to be done. Farrar didn't shy away from the fact that he was advocating a more militant turn. The trend had been to "major on the 'tender' and minor on the 'warrior,' " but "in the trenches you don't want tenderness."[18]

Gordon Dalbey, too, reflected the revitalized militarism among evangelicals in a revised edition of his *Healing the Masculine Soul*. In 1988, he had criticized the "foolish extremes" men's ministries went to, such as hosting fellowship evenings showing films about "the latest jet fighter planes." Sure, this met men where they were, but so would X-rated movies; a Jesus who "healed bodies and blessed 'the peacemakers' " and urged his followers to "turn the other cheek" surely wouldn't be comfortable with fighter-plane movies any more than with X-rated ones. In his 2003 edition, Dalbey blunted his former critique, removing any mention of Jesus as healer and peacemaker. Instead, he added thoughts on how boys must be ushered into a vision "of conflict and warfare."[19]

Other works reveal the extent to which new writers came to rely on common tropes. In 2005, Paul Coughlin published *No More Christian Nice Guy*, a manifesto against alleged distortions of Christian masculinity. Citing Dobson, Weber, Generals MacArthur and Patton, George Gilder, Robert Bly, Teddy Roosevelt, and Mel Gibson's *The Passion*, Coughlin offered a familiar critique of emasculated Christian manhood. He acknowledged that his book testified to men's anger: "They're angry with their culture, their church, and their God, and sometimes their anger is directed at women." But he wanted to transform that anger into a redemptive force. Coughlin took care to distance himself from more extreme views. He affirmed his full support for women's suffrage, countering the apparently popular notion "within the realm of Christian publishing" that a man ought to cast the vote for his entire household. He recognized, too, that prior to 1965 "it was not uncommon for an attractive young woman in the work force to be treated like a piece of flesh, a toy to be used by men." And he acknowledged that men had previously showed troublingly little interest in their families, a problem that organizations like Focus on the Family and Promise Keepers had addressed. He also parted ways with those who advocated a hierarchical authority structure that placed men under the authority of their employers. He couldn't stomach the idea that a boss "holds God's proxy as our employer," although he expressed no such discomfort with a hierarchy of authority based on gender.[20]

Also in 2005, David Murrow's *Why Men Hate Going to Church* urged the church to embrace danger and shed its reputation "as a place for little old ladies of both sexes." Murrow admitted he didn't have the usual qualifications to write books about men and church. He wasn't a pastor, professor, or theologian, he was just "a guy in the pews" who noticed a disturbing trend. (A television producer, Murrow had written and produced Sarah Palin's first television commercial in 2002.) But Murrow had done his reading. He cited Eldredge, Dobson, Dalbey, Lewis, Cole, and Wilson. He, too, celebrated the "wildness of Jesus," praised Mel Gibson's *Braveheart*, and thought the church needed "a few more Teddy Roosevelts." Murrow agreed that aggression was "key to the masculine soul" and that "without men and their warrior spirit in church, *all is lost.*" Murrow didn't have much new to say, but the timing was right; boasting more than 100,000 copies of his book in print, Murrow emerged as a leading voice in the Christian men's movement.[21]

Books on evangelical masculinity were not meant for mere armchair reading. Christian fathers designed initiation rites for sons modeled on medieval knighthood involving expensive steak dinners and commemorated with symbols of great value, such as "a Bible, a shotgun or a plaque." Knights, after all, were "the Promise Keepers of the Middle Ages." Christian men retreated to the "wilderness" to participate in Wild at Heart Boot Camps or engage in "weekend paintball wars," or they fashioned their own events featuring homegrown *"Braveheart* Games," with activities ranging from changing tires on a car to throwing axes and chasing greased pigs. Larger organizations followed suit. At frenzied BattleCry youth rallies, evangelist Ron Luce warned students that communists, feminists, gays, and Muslims threatened to destroy the nation's morality as surely as Osama bin Laden had destroyed the Twin Towers. In language rife with militaristic imagery, Luce called for a "wartime mentality," for young people to awaken to the dangers of "culture terrorists." With guest speakers including Jerry Falwell and Charles Colson, Luce's ministry brought in the old guard to recruit a younger generation to militant Christianity.[22]

Recognizing that their version of evangelical masculinity was out of step with contemporary trends, Promise Keepers rebranded accordingly. To appeal to "The Next Warriors for Christ," the organization replaced promotional images of men hugging, crying, and holding hands, with pictures of sword-wielding men charging on horseback, climbing rocks, and covered in mud, accompanied by the reassuring promise that "This Ain't Your Daddy's PK!" Of course, the organization had only been around for a little over a decade at this point. No longer asking men to "Stand in the Gap," more manly conference titles challenged men to rise up and "Storm the Gates." Given the recent military buildup, some Christians thought the hypermasculine language and militant imagery to be in poor taste. Was this the time for Christian men to be "strutting our biceps and pressing spiritual iron"? For many evangelical men, it was the ideal time.[23]

IN THE EARLY 2000s, white evangelicals were enthusiastic supporters of a military response to the September 11 attacks, but they weren't alone. In October 2001, eight in ten Americans supported a ground war in Afghanistan. The war in Iraq, however, was a harder sell. Connections between Saddam Hussein's regime and America's national security remained sketchy, and many religious groups in the country resisted the administration's efforts to drum up support for another war. The National Council of Churches urged the president to refrain from a preemptive strike; the Vatican warned that preemptive war would be "a crime against peace." Conservative evangelicals begged to differ.[24]

In October 2002, five evangelical leaders sent a letter to President Bush to assure him that a preemptive invasion of Iraq did indeed meet the criteria for just war. Written by Richard Land, president of the SBC's Ethics & Religious Liberty Commission, and signed by fellow evangelicals Charles Colson, Bill Bright, D. James Kennedy, and Carl Herbster, the "Land letter" expressed appreciation for Bush's "bold, courageous, and visionary leadership" and reassured him that his plans for military action were "both right and just." Referencing the appeasement of Hitler, they urged Bush to disarm "the murderous Iraqi dictator" and reminded him that "the legitimate authority to authorize the use of U.S. military force" belonged to the United States government, not the UN. Elsewhere, Land cited Romans 13 to argue that "God ordained the civil magistrate" to punish evildoers.[25]

It wasn't just the evangelical elite who supported a preemptive strike. In 2002, ordinary evangelical Christians were "the biggest backers of Israel and Washington's planned war against Iraq": 69 percent of conservative Christians favored military action, a full 10 percentage points higher than the general population. In 2003, once the war commenced, 87 percent of white evangelical Christians supported Bush's decision to go to war, compared to 70 percent of Protestant mainliners and 59 percent of secular Americans. As one evangelical parishioner explained, Jesus might have preached a gospel of peace, but the Book of Revelation showed that the suffering Messiah turned into the conquering Messiah; in the Bible, God didn't just sanction "war and invasion," God encouraged it. The evangelical parishioner's pastor concurred, adding that President Bush "would fit right into this church . . . being on the same spiritual wavelength counts for a lot."[26]

Steeped in a literature claiming that men were created in the image of a warrior God, it's no wonder evangelicals were receptive to sentiments like those expressed by Jerry Falwell in his 2004 sermon, "God is Pro-War." Having long idealized cowboys and soldiers as models of exemplary Christian manhood, evangelicals were primed to embrace Bush's " 'cowboy' approach" and his "Lone Ranger mentality." God created men to be aggressive—violent when necessary—so that they might fulfill their sacred role of protector.[27]

At the 2004 Republican National Convention, Christian recording artist Michael W. Smith stood on the stage of New York's Madison Square Garden, declaring his love for his president and his country. He then recounted how, only six weeks after the September 11 attacks, he had found himself in the Oval Office with his good friend, President Bush. They spoke of the firefighters and other first responders who had given their lives trying to save others. "Hey W," said the presidential "W" to the singer. "I think you need to write a song about this." Smith did as he was asked. And there, standing before the convention audience as patriotic images flashed on the screen behind him, he performed "There She Stands," a song about the symbol of the nation, the American flag, standing proudly amid the rubble. It was a small rhetorical step to change the feminine "beauty" all men were created to fight for into the nation herself.[28]

Chapter 11

HOLY
BALLS

IN THE YEARS AFTER 9/11, MORE EXTREME expressions of militant masculinity gained traction across American evangelicalism. At GodMen revivals, evangelist Brad Stine challenged men to "kick ass," to "grab your sword and say, 'OK family, I'm going to lead you.'" Profanity was encouraged, "liberals, atheists, and the politically correct" were denigrated, and men were called upon to combat "the wuss-ification of America." Speakers like Paul Coughlin urged Christian men and pastors to be "good," not "nice," and warned that in doing so they would surely make enemies. Forget the Jesus who avoids confrontation, who "turns the other cheek"—that "Bearded Lady" Jesus was a bore, just like the men who followed him. Even their wives found them boring. GodMen participants watched video clips of "karate fights, car chases, and 'Jackass'-style stunts," offered prayers of thanks to God for their testosterone, and raised their voices in "manly" anthems like "Grow a Pair," a song lamenting the feminization of men by "the culture crowd," a song in which men pledged to cowboy up, to join the battle, to jump in the saddle, to grab a sword . . . and, yes, to "grow a pair."[1]

Christian mixed martial arts, too, emerged as a new way to minister to men. The goal of groups like Xtreme Ministries, a church that doubled as a Mixed Martial Arts academy "Where Feet, Fist and Faith Collide," was "to inject some machismo into their ministries—and into the image of Jesus." James Dobson's son Ryan was a promoter.

"The man should be the overall leader of the household," the younger Dobson asserted, but we'd "raised a generation of little boys." Toughening men up in the MMA cage could serve a higher purpose. Some churches hosted fight night MMA viewing parties, others hosted or participated in live events. By 2010, an estimated 700 predominantly white evangelical churches had taken up MMA as a means of outreach. Christian MMA clothing brands like "Jesus Didn't Tap" appeared, along with Christian social networking sites like anointedfighter.com.[2]

To be sure, singing about one's testicles and landing blows to the head for Christ represent the more radical expressions of militant Christian masculinity, but GodMen and Xtreme Ministries only amplified trends that were becoming increasingly common in the post-9/11 era. As militant masculinity took hold across evangelicalism, it helped bind together those on the fringes of the movement with those closer to the center, making it increasingly difficult to distinguish the margins from the mainstream.

THE CHRISTIAN HOMESCHOOL movement remained a steady source of teachings on militant patriarchal authority and Christian nationalism, but by the 2000s it was no longer the remote outpost within the broader evangelical movement that it once had been. Since the early 1980s, Christian homeschooling had been gaining in popularity and influence. In 1994, the movement received a boost when James Dobson joined forces with Michael Farris's Home School Legal Defense Association (HSLDA) to defend the rights of homeschool parents. What sparked Dobson's interest was an amendment to an education bill introduced by a Democratic congressman that would have required homeschool teachers to obtain state certification in each subject they taught, a requirement that would make homeschooling prohibitively difficult. Hosting Farris on his show, Dobson prompted one million callers to contact their representatives in Congress; not only was the proposed legislation defeated, but the House of Representatives responded by passing new legislation guaranteeing greater protections to homeschooling families. Dobson's was "the biggest game in town," Farris recalled, and he considered Dobson's intervention a turning point in the homeschool movement. By 1999, 850,000 children were homeschooled in America; by 2016, the number was at 1.7 million, about two-thirds of whom were religious.[3]

Christian homeschooling remained an effective mechanism for instilling and reinforcing "biblical patriarchy." Within Christian homeschool circles, Bill Gothard continued to operate his IBLP and publish his homeschool curriculum infused with his understandings of masculine authority, female submission, and the need to restore America to its mythical Christian past. Gothard's influence was not small; he estimated that more than 2.5 million people had attended his seminars. A number of leaders of the Christian Right had direct connections to Gothard. Mike Huckabee is an IBLP alumnus; Sarah Palin attended an IBLP conference while mayor of Wasilla, Alaska; and as governor of Texas, Rick Perry spoke at one of Gothard's Advanced Training Institute conferences. Gothard remained in the shadows, preferring to teach his precepts in the context of highly controlled seminars. But in the 1990s, Doug Phillips began to introduce a Gothard-inspired "biblical patriarchy" far beyond the cultlike community Gothard had established.[4]

Doug was the son of Howard Phillips, a Gothard supporter and behind-the-scenes architect of the Moral Majority. Having attended the Reconstructionist Fairfax Christian School, the younger Phillips put his learning to use as an attorney for the HSLDA. Given his pedigree, Doug was like royalty in the Christian homeschool community. In 1998 he founded Vision Forum, a Texas-based organization devoted to promoting biblical patriarchy within the homeschool movement, churches, and in the Christian film industry. Phillips's many publications reveal the influences behind his vision. In 1997 he published *Robert Lewis Dabney: The Prophet Speaks*, a book introducing contemporary audiences to the Southern Presbyterian theologian who had influenced Rushdoony. To Phillips, Dabney was a prophet who boldly stated what many knew to be true but few were willing to say.

He praised Dabney's "prophetic" views on the evils of public education and women's equality, and he found Dabney's anti-feminism "refreshingly virile." Phillips skirted around Dabney's proslavery sentiments, although Phillips, too, diminished the horrors of slavery and denied the genocide of Native Americans. Phillips also revered Theodore Roosevelt, and in 2001 he published *The Letters and Lessons of Teddy Roosevelt for His Sons.* The next year he published *Poems for Patriarchs.* He felt a need to explain that, yes, it was a book of poetry, but the poems were "neither fluffy nor frilly, foppish nor foolish, but virile and often savage." He included poems on God and Christ as warrior kings, and counted Stonewall Jackson among his Christian heroes. He called on men to assume patriarchal leadership "more noble than the valiant deeds of shining knights of yore," and, quoting Charles Spurgeon, he instructed wives to set aside their own pleasure, to sink their individuality into their husbands, to make the domestic circle their kingdom and husbands their "little world," their "Paradise," their "choicest treasure." Phillips believed that patriarchy and patriotism were inextricably connected, and both were God-given duties. Patriarchy was key to the success of nations, and to be "anti-patriotic" was "to be a spiritual ingrate."[5]

Phillips's Vision Forum thrived in the 2000s, producing an array of materials distributed and promoted at homeschool conferences and online. An All-American Boy's Adventure Catalog contained cowboy costumes, knife and tomahawk sets, slingshots, and an "All-American boy's crossbow" to train boys in heroic manhood. The Beautiful Girlhood collection, meanwhile, offered books and DVDs promoting "purity and contentment," "heritage and home," and products such as "Southern lady doll dresses." Vision Forum's gender order was ensconced within a foundational Christian nationalism; the organization led "Faith and Freedom Tours," and for those who could not attend, they produced an array of books and DVDs celebrating Christian patriotism. By 2011, Vision Forum's revenues approached $3.4 million. Phillips also sponsored a Christian Filmmakers Academy and a Christian film festival. Kirk Cameron taught at Phillips's academy and was awarded Best Feature Film at the 2009 San Antonio Independent Christian Film Festival for his 2008 *Fireproof*, a film about a heroic but angry firefighter who feels his wife does not show him sufficient respect and turns to a Christian self-help book to save his marriage. Phillips was meeting the growing demands of an expanding homeschool market, but he was also reaching evangelicals beyond that market niche. His dominionist-inspired teachings celebrating a patriotic, militant Christian masculinity resonated with evangelicals awakened to the "problem" of masculinity by the broader evangelical men's movement, and he found common cause with evangelicals far beyond his immediate circles of influence.[6]

By the 2000s, Phillips emerged as a leading figure in the Quiverfull movement, a pronatalist movement within conservative Protestantism that was especially popular in homeschool networks. It took its name from Psalm 127:4–5: "Like arrows in the hands of a warrior are children born in one's youth. Blessed is the man whose quiver is full of them." Quiverfull women had a critical role to play in birthing an army of God; the culture wars needed as many soldiers as possible. Outbreeding opponents was the first step to outvoting them, and in their reproductive capacities, women served as "domestic warriors." Phillips practiced what he preached. He was the proud father of eight children: Joshua, Justice, Liberty, Jubilee, Faith, Honor, Providence, and Virginia. The Quiverfull movement remained a relatively small faction within conservative Protestantism, numbering only in the low tens of thousands. But the popularity of the Duggar family's *19 Kids and Counting* TLC reality show, which ran from 2008 to 2015, introduced Quiverfull values to the larger American public.[7]

By that time the homeschooling movement more generally had developed into a powerful network intent on equipping children to serve as the next generation's culture warriors. In 2000, Farris founded Patrick Henry College, a college catering to homeschoolers. Although the school accepted fewer than one hundred students a year, in its fourth year of existence it accounted for 7 percent of White House interns. In 2004, Farris and the HSLDA launched Generation Joshua

Arkansas state representative Jim Bob Duggar and his wife
Michelle leading their children to a polling place in Springdale,
Arkansas, in May 2002. AP PHOTO / APRIL L. BROWN.

to recruit homeschooled teenagers as foot soldiers for the Republican
Party. Trained to advance the next iteration of the culture wars, homeschoolers infiltrated the halls of power, finding work in the White
House and on Capitol Hill. Generation Joshua's director, Ned Ryun,
a former speechwriter for George W. Bush and a homeschooled son of
congressman Jim Ryun, predicted that "homeschoolers will be inordi-
nately represented in the highest levels of leadership and power in the
next generation." No longer marginal, they were staking a claim on the
nation itself.[8]

It wasn't just junior culture warriors who were bringing militant
patriarchy into the halls of power. In his investigation of the Family, the secretive group (also known as the Fellowship) that had organized the National Prayer Breakfast since the 1950s, journalist Jeff
Sharlet found evidence of John Eldredge's *Wild at Heart* warrior
code, of knights-in-shining-armor purity culture, and of the Christian Reconstructionist-infused patriarchy of Doug Phillips's Vision
Forum. These sources fed a hypermasculine and authoritarian ethos

within the organization, one that meshed well with their attempts to consolidate power nationally and globally.[9]

THE PACIFIC NORTHWEST was home to another extreme expression of militant evangelical masculinity. Whereas the Christian homeschool movement celebrated a quaint traditionalism, favoring modest attire and a nostalgic ethos, Seattle's Mars Hill Church gained prominence as the leading edge of a forward-looking, tech-savvy evangelicalism. The church was founded in 1996 by twenty-five-year-old pastor Mark Driscoll, and over the next eighteen years Driscoll's empire grew to include fifteen churches in five states along with a global ministry.

Raised Catholic, Driscoll converted to evangelicalism as a college student and quickly made a name for himself as a "theologically hard-line but culturally hip" pastor on the conservative periphery of the "emerging church" movement. Driscoll preached a verse-by-verse literal reading of the Bible and promoted conservative social teachings, but there was nothing stodgy about his style. Mars Hill had the feel of a nightclub, filled with predominantly white twenty- and thirty-somethings with a penchant for tattoos, piercings, beer, and the local indie music scene. Driscoll himself, sporting dark jeans and T-shirts, had the look of a wannabe rock star. Like celebrity evangelists before him, Driscoll mastered cutting-edge communication technologies. "The Internet is the Greek Marketplace of Acts 17," proclaimed the church's visitor guide. "Film and Theology Nights" featured prominently, and for those raised in conservative Baptist, fundamentalist, or Pentecostal churches, Mars Hill offered a refreshing model of cultural engagement. But Driscoll's message wasn't just the old-time religion communicated in a hip new way; his gospel message was infused with militant masculinity.[10]

In language that would have been familiar to many among his flock, Driscoll insisted that real men avoided church because they had no interest in a "Richard Simmons, hippie, queer Christ." But Jesus was no "long-haired . . . effeminate-looking dude"—he was a man like Driscoll's own working-class dad, "a construction worker who swung a hammer for a living," a man with "calluses on his hands and muscles on his frame." Jesus bore no resemblance to "the drag-queen Jesus images that portray him with long, flowing, feathered hair, perfect teeth, and soft skin, draped in a comfortable dress accessorized by matching open-toed sandals and handbag." He was an aggressive, anger-filled leader who picked fights with religious authorities, slaughtered thousands of pigs, ordered his disciples around, and didn't mind causing offense. Jesus was a hero, not a loser, "an Ultimate Fighter warrior king with a tattoo down his leg who rides into battle against Satan, sin, and death on a trusty horse," just like in the Westerns.[11]

Driscoll was indebted to evangelical writers on masculinity who preceded him, but his ideas and rhetoric went far beyond theirs, in many respects. Gone was any language of friendship, tenderness, and personal enrichment; Driscoll wanted nothing to do with the softer side of the men's movement. Instead he made a name for himself as "Mark the cussing pastor." Like Doug Wilson, Driscoll enjoyed shocking his audiences. No one could accuse either man of succumbing to political correctness. Also like Wilson, Driscoll positioned himself as a critic of mainstream evangelicalism. He berated "flaccid church guys" who preferred a fake smile to righteous anger. The Bible spoke of God's anger, wrath, and fury far more than of his love, grace, and mercy, Driscoll insisted. Jesus, too, got angry, even enraged. And Jesus used military terminology when speaking of his church: the church was "an offensive force on the move," storming the gates of hell. In Revelation, Jesus was a conquering warrior. Sure, God was a pacifist, but only at the end of the age, only after he kills all his enemies. In the meantime, God created men for war.[12]

Driscoll also wasn't afraid to talk about sex. Song of Solomon was his favorite part of the Bible, and it was no allegory. To interpret it allegorically would mean that Jesus was trying to "put his hand up your shirt," and he, for one, didn't love Jesus like that. No, Song of

Solomon was a book about erotic love between a man and a woman. In 2007, Driscoll preached a sermon called "Sex: A Study of the Good Bits of Song of Solomon," which he followed up with a sermon series and an e-book, *Porn-again Christian* (2008). For Driscoll, the "good bits" amounted to a veritable sex manual. Translating from the Hebrew, he discovered that the woman in the passage was asking for manual stimulation of her clitoris. He assured women that if they thought they were "being dirty," chances are their husbands were pretty happy. He issued the pronouncement that "all men are breast men. . . . It's biblical," as was a wife performing oral sex on her husband. Hearing an "Amen" from the men in his audience, he urged the ladies present to serve their husbands, to "love them well," with oral sex. He advised one woman to go home and perform oral sex on her husband in Jesus' name to get him to come to church. Handing out religious tracts was one thing, but there was a better way to bring about Christian revival.[13]

Driscoll reveled in his ability to shock people, but it was a series of anonymous blog posts on his church's online discussion board that laid bare the extent of his misogyny. In 2006, inspired by *Braveheart*, Driscoll adopted the pseudonym "William Wallace II" to express his unfiltered views. "I love to fight. It's good to fight. Fighting is what we used to do before we all became pussified," before America became a "pussified nation." In that vein, he offered a scathing critique of the earlier iteration of the evangelical men's movement, of the "pussified James Dobson knock-off crying Promise Keeping homoerotic worship . . ." where men hugged and cried "like damn junior high girls watching Dawson's Creek." Real men should steer clear.[14] For Driscoll, the problem went all the way back to the biblical Adam, a man who plunged humanity headlong into "hell/feminism" by listening to his wife, "who thought Satan was a good theologian." Failing to exercise "his delegated authority as king of the planet," Adam was cursed, and "every man since has been pussified." The result was a nation of men raised "by bitter penis envying burned feministed single mothers who make sure that Johnny grows up to be a very nice woman who sits down to pee." Women served certain purposes, and not others. In one of his more infamous missives, Driscoll talked of God creating women to serve as penis "homes" for lonely penises. When a woman posted on the church's discussion board, his response was swift: "I . . . do not answer to women. So, your questions will be ignored."[15]

Like many other evangelicals, Driscoll was a fan of Mel Gibson's *Braveheart*, but it was the movie *Fight Club* that more directly inspired his approach to ministry. He encouraged men to engage in theological sparring contests, and he goaded men in the audience to throw things at participants and mock men who were not adequately prepared or whose arguments were not sharp enough. Winners were crowned with a Viking helmet. Once, after preaching on manhood for over two hours, Driscoll challenged men to either recommit to the mission of the church or leave, "because you can't charge hell with your pants around your ankles, a bottle of lotion in one hand, and a Kleenex in the other." Driscoll then handed the men two stones, telling them God was "giving them their balls back to get the courage to do kingdom work." The men—at least those who stayed—spoke of this admonishment in glowing terms: "Mark ripped us all a new asshole." According to Driscoll, the change was evident: "We had guys getting saved en masse. We had gay guys going straight. We had guys tossing out porn, getting jobs, tithing, taking wives, buying homes, making babies."[16]

Driscoll thrived on manufacturing a sense of threat posed by outsiders. Prominently identified security guards monitored the sanctuary and flanked Driscoll when he preached, "surveying the audience like a private militia ready to pounce." Male volunteers were recruited to help "protect the body." A sense of physical threat dovetailed with religious and cultural hazards: unorthodox theology, Islam, "sexualized single women" and "effeminate men" all put the church and nation at risk. Driscoll incited fear in order to maintain control. Tolerating no passive consumption, he demanded self-sacrificial service and absolute submission to (his) authority. As in wartime, dissent was quickly snuffed out.

By ratcheting up a sense of alarm, Driscoll justified his demands for discipline, control, and unquestioned power.[17]

A military spirit pervaded the church. Driscoll believed it was his task to keep Christian men battle-ready, an especially critical task in the wake of 9/11. By forming masculine citizen-soldiers, Driscoll could advance Christianity *and* protect the country from Islamic terrorism. To this end, Mars Hill men watched war movies, spoke in a martial dialect, and participated in spiritual warfare "boot camps." Driscoll brought a militaristic model to his ministry, and he brought his ministry to the military, launching a Military Missions outreach for men serving overseas. At a time when the number of women serving in the all-volunteer forces was increasing, Driscoll's sermons on the threat women posed to white, heterosexual men, to national security, and to Christianity resonated with many of his military disciples. With the help of digital media, servicemen in Afghanistan and Iraq became Driscoll's proselytizers, organizing Sunday services on bases and projecting his recorded sermons: "The flood-gates opened with the guys as we worked through porn, masturbating, beer, Calvinism, the exclusivity of Christ, being a husband and daddy, and war."[18]

Driscoll sought to distance himself from earlier culture warriors like Falwell and Dobson, and he liked to bill himself as apolitical. But the trendy packaging masked a culture-warrior mentality every bit as belligerent as that of his predecessors, if not more so. For instance, while he may have welcomed LGBT "seekers" into his church, he denounced gay men as "damn freaks." Some evangelical leaders expressed reservations about Driscoll's crudeness, but many nonetheless professed their admiration. As Al Mohler explained, "wherever the gospel is to be found, we need to be happy about that." Though Mohler thought there was "a difference between being crude and being candid," he admired the "boldness" and "tenacity" with which Driscoll preached "the gospel of Jesus Christ."[19]

The aggressive masculinity Driscoll preached and performed found widespread appeal among young evangelical men in the 2000s. Men encountered these teachings in church camps and small groups, through parachurch ministries like InterVarsity Christian Fellowship, on Christian college campuses, and by listening to Christian radio or perusing the Christian blogosphere. Books like Eldredge's *Wild at Heart* and Josh Harris's *I Kissed Dating Goodbye* were staples for this generation, as were recorded sermons by men like Driscoll and John Piper. Young men listened to their words for hours on end, discussing their teachings in exclusively male contexts. "I formed a lot of my opinions about theology and masculinity in isolation, the ideas were implanted within male only fellowship meetings, and I listened to hundreds of hours of sermons by myself, rarely discussing them with anyone except other men," recalls one former Driscoll fan. Over the course of one and a half years, he started at the beginning and worked his way through all of Driscoll's sermons:

> The hour long, stand up comedy style sermons were engrossing. I would load dozens onto my ipod and listen to them while walking around campus. I spent summertime mowing lawns and would listen to 5–6 sermons a day at times. I remember being fascinated by the way that he would talk about things in the sermons no one was talking about, like how sex plays an important role in marriage, and how "pussified" the church was becoming. . . . I didn't recognize the misogyny in his theology at the time, as a stereotypical beta male, it was like an invitation to become important. . . .

The call to leadership was compelling:

> Up until that point I don't remember people expecting me to do much of anything. I was a lazy student, not particularly athletic or talented in any ways that I was aware of, and there was this whole sub-culture that needed mediocre white guys to just show up and lead because that's what Jesus wanted and all these women were turning the church into wusses. And all I had to do was show up and talk the talk and keep my nose clean.

By listening to men like Driscoll and Piper, young evangelical men became part of a larger movement. They were called to be heroes.[20]

LIKE WILSON AND PHILLIPS, Driscoll was somewhat of an out-lier, an independent operator intent first and foremost on building his own empire. But he also established himself as a highly respected, if controversial, leader among his fellow evangelicals, particularly among young male pastors. It is hard to tell whether Will Ferrell or Mark Driscoll deserves more credit for the "smokin' hot wife" phenomenon that swept through evangelicalism in the 2010s. In 2011, Baptist pastor Joe Nelms garnered national attention when he channeled *Talladega Nights*'s Ricky Bobby in his opening prayer at a NASCAR event, thanking God for his "smokin' hot wife." But praising God for sexy wives in prayers, sermons, and on social media had become common practice among a certain set of conservative evangelical pastors. One megachurch pastor posted a photo of his wife on Instagram captioned with a modified version of Proverbs 31: "her *leather pants* are like water to her husband's soul." For their part, women could attend Christian conferences to learn how to be "a hottie for your honey."[21]

Driscoll inspired by example, but he also helped construct new networks that would leave their imprint on twenty-first-century evangelicalism. Building on a foundation set by R. C. Sproul, John MacArthur, and John Piper, Driscoll helped fuel the movement of the "young, restless and reformed," a revival of Calvinism that swept through American evangelicalism—and denominations like the SBC—in the 2000s. As cofounder of the Acts 29 network and as a founding member of The Gospel Coalition, Driscoll positioned himself at the center of an emerging movement that sought to revitalize evangelicalism with an injection of masculine "New Calvinist" doctrine.[22]

Even as they rejected or deemphasized many elements of the broader confessional tradition of Calvinism and Reformed theology (including infant baptism, covenantal theology, and a more nuanced understanding of biblical authority over against a simplistic commitment to inerrancy), New Calvinists claimed to find in sixteenth-century theologian John Calvin and later Puritan scholars a meatier Christianity that would serve as an antidote to a "softer" evangelicalism. Suppressing the emotive side of evangelical revivalism, they emphasized the existence of hell and the wrath of God, which required Jesus' substitutionary atonement, his bloody death on the cross to atone for humanity's sins. Theirs was a properly masculine theology, the story of a vengeful Father-God taking out his rage on his own Son. Strict gender complementarianism was at the heart of this Calvinist resurgence. For leaders of the movement, patriarchal power was at the core of gospel Christianity; in the words of John Piper, God had given Christianity "a masculine feel."[23]

For all their emphasis on sin, New Calvinists seemed remarkably unconcerned about the concentration of unchecked power in the hands of men. Roger Olson, a Baptist theologian who opposed the Calvinist insurgency, compared the "young, restless, and Reformed" movement to Gothard's Basic Youth Conflicts seminar, observing that there was "a certain kind of personality that craves the comfort of absolute certainty as an escape from ambiguity and risk and they find it in religion or politics of a certain kind." Such people were attracted to an ideology that was "absolutistic, logical (or seemingly so), simple and practical." The notion of "God's chain of command" offered precisely this absolutist certainty. Needless to say, white men were at the top of that chain of command, at least in terms of human relationships.[24]

By 2019, the Acts 29 network founded by Driscoll had planted over 700 churches on six continents, churches committed to upholding "men as responsible servant-leaders in both home and church." Meanwhile, The Gospel Coalition, founded in 2005 by Tim Keller and D. A. Carson, grew into "a towering, thundering goliath," a network of nearly 8000 congregations. TGC's website hosted a battalion of conservative bloggers and garnered around 65 million annual page views on thousands of posts, and TGC organized dozens of conferences that distributed and amplified their message throughout American Christianity and beyond. A hub for the expanding network of conservative evangelical leaders, TGC brought together men like

Driscoll, Piper, Mohler, and other men of prominence within American evangelicalism such as Josh Harris, C. J. Mahaney, Mark Dever, Ligon Duncan, Denny Burk, and Justin Taylor.[25]

New Calvinism was aggressively mission-driven. Spreading through online and organizational networks, this Calvinist resurgence united men across generations and denominations. As one blogger put it, "the Internet has done for Reformed theology what MTV did for hip-hop culture." John Piper, cofounder of CBMW, was "the single most potent factor" in this rise of Reformed theology. Piper's Passion Conference, a Christian worship conference first held in 1997, introduced the pastor and theologian to a generation of young Christians in America and around the world. Piper's book *Desiring God* sold more than 375,000 copies and was "practically required reading for many college-age evangelicals," and his Desiring God website and conferences served as another focal point of the expanding network. Piper's imprimatur could help launch careers; after Driscoll was invited to speak at Piper's conference, he received invitations from Jerry Falwell, Robert Schuller, and Bill Hybels, pastor of the Chicago-area megachurch Willow Creek.[26]

In 2006, Dever, Duncan, Mohler, and Mahaney founded Together for the Gospel (T4G), a biennial conference featuring themselves and other celebrity pastors in the conservative theological orbit, most notably Piper, MacArthur, and Sproul. These men had already established themselves on the Christian conference circuit, but T4G amplified their influence. By 2009, *Time* magazine was labeling "The New Calvinism" one of "10 ideas changing the world right now." As Ted Olsen, managing editor at *Christianity Today* explained, "everyone knows" that the energy and passion in the evangelical world were "with the pioneering new-Calvinist John Piper of Minneapolis, Seattle's pugnacious Mark Driscoll and Albert Mohler, head of the Southern Seminary of the huge Southern Baptist Convention."[27]

What was remarkable was that so many notoriously combative men could find common cause. There were certainly disagreements among leaders on a variety of topics, but they were able to smooth over these differences—including rather significant theological differences—

because of a common reverence for patriarchal authority. For instance, one of the most notable theological differences among leaders concerned the question of cessationism—whether the spiritual gifts of tongues, prophecy, and healing ceased with the apostolic age (a view espoused by MacArthur) or continued into the present (a view expressed by charismatics and many New Calvinists, including Piper, Mahaney, and Grudem). Agreeing that "desperate times called for desperate measures," these men could agree to disagree about speaking in tongues and the gift of prophecy because other issues—including gender complementarianism and church discipline—were more pressing.[28]

DOUG WILSON PROVIDES an interesting case study of the shifting alliances within the evangelical subculture. When he published *Future Men* in 2001, Wilson certainly wouldn't have located himself at the center of evangelicalism. In fact, he was a stalwart critic of mainstream evangelicalism. Although his views on gender and authority aligned in many ways with those of other conservative evangelicals at the time, Wilson often carried those views to extreme, or perhaps logical, conclusions. A woman wearing a man's clothing was "an abomination." If a wife was not properly submissive, it was a husband's duty to correct her. For instance, if dirty dishes lingered in the sink, he must immediately sit her down and remind her of her duty; if she rebelled, he was to call the elders of the church to intervene. In terms of child-rearing, "discipline must be painful." God required the infliction of pain on those dear to us. Homosexuality must be suppressed, not excluding the possibility of the death penalty, though banishment was also an option. Wilson endorsed the concept of "Biblical hatred," a form of militant masculine faithfulness exhibited by one of his heroes of the faith, Scottish minister John Knox.[29]

On issues of race, Wilson's views were similarly extreme. In the 1990s, Wilson had coauthored *Southern Slavery: As It Was*, which questioned the supposed "brutalities, immoralities, and cruelties" of slavery. The slave trade might have been unbiblical, he allowed, but

slavery most certainly was not. To the contrary, the radical abolition-
ists were the ones "driven by a zealous hatred of the Word of God."
Horrific descriptions of slavery were nothing more than abolition-
ist propaganda. The life of a slave had been a life of plenty, of ample
food, good medical care, and simple pleasures, marked by "a degree
of mutual affection between the races" that could never be achieved
through coercive federal legislation. In 2005 he published *Black and
Tan*, a sequel that presented Robert E. Lee as "a gracious Christian
gentleman, a brother in Christ," and claimed that Christian slave owners were "on firm scriptural ground."[30]

In the 1990s, given the audacity of Wilson's claims, his geographic
isolation, and his preference for building his own empire on his own
terms, it would be right to place him at the very fringes of American
evangelicalism. But by the 2000s, with the rise of New Calvinism,
the growing popularity of "biblical patriarchy," and the turn toward
increasingly militant models of masculinity, Wilson found himself within shouting distance of the evangelical mainstream. Wilson
hadn't softened his views or toned down his rhetoric, but this didn't
seem to exclude him from polite company. Not all evangelical leaders
approved of his style, but many considered it forgivable. Some found
it commendable.

John Piper helped smooth Wilson's path from the outer edges into
more respectable circles. In 2009, Piper invited Wilson to speak at
his Desiring God Conference. Suppressing a bit of a chuckle, Piper
noted that Wilson had a way with language, that he was a "risk taker,"
but Wilson got the gospel right. With his "unflinching, unashamed
commitment to the Bible," there was much to like in Doug Wilson.
When controversy surfaced around Wilson's views on race, Piper again
came to his defense. In a video that was at times almost flippant, Piper
pushed back against those who had "perceived" Wilson to have minimized the horrors of slavery. He assured viewers that "Doug hates racism from the core of his gospel soul," and declared his readiness "to
stand with him even if there are differences in historical judgments"
concerning the Civil War and the best way to end slavery.[31]

Long a critic of mainstream evangelicalism, Wilson now found his work (and that of his son, Nate Wilson) covered in *Christianity Today* and *Books & Culture*. In 2007, *Christianity Today* ran a six-part series on Wilson's debates with atheist Christopher Hitchens, raising Wilson's profile. His 2012 novel *Evangellyfish*, a satirical critique of spineless evangelicalism in which nearly every character speaks in Wilson's own distinctly awkward cadences, won *Christianity Today*'s Book Award for Fiction in 2013.[32]

United in their concern about gender and authority, conservative evangelical men knit together an expanding network of institutions, organizations, and alliances that amplified their voices and enhanced their power. Wilson invited Driscoll to speak at his church; Piper invited Wilson to address his pastor's conference; leaders shared stages, blurbed each other's books, spoke at each other's conferences, and endorsed each other as men of God with a heart for gospel teaching. Within this network, differences—significant doctrinal disagreements, disagreements over the relative merits of slavery and the Civil War—could be smoothed over in the interest of promoting "watershed issues" like complementarianism, the prohibition of homosexuality, the existence of hell, and substitutionary atonement. Most foundationally, they were united in a mutual commitment to patriarchal power.[33]

Through this expanding network, "respectable" evangelical leaders and organizations gave cover to their "brothers in the gospel" who were promoting more extreme expressions of patriarchy, making it increasingly difficult to distinguish margins from mainstream. Over time, a common commitment to patriarchal power began to define the boundaries of the evangelical movement itself, as those who ran afoul of these orthodoxies quickly discovered. Evangelicals who offered competing visions of sexuality, gender, or the existence of hell found themselves excluded from conferences and associations, and their writings banned from popular evangelical bookstores and distribution channels. Through deliberate strategies and the power of the marketplace, the exclusion of alternative views would contribute to the radicalization of evangelicalism in post-9/11 America.

Chapter 12

PILGRIM'S
PROGRESS
IN CAMO

I F THERE WAS A CENTRAL HUB TO THE SPRAWLING
network that was twenty-first-century American evangelicalism, it
was Colorado Springs. The "Wheaton of the West," Colorado Springs
had displaced the original Wheaton, a center of a more genteel, establishment evangelicalism, and had surpassed Lynchburg and Orange
County in terms of significance in the evangelical world. In Colorado Springs, the militarization of mainstream evangelicalism was on
full display. And from its evangelical strongholds, the city's faithful
brought their militant faith directly to the US military.[1]

The history of evangelicalism in Colorado Springs can be traced
to the city's founding, but it was in the post-WWII era that the city
began to emerge as a nerve center for a politically engaged, globally
expansive evangelicalism intent on winning the country, and the
world, for Christ. The entrenchment of evangelicalism in Colorado
Springs coincided with the growth of the military in the region. In
1954, the United States Air Force Academy was established in Colorado Springs. The city would eventually house three air force bases,
an army fort, and the North American Air Defense Command. In
the 1960s, the Nazarene Bible College opened its doors, and soon an
array of evangelical, charismatic, and fundamentalist churches, colleges, ministries, nonprofits, and businesses took root. Lured by local

tax breaks and drawn to the growing epicenter of evangelical power, nearly one hundred Christian parachurch organizations sprouted up within a five-mile vicinity of the academy, including Officers' Christian Fellowship, the International Bible Society, Youth for Christ, the Navigators, Fellowship of Christian Athletes, Christian Booksellers Association, Fellowship of Christian Cowboys, Christian Camping International, and, most significantly, Dobson's Focus on the Family.[2]

IN 1991, DOBSON HAD MOVED his organization's headquarters from Pomona, California, to a 47-acre complex in Colorado Springs overlooking the air force academy. When he inaugurated his new headquarters, members of the academy's parachute team parachuted in, presenting Dobson with "the Keys of heaven" at the opening ceremonies. By that time, Dobson had set aside any qualms about direct political engagement. A year after arriving in Colorado, he helped mobilize support for an amendment to the state constitution that would block the passage of gay rights laws. His forces succeeded, at the time. His *Citizen* magazine and his *Family News in Focus* kept followers informed on the latest political events. Meanwhile, with Gary Bauer at its helm, the Family Research Council grew into the most powerful organization of the Christian Right in the nation's capital.[3]

From his base in Colorado Springs, Dobson continued to step up his political activism. In 2003 he came to the defense of Alabama Supreme Court chief justice Roy Moore, an evangelical Christian who had refused to abide by a federal order to remove a monument to the Ten Commandments that he had installed in the Alabama Supreme Court. Speaking in Montgomery, Dobson compared Moore's civil disobedience to that of Rosa Parks: "We as people of faith are also being sent to the back of the bus." It was then that Dobson sensed "a new level of disgust among the country's seventy million white evangelical Christians," and a new willingness to fight. Even at age sixty-seven, this was not a battle he was going to sit out. In order to protect Focus on the Family's tax exemption, Dobson retired from his position as CEO of the organization so he could take up political organizing directly.[4]

Dobson quickly moved from the symbolic battlefield to the electoral one. His first target was Tom Daschle, the Democratic Senate minority leader from South Dakota, for the role Daschle had played in blocking ten of George W. Bush's nominees to the US courts of appeals. In 2004, Dobson threw his support behind John Thune, an evangelical Republican who was an anti-abortion, anti-same-sex marriage candidate. To drum up support for Thune, Dobson organized Focus on the Family–sponsored "Stand for Family" rallies, spoke at a massive Christian music festival, and published "An Important Message from Dr. James C. Dobson" on Thune's behalf in full-page newspaper ads around the state. All told, Dobson reached around one tenth of South Dakota's population. Thune won by a margin of 4508 votes, and he knew what Dobson's endorsement meant: "There is literally a generation of Americans who have grown up with Dr. Dobson," he reflected after his victory. "His voice is golden out there, particularly among Americans who had a conservative value system or worldview. He could speak to them like nobody else could, absent somebody like Billy Graham."[5]

Dobson wielded enormous political power, yet it was nearly invisible outside evangelical circles. "The average person in the establishment is not aware of what Dobson is saying to five or ten million people every week," remarked Richard Viguerie, the GOP's direct-mail mastermind. "That has served us beautifully." Dobson's power was all too apparent to evangelicals themselves, for better and for worse. When asked about their greatest fear, Christian college presidents agreed: the possibility that James Dobson would turn against their school. The lesson was clear: "Don't mess with Dobson or, by extension, with any of the moguls of the Religious Right." With the decline of Falwell's Moral Majority and Robertson's Christian Coalition, Focus on the Family provided a critical fulcrum for evangelical political engagement.[6]

ALSO WITHIN SIGHT of the air force academy stood another evangelical stronghold, New Life Church. One of the nation's most influential megachurches, New Life was founded in 1984 by Ted Haggard, one of "the nation's most politically influential" clergy. His father had established an international charismatic ministry, but Haggard was "born again" at the age of sixteen after hearing Bill Bright preach at Explo '72. After attending Oral Roberts University, Haggard came under the mentorship of Jack Hayford, founding pastor of a Pentecostal megachurch in Van Nuys, California—the church that essentially launched the megachurch model for suburban evangelicalism. Dobson had greater name recognition, but Haggard rivaled his friend and neighbor when it came to influence. He oversaw his own association of around 300 churches, and in 2003 he became president of the National Association of Evangelicals. By that time the organization represented 45,000 churches and 30 million Christians and was the country's most powerful religious lobby.[7]

Like Dobson, Haggard's evangelicalism was explicitly political. He spoke nationally in support of the Iraq war and against abortion, and he embraced free-market capitalism both as an economic model and as essential to the spread of Christianity. Inside New Life's sanctuary, which was decorated in air force silver and blue, large video screens flashed tributes to Haggard, to various politicians and denominational leaders, and to Tony Perkins, Dobson's "enforcer on Capitol Hill." In a two-hour television broadcast before the 2004 election, Haggard worked to turn out the evangelical vote for Bush, and to garner support for the Federal Marriage Amendment that would ban same-sex marriage. Haggard talked with President Bush or his advisers every Monday, giving the administration "the pulse of the evangelical world." On the wall outside his office hung three framed pictures: two of Haggard with the president, and one with Mel Gibson, who prescreened *The Passion* at an event organized by Haggard. According to journalist Jeff Sharlet, who profiled New Life in *Harper's* magazine in 2005, churches like New Life served as ideological crucibles for the Christian Right; ideas "forged in the middle of the country" soon enough made their way to the nation's capital. In this respect, New Life was "not just a battalion of spiritual warriors but a factory for ideas to arm them."[8]

Haggard's church manifested this warfare mentality. In its lobby loomed *The Defender,* "a massive bronze of a glowering angel" wielding a broad sword. Upstairs, children gathered in Fort Victory, a space designed to look like an Old West cavalry outpost. Across the parking lot stood the World Prayer Center's global headquarters, a "spiritual NORAD," and in its atrium stood another bronze warrior angel armed with enormous biceps and packing a sword. The chapel contained computers where visitors entered personal prayers; the center's staff provided more politically oriented prayers—for a marriage amendment, for the appointment of new justices, and for the president. The center also offered prayers for US foreign policy, for God to "crush [the] demonic stronghold and communist regime of Kim Jun II," and for the forces of good to prevail in Iraq.[9]

Those at New Life were aware of the strategic position they occupied. Colorado Springs was a battleground, a "spiritual Gettysburg," explained one man who understood his own role in militarized terms: "I'm a warrior, dude. I'm a warrior for God. Colorado Springs is my training ground." Like the military, New Life employed a rigid chain of command to ensure strict ideological conformity. Male authority and female submission were essential to that hierarchical order. The church also elevated the role of sexual purity, though Haggard insisted that purity didn't diminish pleasure; evangelicals, he boasted, had "the best sex lives" of anyone. All this came together in a larger mission. Evangelicals who flocked to Colorado Springs shared in a mythical dream "populated by cowboys and Indians, monsters and prayer warriors to slay them, and ladies to reward the warriors with chaste kisses."

Haggard's New Life Church was a hotbed of militant evangelicalism. Together, Haggard and Dobson worked to spread this militant faith throughout the US military.[10]

FOR HALF A CENTURY, evangelicals had been working to strengthen the military and imbue it with evangelical values, and they'd been warmly received, particularly by evangelicals already entrenched within the armed forces. By the 2000s, however, some service members began to object to the overt proselytizing and coercive religious atmosphere they encountered within the military. The air force academy in Colorado Springs was ground zero in the battle over religious expression and coercion.

The mission to combat an alleged evangelical takeover was led by Mikey Weinstein, a 1977 honor graduate of the academy, former air force officer, and former legal counsel to the Reagan White House. Weinstein and his family were Jewish, and both of his sons attended the academy, where they encountered aggressive Christian proselytizing at times tinged with anti-Semitic undertones. Weinstein began to gather documentation, and his complaints led to an investigation that revealed a "pervasive" religious intolerance at the academy. A number of questionable activities came to light. Johnny A. Weida, the commandant of cadets, came under scrutiny for creating a call-and-response chant that had cadets shouting "Jesus Rocks." The academy's football coach prayed to the "Master Coach" in the locker room and had a banner emblazoned with the words "Team Jesus." An annual Christmas message in the academy's newspaper proclaimed that "Jesus Christ is the only real hope for the world." Flyers advertised a screening of Mel Gibson's *The Passion of the Christ* at every place setting in the dining hall.[11]

Gibson's film wasn't your run-of-the-mill Hollywood movie. Filled with graphic scenes of Christ's crucifixion, its depiction of Jews struck many critics as anti-Semitic, an allegation that gained traction after Gibson's anti-Semitic rant during a 2006 drunk driving arrest. For many evangelicals, however, watching the movie was an act of devotion. Evangelicals were already fans of Gibson's work. Gibson was Catholic, but evangelicals recognized that they shared the common creed of militant Christianity and heroic masculinity. For many evangelical writers, references to *Braveheart* rivaled biblical references when it came to discerning God's will for men. *The Patriot*, too, offered a heroic vision that was sorely lacking in modern America. But nothing matched evangelicals' fervor for *The Passion*.[12]

Another air force parent, retired colonel David Antoon, was also alarmed at changes that had taken place at the academy. When he'd attended in the late 1960s, the emphasis had been on leadership, not just the art of war. But he was startled by the language he heard from General Weida; in his ninety-minute address, "Weida must have used the term warrior dozens of times," Antoon recalled. (It turned out cadets had a game of ticking off the number of times Weida said "warrior" when he addressed them.) Weida's rhetoric was uncannily similar to that of the literature on evangelical masculinity; according to Weinstein, it was "a page that could well have been lifted from Bobby Welch's playbook *You, the Warrior Leader*."[13]

Welch, a decorated Vietnam vet, had ascended to the presidency of the SBC in 2004. That same year he published his book, a guide to applying military strategy to the spiritual life, with an imprint of the SBC's LifeWay Christian Resources. He opened the book with a quote from SBC megachurch pastor Jerry Vines: "The church is not a passive, milquetoast organization," it was "Militant! Aggressive! Victorious!" The Christian life wasn't to be *compared* to war, it *was* war, and Christians needed to engage in "an all-out offensive assault." Too many Christians believed that a passive, defensive posture was more Christlike, but that left one a sitting target. Offensive tactics had served the cause well in the conservative takeover of the SBC, Welch noted, and he believed the September 11 attacks required a similar mobilization. In this war, too, there would be casualties: "good, sweet, kind people, even children and infants" would be mauled, burned, ravaged by demons. It would be a war filled with "murder, rape, and mayhem," and

Air Force cadets walking past the Academy's Chapel in Colorado Springs, Colorado, in August 2003. AP PHOTO / ED ANDRIESKI.

it wouldn't be won "by parlor games in board rooms" or holy hugs or singing "Kum Ba Ya." Jesus, the Warrior Leader, would lead the assault against "Satan's terrorists." Along with Jesus, Welch looked to figures like Robert E. Lee and KKK Grand Wizard Nathan Bedford Forrest as models of warrior leadership.[14]

It was precisely this evangelical warrior rhetoric that made Antoon's skin crawl. He found this attitude "diametrically opposed" to the values instilled in him decades earlier. Then, fighting and killing had been spoken of "soberly and with humility"—killing was accepted as a fact of war, not exalted. But "somehow that had all been transformed into a kind of holy bloodlust." Antoon identified a source of this infiltration. He'd seen cadets and families at the Cadet Chapel welcomed by "a phalanx of enthusiastic pastors" and recruited to Monday night Bible studies taught by members of New Life Church and Focus on the Family staff bused in for that purpose. The academy, Antoon realized, had become "a giant Trojan horse for evangelicals to get inside the military."[15]

Efforts to address evangelical overreach were met with staunch resistance from evangelicals themselves, inside and outside the military. Under pressure from critics, the academy put together an interfaith team to promote religious diversity, but evangelicals up the chain of command rebuffed these efforts. When reviewing materials the team had compiled, Major General Charles Baldwin, air force chief of chaplains, repeatedly wanted to know why "Christians don't ever win." Baldwin, who had a master of divinity degree from Southern Baptist Theological Seminary and had served at the academy's Cadet Chapel before taking up duties in Washington, also objected to a clip from *Schindler's List* "because it made 'Christians look like Nazis.'" (The scene was replaced with one from Mel Gibson's *We Were Soldiers*.) With support from Focus on the Family's Alliance Defense Fund, evangelical chaplain James Glass brought a legal motion claiming that any effort to curb prayer or proselytizing was a violation of his freedom of speech. Focus on the Family denounced all criticism as unjustified, and "fervently hope[d] that this ridiculous bias of a few against the religion of a majority—Christianity—will now cease."[16]

Increasingly, evangelicalism *was* the religion of the majority within the armed forces. In 2005, 40 percent of active duty personnel identified as evangelical, and 60 percent of military chaplains did. As in other branches of the military, the presence of evangelical chaplains in the air force had increased significantly from 1994 to 2005, and evangelical chaplains brought with them a commitment to evangelism; Brig. Gen. Cecil Richardson, air force deputy chief of chaplains and a member of the Assemblies of God, explained that chaplains would refrain from proselytizing, "but we reserve the right to evangelize the unchurched." He distinguished the two by suggesting that evangelizing "is more gently sharing the gospel," as opposed to "trying to convert someone in an aggressive way." It was a distinction without a difference.[17]

As the air force was coming under fire from critics warning of evangelical infiltration, the academy was still working to recover from revelations of an epidemic of sexual assault within the ranks. Some estimates put the number of women victimized at nearly 20 percent of all female cadets, and it appeared that a systematic cover-up had been going on for years. Victims were blackmailed, threatened, or expelled, while the accused were "allowed to graduate with honors despite multiple accusations." At the time, the sexual assault scandal and the coercive religious atmosphere seemed like two distinct problems, connected only inasmuch as the academy was eager to avoid another public relations fiasco in the aftermath of disclosures of abuse. Yet there was another statistic that suggested the two problems might not be entirely disconnected; one in five cadets felt women didn't belong among them.[18]

WITH THE RENEWED MILITARISM of post-9/11 evangelicalism, pastors like Ted Haggard, Mark Driscoll, and Doug Wilson preached a militant Christian masculinity. But in the age of the War on Terror, pastors weren't necessarily the most effective purveyors of Christian manhood. The military was where boys became men, and where men matured in the Christian faith. Military men, then, could serve as guides for civilian men, and for the church as a whole.

The days of "Olliemania" were long since past, but the renewed militancy of the early 2000s enabled Oliver North to again capitalize on his Christian-military-hero brand. In 2001, North began hosting *War Stories with Oliver North* on Fox News. In 2002, he decided to try his hand at fiction. His novel *Mission Compromised*, billed as a "Tom Clancy-esque" political thriller, bore a remarkable resemblance to North's own experiences: the hero of the story was a hotshot marine tasked with doing "foreign-policy dirty work" to save the world. North published with B&H, an imprint of LifeWay Christian Resources, the publishing arm of the SBC. "I don't proselytize well, and I wouldn't pretend to be a biblical scholar," North conceded, but by publishing with B&H he was free to develop his story's religious dimensions. "Faith and fiction can work together," he explained. B&H, meanwhile, saw North's books as a way to break into the mainstream market. B&H published other works of fiction, but none by authors with as much "stature and selling potential" as North; to promote the book, North visited 58 cities over the course of thirty days, traveling the country on a bus formerly used by Dolly Parton's band, dubbed the "Dolly-Ollie bus." Banking on a bestseller, B&H reportedly issued a first printing of 350,000 copies.[19]

North continued to publish installments in his fiction series alongside a number of nonfiction titles including *A Greater Freedom: Stories of Faith from Operation Iraqi Freedom* and *American Heroes in the Fight Against Radical Islam*. The latter criticized Americans for being squeamish about pointing out that those trying to destroy the American way of life were, "almost exclusively, radical Muslim males." The primary purpose of the book, however, was to showcase the heroism of American soldiers fighting against Islam. North insisted that it wasn't about glorifying war; war was terrible, of course. He simply wanted to show brave American soldiers as they really were, as "part of the brightest, best educated, trained, led, and equipped military any nation has ever had." And they were deeply religious. North told of a "little choir of Marines" performing "the manliest rendition of 'Amazing Grace' " he'd ever heard, and of servicemen tucking Bibles into their flak jackets and flocking to chapel services, Bible studies, and prayer sessions. In combat, men might "take vulgar language to the level of a new art form," but when the shooting stopped, they could be found reading their Bibles in a quiet moment.[20]

In *American Heroes* North also recounted a conversation with a Parisian reporter who had accused President Bush of "swashbuckling around the planet like President John Wayne." North was clearly delighted by the comparison, though he was fairly certain the reporter was thinking of Ronald Reagan, not John Wayne. It was an honest mistake. On another occasion, a European female news correspondent was overheard asking—or was it telling—one of the marines that she had "never seen so much bravado, machismo, or arrogance" in her life. The young NCO appeared to mull over her grievance before replying, "Yes ma'am, that's why they call themselves U.S. Marines." Sometimes truth was better than fiction, if North's accounts of these conversations could be believed.[21]

North persisted in blaming the American media for failing to support the troops—for neglecting to cover the heroes' welcome they received in Iraq and focusing instead on the looting, "the destruction of 'cultural sites,'" and problems getting water and electricity up and running again. All this seemed "grievously unfair to these boys-turned-men who had fought so hard and sacrificed so much." To make matters worse, the media was implying that US soldiers died for nothing, a technique "perfected during Vietnam," he maintained. Vietnam wasn't lost during Tet '68; it was lost "in the pages of America's newspapers, on our televisions, our college campuses—and eventually in the corridors of power in Washington." For those who claimed to support the troops but not the war in Iraq or Afghanistan, North had nothing but contempt. Thankfully, President Bush never wavered in his support for the troops. His field commanders "were cut from the same tempered steel." Real leaders knew to ignore "the bashing they got for being too aggressive." They knew how to keep after the enemy.[22]

North had written *American Heroes* with the assistance of Chuck Holton. A one-time Airborne Ranger, Holton was a popular writer in the same genre. In 2003, Holton had begun reporting for the Christian Broadcasting Network as "adventure correspondent," and that same year he published *A More Elite Soldier*. Stu Weber, stalwart of the evangelical men's movement, called Holton's book "*Pilgrim's Progress* in camouflage"—an account of a soldier's journey into manhood, and into spiritual maturity. According to Holton, "life *is* combat," and combat wasn't for the weak; in basic training, the weak were eliminated. When Holton put on his black beret it symbolized his status as a member of an elite group of warriors, a unit "set apart and held to higher standards" in order to defend the freedom of their countrymen, many of whom were oblivious to or ungrateful for their sacrifice. The pride Holton felt in being an elite soldier was inextricably linked to this concept of being set apart by God, "called out of the ranks of ordinary soldiers, and given a more difficult assignment to fulfill for Him." In accepting this mission, Holton had entered a brotherhood of shared belief, hardship, and purpose. Of course war was distasteful, yet still "somehow glorious." Most of life's obstacles could be overcome "by exerting a little over ten pounds of pressure with a trigger finger." Upon reflection, Holton realized that Jesus himself would have made "an outstanding NCO."[23]

That same year Holton coauthored *Stories from a Soldier's Heart: For the Patriotic Soul*. The book included stories from John McCain, Stu Weber, and Bill Gothard, along with a confessional written by a former Vietnam-era protestor who acknowledged the "extreme narcissism" of the counterculture and expressed regret for failing to properly honor the men who served their country. Eldredge's influence on these authors was clear: "Deep down, all guys want to be warriors," to engage in "an epic battle," to be the hero. *Braveheart*'s William Wallace offered words of wisdom: "Every man dies, but not every man truly lives." The message of this collection was the same as that of Holton's *A More Elite Soldier*: the American soldier modeled true Christian manhood.[24]

Like North, Chuck Holton tried his hand at fiction, too. His fictional universe was populated by heroic military men and vulnerable women drawn to their physical strength. It was a world where a diabolical Islamic menace posed an imminent threat. Fortunately, there were brave and good men "willing to do the dirty work necessary to keep evil men at bay." Make no mistake—this was a gruesome task. But since evil men understood no language but violence, "good men must open the dialogue and finish the argument in that language." Holton believed it was critical that the military "be given the latitude and resources to do the job right." In his 2009 novel *Meltdown*, one of Holton's characters, a colonel, takes aim at "namby-pamby politicians" who lacked "the stones" necessary "to chase the jihadis back into their caves for good," preferring instead to conduct tiresome investigations "into whether our troops were being gentle enough with the savages who were out to murder them." This wasn't just cowardly, it was treasonous. And what of peaceful Muslims in America? He wasn't seeing any. Holton published his fictional series with Multnomah, a Christian publisher that also published Stu Weber, James Dobson, Steve Farrar, Josh Harris, and John Piper.[25]

IN COLORADO SPRINGS, militant masculinity was entrenched within the heart of American evangelicalism. From the evangelical bastions of New Life Church and Focus on the Family, this militant faith was exported to the military itself. Meanwhile, military men were refashioning Christianity in their own image, and offering their own brand of militant evangelicalism for broader consumption. As the writings of Oliver North and Chuck Holton attest, this militant faith was often virulently Islamophobic. Men like James Dobson and Ted Haggard also traded in anti-Islamic tropes. As in the Cold War era, for all their militant rhetoric and supreme confidence that God was on their side, evangelicals seemed curiously fearful. In twenty-first century evangelicalism, the threat of radical Islam loomed large. Yet upon closer examination, this fear appears suspect. On the part of evangelical leaders, at the very least, fear of Islam appeared to be nothing more than an attempt to drum up support for the militant faith they were hawking.

Chapter 13

WHY WE WANT
TO KILL YOU

I N THE WAKE OF SEPTEMBER 11, ISLAM REPLACED communism as the enemy of America and all that was good, at least in the world of conservative evangelicalism. "The Muslims have become the modern-day equivalent of the Evil Empire," explained the NAE's Richard Cizik. Evangelicals' pro-Israel sympathies had fueled anti-Muslim sentiments even before the terrorist attacks, and in the 1990s, as evangelicals looked for alternatives to a foreign policy agenda long framed by Cold War categories, many had turned their attention to the persecution of Christians in other nations, attention that often ended up focusing on the oppression of Christian minorities in Islamic countries. After September 11, the long history of Christian Zionism and heightened interest in the fate of global Christians became inter-twined with evangelicals' commitment to defend Christian America. Once again, the line between good and evil was clearly drawn. In the days after the attack, President Bush spoke of ridding "the world of evil-doers," and he warned Americans that "this crusade, this war on terrorism, is going to take a while." Some found this rhetoric disturb-ing, prompting Bush to set aside talk of crusades and take pains to distinguish Islamic extremism from the faith as a whole. But to con-servative evangelicals, such language made perfect sense.[1]

Billy Graham's son Franklin called Islam "a very evil and wicked religion." Pat Robertson assured his viewers that Muslims were "worse than the Nazis." James Dobson began to characterize Islamic fundamentalism as one of the most serious threats to American families, explaining that "the security of our homeland and the welfare of our children" were, after all, "family values." Ted Haggard agreed, insisting that spiritual warfare required "a virile worldly counterpart" lest his kids "grow up in an Islamic state." In the fall of 2002, 77 percent of evangelical leaders held an overall unfavorable view of Islam, and 70 percent agreed that Islam was "a religion of violence." Two-thirds also believed that Islam was "dedicated to world domination."[2]

The Christian publishing industry helped fuel evangelical fear and strengthen support for preemptive war. Alongside Bible studies and devotionals, Christian bookstores stocked foreign policy titles such as *From Iraq to Armageddon* and *Iran: The Coming Crisis*, along with books such as *Secrets of the Koran, Married to Muhammed*, and *The Islamic Invasion. New Man*, the magazine of the Promise Keepers movement, carried ads for Mike Evans's *The Final Move Beyond Iraq: The Final Solution While the World Sleeps*, which issued a call for Americans to awaken to the threat of Islamofascism, "the greatest threat America has faced since the Civil War." The message was clear: the Islamic threat demanded a robust military response. Even the Quiverfull movement participated in this rhetoric, noting that children would provide combatants in the war against Islam. And, of course, authors like Oliver North and Chuck Holton turned to fiction to stir up fear of radical Islam. But evangelicals also peddled fiction as fact in their effort to raise the alarm about the threat Islam posed to America, and to American Christians in particular.[3]

IN THE AFTERMATH OF 9/11, several "ex-Muslim terrorists" took the evangelical speaking circuit by storm, offering audiences a firsthand account of the Islamic threat. The most influential of these were the Caner brothers, Ergun and Emir, whose 2002 book *Unveiling Islam: An Insider's Look at Muslim Life and Beliefs* was a runaway bestseller in evangelical circles. The brothers had converted to Christianity in their teens, after Ergun attended a Baptist revival meeting, and they ended up at Criswell College in Dallas, where they met Paige Patterson, Criswell's president. Patterson became like "a surrogate father," and when Patterson left Criswell in 1991 to take up a position at Southeastern Baptist Theological Seminary, they followed. It was Patterson who convinced them to write *Unveiling Islam* after the terror attacks, and in its first year the book sold 100,000 copies; it would eventually approach 200,000 in sales.[4]

In *Unveiling Islam*, the Caners told of growing up as devout Muslims, but after the attacks on America they felt compelled to expose the faith as violent and dangerous. War was "not a sidebar of history for Islam," they wrote, but "the main vehicle for religious expression." Muslims quickly raised red flags concerning a number of assertions in the book, accusing the brothers of "either purposely or ignorantly" presenting "half-truth after half-truth, mischaracterization after mischaracterization and falsehood after falsehood." But the book told conservative evangelicals exactly what they wanted to hear.[5]

Inspired by the Caners' book, Jerry Vines, former president of the SBC, denounced Islam in provocative language: "Christianity was founded by the virgin-born son of God, Jesus Christ. Islam was founded by Muhammad, a demon-possessed pedophile who had 12 wives, the last of which was a 9-year-old girl." Speaking on the eve of the Southern Baptists' annual convention in 2002, Vines denied that Muslims and Christians worshiped the same God: "Allah is not Jehovah," he insisted, and "Jehovah's not going to turn you into a terrorist." (When President Bush addressed the SBC gathering via satellite the next day, praising Baptists as "among the earliest champions of religious tolerance and freedom," the irony was not lost on some observers.) Vines's claims struck many as extremist, but he quickly drew the support of fellow evangelicals. Falwell jumped to his friend's defense, explaining how Vines had hard evidence from *Unveiling Islam*. "If you want to raise the ire of the mainstream press and the swarm of politically-correct organizations in this nation, just criticize Islam [as Dr. Vines learned]," Falwell wrote to his newsletter subscribers. When asked about his support for Vines a few months later, Falwell didn't mince words: "I think Mohammed was a terrorist." Falwell's remarks unleashed a global furor. The Iranian foreign minister condemned Falwell's comments, intimating that they were "part of a propaganda war by the US mass media and the Zionists" intent on sparking "war among civilisations." The British foreign secretary called Falwell's comments "outrageous and insulting." In India and Kashmir protests erupted; in the Indian town of Solapur violence left at least eight people dead. Falwell ended up apologizing, claiming he "intended no disrespect to any sincere, law-abiding Muslim."[6]

In 2003, Falwell hired Ergun Caner to teach at Liberty University's School of Religion, and in 2005 Caner was appointed dean of the school's seminary, the first former Muslim to head an evangelical seminary. Caner saw himself as part of "a new generation of new evangelists who are provocative, cultural and yet conservative"—a generation who would "sit in the back of the bus no more." He gained a reputation for his "sometimes politically incorrect style." Speaking before predominantly white evangelical audiences, Caner was known to mock black Christians and make fun of Mexicans—they were good for roofing and lawn care. Under Caner's dynamic leadership, seminary enrollment tripled. The Caner brand of Islamophobia continued to sell, and the brothers became among the most sought-after speakers on the evangelical circuit. Televangelist John Ankerberg promoted Caner's teachings across his media empire, reaching an estimated 147 million viewers along with millions more through his global radio and online presence. Booked years out at evangelical churches and schools, the Caners were also invited to speak to law enforcement and active-duty military.[7]

The more Caner spoke, the more he embellished his story, spinning yarns of growing up in Turkey and being trained as a jihadist intent on destroying Christian civilization. Eventually Caner's tales started to catch up with him. Muslim and Christian bloggers began to dispute many of his claims. He hadn't grown up in Turkey, but rather had been born in Sweden and at age three moved to Ohio. After his parents' divorce he was raised by his Swedish Lutheran mother. He'd never been involved in Islamic jihad, he hadn't bravely debated dozens of Muslims, and his thick Middle Eastern accent was a sham. Moreover, he got basic facts wrong about Islam. In the spring of 2010, Liberty University investigated allegations against Caner but declined to take action; Liberty's board concluded that he'd "done nothing theologically inappropriate." Not about to let facts get in the way of a greater truth, Focus on the Family decided to rerun a 2001 interview with Caner in which he had put forward many of the now-disputed claims. Critics, however, refused to back down, and in the summer of 2010 Liberty bowed to pressure and demoted Caner, though he would stay on as professor. Even then, they attributed the move to "discrepancies related to matters such as dates, names and places of residence," hardly the full-throated censure critics were demanding.[8]

The Caner brothers weren't the only "self-proclaimed former Islamic terrorists" making the rounds on the evangelical speaking circuit in the wake of 9/11. Together, Walid Shoebat, Zachariah Anani, and Kamal Saleem formed their own "traveling anti-Muslim sideshow." Shoebat, a Palestinian American evangelical convert, claimed to have been a member of the PLO and to have bombed an Israeli bank. Anani, a Lebanese-born Canadian, claimed to have joined a militia at the age of thirteen, "trained to become a black belt and an expert with daggers and knives," and to have killed hundreds of people before meeting a Southern Baptist missionary and getting saved. It was Saleem's story, however, that was most remarkable—so remarkable that one journalist dubbed him the "Forrest Gump of the Middle East." Born in Lebanon, Saleem claimed to have been recruited by the PLO *and* the Muslim Brotherhood, taught to shoot an AK-47 by none other than Palestinian nationalist resistance leader and cofounder of Fatah, Abu Jihad, and touted as a model warrior by Yasser Arafat himself. By his own account, Saleem then moved to the United States to wage "Cultural Jihad on America." He went to the Bible Belt so he could "take on the best of the best." But then a Christian physician—and the voice of

Jesus—led to his conversion to evangelical Christianity. He became an evangelist spreading the good news of the gospel and warning of an ominous Islamic threat.[9]

It was after Saleem came to his Christian college campus that Doug Howard, an expert on the Ottoman empire, began to look more closely at Saleem's backstory. Saleem had claimed to be a descendent of "the Grand Wazir of Islam," but Howard knew there was no such thing as a "Grand Wazir." He discovered that Saleem's real name was Khodor Shami, that he had worked for Pat Robertson's CBN for sixteen years and in 2003 had joined the staff at Focus on the Family. In 2006 he'd founded his own nonprofit, Koome Ministries, from which he drew a salary and a generous expense account. Determined to get to the bottom of Saleem's nonsensical claims, Howard contacted Jim Daly, president of Focus on the Family, in the fall of 2007. Focus on the Family had been actively promoting an anti-Islamic agenda as part of its ministry, so Howard was surprised to learn that they, too, had become skeptical of Saleem's claims—not only his tales of a violent terrorist past, but even his claim to have kicked a game-winning field goal for the Oklahoma Sooners. (Saleem/Shami never played for the Sooners.) They had not, however, gone public with their doubts. Nor were they eager to do so.[10]

The narratives of Saleem's fellow "former terrorists" didn't hold up any better under scrutiny. In the words of a former Canadian security expert, Anani was "not an individual who rates the slightest degree of credibility." The *Jerusalem Post*, meanwhile, called into question Shoebat's entire story. It turns out that religion played little role in his upbringing and there was no record of him bombing a bank. As Howard put it, "the most extreme thing he ever did was attaching Palestinian flag stickers to utility poles around town."[11]

Despite the numerous holes in their stories, all three "ex-terrorists" remained sought-after authorities in evangelical circles. Shoebat was "a favorite of the 'Left Behind' crowd," addressing Tim LaHaye's Pre-Trib Research Center and John Hagee's Christians United for Israel events. He was also a featured speaker at the 2008 BattleCry convention, the

initiative founded in the mid-2000s to recruit a younger generation
of culture warriors, backed by Pat Robertson and Charles Colson.
All three continued to speak at Christian colleges, conferences, and
churches, and on Christian radio and television. They appeared on
major news networks as experts on terrorism, spoke at prestigious uni-
versities and, in 2008, at the air force academy in Colorado Springs.[12]

The popularity of these "ex-Muslim terrorists" casts in stark relief
the dynamics of an evangelical politics of fear. Trafficking in a pornography of violence, these "experts" divulged graphic stories purportedly
revealing the sadistic violence of Islam, and in doing so dehumanized
Muslims while goading Americans (and especially American Christians) to respond with violence of their own. With books like the not-
so-subtly-titled *Why We Want to Kill You*, they positioned American
Christians as victims, thereby justifying an extreme response. They
accused any and all detractors of having ties to Islamic terrorism and
used imagined threats of violence to bolster their own credibility.
Anani claimed to have survived fifteen attempts on his life. Saleem
claimed that the Muslim Brotherhood "put a $25 million bounty on
his head" and warned that he had "a band of dangerous middle East-
erners on his trail." (Local law enforcement had no record of purported
assassination attempts.)[13]

It's not hard to see what this titillating narrative of imagined violence got the "ex-terrorists." They sold books, collected speaking fees,
and padded their own pockets. But what did it do for evangelicals
who promoted their books, engaged them as speakers, and gave them
a platform?[14]

Stoking fear in the hearts of American Christians played into the
hands of conservative evangelical leaders, too. Just as Jack Hyles, Jerry
Falwell, and Mark Driscoll had stage-managed in their own churches,
evangelicals in post-9/11 America enhanced their own power by ratcheting up a sense of threat—a tactic that only worked within a militarized framework. Leaders claimed the moral high ground while
validating their own aggression. In this way, the popularity of fraudulent ex-Muslim terrorists casts into stark relief the relationship between

militarism and fear. Were evangelicals embracing an increasingly militant faith in response to a new threat from the Islamic world? Or were they creating the perception of threat to justify their own militancy and enhance their own power, individually and collectively? By inciting fears of an Islamic threat, men like Falwell, Patterson, Vines, and Dobson heightened the value of the "protection" they promised—and with it, their own power.

Not all evangelicals jumped on the anti-Muslim bandwagon. In 2007, nearly 300 Christian leaders signed the "Yale Letter," a call for Christians and Muslims to work together for peace. Published in the *New York Times*, the letter was signed by several prominent evangelical leaders, including megachurch pastors Rick Warren and Bill Hybels, *Christianity Today* editor David Neff, emerging church leader Brian McLaren, Jim Wallis of Sojourners, and Rich Mouw, president of evangelical Fuller Seminary. Notably, Leith Anderson, president of the NAE, and Richard Cizik, the NAE's chief lobbyist, also signed the letter.[15]

Other evangelical leaders, however, voiced strenuous opposition. Al Mohler, president of Southern Baptist Theological Seminary, found no need to apologize for the War on Terror or to confess any sins "against our Muslim neighbors." It was all quite confounding to him: "For whom are we apologizing and for what are we apologizing?" Dobson's *Citizen* magazine criticized the Yale Letter for claiming that the two faiths shared a deity, and for showing weakness and endangering Christians. Apologizing for past violence against Muslims would make Christians in Muslim countries more vulnerable to violence, he reasoned. Focus on the Family urged like-minded critics to register their displeasure with the NAE and included the NAE's PO box for their convenience. Dobson and other conservative evangelicals pressured the NAE to oust Cizik that year, both for his attempts at Muslim-Christian dialogue and for his activism on global warming. This was easily accomplished the next year, when Cizik came out in support of same-sex civil unions.[16]

Most evangelicals appeared to side with Dobson and Mohler. In

2007, white evangelical Protestants continued to register more negative views of Muslims than other demographics, and to persist in their
belief that Islam encouraged violence. A 2009 survey also revealed
that evangelicals were significantly more likely than other religious
groups to approve of the use of torture against suspected terrorists.
Sixty-two percent agreed that torture could be justified "often" or
"sometimes," compared to 46 percent of mainline Protestants and
40 percent of unaffiliated respondents. The widespread embrace of a
militant Christian nationalism would have far-reaching consequences
in the age of terror.[17]

SCATTERED THROUGHOUT THE MILITARY, including at the
highest levels of leadership, evangelicals who had embraced a militant
interpretation of their faith used their positions of power to advance
their religious agenda, which they saw as wholly fused with their military mission. Such was the case for Lt. Gen. William G. (Jerry) Boykin.

In the course of a storied military career, Boykin served in an Airborne division in Vietnam and as a Delta Force commander, participated in the failed Iranian hostage rescue in 1980 and in the invasion
of Grenada, and took part, too, in the mission to apprehend Panama-
nian dictator Manuel Noriega and the failed 1993 Somalian mission
of "Black Hawk Down." He later served at the CIA, and from 2002
to 2007 as under secretary of defense for intelligence under President
Bush. In that capacity he played an important role in the War on
Terror.[18]

In the wake of 9/11, President Bush worked to consolidate control
over the military and intelligence communities. His immediate concern was the war in Iraq, but the administration had declared war on
"bad guys" everywhere, and he and his national security advisors were
already looking ahead to Iran. By issuing executive orders and placing the War on Terror under the Pentagon's control, Bush essentially
enabled Donald Rumsfeld to pursue the war off the books, free from
restrictions imposed on the CIA, including the oversight of Senate

and House intelligence committees. Rumsfeld had two key deputies in this effort: Stephen Cambone, a neoconservative defense intellectual known for his dictatorial style, and Jerry Boykin.[19]

Cambone set out to circumvent both the CIA and the State Department, and with his special-ops experience, Boykin "was the action hero" at Cambone's side. The partnership was, according to one military intelligence source, "a melding of 'ignorance and recklessness.'" This sort of workaround wasn't unprecedented. A secret counter-insurgency program called the Phoenix Program had been instituted during the Vietnam War, and in the 1980s a covert unit had been created after the failed attempt to rescue American hostages in Iran; deployed against the Sandinistas in Nicaragua, it helped lay the groundwork for the Iran-Contra connection. In the twenty-first century, under Rumsfeld's leadership, the Pentagon was ready to fight fire with fire. "The only way we can win is to go unconventional," explained an American advisor to the civilian authority in Baghdad. "We're going to have to play their game. Guerrilla versus guerrilla. Terrorism versus terrorism. We've got to scare the Iraqis into submission." Another official concurred: "It's not the way we usually play ball, but if you see a couple of your guys get blown away it changes things. We did the American things—and we've been the nice guy. Now we're going to be the bad guy, and being the bad guy works." Not everyone agreed. As one Pentagon advisor put it, "I'm as tough as anybody, but we're also a democratic society, and we don't fight terror with terror." Rumsfeld, however, had been given the power to effectively establish "a global free-fire zone."[20]

A devout evangelical, Boykin pursued his assignment zealously. And he wasn't afraid to talk about it. He was a frequent speaker at conservative Christian events, especially at Baptist and Pentecostal churches, and he nearly always appeared in uniform. A "circuit rider for the religious right," he worked in tandem with the Faith Force Multiplier, a group whose manifesto advocated applying military principles to evangelism. Boykin depicted the War on Terror as "an enduring battle against Satan" and assured fellow Christians that God had placed President Bush in power, "that radical Muslims hate America," and that the military was "recruiting a spiritual army" to defeat its enemy. Part of Boykin's mission involved evading the Geneva Conventions, and he appeared to be working to replace international law with his own notion of biblical law. He understood himself to be in God's direct chain of command. President Bush, too, was "appointed by God" to root out evildoers. Clearly, they answered only to the highest power.[21]

When word of Boykin's speeches came out, Arab and Muslim groups accused him of bigotry and demanded his removal. Members of the Senate Armed Services Committee called for an inquiry and for Boykin to step down until cleared of wrongdoing, but Rumsfeld backed Boykin, and he retained his position. The report concluded that Boykin had violated three internal regulations, but the substance of his remarks was not addressed; a senior defense official called the report a "complete exoneration," finding Boykin responsible only for a few "relatively minor offenses," technical and bureaucratic matters. Boykin emerged from the situation largely unscathed. Chuck Holton later had his fictional colonel come to Boykin's defense: "Boykin got flambéed in the press for telling it like it is," for saying "this war is against radical Islam, and the press tried to crucify him for it."[22]

Boykin, however, had other things on his mind. At the height of the scandal, he was also engaged in a covert operation to "gitmoize" the Abu Ghraib prison in Iraq. Boykin had flown to Iraq to meet with the commander of Guantanamo, who had been called to Baghdad to brief military commanders on interrogation techniques. Under Rumsfeld's command, Cambone introduced these methods—both physical coercion and sexual humiliation—at Abu Ghraib to extract intelligence on the Iraqi insurgence. All of this was carried out secretly within the Defense Department. When news, including photographs, leaked of the tactics being employed, members of the 372nd Military Police Company took the fall. Boykin remained at his post until his retirement in 2007.[23]

Even after his retirement, Boykin pressed his agenda. He founded Kingdom Warriors, an organization to promote militarized Christianity, and he accepted a position as executive vice president of the Family Research Council. He also published *Never Surrender: A Soldier's Journey to the Crossroads of Faith and Freedom*, a book endorsed by kindred spirits Oliver North and Stu Weber. Boykin decided not to submit the book to the Pentagon for advance review and ended up receiving "a scathing reprimand" after a criminal investigation revealed that the book disclosed classified information. Boykin was unrepentant, insisting that the censure was payback for his vocal objections to the Pentagon, particularly his opposition to the integration of women in the military. In 2014 Boykin published another book, coauthored with "terrorism expert" Kamal Saleem. CBN featured Boykin and Saleem on *The Watchman*, a program devoted to exposing how "radical Islam" was on the march around the world, and the Family Research Council touted their dystopian exploration of "what happens when Islam rules" as an "exciting merger of reality and fiction."[24]

EVANGELICALS WEREN'T the only ones renegotiating their views on foreign policy in the post–Cold War era, nor were they the only ones who thought President Clinton's pursuit of humanitarian wars and peacekeeping missions betrayed American interests and values. During the 1990s, a group of young conservative intellectuals developed a plan for how America should brandish its unrivaled military and economic power, and though they were not particularly religious, these self-described neoconservatives did have faith—an expansive faith in American power. And they had their own patron saints: Teddy Roosevelt and Ronald Reagan. They believed that there was a direct connection between domestic and global issues, and, by invoking patriotism to encourage sacrifice, they sought to instill "military virtues" in the American public. For these neocons, the military embodied the nation's highest ideals even as it unleashed violence and death, and there was no contradiction. War would provide Americans with "moral clarity."[25]

The neoconservative agenda meshed exceedingly well with evangelical militarism. To the chagrin of neoconservatives, Bush had campaigned on a more restrained foreign policy, but the terror attacks had changed everything. In his 2002 State of the Union, the evangelical president christened Iraq, Iran, and North Korea the "axis of evil" and suggested that preemptive war might be in order. Prominent neocons, including Paul Wolfowitz, Paul Bremer, and Stephen Cambone, were already ensconced in the administration, and Secretary of Defense Donald Rumsfeld and Vice President Dick Cheney were sympathetic to neocons' calls for military action. The invasion of Iraq provided the state of perpetual war that neoconservatives—and many evangelicals—had longed for. And it transformed President Bush into a warrior president, an identity memorably enacted in his "Mission Accomplished" speech on the deck of the USS *Abraham Lincoln*.[26]

Whereas in previous generations a sense of the inherent risk of war had prevailed, a sense that war could lead to unintended consequences and that military power was "something that democracies ought to treat gingerly," by the early 2000s this sense had all but disappeared. With evangelicals in the vanguard, Americans had come to see the military as a bastion of "traditional values and old-fashioned virtue," a view only possible by turning a blind eye to reports of military misconduct and sexual abuse within the ranks. Members of the military tended to agree with assessments of their superior virtue, although some senior officials did express reservations, suggesting that such tendencies were not healthy in armed forces serving a democracy. But there were no serious checks on this inclination. When civilians become the leading militarists, the very concept of civilian control of the military loses its potency.[27]

AFTER THE CONFUSION and frustration of the 1990s, conservative evangelicals had regained their footing in 2001. The election of George W. Bush placed a kindred spirit back in the White House, and the terror attacks ensured that foreign policy was once again framed by a clear battle between evildoers and Christian America. By the end of Bush's second term, however, evangelical confidence once again began to falter. As the death toll mounted among US forces in Iraq, support for the war diminished among Americans generally, and among American evangelicals. Evangelicals still supported the war at rates significantly higher than the general public, but between September 2006 and January 2007 white evangelical Protestants who believed the United States made the right decision in using force in Iraq to oust Saddam Hussein dropped from 71 percent to 58 percent. White evangelical support for the president reflected a similar disenchantment. Seventy-nine percent of white evangelicals had supported Bush's 2004 reelection, but as his warrior status diminished, his approval rate steadily declined.[28]

Support for the president dropped most precipitously among younger white evangelicals. In 2002, 87 percent of white evangelicals ages eighteen to twenty-nine approved of the president's job performance; by August 2007, his approval rating among this group had dropped by 42 percentage points, with most of the decline (25 points) occurring since 2005. Younger evangelicals weren't just unhappy with the president; since 2005, Republican Party affiliation among this demographic had dropped by 15 percentage points. For leaders of the Christian Right this was cause for alarm. As the end of Bush's presidency neared, they looked ahead with trepidation. To their dismay, they were presented with two unsatisfactory choices for his successor.[29]

Chapter 14

SPIRITUAL
BADASSES

SENATOR JOHN MCCAIN WAS A REPUBLICAN WAR
hero who attended a Southern Baptist megachurch, but he had
never embraced culture-wars evangelicalism. In 2000, when running
against George W. Bush in the Republican primary, he had denounced
those who practiced "the politics of division and slander" in the name
of religion, party, or nation, and he urged voters to resist "agents of
intolerance," by which he meant men like Pat Robertson and Jerry Falwell. The next day McCain lost the Virginia primary, and nine days
later he withdrew his candidacy. For the 2008 election, McCain tried
to smooth things over with the Religious Right, even giving the commencement address at Falwell's Liberty University. But it was clear to
evangelicals that McCain was not one of them. James Dobson certainly
wasn't buying it. Flexing his own political muscle, Dobson insisted that
he "cannot and will not" vote for McCain, whom he deemed insufficiently conservative on social issues. Yet for Dobson, and for most
evangelicals, the Democratic candidate was far more troubling.[1]

An African American with the middle name of Hussein, Barack
Obama challenged the values—spoken and unspoken—that many
white evangelicals held dear. As an adult convert to Christianity, he
could speak with eloquence and theological sophistication about his
faith, but for many evangelicals this mattered little. For some, racial
prejudice shaped their political leanings. But even for those who did
not hold explicit racist convictions, their faith remained intertwined

with their whiteness. Although white evangelicals and black Protestants shared similar views on a number of theological and moral issues, the black Protestant tradition was suffused with a prophetic theology that clashed with white evangelicals' Christian nationalism. It's worth remembering that for both Barack and Michelle Obama, their unforgivable sins—at least as far as conservative white evangelicals were concerned—involved their critique of America. For Michelle, it was a confession she made while stumping for her husband; reflecting on the engagement of his supporters, she declared that, "for the first time" in her adult life, she was proud of her country because "it feels like hope is finally making a comeback." Conservatives pounced. Hadn't Michelle been an adult when the Cold War was won? Was there nothing to be proud of in the last twenty-five years of American history? For her part, Cindy McCain was quick to assert that she had *always* been proud of her country.[2]

For Barack Obama, it was a controversy involving his pastor, the Reverend Jeremiah Wright, that threatened to derail his campaign. Shortly after the September 11 attacks, Wright had reminded Americans that their country had displaced Native Americans by way of "terror," had bombed Grenada, Panama, Libya, Hiroshima, and Nagasaki, and had supported state terrorism against the Palestinians and in South Africa. Quoting Malcolm X, he warned that "America's chickens are coming home to roost." A 2003 sermon also came to light in which Wright uttered the memorable phrase "God damn America"—a phrase he qualified by adding, "as long as she keeps trying to act like she is God and she is supreme!" That sermon was a tirade against militarization, against those "blinded by a culture of war." War, the military, colonization, occupation, regime change—none of these things would bring peace, Wright insisted. They would only bring more violence. Wright critiqued the "few Muslims" who called for jihad, but he also criticized Christians calling for "crusade," Christians who condoned the killing of civilians, collateral damage, "shock and awe" tactics, preemptive strikes, and the unilateral takeover of another nation while secure in the notion that the ends justified the means, that God would bless their efforts. Wright, too, condemned the nation's legacy of racism, the lie that all men were created equal when it only really applied to white men. And he called out more recent lies, like those orchestrated by Oliver North, and the false pretenses used to justify the Iraq War: "This government lied in its founding documents and the government is still lying today." To white evangelicals steeped in Christian nationalism, this was blasphemy.[3]

To quell the controversy, Obama gave one of the most powerful speeches of his political career. He professed his "unyielding faith in the decency and generosity of the American people" even as he acknowledged the Constitution's unfinished work, the need to extend liberty and justice to all people. He criticized his pastor's "incendiary language" that denigrated "both the greatness and the goodness of our nation," and he denounced "the perverse and hateful ideologies of radical Islam." Yet he insisted that there was more to Wright than such rhetoric suggested; his church contained "in full the kindness and cruelty, the fierce intelligence and the shocking ignorance, the struggles and successes, the love and yes, the bitterness and bias that make up the black experience in America," and he could no more disown Reverend Wright than he could disown the black community, or his white grandmother. "These people are a part of me. And they are a part of America, this country that I love." Obama's avowal of love for country was enough for many Americans, but not for most evangelicals.[4]

Within the evangelical community, Dobson emerged as Obama's fiercest critic. In June 2008 he lashed out at Obama on his radio program, accusing him of distorting the Bible to fit his worldview, of having a "fruitcake interpretation of the Constitution," and of appealing to the "lowest common denominator of morality." Dobson especially took issue with a speech Obama had given in 2006 in which he had defended the right of people of faith to bring their religious beliefs into the public square, while also pointing out that Christians disagreed among themselves on how best to do so. Whose Christianity would win out? "Would we go with James Dobson's, or Al Sharpton's?" Obama had asked. "Which passages of Scripture should guide our public policy?" Should Old Testament passages dictate that slavery was acceptable but eating shellfish was not? "Or should we just stick to the Sermon on the Mount—a passage that is so radical that it's doubtful that our own Defense Department would survive its application?" Dobson was not amused.[5]

It wasn't clear, however, if Dobson's opinion still mattered. With young evangelicals' apparent defection from the politics of the Religious Right, and from the Republican Party, it seemed by 2008 that "the old lions of the Christian Right" were "suddenly sputtering," as one journalist remarked. During the campaign, some evangelicals came to Obama's defense. Before his departure, the NAE's Richard Cizik had provided assurances that Obama was indeed "a fellow brother in Christ." Megachurch pastor Rick Warren welcomed Obama to his church, and a number of evangelicals worked to broaden "values issues" to include poverty, the environment, and health care. It was McCain's surprising choice of Alaska governor Sarah Palin as his running mate that helped the old guard regroup, remaking the election into a familiar culture-wars contest. McCain's pick changed Dobson's tune. The selection of Palin was "one of the most exciting days" of his life. Palin quickly drew praise from Family Research Council Action president Tony Perkins, from the Christian Coalition's president Roberta Combs, and from Richard Land.[6]

Palin's candidacy, however, raised the issue of gender. For evangelicals who believed in male headship, was it appropriate for a woman to be in such a position of power? If the alternative was Barack Obama, then the answer they gave was yes. Days before the 2008 election, John Piper wrote a blog post with the title, "Why a Woman Shouldn't Run for Vice President, but Wise People May Still Vote for Her." Piper made clear that he still believed that "the Bible summons men to bear the burden of primary leadership, provision, and protection," and that "the Bible does not encourage us to think of nations as blessed when women hold the reins of national authority." But a woman could hold the highest office if her male opponent would do far more harm by "exalting a flawed pattern of womanhood."[7]

However, for most evangelicals, supporting Palin wasn't really a lesser-of-two-evils scenario. Raised in nondenominational evangelicalism with a dose of Pentecostalism, Palin was a self-described "Bible-believing Christian," a down-to-earth candidate ("just your average hockey mom") who appealed to plain-folk evangelicals, to those tired of being disparaged by "liberal elites." She was also a creationist, she was staunchly pro-gun and anti-abortion, and she had just given birth to her fifth child, who had Down syndrome. But Palin didn't only, or even primarily, project a maternal image. A former beauty queen, she embodied an ideal of feminine beauty that had been elevated to a new level of spiritual—and political—significance. She was the ultimate culture warrior, a Phyllis Schlafly for a new generation, a moose-hunting pit bull in lipstick who could give feminists a run for their money, without compromising her sex appeal. In this way, Palin embodied the conservative ideal that "their" women knew how to please men. And Palin delighted in undermining the masculinity of liberal men, especially Barack Obama. Many voters found Palin's unpredictability and general ignorance of world affairs disqualifying, but to many evangelicals, she was, in the words of Richard Land, "a *rock star.*"[8]

SEVENTY-FOUR PERCENT of white evangelicals voted for the McCain/Palin ticket. But 24 percent of white evangelicals—up 4 percent from 2004—broke ranks and voted for Obama. The Obama campaign had targeted moderate white evangelicals, the sort who had been voting Republican for twenty years but who wanted to expand the list of "moral values" to include things like poverty, climate change, human rights, and the environment. Obama doubled his support among white evangelicals ages eighteen to twenty-nine compared to Kerry's in 2004, and nearly doubled his support among those ages thirty to forty-four. Scholars and pundits alike started to declare the end of the culture wars, and to look ahead to "the end of white Christian America." The old guard was shaken.[9]

But militant evangelicalism was always at its strongest with a clear enemy to fight. Two weeks before the election, with an Obama victory appearing likely, one Colorado Springs pastor reminded fellow evangelicals of this: "This could be the best thing that ever happened to the evangelical cause. . . . We're used to being against the tide." He was right. The presidency of Barack Obama would strengthen evangelicals' sense of embattlement and embolden the more militant voices within the movement.[10]

Race had been central to the formation of white evangelicals' political and cultural identity, and so it's not surprising that evangelical opposition to the first African American president would reflect a belief in his "otherness." Explicit expressions of racism were rare, but among conservatives generally, the birther movement gained traction, questioning the legitimacy of Obama's citizenship. Within evangelical circles, Franklin Graham added fuel to the fire by agreeing that the president had "some issues to deal with" regarding his birth certificate. Graham also questioned the legitimacy of Obama's Christian faith. For Christian nationalists, casting doubt on Obama's faith functioned in the same way as questioning the legitimacy of his citizenship. The president's problem, according to Graham, was that "he was born a Muslim"—the "seed of Islam" had passed through his father to him, and "the Islamic world sees the president as one of theirs." Graham saw "a pattern of hostility to traditional Christianity by the Obama administration" while Muslims seemed to be "getting a pass."[11]

Other evangelicals, too, depicted the president as a Muslim sympathizer. Gary Bauer claimed the president was more interested "in defending the reputation of Islam" than in "saving the lives of Christians," and he thought it prudent to advise Obama that defending Islam was not "in his job description." Conservative evangelicals took issue with the president's reluctance to use the words "Islamist extremism," and recoiled as he "glowingly gushed about the Quran multiple times" during his 2009 Cairo speech. By 2010, more white evangelicals believed Obama was a Muslim (29 percent) than believed he was a Christian (27 percent). A full 42 percent claimed not to know.[12]

The specter of a Muslim in the White House further entrenched the Islamophobia already widespread within the Christian Right. During Obama's first year in office, Phyllis Schlafly hosted a "How to Take Back America Conference." The conference included the usual sessions on "How to Counter the Homosexual Extremist Movement," "How to Stop Socialism in Health Care," and "How to Recognize Living Under Nazis & Communists," but General Jerry Boykin was also invited to address the conference on the threat of Islam. The next year, Boykin contributed to a report on "Shariah: The Threat to America," published by a neoconservative think tank. The report warned of Muslim schemes to impose shariah law and claimed that most Muslim social organizations were "fronts for violent jihadists." The center's director noted considerable interest on the part of "local law enforcement intelligence, homeland security, state police, National Guard units and the like," even as terrorist experts critiqued the report as "inaccurate and counterproductive."[13]

During Obama's first term, conservative evangelicals worked to woo back wayward members of the younger generation. Two years after Obama was elected, Wayne Grudem, cofounder of the Council for Biblical Manhood and Womanhood, former president of the Evangelical Theological Society, and one of the leading proponents of gender complementarianism, decided to weigh in on politics directly. Until then, Grudem had focused primarily on theology and gender, writing several books promoting "biblical manhood and womanhood," serving as general editor for the ESV Study Bible, and penning an evangelical approach to systematic theology. In 2010, he published what amounted to a systematic guide to politics; weighing in at over six hundred pages, the book offered an exhaustive guide to the "biblical" view on all things political. Grudem denounced abortion and LGBT rights and defended religious freedom and national sovereignty. Illegal immigration was a problem, but so were the "too many" legal immigrants who didn't seem to be assimilating. He recommended immediately and effectively closing the borders, especially the border with Mexico. For Grudem, loving one's neighbors meant going to war to protect them from "evil aggressors." Military strength was a blessing, and it was wrong not to use it, especially in the case of the nation's greatest threat, Islamic terrorism. Treating terrorism as a "law-enforcement problem" wouldn't work; preemptive war was required. For those less inclined to purchase a weighty tome on Christian politics, the basic contours of the political worldview Grudem delineated were readily available in dozens of books on evangelical masculinity published in the 2000s. Faithful Christian manhood might start in the family, but it didn't end there.[14]

Hoping to stem the Leftward drift of younger evangelicals, Grudem made a point of criticizing those tempted to vote candidate over party, a transgression too many evangelicals had committed in 2008. In 2012, he and his conservative allies did see a small decrease in evangelical defections (Obama's share of the white evangelical vote dropped to 21 percent), but they failed to vote Obama out of office. Resentment festered. As President Obama was being sworn in for his second term, Mark Driscoll tweeted that he was praying for a president who would be placing "his hands on a Bible he does not believe to take an oath to a God he likely does not know."[15]

In Obama's second term, evangelical opposition manifested around the issue of religious freedom, and for evangelicals, "religious freedom" didn't apply equally to all faith traditions; their defense of religious freedom was linked to their defense of "Christian America" and to their conservative gender regime. Already in Obama's first term in office, the Affordable Care Act's contraceptive mandate signaled that hostile government overreach could coerce Christians into participating in practices they abhorred. In 2012, the ACLU brought a suit against the conservative Christian owner of the Masterpiece Cakeshop for refusing to bake a cake for a same-sex wedding. In the summer of 2015, the Supreme Court ruled in favor of same-sex marriage, ensuring that more Christian business owners would be forced to violate their consciences in this way. Weeks later, a county clerk in Kentucky named Kim Davis became a cause célèbre among religious conservatives when she refused to issue marriage licenses to same-sex couples.

The next year, the administration sued North Carolina over the state's controversial "bathroom bill" restricting individuals to use facilities matching their sex assigned at birth. Evangelicals were taken aback at the pace of their apparent marginalization, but they weren't about to give up the fight.[16]

True to form, conservative evangelical leaders worked to galvanize followers by stoking a sense of embattlement and issuing calls for greater militancy. They drew on a familiar script. After the Pentagon lifted the ban on women in combat in 2013, John Piper called Obama's support for the move "a shame on the president's manhood." At a 2014 National Day of Prayer event, Dobson labeled Obama "the abortion president." Dobson's fury at the threat of transgender restrooms reflected longstanding assumptions about unrestrained male sexuality, female vulnerability, and predatory behavior. Blaming "Tyrant Obama" for his dictatorial attempts to alter how women and men relate to one another and how children perceive their own gender identity, Dobson could hardly contain himself: Who would have thought the day would come "when boys could meander into the private sanctuary of girls' toilets," when "sex-absorbed junior high boys" could ogle girls' bodies in the shower? "Have we gone absolutely mad?" In language reminiscent of that voiced by ERA opponents three decades earlier, Dobson issued a desperate call to action to American men to defend their wives from men who dressed like women in order to peer over bathroom stalls, and their little girls from men "who walk in unannounced, unzip their pants and urinate in front of them." If any of this had happened a century ago, "someone might have been shot. Where is today's manhood? God help us!" General Boykin concurred: "The first man who goes in the restroom with my daughter will not have to worry about surgery." The Family Research Council executive vice president claimed to be surprised when the LGBT community responded by calling him out for inciting violence.[17]

It wasn't as though evangelical men hadn't already been heeding Dobson's call. From authors and pastors to men in the pews, evangelical men had been promoting and performing a militant Christian masculinity with increasing fervor. During the Obama years, new voices joined a now-familiar refrain.

Eric Metaxas emerged as a leading voice on Christian masculinity in the Obama era. Metaxas wasn't new to the world of evangelical publishing, or to evangelical culture more generally. Raised in the Greek Orthodox Church, Metaxas got his start writing children's books. In 1997 he began working as a writer and editor for Charles Colson's *BreakPoint* radio show, and he then worked as a writer for *VeggieTales*, a children's video series where anthropomorphic vegetables taught lessons in biblical values and Christian morality. (Bob the Tomato and Larry the Cucumber became household names in 1990s evangelicalism.) Belying his *VeggieTales* pedigree, Metaxas brought a new sophistication to the literature on evangelical masculinity. As a witty, Yale-educated Manhattanite, Metaxas cut a different profile than many spokesmen of the Christian Right. If Metaxas's writing wasn't exactly highbrow, his was higher-brow than most books churned out by Christian presses. More suave in his presentation than the average evangelical firebrand, Metaxas was a rising star in the conservative Christian world of the 2000s. After Colson's death in 2012 he took over *BreakPoint*, a program broadcast on 1400 outlets to an audience of eight million. That year he also gave the keynote address at the National Prayer Breakfast, where he relished the opportunity to scold President Obama to his face, castigating those who displayed "phony religiosity" by throwing Bible verses around and claiming to be Christian while denying the exclusivity of the faith and the humanity of the unborn. In 2015 he launched his own nationally syndicated daily radio program, *The Eric Metaxas Show*.[18]

Metaxas specialized in writing about Christian heroes. His 2007 book, *Amazing Grace: William Wilberforce and the Heroic Campaign to End Slavery*, helped secure his position in the evangelical world. In Metaxas's narrative, evangelical Christians were the good guys; sharing "God's perspective on the subject," they rejected "the abominable racial views" held by non-Christians and "cultural Christians." In 2011 he

Eric Metaxas delivering the keynote at the 60th annual National Prayer Breakfast at the Washington Hilton on February 2, 2012. REUTERS / LARRY DOWNING.

published *Bonhoeffer: Pastor, Martyr, Prophet, Spy*. Metaxas's version of Dietrich Bonhoeffer bore an uncanny resemblance to conservative American evangelicals, in that he battled not only Nazis but the liberal Christians purportedly behind the rise of Nazism. Once again, evangelicals emerged as heroes. Evangelicals loved the book. Meanwhile, historians panned it; the director of the U.S. Holocaust Museum's Programs on Ethics, Religion, and the Holocaust described it as "a terrible oversimplification and at times misinterpretation of Bonhoeffer's thought, the theological and ecclesial world of his times, and the history of Nazi Germany."[19]

In his 2013 book, *7 Men: And the Secret of Their Greatness*, Metaxas revealed the larger purpose behind his biographies. He wanted to clear up the confusion around "the idea of manhood" by addressing two "vitally important questions": *What is a man? And what makes a man great?* The answer started with none other than John Wayne. Wayne was the "icon of manhood and manliness." He had "toughness and swagger," but he used his strength to protect the weak. Generations of men were inspired by his model of masculinity, until something happened. That something was the 1960s.[20]

The transformation probably had something to do with Vietnam or Watergate, Metaxas mused. Until Vietnam, wars were seen as worth fighting and patriotic Americans dutifully defended the country and its freedoms. Vietnam changed all that. "Ditto with Watergate," which presented us with a president acting not at all presidential. Since that time, people had focused on the negative when it came to famous people, and it was hard to have heroes in a climate like that. Making matters worse, Americans had extended this critique back through history. No longer heralded as a selfless and heroic Founding Father, George Washington was denounced as a wealthy landowner and hypocritical slave owner. Instead of celebrating Christopher Columbus as the "intrepid visionary" he was, Americans now pilloried the explorer as a murderer of indigenous peoples. Metaxas conceded that "idol worship" wasn't a good thing, but being "overly critical" of good men could also be incredibly destructive.[21]

For Metaxas, the decline of heroic masculinity undermined Christian nationalism and eroded patriarchal authority. Just compare the 1950s television show *Father Knows Best* with the way the mainstream media had come to depict fathers, "either as dunces or as overbearing fools." But the country was paying the bitter price for their rejection of authority. Young men especially needed heroes and role models to see "what it means to be a real man, a good man, a heroic and brave man." Metaxas wasn't saying anything evangelicals hadn't been saying for fifty years. But with Barack Obama in the White House, and with evidence abounding that evangelicals were losing the culture wars, the message resonated widely.[22]

If Metaxas offered a comparatively highbrow discourse on heroic masculinity, the Robertsons offered a decidedly lowbrow version. *Duck Dynasty*, the reality television show featuring the Robertson family, debuted in 2008, and by 2013 it had become one of the most popular shows on television, with its fourth season premier drawing almost twelve million viewers, more than the highest viewed episodes of criti-cal favorites *Breaking Bad* and *Mad Men* combined. It was a show that celebrated faith, family, and duck hunting. In the Robertson clan, there was no gender confusion. Men were men: big, burly, bearded men. And women were women: perfectly accessorized wives and daughters who welcomed their husbands home after a long day's work with a home-cooked meal. Phil Robertson, the family patriarch, had been a college football quarterback; his brother, "crazy" Uncle Si, was a Vietnam vet. There were rifles and crossbows, multiple varieties of jerky, and not a whiff of elitism.[23]

Duck Dynasty was a show made for Red State Americans. And for American Christians. Phil Robertson, the family patriarch, was a self-described Bible-thumping convert, and his son Al was a pastor. Onscreen and off, the entire Robertson clan committed themselves to "faith, family, fellowship, forgiveness, and freedom." The show itself wasn't in-your-face Christian, due in part to A&E's judicious edit-ing. "We don't want to make it like 'The 700 Club for Rednecks,'" Al explained. Onscreen, the Robertsons shared their faith with a lighter touch, but as celebrities they weren't afraid to address controversial issues more directly. In a speech to a pregnancy center that drew atten-tion in 2013, Phil denounced abortion and the hippies responsible for a movement that "lured 60 million babies out of their mothers' wombs." Later that same year, in an interview with *GQ*, he suggested that homo-sexuality would lead to "bestiality, sleeping around with this woman and that woman and that woman and those men," and included a few choice words on his own preference for vaginas over anuses. Without an editor to scrub his dialogue, Phil's unadulterated words caused an uproar in some circles. But among many of his conservative Christian fans he emerged as a new kind of culture warrior—one who wasn't concerned about "respectability," who wasn't trying to engage "the establishment," who wasn't afraid to say it like it was.[24]

The Christian publishing industry took note. In 2013, the Robert-son clan authored *The Duck Commander Devotional*. The next year Jase Robertson published *Good Call: Reflections on Faith, Family, and*

Fowl, and Thomas Nelson published the *Duck Commander Faith &*
Family Bible, a New King James Version available in hardcover. In
2015 Thomas Nelson published Jep and Jessica's book on faith and
family, and seventeen-year-old Sadie's book on the same. The Robertsons' books were available at LifeWay books and at retailers like
Walmart. Already in the 1990s, Thomas Nelson had recognized that
they shared a "family values" base with Walmart, and they entered
into a partnership; within ten years the big-box retailer had become
the nation's largest supplier of Christian merchandise, selling over a
billion dollars annually. Christianbook.com also carried an array of
Duck Commander titles, plus DVD collections, hoodies, cookbooks,
greeting cards, lunch napkins, and dessert plates.[25]

Some evangelicals worried about the "cultural Christianity" these
Louisiana good ol' boys portrayed, but the Robertsons weren't just
"cultural Christians." They were devout, practicing evangelicals who,
in good evangelical fashion, saw their celebrity as a means of spreading their faith. But the very distinction requires scrutiny. By the early
2000s, was it even possible to separate "cultural Christianity" from a
purer, more authentic form of American evangelicalism? What did it
mean to be an evangelical? Did it mean upholding a set of doctrinal
truths, or did it mean embracing a culture-wars application of those
truths—a God-and-country religiosity that championed white rural
and working-class values, one that spilled over into a denigration of
outsiders and elites, and that was organized around a deep attachment
to militarism and patriarchal masculinity?[26]

WHILE METAXAS PONTIFICATED on the virtues of heroic masculinity from his Manhattan perch, and the Robertsons reached large
swaths of Red State America with their own brand of the same, dozens
of other evangelical men (and they were overwhelmingly men) continued to churn out large quantities of indisputably middlebrow literature
on Christian masculinity. The warrior as a model of Christian manhood remained ubiquitous, and a militaristic view of Christian mas-

culinity went largely unchallenged in conservative evangelical circles. Within this genre, real-life military warriors continued to bring an aura of authenticity that mere pastors couldn't match.

In 2015 John McDougall, an army chaplain, West Point graduate, and veteran of Iraq and Afghanistan, published *Jesus Was an Airborne Ranger: Find Your Purpose Following the Warrior Christ*. Stu Weber, a fellow Ranger who first met McDougall at West Point, contributed the book's foreword. Setting aside the pretty-boy Sunday-school Jesus no real man could relate to, McDougall made clear that his savior was no Mister Rogers. He was a warrior who knew how to channel aggression when he needed to. "In Ranger vernacular, Jesus was a badass," a "forceful man" who called other men to "vigorously advance his kingdom"—as "spiritual badasses"—in their homes, communities, and world. There was nothing prim and proper about this Jesus. He was "a wild-at-heart Ranger on a mission," a rural laborer who knew how to work hard and play hard. To sum up, "You can't spell *Ranger* without the word *anger*."[27]

That same year, Weber teamed up with fellow real-life warrior Jerry Boykin to write *The Warrior Soul*. The Bible was filled with the vocabulary of war, with "attacks, wounds, blood, sacrifice, swords, battles, victories," and for Christians there would be no peace until Christ the victor ushered in peace. Until then it was up to them to join the fight. "Should you *stand*—take action—against the murder of children by abortion? Of course you should!" Figure out how. The same applied to the Christian bakery fined for refusing to bake a cake for a same-sex "'marriage' ceremony." It was time to show up. War required sacrifice. What might that look like for the armchair reader? Perhaps a significant donation to the Family Research Council. (Boykin served as executive vice president.) "Write some well-directed checks, warrior." Or it might look like joining the fight against terror by informing oneself on the dangers of Islam: "Can you intelligently address Sharia law and the threat posed to our faith and culture?"[28]

Weber and Boykin had opinions on actual war, too. The Bible taught that it was a mistake to settle for quick and cheap peace. Just look at ancient Israel: when Israel was reluctant "to sacrifice sufficiently" they failed to conquer the land. In case readers failed to see the application to the present day, they made themselves plain: America's reluctance to recognize the Islamic threat placed the nation in peril. Of course there were "moderate" Muslims who didn't share this violent worldview, but these were "bad Muslims"—much like mainline Christians who had abandoned historical Christian fundamentals were "bad Christians." Ignoring the threat of violent Islam could be lethal.[29]

Weber and Boykin also took a swipe at civilian control of the military. Determining the morality of war was best left to warriors themselves: "Despite their considerable pontification on the subject, philosophers aren't necessarily the best judges of what makes a war just." Warriors had "a unique perspective of the nature of warfare," and they were the ones who should decide "what makes war just." Moreover, God himself had "a special place in his great heart for warriors and their soldiering"—after all, his son Jesus was "a truly exceptional warrior." Both Christian theology and "this constitutional republic" reserved "a high and honored place for the warrior."[30]

REMINISCENT OF THE WANING YEARS of the Reagan administration, conservative evangelicals had struggled to mobilize as the George W. Bush presidency came to an end. But the Religious Right had always thrived on a sense of embattlement, and in that respect, the Obama White House was heaven-sent. Between demographic changes portending an end to "white Christian America," the apparent erosion of loyalty among young evangelicals, and steady assaults on their conception of religious liberty, white evangelicals perceived clear and present dangers to their very existence. Or at least to their social and political power. Obama's election had issued a warning call to evangelical leaders. Leaving nothing to chance, they made the most of the moment, working arduously to stoke further fear and resentment. By the end of Obama's eight years in office, even as the president's overall approval ratings had been among the highest in recent presidential history, white evangelicals remained his most stalwart critics. Seventy-four percent viewed him unfavorably, compared to 44 percent of Americans generally. Perhaps more importantly, conservative evangelicals had reinvigorated their posture of embattlement. Drastic times would call for drastic measures. When 2016 came around, they were primed for the fight. They just needed the right warrior to lead the charge.[31]

Chapter 15

A NEW
HIGH PRIEST

FOR EVANGELICALS WHO HAD COME TO DESPISE
President Obama and all that he stood for, it was hard to imagine
anyone worse. And then Hillary Clinton declared her candidacy.

Clinton was a devout Christian, but the wrong kind. She spoke
about her Methodist faith frequently during the 2016 campaign, reciting favorite passages of Scripture with ease. Tapping into a tradition of
American civil religion, she reminded Americans that they were great
because they were good, and she urged them to summon the better
angels of their nature. On the campaign trail she seemed especially at
home among black Protestants, whose prophetic faith tradition bore
many similarities to her own progressive Methodism. But for white
evangelicals, Clinton was on the wrong side of nearly every issue. A
feminist and a career woman, she thought it took a village to raise a
child. She promoted global human rights and women's rights at the
expense of US sovereignty, at least in the eyes of her critics. And she
was pro-choice. The fact that she read the same Bible didn't register
for most evangelicals, and her faith testimony came across as political
pandering, or just plain lying.

After leaving the White House, Clinton had achieved notable political success in her own right, first as a New York senator and then as
Secretary of State. By 2012, she was more popular than either President
Obama or Vice President Biden. But the attack against US government
facilities in Benghazi that year, and Republicans' subsequent attempts

to pin the blame on her for the attack—and an alleged cover-up—
helped conservatives build a case against Clinton as unfit to defend the
nation. Her use of a private email server for official communications
would further feed this narrative, once those revelations emerged. As
the 2016 election got under way, it was clear that Clinton would not
be winning over her evangelical detractors.[1]

Not that she seemed to be trying all that hard. On the issue of abortion, Democrats had long campaigned under the mantra "safe, legal,
and rare," but in 2016, "rare" seemed to disappear from their lexicon.
When asked about abortion during a debate, Clinton didn't hedge.
As president, she would defend Planned Parenthood, *Roe v. Wade*,
and "women's rights to make their own health care decisions," even
in the case of late-term abortions. At best, her unapologetic response
struck evangelicals as tone deaf. At worst, it confirmed their darkest
fears about what a Clinton presidency would mean. Conservatives
also painted Clinton as a virulent opponent of religious freedom, only
heightening their anxiety over the election and what it would mean for
the future of the Supreme Court.[2]

Then there was the matter of her gender. John Piper had given a
special dispensation to vote for the McCain/Palin ticket, but Hillary Clinton was no Sarah Palin. All policy issues aside, the fact that
Clinton was a woman disqualified her in the eyes of many conservative evangelicals. But in the 2016 election, evangelical views of gender
didn't just affect Clinton's appeal—or lack thereof. Gender was also a
key factor in shoring up support for the unconventional, morally challenged Republican candidate, Donald J. Trump.

EVANGELICAL INFATUATION with Donald Trump wasn't
instantaneous, and it didn't start with leadership. Initially, prominent
evangelicals preferred more traditional Republican candidates, and
they had plenty to choose from.

Candidate Mike Huckabee wasted no time in denouncing same-
sex marriage, reproaching "trashy" women who swore, criticizing the

Obamas for letting their girls listen to Beyoncé, warning that ISIS was a greater threat than the "sunburn" people might get from climate change, and declaring "war against a 'secular theocracy.'" Ben Carson, too, was popular among evangelicals. An African American conservative, Carson knew how to play to the white evangelical crowd. He suggested that a Muslim should be disqualified from serving as president, defended the right to fly the Confederate flag, compared political correctness to the practices of Nazi Germany, and suggested that the Holocaust would not have happened if Jews had been armed. Carson appealed to evangelicals who claimed, and often sincerely believed, that they held no racist convictions, without requiring them to sacrifice any of their social and political commitments. Marco Rubio, meanwhile, was making a strong play for the evangelical vote. He had gathered a "religious liberty advisory board" that included Wayne Grudem and other evangelical academics and faith leaders, and his appeal was especially strong among northern establishment evangelicals—the Wheaton and *Christianity Today* types.[3]

Texas senator Ted Cruz also emerged as a contender. The son of a traveling evangelist, Cruz was raised in the dominionist tradition, and even more than Huckabee, Rubio, and Carson, he knew how to stoke the fears of conservative Christians. Cruz drew stark distinctions between good and evil; he, of course, was on God's side, opposing the forces of evil. He talked of the need to "Restore America" and he echoed the militarized vocabulary that had come to permeate American evangelicalism. The nation was "under attack" and it was only going to get worse. With the death of Supreme Court Justice Antonin Scalia, Cruz painted a doomsday scenario of what could happen with a liberal appointment to the Court: unlimited abortion-on-demand, the end of religious freedom, the Second Amendment disappearing from the Constitution. After his victory in the Iowa caucuses, Cruz drew endorsements from James Dobson, Tony Perkins, Gary Bauer, and Glenn Beck. General Jerry Boykin agreed to serve as a national security advisor to his campaign.[4]

Around this time, Russell Moore, president of the SBC's Ethics &

Religious Liberty Commission and a Rubio supporter, summed up the evangelical vote: "I would say that Ted Cruz is leading in the 'Jerry Falwell' wing, Marco Rubio is leading the 'Billy Graham' wing and Trump is leading the 'Jimmy Swaggart' wing." With the last remark, Moore was referring to prosperity gospel Pentecostals, but also no doubt alluding to Swaggart's sex-with-prostitute scandals. But Iowa evangelical political operative Bob Vander Plaats cautioned against pigeonholing evangelicals in this way. "I don't think we want to divide Christianity along those lines," he advised. "We all break off the same church." In the words of fellow operative David Lane, "Politics is about addition and multiplication, not subtraction and division." Vander Plaats and Lane were right. Before long the evangelical vote began to coalesce. Behind Donald Trump.[5]

Why Trump, many wondered, including many evangelicals themselves. For decades, the Religious Right had been kindling fear in the hearts of American Christians. It was a tried-and-true recipe for their own success. Communism, secular humanism, feminism, multilateralism, Islamic terrorism, and the erosion of religious freedom—evangelical leaders had rallied support by mobilizing followers to fight battles on which the fate of the nation, and their own families, seemed to hinge. Leaders of the Religious Right had been amping up their rhetoric over the course of the Obama administration. The first African American president, the sea change in LGBTQ rights, the apparent erosion of religious freedom—coupled with looming demographic changes and the declining religious loyalty of their own children—heightened the sense of dread among white evangelicals.

But in truth, evangelical leaders had been perfecting this pitch for nearly fifty years. Evangelicals were looking for a protector, an aggressive, heroic, manly man, someone who wasn't restrained by political correctness or feminine virtues, someone who would break the rules for the right cause. Try as they might—and they did try—no other candidate could measure up to Donald Trump when it came to flaunting an aggressive, militant masculinity. He became, in the words of his religious biographers, "the ultimate fighting champion for evangelicals."[6]

When he announced his candidacy in the summer of 2015, Trump made clear that his campaign would not be politics-as-usual. He ridiculed his opponents and carped about the country not having victories anymore, about it becoming "a dumping ground for everybody else's problems." He talked of Mexican "rapists" and drugs and crime and terrorists crossing the border, "because we have no protection." Mexico and China were taking "our jobs," the country was getting weaker and our enemies stronger. "Even our nuclear arsenal doesn't work." America needed a leader, "a truly great leader," a leader who could bring back jobs, bring back the military, and revive the American dream—which was dead. Trump promised to "bring it back bigger and better and stronger than ever before." He promised to "Make America Great Again."[7]

Trump's opening barrage was shocking enough, but his rhetoric only devolved over the course of a heated primary season. He fulminated on Twitter, derided Cruz's wife for her physical appearance, and ended up boasting about the size of his penis on national television during a primary debate. The more raucous the campaign grew, the more emboldened Trump became. And the more evangelicals seemed to fall in behind him.

Even before the first primary debate, mounting evidence pointed to Trump's popularity among white evangelicals. A poll conducted in July 2015 found 20 percent of Republican-leaning white evangelicals supporting Donald Trump, compared to 14 percent for Scott Walker, 12 percent for Huckabee, and 11 percent for Jeb Bush. Marco Rubio came in at 7 percent, and Ted Cruz at just 5 percent. Journalists struggled to explain the baffling phenomenon of evangelical support for "the brash Manhattan billionaire" who seemed to stand for everything they despised. What could compel "family-values" evangelicals to flock to this "immodest, arrogant, foul-mouthed, money-obsessed, thrice-married, and until recently, pro-choice" candidate? Many evangelical leaders shared this bewilderment. Not a few remained skeptical of reports of evangelical support. "I haven't talked to a pastor yet who is supporting Donald Trump," insisted Russell Moore. "I think what's happening right now is that we're in the reality TV phase of the presidential campaign where people are looking to send a message rather than hand over the nuclear codes to a person." Trump knew how to get attention, and he knew how to tap into anger and resentment. Evangelicals were just sending a message.[8]

But as evangelical support for Trump proved to be more than a passing fancy, evangelical leaders confronted the limits of their own influence. This was true on a national level, with the old guard discovering that their endorsements of Rubio or Cruz didn't seem to be quelling the surge of support for Trump, and on the local level, as pastors realized the limits of their power even within their own congregations. "It's the most amazing thing I've ever seen," wrote evangelical activist Randy Brinson. "It's like this total reversal of the shepherd and the flock," with congregants threatening to leave their churches if their pastors opposed Trump.[9]

By early 2016, a few leaders were starting to get on board with grassroots enthusiasm for the unconventional candidate. Jerry Falwell Jr. and Robert Jeffress were two of Trump's earliest and most brazen supporters. In January, Falwell invited Trump to speak at Liberty University's convocation. Several months earlier Cruz had launched his campaign at Liberty, but now the enthusiasm for Trump was far greater. Introducing Trump, Falwell spoke of his father's support for Ronald Reagan over Southern Baptist Jimmy Carter: "When he walked into the voting booth, he wasn't electing a Sunday school teacher or a pastor or even a president who shared his theological beliefs." He was electing a leader. "After all, Jimmy Carter was a great Sunday school teacher, but look at what happened to our nation with him in the presidency. Sorry."[10]

Then it was Trump's turn. Rejecting the teleprompters, Trump was ready to have some fun. After some rambling self-congratulatory remarks about his crowd size, and then more self-congratulatory remarks on his poll numbers ("we've done great with the evangelicals"), he made his pitch. "We're going to protect Christianity, and I can say that. I don't have to be politically correct." He then quoted "two Corinthians," to the amusement of his critics. The media jumped on the gaffe, but it didn't seem to distract those in attendance from his key message: He would protect them.[11]

What Trump lacked in eloquence he made up for in passion. Christianity was "under siege." In Syria, "they're chopping off heads." Identifying himself as a proud Christian, he urged Christians to band together for protection, because "very bad things are happening." Christians already had the numbers—"70 percent, 75 percent, some people say even more"—they just needed to claim their power. Knowing how to woo the evangelical voter, Trump turned his attention to the military. Lamenting that the military was "the least prepared it's been in generations," he promised to "build it big, build it strong," so strong that nobody would want to mess with America. He denigrated generals who said it would take a long time to defeat ISIS. He wanted the sort of general "where we knock the hell out of them fast." The audience erupted in cheers. "We're going to be strong," he promised. "We're going to be vigilant," with strong borders, powerful borders, putting an end to weakness, to vulnerability, to a lack of respect. Trump might not be the best Christian, but as a Christian nationalist he could more than hold his own.[12]

This wasn't Trump's first visit to Liberty's campus. In 2012, he had given the school's commencement address. Then, too, the younger Falwell (Falwell senior had died in 2007) had welcomed Trump "to raucous applause," calling the businessman "one of the great visionaries of our time" and praising him for forcing Obama to release his birth certificate. The fawning was mutual. In that address Trump had joked about divorce and prenups, toyed with running for president, and urged students to "get even" if someone wronged them in business. The latter comment sparked some controversy in the media, but Falwell assured critics that the statement was compatible with Christian teaching in that it was representative "of the 'tough' side of Christian doctrine and the ministry of Christ."[13]

For evangelicals, there were warriors on the actual field of battle, and there were those who emerged victorious in the rough-and-tumble world of capitalism. The same rules applied in each arena; daring, vision, and an "aptitude for violence and violation" generated success in both war and business. The warrior and the businessman were both worthy of emulation, and both entitled to command.[14]

A few days after Trump's 2016 visit to Liberty, he arrived at Dordt College, where he made his claim about being able to stand in the middle of Fifth Avenue and shoot somebody without consequence. Three days later, Falwell officially endorsed Trump. His endorsement brought some controversy at the time. Mark DeMoss, chair of Liberty's governing board, insisted that Trump's bullying and personal insults were inappropriate, especially "for anyone who claims to be a follower of Christ." Penny Nance, president of Concerned Women for America, "strongly" disagreed with Falwell's endorsement out of her "deep concerns about Donald Trump's commitment to life and his respect for women."[15]

Falwell and Trump may have had more in common than a penchant for "tough Christianity." Reports surfaced that Falwell had been in conversation with Michael Cohen, Trump's fixer, for help in dealing with compromising photographs that had come to light in connection with a real estate lawsuit against Falwell. Falwell denied the existence of compromising photos, and a source close to Falwell denied that he had any knowledge of Cohen's intervention on his behalf. Still, the mere existence of the rumors was enough to suggest to some that Falwell's support for Trump in 2016 was part of a backroom deal. There was, however, no evidence of a quid pro quo arrangement. More importantly, for the average evangelical voter, no blackmail would be necessary to earn their loyalty. That week, a survey revealed that Trump had the support of 37 percent of evangelicals, nearly double that of Cruz.[16]

Jeffress, too, was one of Trump's most stalwart supporters. First Baptist Dallas had a storied past when it came to conservative evangelicalism. For nearly half a century the church had been pastored by W. A. Criswell, the onetime staunch segregationist who had teamed up with Paige Patterson to help orchestrate the conservative takeover of the Southern Baptist Convention. A magnet for wealthy conservative business leaders—and the longtime home church of Billy

Graham—First Baptist had grown into an influential urban mega-church and hub of the Religious Right. A combative culture warrior, Jeffress had written a book in 2014 suggesting that Obama's support for same-sex marriage was paving the way for the Antichrist. In January, Jeffress had offered the opening prayer at Trump's Dordt College address. The next month he appeared with Trump at a Dallas campaign stop, assuring fellow evangelicals that they would "have a true friend in the White House." Like Falwell, he reminded evangelicals of 1980, when conservative Christians were presented with two choices: a born-again Baptist Sunday school teacher and "a twice-married Hollywood actor" who had signed "the most liberal abortion bill in California history." Evangelicals chose Reagan because they were looking for a leader. When it came to defeating terrorism or the Iran nuclear deal, Jeffress "couldn't care less about that president's tone or his language." It was Jeffress who so memorably quipped that he wanted "the meanest, toughest, son-of-a-you-know-what" in that role.[17]

Writing in the *Baptist News*, Alan Bean later reflected that Jeffress embraced a "Jesus/John Wayne dualism." Trump's biblical ignorance was boundless, but Jeffress wasn't interested in a president who would govern according to Jesus' Sermon on the Mount. Nor did he think that the Bible had anything to say about governments needing to forgive or "turn the other cheek." The role of government was "to be a strongman to protect its citizens against evildoers." Sure, Trump was a notorious womanizer, married three times. So was John Wayne. Wayne was "an unapologetic racist," Bean added, "and Trump stands proudly in that tradition." Both men represented white manhood "in all its swaggering glory." Trump was "the John Wayne stand-in" his evangelical supporters were looking for.[18]

Bean wasn't the only one to see Trump as in the mold of John Wayne. Wayne's own daughter agreed. Days after his Liberty appearance, and just days before Jeffress (unofficially) and Falwell (officially) endorsed him, Trump accepted Aissa Wayne's endorsement. Standing in front of a fake desert background and a wax statue of the gun-toting Wayne at the John Wayne Museum in Winterset, Iowa, Trump

Donald Trump kisses John Wayne's daughter Aissa during a news conference at the John Wayne Museum in Winterset, Iowa, January 19, 2016. AP Photo / Jae C. Hong.

intoned: "When you think about it, John Wayne represented strength, he represented power, he represented what the people are looking [for] today because we have exactly the opposite of John Wayne right now in this country."[19]

EVANGELICALS OPPOSED TO TRUMP tried in vain to redirect their coreligionists. Even before Trump secured the nomination, Russell Moore likened Trump's attitude toward women to "that of a Bronze Age warlord." Moore had a hard time believing that fellow evangelicals could support this man. When polls said otherwise, he cried foul. Just after Trump handily won the South Carolina primary, besting Ted Cruz by six percentage points among white evangelicals and Marco Rubio by nearly twice that much, Moore offered his own spin: Many people telling pollsters they were evangelical "may well be drunk right now, and haven't been into a church since someone invited them to Vacation Bible School sometime back when *Seinfeld* was in first-run episodes." The word "evangelical" had been "co-opted by heretics and lunatics" and diluted by evangelicals-in-name-only, and none of this should be confused with true evangelicalism. When the dust settled after the election, the time would come "to make 'evangelical' great again." Moore used his platform to denounce the scapegoating of religious minorities and the racist and anti-immigrant undertones of Trump's campaign: "The man on the throne in heaven is a dark-skinned, Aramaic-speaking 'foreigner' who is probably not all that impressed by chants of 'Make America great again.' " Trump, confident in his evangelical base, shot back on Twitter: "Russell Moore is truly a terrible representative of Evangelicals and all of the good they stand for. A nasty guy with no heart!"[20]

Denny Burk, president of CBMW, insisted that "men of principle" should do what they could to keep Trump away from the presidency: "If ever the country needed its statesmen to be men of courage, it is right now." Michael Gerson, former speechwriter for George W. Bush, pleaded with his fellow evangelicals that they must not "bear the mark of Trump." He noted that it was, to put it mildly, "unexpected for evangelicals to endorse a political figure who has engaged in creepy sex talk on the radio, boasted about his extramarital affairs, made a fortune from gambling and bragged about his endowment on national television." How could evangelicals identify with a man who fueled racist tension, endorsed religious discrimination, advocated war crimes, and promoted incivility and intolerance, a man "who holds a highly sexualized view of power as dominance, rather than seeing power as an instrument to advance moral ends"?[21]

Perhaps Gerson hadn't been paying attention. Trump was hardly the first man conservative evangelicals had embraced who checked off this list of qualifications. With the forces of evil allied against them, evangelicals were looking for a man who would fight for them, a man whose testosterone might lead to recklessness and excess here or there, but that was all part of the deal. Not all evangelicals were as puzzled as Gerson and Moore. "Evangelicals see what's going down," explained a senior advisor to Huckabee, before Huckabee—the onetime Baptist pastor—exited the race; they were looking for somebody "to be strong and stern," somebody with an aggressive leadership style.[22]

Before long, "real" evangelical leaders began to fall in line. Less than a month before the Republican Convention, Dobson, who had initially endorsed Cruz, testified on behalf of Trump's nascent faith. Granted, the candidate didn't exactly talk the talk. "He used the word 'hell' four or five times" in his meeting with conservative Christian leaders, Dobson acknowledged, and "he doesn't know our language." And yes, he'd had a rough time on the campaign trail, getting tripped up on questions about whether he'd ever asked for forgiveness (no), or what his favorite Bible verse was ("I don't want to get into specifics"). But Dobson had on good authority that Trump had recently come "to accept a relationship with Christ." He was, in Dobson's words, "a baby Christian." When it came to Trump's obvious shortcomings, Dobson urged evangelicals to "cut him some slack."[23]

Wayne Grudem, author of the primer on "biblical politics," had spoken out against Trump in the winter of 2016, but by July he'd penned an essay arguing that voting for Trump was *not* the lesser of two evils, but rather "a morally good choice." True, he was egotistical, vindictive, and bombastic. And yes, he was married three times and unfaithful. But none of these things should disqualify him; Trump was "a good candidate with flaws." He wasn't racist or misogynistic or anti-Semitic or "anti-(legal) immigrant." He was "deeply patriotic," a successful businessman, and he'd "raised remarkable children." Grudem then went on to list over a dozen policy reasons to support Trump.[24]

By this point, Trump had announced the selection of Indiana governor Mike Pence as his running mate. Pence, a dyed-in-the-wool conservative evangelical, explained why he'd agreed, "in a heartbeat," to join the ticket: Trump embodied "American strength," and he would "provide that kind of broad-shouldered American strength on the global stage as well." Pence himself might have lacked a certain ruggedness, but he was ready to ride Trump's broad coattails into the White House. "Broad-shouldered" became Pence's favorite go-to phrase on the campaign trail, and he would also point to similarities between Trump and Teddy Roosevelt—two men who "dared ... to make America great." Other evangelicals voiced the same admiration Pence did.[25]

Eric Metaxas's change of heart is a case in point. Early on, when Trump's candidacy still seemed like a joke, Metaxas had issued a number of satirical tweets mocking Trump's deficient faith formation. Only after Trump secured the nomination did Metaxas publicly express his support: "With all his foibles, peccadilloes, and metaphorical warts, he is nonetheless the last best hope of keeping America from sliding into oblivion, the tank, the abyss, the dustbin of history, if you will." Metaxas never looked back. If Hillary Clinton were to be elected, he wagered the country had less than two years before it would cease to exist. "Not only can we vote for Trump, we must vote for Trump." Metaxas's endorsement shocked many conservatives who knew him. How could Bonhoeffer's biographer support a man like Trump? In his own book, after all, he had described Hitler's rise to power in words that rang eerily familiar: "The German people clamored for order and leadership. But it was as though in the babble of their clamoring, they had summoned the devil himself, for there now rose up from the deep wound in the national psyche something strange and terrible and compelling." Metaxas agreed that his Bonhoeffer biography invited "some unpleasant parallels w/ the current election," but not those one might expect. He saw no connection between Trump and Hitler, but he did refer to Trump's opponent as "Hitlery Clinton." He suggested, too, that his critics bore a striking resemblance to Nazis. It wasn't Trump and his followers who were guilty of racism and xenophobia; it was the "Beltway and Manhattan elites" who practiced a "new and accepted tribalism and xenophobia" against "white European 'Christian' varieties." Metaxas derided his critics as "vile," "obscene," "impotent." The Yale-educated Manhattanite positioned himself "on the side of the common folk against 'elites.'" At the time of the Republican National Convention, Metaxas reiterated his support for Trump. He may be no "great man of virtue," but he loved America. It wasn't really about his sexual ethics or humility or narcissism: "When you are in a war mentality, you say 'who is going to stand up where we need to stand up.'" Metaxas's protestations aside, it did indeed seem to be about Trump's sexual ethics, his lack of humility, his narcissism. What Metaxas admired in Trump appeared to be precisely the fact that he was no great man of virtue, traditionally defined. But he was the perfect embodiment of a different set of masculine "virtues" that evangelical men had been touting for nearly half a century.[26]

By that point Metaxas was in good company; at the time of the convention, 78 percent of white evangelicals were backing Trump.[27]

AS THE ELECTION NEARED, the evangelical vote for Trump seemed secure. In fact, the more unconventional, bombastic, and offensive he became, the more evangelicals seemed to rally to his side.

In September, Trump took a momentary pause from campaigning to attend Phyllis Schlafly's funeral. Although the times had changed, the matriarch of the Religious Right, in her waning years, had not. During the Obama administration she continued to denounce "the stupidity of feminists" for getting rid of "all the manly men." Most women liked "big, strong, John-Wayne-type men," the kind of men who "put out fires, fight in combat, protect their wives and children against intruders, and save damsels in distress." For too long feminists had made men "afraid to be manly," but it was time for women to say: "we love manly men." Schlafly knew a manly man when she saw one. She had been an early Trump supporter during the primaries, and she had spoken in support of Trump at the RNC in Cleveland, connecting Trump, in the words of his evangelical biographers, to "fifty years' worth of anti-establishment, grassroots, Christian, Republican Party politics." Trump eulogized Schlafly as a "truly great American patriot," a hero of the Christian Right. The day after Schlafly's death her final book was released: *The Conservative Case for Trump*.[28]

Remarkably, Trump had become the standard-bearer of the Christian Right. Four weeks before the election, however, the release of the *Access Hollywood* tape threw everything into question. The video, recorded in the NBC Studios parking lot in 2005, contained footage of Trump bragging about his attempts to seduce a married woman, of kissing women without their consent, of assaulting women—because "when you're a star, they let you do it. You can do anything ... grab 'em by the pussy." This wasn't the first hint of Trump's sexual impropriments, but the *Access Hollywood* tape made the candidate's sexual indiscretions impossible to ignore. Surely this admission of sexual assault represented a problem for his evangelical supporters, many outsiders assumed.[29]

In the immediate aftermath, some evangelicals did waver in their support. Grudem rescinded his earlier endorsement, regretting that he had not more strongly condemned Trump's moral character, and reminding Christians that God intended men to "honor and respect women, not abuse them as sexual objects." Yet Grudem was clearly tortured over his decision. Not sure what to do, he decided to pray about it. Ten days later, he asked for his original endorsement to be reposted.[30]

Other evangelical leaders were steadier, finding ways to diminish or dismiss concerns from the start. Ralph Reed, head of Trump's religious advisory board, admitted that as the father of two daughters he was "disappointed by the 'inappropriate' comments," but Clinton was still worse. He surmised that "a 10-year-old tape of a private conversation with a TV talk show host" ranked "pretty low" on faith voters' hierarchy of concerns. Franklin Graham acknowledged that Trump's "crude comments" from "more than 11 years ago" could not be defended, but then again neither could "the godless progressive agenda" of Clinton and Obama. Eric Metaxas tweeted out his initial response: "BREAKING: Trump caught using foul language, combing his hair oddly." He later deleted the tweet, agreeing that the comments were "ugly stuff," but he did not rescind his support. David Brody of the Christian Broadcasting Network offered another line of defense: "This just in: Donald Trump is a flawed man! WE ALL sin every single day. What

if we had a 'hot mic' around each one of us all the time?" Robert Jeffress acknowledged that Trump's comments were "lewd, offensive, and
indefensible," but they still weren't enough to make him vote for Clinton. Sure, he might not pick Trump for a Sunday school teacher, but
that wasn't the point.[31]

Some evangelicals despaired of support for Trump within their own
ranks. Evangelicals' love for Trump was "a disgrace," Russell Moore
maintained, "a scandal to the gospel of Jesus Christ and to the integrity
of our witness." John Piper, too, parted ways with many of his conservative brethren in refusing to endorse Trump. In the days before the
election, he denounced "the flagrant wickedness of both party candidates" and refused to vote for either. Ed Stetzer made a last-ditch
attempt to dissuade his fellow evangelicals from "selling their souls" by
voting for Trump. Writing in *Christianity Today*, the executive director of Wheaton's Billy Graham Center warned evangelical readers: "If
you find that you have overlooked or dismissed many of the morals and
values that you have held dear in the past, then it just may be that your
character has been Trumped."[32]

Some evangelical women were also vocal critics of Trump. The day
after the tape was released, Beth Moore, beloved author of popular
women's Bible studies, expressed her horror at Christian leaders who
seemed to think objectification and abuse of women was no big deal.
Jen Hatmaker, a best-selling author, blogger, pastor, and all-around
"avatar of the New Christian Woman," castigated evangelical men who
defended Trump: "We will not forget. Nor will we forget the Christian
leaders that betrayed their sisters in Christ for power." Christian talk-
show host Julie Roys agreed: "I honestly don't know what makes me
more sick. Listening to Trump brag about groping women or listening
to my fellow Evangelicals defend him."[33]

But on November 8 it became clear that the vast majority of evangelicals had come back around. Exit polls revealed that 81 percent
of white evangelical voters had handed Trump the presidency. Once
again, reports of the death of the Religious Right had been greatly

exaggerated. The "Moral Majority" had reasserted itself, electing the least moral candidate in memory to the highest office of the land.[34]

IN THE DAYS AND WEEKS that followed, journalists, pundits, and evangelicals themselves struggled to come to terms with the role evangelical Christians had played in the election of Donald Trump. A number of theories emerged.

Evangelical elites again raised the specter of "fake evangelicals"—of "culture Christians" masquerading as real evangelicals. No true, Bible-believing, family-values evangelical could vote for a man like Trump, they insisted. The pollsters were using flawed categories. People who knew nothing of the finer points of doctrine were being thrown in with real evangelicals, muddying the category. Early in the primary season, #NeverTrump evangelicals had taken comfort in polls suggesting that those who attended religious services more frequently were less likely to support Trump, but this comfort proved ephemeral. A survey conducted in June 2016 revealed that churchgoing Republican voters were as likely to support Trump as those who attended less frequently; in fact, "nearly nine-in-ten GOP registered voters who attended religious services weekly" were backing Trump at that point. Still, the narrative of "true evangelicals" resisting Trump endured among establishment types. Outside critics pushed back, accusing defenders of "respectable evangelicalism" of "evangelical gerrymandering"—of tinkering with definitions in order to avoid asking hard questions about the nature of their own movement, even as the movement "they helped conjure burns down the country." Subsequent polls offered little support for claims that "real evangelicals" weren't true supporters; one hundred days into Trump's presidency, 80 percent of churchgoing white evangelicals still approved of Trump (a figure that was slightly higher than that for evangelicals who attended less frequently).[35]

In the aftermath of Trump's election, many pundits pointed to economic motivations behind support for Trump more generally, and some applied this reasoning to his white evangelical base as well. But surveys before and after the election disproved this theory. Fears about cultural displacement far outweighed economic factors when it came to support for Trump. In fact, among white working-class Americans, economic hardship predicted support for Hillary Clinton rather than for Trump. Among white evangelicals, economic anxiety also didn't register as a primary reason for supporting Trump. Although evangelicals may have celebrated rural and working-class values, many were securely middle-class and made their home in suburbia. More than economic anxieties, it was a threatened loss of status—particularly racial status—that influenced the vote of white evangelicals, and whites more generally. Support for Trump was strongest among those who perceived their status to be most imperiled, those who felt whites were more discriminated against than blacks, Christians than Muslims, and men than women. In short, support for Trump was strongest among white Christian men. The election was not decided by those "left behind" economically, political scientists discovered; it was decided by dominant groups anxious about their future status. This sense of group threat proved impervious to economic arguments or policy proposals. Research discounting the role of economic hardship in predicting support for Trump reinforces earlier research into white evangelical political behavior. For evangelicals, cultural alignments dictated responses to economic circumstances, rather than the other way around.[36]

Many evangelicals themselves claimed to have "held their noses" when they voted for Trump as the lesser of two evils. It is true that concerns about Clinton's moral character, corruption, and deficiencies on national security had reached a fevered pitch among conservative evangelicals, though it's worth noting that similar—or significantly more serious—questions about Trump's character, corruption, and security liabilities were more easily dispatched. Still, there was the Supreme Court to consider. Certain "character flaws" might be overlooked in the interest of defending religious freedom and protecting the lives of the unborn. Trump would indeed come through on this front as far as evangelicals were concerned. Yet in the weeks and months after the election, after the specter of Hillary Clinton had been vanquished and court appointments secured, few evangelicals seemed willing to critique behaviors they might otherwise have been expected to find repulsive, or at the very least troubling. White evangelical support held steady for the man who redefined the meaning of "presidential." In the aftermath of the election, it was #NeverTrump evangelicals who ended up on the defensive. Russell Moore found his job in jeopardy when more than one hundred SBC churches threatened to withhold donations unless he resigned. (When Trump invited evangelical leaders to a Rose Garden ceremony to celebrate his executive order on religious freedom, Moore was not in attendance—a matter of grave concern to members of his denomination looking for access and influence.) Moore retained his position, but only after undertaking an extensive "apology tour" to expiate the unflattering things he had said about Trump and his evangelical supporters.[37]

For some, the question of evangelical support for Trump had a simpler explanation: rank hypocrisy. Indeed, in the weeks between the release of the *Access Hollywood* tape and the election, PRRI (Public Religion Research Institute) social scientists identified a curious "Trump effect." Five years earlier, only 30 percent of white evangelicals believed that "a person who commits an 'immoral' act could behave ethically in a public role." The month before the election, 72 percent believed this was possible. According to the PRRI's Robert P. Jones, "This dramatic abandonment of the whole idea of 'value voters' is one of the most stunning reversals in recent American political history."[38]

However, for many evangelicals, Donald Trump did not represent the betrayal of many of the values they had come to hold dear. His testosterone-fueled masculinity aligned remarkably well with that long championed by conservative evangelicals. What makes for a strong leader? A virile (white) man. And what of his vulgarity? Crudeness? Bombast? Even sexual assault? Well, boys will be boys. God-given testosterone came with certain side effects, but an aggressive and even reckless masculinity was precisely what was needed when dealing with the enemy. If you wanted a tamer man, castrate him. Among those who embraced this sort of militant masculinity, such character traits

Willie Robertson speaking on behalf of Donald Trump at a campaign rally at the Oklahoma State Fair in Oklahoma City, September 25, 2015. AP PHOTO / J PAT CARTER.

paradoxically testified to Trump's fitness for the job. Some white evangelicals did end up "holding their nose" to vote for Trump, but for many, he was exactly what they had been looking for. Or at least close enough. Some stated this explicitly; for others, the affinities were apparent in the language they used to explain or excuse their support for Trump. He was strong, he wouldn't bow to political correctness, he was their "ultimate fighting champion."[39]

Just a little over a year after Trump's inauguration, two of his evangelical supporters published *The Faith of Donald J. Trump: A Spiritual Biography*. Given the paucity of evidence available on the topic, David Brody (a journalist at Christian Broadcasting Network) and Scott Lamb (a vice president at Liberty University) went to creative lengths to craft a portrait of the president that would appeal to evangelicals and assuage any misgivings some might still harbor. Though they conceded his lineage might be a little sketchy, according to "family history," Trump's ancestors included "an incredible soldier who fought the English at the Battle of Bannockburn (depicted as the final scene of Mel

Gibson's *Braveheart*)." There was also "a good chance" that Trump had "Viking blood running through his veins." His Scotch ancestry, too, linked Trump to "the land of John Knox," a man of God who "spoke truth to power," a man (like other Scots) known for his "straight talk," a man celebrated by the likes of Doug Wilson and Doug Phillips.[40]

Having established Trump's Scottish *and* Viking virility, Brody and Lamb turned their attention to his childhood. Of key interest here was whether or not young Donald had been "a Spock baby." Had his parents been influenced by Benjamin Spock's rejection of "rules, regulations, schedules, and spankings?" Although they lacked direct evidence, Brody and Lamb did not lack certainty: "In a word: No. Sure, a copy of the book might have found its way into the Trump household, but 'newfangled parenting methods' is not the way anyone who knew Fred and Mary Anne describes their style of parenting. They were old school." They were parents who dared to discipline.[41]

The authors neglected to mention Trump's draft deferment, but they made much of his attendance at the New York Military Academy as a high school student, where he came under the authority of a WWII vet, "a regular George Patton" whose style was reminiscent of the opening scene in the movie *Full Metal Jacket*. Trump adored General Patton and General MacArthur, they made clear.[42]

Brody and Lamb also made much of Trump's rootedness in traditional American values. They quoted Michele Bachmann at length on Trump's "1950s sensibilities," by which she meant that he really did "believe in a strong America because he grew up being proud of the United States—'a John Wayne America.'" Unfortunately, children today were being taught that the United States was "an evil country and that somehow we've hurt the rest of the world," but this was "one of the biggest lies" young people were being told. America had been "a force for good." Brody and Lamb concurred:

> Trump believes in "strength" and a "strong America" that corresponds to traditional masculinity. The "John Wayne America" ideal man sits tall in the saddle; doesn't whine or complain; fights

and dies for things that matter; exhibits courage in the face of danger; works hard—maybe even an unbalanced amount; provides for his family; builds things (institutions, buildings, businesses) that others inhabit; leaves the world a better place; may speak with machismo—but never effeminacy; and communicates hope even when it defies logic.

Trump believed "in a black-and-white world of right and wrong, good and evil." It was like in the movies, where you always knew the good guys from the bad guys, and you knew America was on the side of the righteous. Trump, in other words, was a real man, a man whose rugged masculinity was forged in 1950s America, a time when all was right with the world.[43]

In 2016, nearly three-quarters of white evangelicals believed America had changed for the worse since the 1950s, a more pessimistic view than any other group. They were looking for a man who could put things right, a man who could restore America to a mythical Christian past. Like Bachmann, they believed that God had blessed America and they believed Trump understood this; he wasn't ashamed of Christian America. Trump wasn't just a nationalist, he was a Christian nationalist, and he wasn't afraid to throw his weight around.[44]

Evangelicals hadn't betrayed their values. Donald Trump was the culmination of their half-century-long pursuit of a militant Christian masculinity. He was the reincarnation of John Wayne, sitting tall in the saddle, a man who wasn't afraid to resort to violence to bring order, who protected those deemed worthy of protection, who wouldn't let political correctness get in the way of saying what had to be said or the norms of democratic society keep him from doing what needed to be done. Unencumbered by traditional Christian virtue, he was a warrior in the tradition (if not the actual physical form) of Mel Gibson's William Wallace. He was a hero for God-and-country Christians in the line of Barry Goldwater, Ronald Reagan, and Oliver North, one suited for *Duck Dynasty* Americans and American Christians. He was the latest and greatest high priest of the evangelical cult of masculinity.

Chapter 16

EVANGELICAL
MULLIGANS:
A HISTORY

THREE MONTHS INTO DONALD TRUMP'S presidency, three-quarters of white evangelicals approved of his job performance, nearly twice as high as his approval rating among the general public. Trump's evangelical support was strongest among regular churchgoers. Most evangelicals appeared to be far less conflicted about their crude, egotistical, morally challenged president than many had imagined them to be. But this shouldn't have come as a surprise.[1]

Since the 1960s and 1970s, evangelicals had championed discipline and authority. To obey God was to obey patriarchal authorities within a rigid chain of command, and God had equipped men to exercise this authority in the home and in society at large. Testosterone made men dangerous, but it also made them heroes. Within their own churches and organizations, evangelicals had elevated and revered men who exhibited the same traits of rugged and even ruthless leadership that President Trump now paraded on the national stage. Too often, they had also turned a blind eye to abuses of power in the interest of propping up patriarchal authority. In the 2010s, a number of high-profile cases revealed the darker side of the aggressive, testosterone-fueled masculine "leadership" evangelicals had embraced within their own homes, churches, and communities.

MARK DRISCOLL WAS PERHAPS the clearest embodiment of militant evangelical masculinity in the early 2000s. Ruling his Mars Hill empire with military discipline, he inspired a generation of conservative pastors and young Christian men. But in 2013, his empire started to come undone. The first sign of trouble came with accusations of plagiarism. Then came *World* magazine's revelation that his church had spent $210,000 to buy his book *Real Marriage* a spot on the *New York Times* Best Sellers list. Only then, when Driscoll no longer seemed invincible, did twenty-one former Mars Hill pastors have the courage to come forward to accuse Driscoll of an abusive leadership style, of lacking self-control and discipline, of being arrogant, domineering, quick-tempered, and verbally violent. With allegations mounting, the Acts 29 network announced in August 2014 that it had removed Driscoll and Mars Hill Church from its network. Later that month Driscoll resigned his pastorate.[2]

The response of other evangelical men to Driscoll's fall from grace was revealing. The day after Driscoll resigned, Doug Wilson defended his friend and colleague: "I liked Mark Driscoll before and I like him now." Wilson thought he knew what was behind "the Driscoll dogpile": Driscoll was guilty of the sin of being an alpha male. He was "a tough guy," and his "out-there masculinity provoked resentment among others." In essence, Driscoll's downfall could be seen as "the revenge of the beta males." John Piper, too, came to Driscoll's defense. Although he confessed to harboring certain reservations concerning Driscoll's "leadership attitude" and "unsavory language," and regarding certain "exegetical errors," he did not regret befriending Driscoll, speaking at his events, or hosting him at his Desiring God Conference. Instead, he chided Driscoll's detractors and reminded followers that everyone needed renewal and restoration, not just Driscoll. What happened in Seattle was a tragedy: "It was a defeat for the gospel, it was a defeat for Mark, it was a defeat for evangelicalism, it was a defeat for Reformed theology, for complementarianism. It was a colossal

Satanic victory." Yet Piper reminded followers that God still used people to "speak gospel truth" despite their flaws. The Gospel Coalition cofounder and vice president Tim Keller seemed to agree. He admitted that "the brashness and the arrogance and the rudeness in personal relationships" had been obvious from Driscoll's earliest days, yet he still found opportunity to credit Driscoll with building up "the evangelical movement enormously."[3]

Driscoll wasn't the only alpha male in evangelical circles to run into trouble in the 2010s. In 2011, C. J. Mahaney, president of Sovereign Grace Ministries (SGM), a church-planting association of eighty predominantly white, Reformed evangelical churches, board member of The Gospel Coalition and CBMW, and cofounder of Together for the Gospel, took a six-month leave after other SGM pastors charged him with "expressions of pride, unentreatability, deceit, sinful judgment and hypocrisy." His alleged sins included bullying and attempting to blackmail his ministry's cofounder to keep him from expressing doctrinal disagreements. After that brief hiatus, Mahaney was welcomed back and reinstated.[4]

In 2016, Driscoll's good friend Darrin Patrick, author of *The Dude's Guide to Manhood*, member of The Gospel Coalition, and vice president of the Acts 29 network, was fired from his St. Louis megachurch for his domineering and manipulative leadership style. In 2018, evangelical megachurch pastor and champion of complementarianism John MacArthur ran into trouble when accreditors placed his Master's University and Seminary on probation for operating under a "pervasive climate of fear, intimidation, bullying, and uncertainty." Accreditors also flagged his institution's failure to comply with requirements of the Violence Against Women Act. In 2019, SBC megachurch pastor James MacDonald, author of *Act Like Men*, took an "indefinite sabbatical" after a *World* magazine investigation uncovered patterns of bullying, angry outbursts, abusive speech, intimidation, and financial mismanagement. Then, audio clips were released in which MacDonald lashed out at *Christianity Today* for its coverage of the evolving scandal. His choice of words is revealing: "CT is Anglican, pseudo-dignity,

high church, symphony-adoring, pipe organ-protecting, musty, mild
smell of urine, blue-haired Methodist-loving, mainline-dying, women
preacher-championing, emerging church-adoring, almost good with
all gays and closet Palestine-promoting Christianity, so of course they
attacked me."[5]

DRISCOLL, MAHANEY, PATRICK, MacArthur, and MacDon-
ald had all risen to prominence through their aggressive promotion
of patriarchal power. To those who cared to notice, it was clear that
Trump wasn't the first domineering leader to win over evangelicals. Yet
what most puzzled observers when it came to evangelical devotion to
the president wasn't their eagerness to embrace a brash, aggressive, even
authoritarian leader. Rather, it was the apparent willingness of "family values" voters to support a man who seemed to make a mockery of
those values, the willingness of the self-proclaimed "moral majority"
to back such a blatantly immoral candidate. The release of the *Access
Hollywood* tape just weeks before the election had done little to shake
evangelicals' loyalty, nor had allegations leveled by at least sixteen
women who had accused Trump of sexual misconduct that included
harassment and assault. In the months after Trump took office, the
puzzle of evangelical support for morally challenged men persisted.[6]

First there was Roy Moore. In 2017, Moore ran in a special election to fill the Senate seat vacated by Jeff Sessions after Sessions was
appointed attorney general. Back in the early 2000s, Moore had gained
hero status among conservative Christians for ignoring a court order
to remove the monument of the Ten Commandments he had installed
in the Alabama Supreme Court. In 2011, he had contributed to one
of Doug Phillips's textbooks and appeared in an accompanying Vision
Forum video. And in the run-up to the special election, Moore's old
friend James Dobson endorsed him as "a man of proven character and
integrity," a "champion for families" who would "govern the nation
with biblical wisdom." But then stories surfaced detailing Moore's long
history of sexual misconduct; in one case, he had allegedly pursued a

relationship with a fourteen-year-old girl. In Alabama, however, evangelical support for the culture warrior remained firm. Some cast doubt on the women's stories, while others saw no problem with a then-thirty-two-year-old man courting a fourteen-year-old girl. After all, hadn't Jesus' mother Mary been a teenager when she married Joseph? This was too much for Russell Moore (no relation to Roy): "Christian, if you cannot say definitively, no matter what, that adults creeping on teenage girls is wrong, do not tell me how you stand against moral relativism." Yet once again Russell Moore found himself in the minority; one poll suggested that 37 percent of the state's evangelicals were *more* likely to vote for Moore in the wake of the allegations. In the end Moore lost his bid, the first Republican to lose a Senate race in Alabama since 1992, but white evangelicals had voted for him at the remarkably resilient rate of 80 percent.[7]

No sooner had Roy Moore been put to rest than national attention turned to Stormy Daniels, a porn star who had been paid $130,000 in hush money in the weeks before the 2016 election to avoid going public about her 2006 affair with Trump. By this point in time there was nothing shocking about allegations of Trump's sexual conduct, and the response of Trump's evangelical supporters was also predictable. Tony Perkins, president of the Family Research Council, explained that evangelicals "gave him a mulligan"—"they let him have a do-over." Why? Evangelicals were "tired of being kicked around by Barack Obama and his leftists," Perkins groused, and they were "finally glad that there's somebody on the playground that is willing to punch the bully."[8]

Several months later, in the summer of 2018, the nomination of Brett Kavanaugh to the Supreme Court again centered the nation's attention on allegations of sexual abuse. When Christine Blasey Ford accused Kavanaugh of sexual misconduct dating back to their high school days, white evangelicals found all sorts of reasons to doubt her testimony. (Around this time there appeared to be a sudden uptick in sermons on Potiphar's wife, the biblical woman who had falsely accused the righteous Joseph after he resisted her sexual advances.)

Moreover, close to half of all white evangelicals thought Kavanaugh should be confirmed *even if* the allegations proved true. Once again, observers were left wondering: How could evangelicals—who for half a century had campaigned on "moral values," who had called on men to "protect" women and girls—find so many ways to dispute, deny, and dismiss cases of infidelity, sexual harassment, and abuse? Was this simply the case of political expediency, or naked tribalism, eclipsing "family values"?[9]

History, however, makes plain that evangelicals' tendency to dismiss or deny cases of sexual misconduct and abuse, too, was nothing new. Reminiscent of the 1980s, the 2000s saw a spate of sex scandals topple evangelical leaders. In many cases, the abuse or misconduct stretched back years, even decades. Many of the men implicated in the abuse, or in covering up cases of abuse, were the same men who had been preaching militant masculinity, patriarchal authority, and female purity and submission. The frequency of these instances, and the tendency of evangelicals to diminish or dismiss cases of abuse in their own communities, suggests that evangelicals' response to allegations of abuse in the era of Trump cannot be explained by political expediency alone. Rather, these tendencies appear to be endemic to the movement itself.

Those lamenting evangelicals' apparent betrayal of "family values" fail to recognize that evangelical family values have always entailed assumptions about sex and power. The evangelical cult of masculinity links patriarchal power to masculine aggression and sexual desire; its counterpoint is a submissive femininity. A man's sexual drive, like his testosterone, is God-given. He is the initiator, the piercer. His essential leadership capacity outside the home is bolstered by his leadership in the home, and in the bedroom. The responsibility of married women in this arrangement is clear, but implications for women extend beyond the marriage relationship. Women outside of the bonds of marriage must avoid tempting men through immodesty, or simply by being available to them, or perceived as such. Within this framework, men assign themselves the role of protector, but the protection of women and girls is contingent on their presumed purity and proper submission to masculine authority. This puts female victims in impossible situations. Caught up in authoritarian settings where a premium is placed on obeying men, women and children find themselves in situations ripe for abuse of power. Yet victims are often held culpable for acts perpetrated against them; in many cases, female victims, even young girls, are accused of "seducing" their abusers or inviting abuse by failing to exhibit proper femininity. While men (and women) invested in defending patriarchal authority frequently come to the defense of perpetrators, victims are often pressured to forgive abusers and avoid involving law enforcement. Immersed in these teachings about sex and power, evangelicals are often unable or unwilling to name abuse, to believe women, to hold perpetrators accountable, and to protect and empower survivors.[10]

ONE OF THE FIRST SEX SCANDALS to rattle twenty-first-century American evangelicalism struck at the heart of evangelical power. In 2006, male escort Mike Jones went public with the news that Colorado Springs megachurch pastor Ted Haggard had been paying him for sex for the past three years—the approximate period during which Haggard had been serving as head of the National Association of Evangelicals. Haggard, the pastor of the muscular-angel-bedecked New Life Church, had at the time been lobbying for Colorado Amendment 43, a ban on same-sex marriage, and it was Haggard's hypocrisy that prompted Jones to go public.[11]

Fellow evangelicals jumped to Haggard's defense. James Dobson accused the media of spreading unsubstantiated rumors in order to derail the marriage-protection amendment. When it became clear that Jones's allegations could indeed be substantiated, Mark Driscoll offered a different line of defense. Although no women were involved in this sex scandal, that didn't keep Driscoll from finding a woman to blame. It wasn't unusual, he explained, "to meet pastors' wives who really let themselves go." Women who knew their husbands were "trapped into fidelity" could become lazy. Moreover, a wife who wasn't "sexually available to her husband in the ways that the Song of Songs is so frank about" might not be responsible for a husband's sin, but she certainly wasn't helping him.[12]

Not every evangelical sex scandal made the national news, but a dedicated cadre of bloggers and local journalists worked to bring to light abuses that otherwise might have remained in the shadows. One of these involved Joe White, president of Kanakuk Kamps, popular evangelical camps that combined cowboy and sports motifs to disciple young Christians. White's work at the camps—and Dobson's enthusiastic support for that work—positioned him as one of Promise Keepers' early celebrity speakers. But in 2011, allegations of abuse began to surface. It turned out that White's camp director, Pete Newman, had been molesting dozens of boys for years. White allegedly knew of Newman's actions (including his penchant for riding four-wheelers while naked, and with naked "kampers"), yet Kanakuk continued to back Newman as a "devoted husband, loving, beloved friend and mentor to youth." Newman, meanwhile, promoted himself across the nation as an expert on sexual purity, and it was at purity conferences that he allegedly engaged in inappropriate sex talks and mutual masturbation with boys. (He was known for having one-on-one "Bible studies" with boys in his hot tub.) Newman was convicted of child sex abuse crimes and is serving two life sentences. Critics likened White's role in the affair to that of Joe Paterno in the Jerry Sandusky sex abuse scandal. Like Paterno, White was a "god-like" figure in his conservative Christian orbit, and he was accused of allowing Newman to use his "mantle of authority" to prey on children. But White remained a sought-after speaker in evangelical circles even after the allegations had come to light.[13]

Before long, C. J. Mahaney was back in the news. He had been reinstated after his six-month leave for bullying and other aggressive behavior, but his problems were far from over. In 2012, a class-action suit was filed against Mahaney and SGM for cultivating an "environment conducive to and protective of physical and sexual abuse of children," and the details of the case threw into stark relief the dynamics of abuse within authoritarian, patriarchal communities. Plaintiffs described how women and children were "threatened and ostracized if they resisted efforts to 'restore' their abusive husbands and fathers to a position of 'leadership' in the family," and according to a former member of a Sovereign Grace church, victims' families were compelled or misled into not pursuing legal action. If charges were brought, church leaders wrote letters requesting leniency, or urged victims' families to do so. Families were pressured to forgive perpetrators, and "even children as young as three were forced to meet their abusers for 'reconciliation.'" One woman was informed by church leaders that her husband's urge to molest their ten-year-old daughter could be attributed to her own failure to meet his sexual needs; she was told to take her husband back, lock her daughter's bedroom, and have sex with him regularly. Accusations also included domestic violence, fathers beating children (even into adulthood), youth pastors abusing church children, and extensive efforts to keep victims from reporting abuse to the authorities. As Mahaney's protégé, purity guru Josh Harris had taken charge of Mahaney's Covenant Life Church a few years earlier as Mahaney shifted his attention to his larger church network. In that capacity, Harris was also implicated in failing to address the rampant abuse within the SGM community.[14]

In the assessment of former member T. F. Charlton, "the combination of patriarchal gender roles, purity culture, and authoritarian clergy that characterizes Sovereign Grace's teachings on parenting, marriage, and sexuality" created an environment where women and children—especially girls—were "uniquely vulnerable to abuse." Like many other proponents of militant patriarchy, Mahaney loved to write about sex. He opened his 2004 book, *Sex, Romance, and the Glory of God*, with a discussion of the gift of sex based on Song of Solomon, and he insisted that it was part of masculine leadership to teach wives what the Bible says about sex. He quoted Doug Wilson on the subject of sexual expectations, and like Marabel Morgan and the LaHayes, he included advice urging women to look after their appearances and to obey God by giving their bodies to their husbands, even if they didn't feel like it. He was, in other words, treading on well-traveled ground. The 1980s book on Christian child discipline, *God, the Rod, and Your Child's Bod*, was also "in heavy use" at SGM. The book offered parents guidelines for using harsh corporal punishment to ensure instant and "joyful" submission to authority. As Charlton recognized, "submission theology protects the privileges of the powerful."[15]

C. J. Mahaney enjoyed an outpouring of support from his friends and fellow pastors in the midst of the allegations leveled against him, despite the fact that Brent Detwiler, one of Mahaney's former associates, had sent a letter to key evangelical leaders urging them to stop promoting Mahaney until pending charges were resolved. Piper received the letter, but shortly thereafter decided to demonstrate his public support for Mahaney by preaching at his new Sovereign Grace Church in Louisville, Kentucky. There Piper offered a heartfelt endorsement of his friend, praising what God was doing through him and declining to mention the decades-long history of abuse for which Mahaney was being called to account. Other evangelical men likewise rejected Detwiler's plea. Al Mohler and his fellow Together for the Gospel founders attested to Mahaney's integrity, and to his "vast influence for good" among "Gospel-minded people." The president of CBMW and leaders at The Gospel Coalition likewise expressed support, the latter pointing out that "high-profile Christians are sometimes targeted not because they are guilty, but because they are well known." People who "hate the gospel" only stood to gain when Christian leaders were "unfairly attacked and diminished."[16]

In 2016, Mohler again defended Mahaney, and his invitation to speak at the Together for the Gospel Conference. In introducing Mahaney, he made light of the allegations—joking about Googling to see what he could find about Mahaney online—to the delight of thousands of conference attendees. Instead, he lauded the "massive influence" of Sovereign Grace Ministries and praised Mahaney as a model of endurance, kindness, and steadfastness—"biblically defined as being immovable where the Christian man should be immovable, in the faith, in the truth, in Christ." He assured Mahaney that he had

"10,000 friends" in the room. The allegations against Mahaney and his ministry never made it to trial due to a ruling on the statute of limitations, but this technicality convinced state legislators of the need to change the law in this respect.[17]

Mahaney's friends were loyal because of a shared stake in a patriarchal "gospel," and also, it turns out, because Mahaney had been lining their pockets. According to Detwiler, "Mahaney made a habit of doubling his friends' honoraria (speaking fees) while also providing them with lavish hotels, flight arrangements, new computers, and other gifts." He gave Mark Dever's church $10,000, and he and Sovereign Grace donated "$200,000 *or more*" to Southern Baptist Theological Seminary, where Al Mohler, one of Mahaney's strongest supporters, served as president.[18]

The most conservative corners of the evangelical subculture were also not immune to scandal. Far from it: the more an evangelical leader emphasized male authority and female submission, the more twisted his justifications for any personal scandal.

In 2014, Bill Gothard stepped down from his Institute in Basic Life Principles after more than thirty women—including some minors— accused him of molestation and sexual harassment. For over fifty years, Gothard had advocated modesty, parental authority, strict discipline, and other such "family values." In 2016 ten women filed a suit against Gothard, charging him and ministry leaders with sexual harassment, abuse, and cover-up; one woman accused Gothard of rape. Gothard maintained his innocence. Conveniently, in his own writings Gothard had insisted that God had established "very strict guidelines of responsibility" for victims of abuse: if a woman failed to cry out for help, she was "equally guilty with the attacker." In 2018 the suit against Gothard was dropped, "due to the unique complexities of this case, including the statutes of limitation," but the plaintiffs wanted to make "abundantly clear" that they were not in any way recanting their allegations; they had calculated the costs, emotional and financial, and decided the costs outweighed the benefits of proceeding.[19]

The year before Gothard stepped down from IBLP, his protégé, Doug Phillips—the married Christian homeschool leader and Quiverfull proponent—resigned from his own Vision Forum Ministries after admitting to a "lengthy inappropriate relationship." The next year, the young woman he was involved with—Lourdes Torres-Manteufel—filed a lawsuit against Phillips and his ministries, accusing him of treating her "as a personal sex object." According to the complaint, Phillips began grooming Torres when she was fifteen, establishing himself as "the dominant authority figure in Ms. Torres's life and family," positioning himself as "her spiritual father" and dictating where she lived, worked, worshiped, and spent her time. The case detailed how Phillips's patriarchal movement taught that women should be under the absolute control of men, and how he kept followers from interacting with outside authorities by fostering "a pervasive sense" that they were "engaged in a cosmic war." Phillips established his own "church-court system," and any disputes were brought before a board of male elders, without any of the protections offered in secular courts. Following in Gothard's footsteps, Phillips's community labeled gossip "a very serious sin," effectively shielding perpetrators. Enmeshed in the patriarchal purity culture, Torres was in a no-win situation. If she rejected Phillips's authority, she placed herself outside her community and in opposition to the will of God, yet in submitting to that authority she became "damaged goods" in the eyes of her family and her community.[20]

The accusations against Phillips left many of his acolytes reeling: "He was our hero—the man who could lead us to victory through this horrific war." Doug Wilson, however, came to the defense of his fellow leader in the Christian homeschool movement. To begin with, Wilson argued, it was not appropriate to refer to Torres as a "victim." She was an adult, and thus, "if his attentions were not entirely unwelcome, she was a player in the vice, not a victim." If Phillips's attentions *had* been entirely unwelcome—if she had been "freaked out by the creepster"—Wilson wondered why "she wasn't down the road at the first opportunity . . . with Doug Phillips receiving notification of her opinion of what transpired via the sound of sirens." That hadn't happened, and so if there was a victim in this story, it was Phillips's wife, "with both Phillips and Torres victimizing her."[21]

Wilson had a long history of victim blaming. In his 1997 book on "biblical courtship," he had expounded on the common view that immodest women were responsible for men's actions. As he put it, girls should "cover up" and not dress in a way that "a godly man has to duck down alleys or climb trees to get away from her." Wilson didn't believe men should go to lunch with a female coworker; though he hated "to belabor the obvious," he felt it necessary to point out that "under the clothes, their bodies are different, and hers looks like it would be a lot more fun than some male co-worker's body." Moreover, Wilson suggested that women who rejected submissive femininity were "unprotected"; women who refused masculine protection were "really women who tacitly agree on the propriety of rape." Wilson also liked to draw attention to false accusers, real or imagined. Earlier, in his defense of Driscoll, he had pointed out that prominent figures like Driscoll were "regularly toppled," whereas false accusers rarely were. His award-winning 2012 novel *Evangellyfish*, a book filled with sexual escapades recounted with apparent relish, turned on not one but two women who faked sexual assault.[22]

Like many conservative pastors, Wilson believed that "civil disputes" like Phillips's should be settled among Christians, not in courts "run by unbelievers." Failing that, he thought it prudent that society find "wise and godly men" to serve as judges, so that they could determine, in cases of alleged statutory rape, if "the one raped is almost of age." It turns out Wilson had some experience with the court system. In 2011, he had performed the marriage of Steven Sitler to a young woman in his congregation. Sitler had been convicted in 2005 of child molestation, and at the time Wilson had advocated for leniency in sentencing. (Sitler had been a student at Wilson's New Saint Andrews College and had attended Wilson's church.) Sitler received a life sentence, but was released on probation after only twenty months; three years later, an elder at Wilson's church arranged a meeting with the young woman who would soon become his wife. The couple eventually had a son, but in 2015 the court ordered that Sitler be restricted to chaperoned visits due to inappropriate sexual contact with his own child. When Wilson's wisdom in marrying Sitler to a young woman in his church was questioned, Wilson hit back: the Sitler case was just "an easy way for enemies of our ministry to attack us." He denied that his church was "protecting, covering, or advocating molestation of children." The church existed to minister to broken people. Yet Wilson rejoiced in the "slander"; he and his wife celebrated with a bottle of single-malt scotch, and he used the attention to promote his latest book—which took up the subject of justice.[23]

As Wilson readily admitted, this wasn't the first time he had been embroiled in scandal. The Sitler case brought to mind an earlier incident, that of Jamin Wight. Like Sitler, Wight was a former homeschool student. While enrolled in Wilson's ministerial training program, the twenty-four-year-old boarded with a homeschooling family who were members of Wilson's church, and during that time Wight groomed and sexually abused a young girl, starting when she was fourteen. While Wilson acknowledged Wight's "sin," he also blamed the victim's father for failing to protect his daughter. At his sentencing, Wilson appeared with Wight in court; Wight's charges were reduced to felony offense of injury to a child, and he reached a plea to serve four to six months. The judge in the case was apparently convinced that what had happened was best described as a "homeschool teenage love affair," rather than a crime.[24]

In 2015, the Duggar family, devotees of Gothard's teachings and stars of the TLC reality show *19 Kids and Counting*, became embroiled in their own scandal when reports surfaced that oldest son Josh had molested four of his sisters, as well as the family babysitter. His father, who had known about the abuse years earlier and had sent him to a Christian counselor, insisted that "he was just curious about girls and he had gone in and just basically touched them over their clothes while they were sleeping." His sisters, too, minimized his actions, and his mom Michelle went on Fox News to explain that everyone has made

mistakes—"That's why Jesus came." She felt there was an agenda at
work, that people were eager to slander the family. At the time, Josh
Duggar was executive director of FRC Action, the lobbying arm of
the Family Research Council, an organization known for anti-LGBT
activism and for linking homosexuality with child abuse. In light of
the revelations, Duggar resigned and, with advertisers fleeing, TLC
canceled *19 Kids and Counting.*[25]

Across conservative evangelicalism, it was not uncommon for allegations of assault to be met with skepticism or otherwise covered up
or dismissed. In 2014, an independent report found that Bob Jones
University had been telling victims not to report sexual assault to the
police so as not to harm their families, churches, and the university.
For decades, too, they'd told victims they were to blame for their abuse.
That same year, *The New Republic* published a report on sexual assault
at Patrick Henry College, the school founded by Michael Farris to
serve as a pipeline for homeschooled Christian culture warriors. The
previous year, the college had required all students to attend a lecture
in which a professor spoke of "witch hunts" waged against men even
as "seductresses" lured men into "honeytraps." "Recreational sex in the
evening turns into accusations of 'rape' in the morning, even when it
was entirely consensual." Another PHC professor explained, "When
you have a culture of license where you can't tell the difference between
what's full rape or fake rape and what's real rape," it was hard to deal
with rape at all. This reasoning echoed that of Missouri Republican
Todd Akin, who had provoked outrage during his 2012 Senate campaign when he sought to distinguish "legitimate rape" from most rape
allegations—a distinction that was common at places like PHC, where
the burden of guilt rested on female victims.[26]

Elsewhere in the world of conservative evangelicalism, additional
cases of abuse were coming to light. Among the more harrowing were
those surfacing within the Independent Fundamental Baptist movement, the coalition whose flagship church was First Baptist of Hammond, Indiana. As far back as 1972, influential pastor Jack Hyles had
been telling Christian parents to toughen up their boys, advocating

corporal punishment and training in firearms in order to raise a generation of young men who wouldn't capitulate to enemies like the North Vietnamese. His was a gospel of masculine power and female submission. As pastor of First Baptist, Hyles became the de-facto leader of a network of IFB churches, and the authoritarian curriculum developed at his college was exported across the country. Already in 1989, signs of trouble surfaced when an evangelical magazine alleged that he had been carrying on an affair with his secretary. News of the scandal spread through the religious world and the mainstream media: "The great Jack Hyles, the man of God, whose schools had dating rules so strict that you could earn a demerit by accidently touching the end of a pencil held by someone of the opposite sex, was committing adultery." Hyles denied the allegations, and members of his church rose up in his defense. Some, however, broke with Hyles. One member, Voyle Glover, wrote a book called *Fundamental Seduction*, detailing Hyles's offences and the "Watergate-like coverup" of sexual abuse at the church. Glover was threatened, called the Antichrist, and excrement was left on his doorstep.[27]

Allegations also dogged Hyles's son, Dave Hyles. Stretching back to the 1970s, stories surfaced suggesting that he'd carried on affairs with more than a dozen churchwomen. Later reports alleged that he preyed on young girls, too. One woman recalled her own assault at the age of fourteen. "He was a man of God," she recounted, and even though it felt wrong, she knew it must be what God wanted: "He compared himself to David in the Bible and how he was anointed, and said this is what I was supposed to do . . . to take care of him because he was the man of God." After shuffling his son off to another church, Jack Hyles began to groom his son-in-law, Jack Schaap, to take the helm; the congregation, too, had been primed to embrace a pastor like Schaap. After Hyles's death in 2001, Schaap—"a virtual Hyles clone"—received "a hero's welcome." Like Driscoll, Schaap cultivated an aggressive masculinity on all fronts. He rebuked members for not tithing enough, volunteering enough, or evangelizing enough. As he consolidated his power, he became more brazen, infusing his sermons with graphic sex-

ual material to the point that they seemed vulgar, even "pornographic."
In 2010, in front of thousands of teenagers gathered for a youth conference, Schaap preached a sermon on the "Polished Shaft." Holding
a shaft of an arrow in one hand and a cloth in another, he placed the
stick near his groin and simulated masturbation; by "yielding to God,"
by allowing God to "polish his shaft," promised pleasures would be his.
When the video was posted on YouTube, viewers found the display
shocking; to members of First Baptist, "it was all in a day's preaching."[28]

In 2012, Schaap pleaded guilty to crossing state lines to have sex
with a sixteen-year-old girl he was counseling. Investigations revealed
"a deeply embedded culture of misogyny and sexual and physical
abuse" at First Baptist. More than a dozen men with connections to the
church—including several preaching in churches across the country—
were implicated in a series of lawsuits and arrests involving rape, sexual
molestation, and the abuse of children. A "cultlike culture" led to a
culture of corruption, including "pedophilia, violence, defamation of
the innocent to protect the guilty . . . defiance against lawful authority." This institutional culture caused "good people," sincere Christians
who had "hearts for the Lord," to defend and enable abusers. Even after
Schaap's conviction, many of these "good people" blamed his victim,
whom they labeled a "temptress."[29]

DESPITE MOUNTING EVIDENCE to the contrary, in the early
2000s many evangelicals persisted in the belief that sexual abuse was a
problem plaguing the Catholic church, and that any instances within
their own communities were exceptions that proved the rule. But in
2018, the #MeToo movement came to American evangelicalism. The
increasing frequency and scale of revelations of abuse within their own
circles made this assertion more difficult to sustain.

It started after Jules Woodson, inspired by the larger cultural reck-
oning, sent her former youth pastor Andy Savage an email holding
him accountable for sexually assaulting her nearly two decades earlier,
when she was seventeen. In front of his Memphis megachurch, in a

highly orchestrated event that couched his trespass in terms of redemption, Savage confessed to a "sexual incident"; members responded with a standing ovation. Caught on video, this jarring response prompted a backlash among outside observers, garnering the attention of the *New York Times* and other media outlets. In light of the outrage, Savage resigned his pastorate and decided to step away from ministry.[30]

Weeks later, Willow Creek megachurch pastor Bill Hybels was in the news after seven women accused him of sexual misconduct and abuse of power. Allegations went back decades, but the church had failed to address them. When the story broke, church leadership initially cast doubt on the women's stories, and Hybels, too, received a standing ovation from his congregation. Accumulating evidence eventually forced his resignation. Hybels represented the more progressive wing of evangelicalism, demonstrating that egalitarians were not immune to sexual misconduct. Although he positioned himself as an egalitarian, however, Hybels was a man known for wielding power. Having perfected a demanding, top-down leadership structure, he then exported that structure across a network of thousands of seeker-friendly congregations. He was both architect and product of a larger evangelical culture. It was Dobson, according to Hybels, who convinced him of the need to view pornographic videos, which he then required his female assistant to watch with him.[31]

Before the dust had settled on the Hybels case, a new scandal reached the bastion of conservative evangelicalism, the SBC. Allegations centered on Paige Patterson, revered patriarch and president of Southwestern Baptist Theological Seminary, and one of the leaders of the conservative takeover of the SBC four decades earlier. Patterson exerted enormous power within the evangelical world. A stalwart defender of Christian patriarchy, Patterson liked to don a cowboy hat and display big-game trophies in his office. It turns out he also had a history of commenting on young women's appearances and advising abused women to stay with their abusers, and he had once told a student not to report her rape to the police and to forgive her rapist. (A later report would reveal that Patterson also had a history of downplay-

ing allegations of sexual assault. Together with Jerry Vines, Patterson
had facilitated the rise of SBC pastor Darrell Gilyard, despite multiple
accusations of rape, molestation, and other forms of sexual misconduct
alleged against Gilyard. Although Patterson oversaw Gilyard's resignation from Victory Baptist Church in 1991, this was four years after
allegations first surfaced, and even then, Patterson characterized many
of the accusations as untrue, called attention to the "sins" of alleged
victims, and praised Gilyard as a "spokesman of God." Emboldened
by the support of men like Patterson and Vines, Gilyard had threatened to "go after [the] jugular" of one of his accusers.) Meanwhile, Patterson's coconspirator in the conservative takeover of the SBC, Paul
Pressler, was facing his own charges of covering up inappropriate sexual
conduct (with Patterson's help), and of molesting or soliciting sex from
men and boys dating back to the 1970s.[32]

Over the next several months, it became clear that the problem
of abuse within evangelicalism was not just one of a few high-profile
leaders. In December 2018, the Fort Worth *Star-Telegram* uncovered
at least 412 allegations of sexual misconduct linked to 187 Independent Fundamental Baptist churches and affiliated institutions, stretching across forty states and Canada. Victims suggest the number is far
greater but suppressed by a culture of silence. At least forty-five alleged
abusers continued in ministry positions even after accusations came to
light, transferred from one church to another to evade accountability.
Within this network, "men of God" ruled by fear. To question the pastor was to question God. Victims were accused of being "promiscuous,"
were ostracized, and were at times made to apologize in front of their
congregations.[33]

The institutional culture of Independent Fundamental Baptists represented the more authoritarian tendencies of conservative evangelicalism, but it existed as part of a larger evangelical culture that celebrated
patriarchal authority—a culture that dictated the values and directed
the actions of "good people" in ways that could displace compassion
and justice with blind obedience to authority. For a community that
believed in the existence of sin, conservative evangelicals were curiously

nonchalant about the dangers of unchecked power when that power was placed in the hands of a patriarch.

Two months later, the *Houston Chronicle* published an investigation revealing extensive patterns of abuse within the SBC. For decades, victims had attempted to hold perpetrators accountable, but to little avail. Predators remained in positions of power, even after their actions had been exposed. Churches failed to notify law enforcement, or to warn other churches of allegations. Since 1998, around 380 perpetrators within the SBC had left a trail of more than 700 victims. In the wake of these revelations, a number of SBC leaders denied collective culpability, drawing attention to the autonomy afforded local churches within the SBC. Yet the SBC had a record of promptly "removing from fellowship" churches that hired female pastors, even as they appeared unable to discipline those that hired known sex offenders. Many victims had been urged to forgive their abusers, and it was victims, rather than predators, who frequently ended up shunned by their churches. As one SBC victim testified, the crisis of abuse in the church was "an epidemic powered by a culture of our own making."[34]

It was precisely this pattern that led Rachael Denhollander to label the church "one of the worst places to go for help" for victims of abuse. Widely celebrated for bringing USA Gymnastics doctor and serial abuser Larry Nassar to justice, Denhollander stunned the evangelical world in 2018 when she contended that, had her abuser been an evangelical pastor, she knew she would have been "actively vilified and lied about by every single evangelical leader out there." Denhollander, who identifies as "a very conservative evangelical," made this allegation after she and her husband had raised questions about their own church's role in rehabilitating C. J. Mahaney and his Sovereign Grace network. In response to their concerns, their home church had informed them that it was no longer the right place for them.[35]

In her powerful victim statement at the Nassar trial, Denhollander had rebuked Nassar for asking for forgiveness without repentance. She said the same was true of churches. God was a God of forgiveness, but also a God of justice, and churches' tendency to cover up abuse and quickly "forgive" perpetrators, often for the sake of the church's witness, was misguided. "The gospel of Jesus Christ does not need your protection," she insisted. Jesus only requires obedience—obedience manifested in the pursuit of justice, in standing up for the victimized and the oppressed, in telling "the truth about the evil of sexual assault and the evil of covering it up."[36]

EVANGELICAL LEADERS were growing increasingly alarmed by the "avalanche of sexual misconduct" allegations that showed no sign of letting up. In the spring of 2018, Al Mohler felt as though bombs were dropping, left and right, and only God knew how many would fall and where they would land. The media spotlight had brought "the terrible swift sword of public humiliation," and Mohler admitted that he had been unprepared for the deluge; he hadn't seen it coming. Perhaps he should have. Just two years earlier he'd made light of allegations against his good friend, C. J. Mahaney.[37]

In his bewilderment, Mohler found himself asking if theology might be to blame. Was complementarianism "just camouflage for abusive males and permission for the abuse and mistreatment of women?" Quickly answering his own question, he declared that, no, the same Bible that expressed God's concern for victims also revealed "the complementarian pattern of male leadership in the home and the church." Mohler was not about to abandon patriarchy. For his part, Russell Moore thought it prudent to point out that God was revealing that there was "no ideological safe harbor," as it was clear that abuse occurred in egalitarian strongholds and outside the church. It wasn't just a complementarian problem.[38]

John Piper also decided that evangelicalism's #MeToo movement was a good time to defend patriarchy. In a Desiring God podcast recorded in March 2018, he blamed egalitarianism for leaving women vulnerable. Complementarianism charged men "to care for and protect and honor women," but Christian and non-Christian egalitarians had stripped women of that protection. He remained convinced that "manly valor" would restrain male vice. Yet Piper himself had a less-than-stellar record when it came to dealing with abuse. In 2009, when asked whether a woman should submit to abuse, he hedged. It depended on "what kind of abuse." Was a woman's life in danger, or was this merely "verbal unkindness"? If her husband was asking her to engage in "group sex or something really weird, bizarre, harmful," then she might very gently refuse to submit, but if the abuse was just hurting her and not requiring her to sin, then she should endure "verbal abuse for a season"—and "perhaps being smacked one night." Only then should she seek help . . . from the church.[39]

In assessing the role of complementarianism generally, some evangelicals argued for the need to separate out more extreme formulations of complementarianism—"hypercomplementarianism"—from a more moderate "biblical complementarianism." In 2010, for example, Nathan Finn, a professor at Southeastern Baptist Theological Seminary, complained in the pages of CBMW's journal that it was unfair to group organizations like CBMW, Together for the Gospel, and Focus on the Family with figures like Doug Phillips and the Duggar family, with "the patriarchs and theonomists of the movement's far-right extreme." Though he allowed that "some of the convictions and terminology overlap," he maintained that "the application is vastly different," and confusing the two produced nothing but a "complementarian caricature." Finn did, however, urge CBMW readers to be clearer about their beliefs so that their "normative complementarian" movement would not be lumped in with the wider patriarchy movement.[40]

Finn was correct to locate Phillips and the Duggars at the edges of conservative evangelicalism. Yet a decade hence, it is the relationship between the centers and the margins that demands scrutiny. Those who occupy what center there is have largely failed to define themselves against the more extreme expressions of "biblical patriarchy," and there are reasons for this. With the escalation of the culture wars in the 2000s, stronger affinities—both theological and cultural—bound together "normative complementarians" and "biblical patriarchs" than Finn cared to admit, and this was not happenstance. For decades, networks had been forged and alliances secured, linking the center and peripheries. At the same time, a vast consumer market cared little for such distinctions. One no longer needed to attend a Bill Gothard seminar to tap into his extremist ideology; one could buy Phillips's latest DVD online. Or watch reality television. The Duggars, after all, were a national phenomenon.

When it came to evangelical masculinity, the ideological extreme bore a remarkable resemblance to the mainstream. In the end, Doug Wilson, John Piper, Mark Driscoll, James Dobson, Doug Phillips, and John Eldredge all preached a mutually reinforcing vision of Christian masculinity—of patriarchy and submission, sex and power. It was a vision that promised protection for women but left women without defense, one that worshiped power and turned a blind eye to justice, and one that transformed the Jesus of the Gospels into an image of their own making. Though rooted in different traditions and couched in different styles, their messages blended together to become the dominant chord in the cacophony of evangelical popular culture. And they had been right all along. The militant Christian masculinity they practiced and preached did indelibly shape both family and nation.

CONCLUSION

I N 2008, THE GAITHER VOCAL BAND, A LEGENDARY southern gospel vocal group with roots in the contemporary Christian music scene of the 1980s, released the single "Jesus and John Wayne." The song set up a contrast between a mother's gentle faith and a father's toughness, between a cowboy and a saint, and the singer found himself somewhere between the two. True to the Gaithers' brand, it was a nostalgic ballad; by that point in time, for many of their evangelical fans, little separated Jesus from John Wayne. Jesus had become a Warrior Leader, an Ultimate Fighter, a knight in shining armor, a William Wallace, a General Patton, a never-say-die kind of guy, a rural laborer with calluses on his hands and muscles on his frame, the sort you'd find hanging out at the NRA convention. Jesus was a badass.[1]

This Jesus was over half a century in the making. Inspired by images of heroic white manhood, evangelicals had fashioned a savior who would lead them into the battles of their own choosing. The new, rugged Christ transformed Christian manhood, and Christianity itself.

Weaving together intimate family matters, domestic politics, and a foreign policy agenda, militant masculinity came to reside at the heart of a larger evangelical identity. Over the years, Christians have been drawn into this cultural and political identity in many ways. Christian men attended men's ministries to become better fathers and more faithful Christians. Christian parents sought help raising children.

Christian women looked to books and seminars to learn how to be better wives. The resources they found introduced them to a larger world
of evangelical "family values"—to traditional visions of masculinity
and femininity, and to a social order structured along clear lines of
patriarchal authority.

FROM THE START, evangelical masculinity has been both personal and political. In learning how to be Christian men, evangelicals
also learned how to think about sex, guns, war, borders, Muslims,
immigrants, the military, foreign policy, and the nation itself.

Consider, for instance, gun rights. Writers on evangelical
masculinity have long celebrated the role guns play in forging Christian manhood. From toy guns in childhood to real firearms gifted in
initiation ceremonies, guns are seen to cultivate authentic, God-given
masculinity. A 2017 survey revealed that 41 percent of white evangelicals own guns, a number higher than members of any other faith
group and significantly higher than the 30 percent of Americans overall who own firearms. In 2018, the National Rifle Association elected
none other than Oliver North as president. Introduced as "a legendary warrior for American freedom," North opened the annual meeting with a patriotic and unapologetically Christian invocation. At the
meeting's prayer breakfast, he reminded members that they were "in a
fight . . . in a brutal battle to preserve the liberties that the good Lord
presents us with." At the same meeting, former Major League first
baseman Adam LaRoche pontificated that Jesus was no pacifist. Jesus
came not to bring peace, but a sword. LaRoche was sporting a black
T-shirt emblazoned with the message "Jesus loves me and my guns."[2]

It's not just the religious rhetoric that is striking here, or the fact
that it could have been lifted straight out of dozens, if not hundreds,
of books on evangelical masculinity. A common sense of embattlement
also links the rhetoric of the NRA to that of conservative white evangelicalism. For both, a bunker mentality strengthens identity and loyalty, and fuels militancy. Even though conservatives have dominated

public policy on gun control for decades, a persecution narrative rooted in a sense of cultural decline has long mobilized gun rights advocates and driven gun sales, especially during Democratic administrations. For conservative white evangelicals, guns carry a symbolic weight that can only be understood within this larger culture of militancy.[3]

Or consider evangelical views on immigration and border security. More than any other religious demographic, white evangelicals see immigrants in a negative light. Two years into Trump's presidency, more than two-thirds of white evangelicals did not think the United States had a responsibility to accept refugees. In 2019, nearly the same percentage supported Trump's border wall. Given that the Bible is filled with commands to welcome the stranger and care for the foreigner, these attitudes might seem puzzling. Yet evangelicals who claim to uphold the authority of the Scriptures are quite clear that they do not necessarily look to the Bible to inform their views on immigration; a 2015 poll revealed that only 12 percent of evangelicals cited the Bible as their primary influence when it came to thinking about immigration. But this does not mean that religion does not matter. Evangelicals may self-identify as "Bible-believing Christians," but evangelicalism itself entails a broader set of deeply held values communicated through symbol, ritual, and political allegiances.[4]

From the Cold War to the present, evangelicals have perceived the American nation as vulnerable. Tough, aggressive, militant men must defend "her." The border is the line of defense, a site of danger rather than a place of hospitality. Since the 1960s, evangelicals, too, have exhibited a dogged commitment to "law and order." What started as a backlash against hippies, antiwar protestors, civil rights activists, and urban minorities evolved into a veneration of law enforcement and the military. It's no surprise, then, that the majority of evangelicals would agree that "building walls is not non-Christian," that there is "nothing anti-gospel about protecting our nation from those who would do our nation harm," and that those perceived as threats are members of nonwhite populations.[5]

Despite evangelicals' frequent claims that the Bible is the source of their social and political commitments, evangelicalism must be seen as a cultural and political movement rather than as a community defined chiefly by its theology. Evangelical views on any given issue are facets of this larger cultural identity, and no number of Bible verses will dislodge the greater truths at the heart of it.

Rather than seeing culture as pitted against theology, however, we should treat the interplay between the two as what ultimately defines evangelicalism. Here, recent debates over the nature of the Triune God—Father, Son, and Holy Spirit—are illuminating. Having pronounced patriarchal authority and female submission nonnegotiable "gospel truths," some complementarian theologians went a step further. In 2016, CBMW's Wayne Grudem and Bruce Ware advanced a theology of the Trinity that made Jesus "eternally subordinate" to God the Father, in order—according to critics—to justify the eternal, God-ordained subordination of women to men. Grudem and Ware might have been following in the footsteps of Elisabeth Elliot, who had written about this notion in the 1970s, but in doing so they were parting ways with roughly two millennia of Christian orthodoxy. Even some fellow complementarians labeled this innovation "heresy," or "idolatry." Many of those affiliated with CBMW, however, sided with Grudem and Ware. For critics, this raised an important question: were men defending patriarchy because they believed it to be biblical, or were they twisting the Scriptures in order to defend patriarchy?[6]

Many of the new orthodoxies are subtler than this. Masculine authority, militarism, and the sexual and spiritual subordination of women have simply been part of the air evangelicals breathe for decades. In Sunday schools and Vacation Bible Schools boys learn to be superheroes for Christ, and girls to be beautiful princesses. Children sing "I'm in the Lord's Army" while marching in formation. In church youth groups, boys train to use guns and bows, girls to apply makeup, shop, and decorate cakes. Churches host special Mother's Day services, handing out flowers or sweet pastries and poems to women in the congregation. On Father's Day, they grill wild game, or host "dad contests" where men toss footballs, click TV remotes, and compete in simulated hunting games, the winner taking home a box of steaks. One Kansas church hosts an annual Smoking Barrel event, where men and boys shoot guns and eat smoked meat. Church deer-hunting events are common, sometimes involving the smearing of blood as a masculine rite of passage. Christian schools, often boasting mascots like Knights, Eagles, or Crusaders, host chapel services featuring weightlifters for Jesus or local groups of WWF look-alikes who tear apart phone books and jump through walls of ice, all in the name of Christ. National men's conferences bring men together with their favorite Christian authors for worship and ax throwing. Churches host Fight Club ministries, or they come up with their own homegrown versions of manly men's groups. One church rebranded their men's retreat as a "men's advance"—because "men don't retreat." To study the Bible, men come together as "Knights of the Round Table," women as "Handmaidens of the Lord."[7]

The world of Christian retail reflects and reinforces these dynamics. DaySpring Christian cards specialize in pastel-themed greeting cards for women, and they've also developed a *Duck Dynasty* product line marketed to men. Nelson Bibles publishes "Biblezines" for teenagers that contain the text of the Old or New Testament along with "Christian lifestyle advice" for boys and girls. Emblazoned against an image of horsemen riding into battle, the boys' version urges boys to "Fight the Fight" and boasts of stories about "Epic battles of the Old Testament" and "Men of the Sword: How Unstoppable Warriors Got So Awesome." The girls' New Testament (with pretty, smiling girls on the cover) provides a list of "beauty secrets," advice and quizzes on topics like "Are You Dating a Godly Guy?" and a "Guys Speak Out" section so girls can hear what young men have to say "on tons of important issues."[8]

The gendered nature of the evangelical marketplace is on vivid display as close as your nearest Hobby Lobby store. Owned by a powerful evangelical family, Hobby Lobby recently helped spearhead opposition to the Affordable Care Act's contraceptive mandate, and the company's profits have helped fund the new Museum of the Bible in the nation's capital. But in the evangelical world, the craft store's influence extends far beyond the Beltway. In the past decade, the local Christian bookstore has declined along with other brick-and-mortar outlets as Christian retail has migrated to online retailers including LifeWay, Christianbook.com, and, increasingly, Amazon.com. Together with Walmart, Hobby Lobby has also claimed a slice of the religious market by pioneering an era of big-box Christian retail. Effortlessly bridging the sacred and the secular, Hobby Lobby is beloved by crafters and white Christian women alike (the categories are not mutually exclusive). Book displays near the registers stock an impressive array of ESV and NIV Bibles pitched to specific market segments (teen girls, crafters, and "Every Man"), along with devotionals, Christian romance novels, and the latest offerings from Franklin Graham and Chip and Joanna Gaines.

Beyond the book displays extend aisle upon aisle of gender-specific merchandise. For little girls there's an entire section of pink princess-themed products, wall plaques declaring that little girls are made of "bows, bling, & sparkly things," and other items reminding girls that true beauty comes from within, from "a gentle and quiet spirit." Grown women can find glittery coffee tumblers adorned with odes to lipstick, mascara, coffee, and Jesus. Stroll over to the men's section and you'll find an impressive assortment of fake Texas longhorn skulls, resin cowboy boot decor, bullet-shaped drawer pulls, a "bolt action" shotgun-shaped grilling spatula, and plaques galore celebrating the army and marines, Ronald Reagan, and the Second Amendment. One wall plaque boldly proclaims: "I stand for the National Anthem," stenciled against a weathered red-white-and-blue American flag. There is also assorted "man cave" signage—and a shelf devoted to John Wayne memorabilia.

Non-evangelicals and non-Christians also shop at Hobby Lobby, and much of the merchandise lining the shelves isn't explicitly "Christian" in any overt sense. Yet, for evangelical women, shopping at Hobby Lobby can be akin to an act of religious devotion, and objects that find their way into evangelical homes reinforce the gender ideals at the center of conservative evangelicalism. The message conveyed through these products is clear. Women should be beautiful and love Jesus (even though they're likely to be "hot messes"). A touch of lipstick, some caffeine, and a strong man can help make things right. Hobby Lobby masculinity, meanwhile, is a mix of gun-toting bravado, nostalgic imperial conquest, and flag-waving (white) Christian nationalism.[9]

Conservative evangelicals have long positioned themselves against "the secular," but as the cultural evangelicalism of Hobby Lobby indicates, sacred and secular can be difficult to distinguish. For many evangelicals, the masculine values men like John Wayne, William Wallace, Ronald Reagan, Rush Limbaugh, Jordan Peterson, and Donald Trump embody have come to define evangelicalism itself.

WHILE DOMINANT, the evangelical cult of masculinity does not define the whole of American evangelicalism. It is largely the creation of white evangelicals. The vast majority of books on evangelical masculinity have been written by white men primarily for white men; to a significant degree, the markets for literature on black and white Christian manhood remain distinct. With few exceptions, black men, Middle Eastern men, and Hispanic men are *not* called to a wild, militant masculinity. Their aggression, by contrast, is seen as dangerous, a threat to the stability of home and nation.[10]

Evangelical masculinity serves as the foundation of a God-and-country Christian nationalism, but that hasn't stopped American evangelicals from exporting aspects of this ideology globally, to places like Uganda, India, Jamaica, and Belize. Evangelicals in Brazil, drawing on their own culture of machismo and borrowing from the playbook of American evangelicals, helped install Jair Bolsonaro—a thrice-married strongman known for his misogynistic statements, his antigay agenda, and his defense of "traditional" family values—as the nation's president. Over the past decade, groups like Focus on the Family, the Home School Legal Defense Association, the Alliance Defending Freedom, and the Billy Graham Evangelistic Association have funneled more than $50 million into right-wing European organizations. American evangelicals have also forged ties with Vladimir Putin, who is known for flaunting his bare-chested masculinity, and with conservative elements in the Russian Orthodox Church; in 2014, the Billy Graham Evangelistic Association's *Decision* magazine featured Putin on its cover, and Franklin Graham praised the Russian president for standing up to the "gay and lesbian agenda." The next year, Graham met with Putin in Moscow, an occasion that prompted him to praise Putin as a defender of "traditional Christianity" while accusing President Obama of promoting atheism. In foreign policy as in domestic politics, the cult of masculinity can transform loyalties and reshape alliances.[11]

For conservative white evangelicals steeped in this ideology, it can be difficult to extricate their faith, and their identity, from this larger cultural movement. As one man who grew up awash in evangelical masculinity and 1990s purity culture later reflected, "I lived and breathed these teachings, and they still shape me in ways I don't understand even 20 years after rejecting them intellectually."[12]

For those who have come to reject aspects of this belief system, motivations have varied. For some men, a wild, aggressive masculinity has always been untenable. One man with a physical disability recalls feeling that there was no place for him in the evangelicalism of the 2000s. If you weren't "a sports or hunting fanatic in an evangelical church," your position was marginal, as he put it. Another man, too, recounted that those who weren't particularly athletic, who weren't looking to "jump across ravines and climb rock walls" could feel like inauthentic men and second-class Christians.[13]

Militantly patriarchal expressions of the faith thrived in male-only discussion spaces, and so for some men, it was by listening to Christian women that the darker aspects of evangelical masculinity became visible. For one man, it was the surprise of meeting loving, Christian couples who rejected the teachings of complementarianism that led him to rethink the teachings of men like John Piper and Mark Driscoll.[14]

Over time, many of those influenced by purity culture also began to reassess their spiritual and sexual formation. Those who had saved sex (and even kissing) for marriage discovered that marriage—and marital sex—didn't always live up to expectations. Many came to reject the culture of shame and blame. Women including Sarah Bessey, Dianna Anderson, Samantha Field, Linda Kay Klein, Libby Anne, and groups such as Homeschoolers Anonymous began to expose the damage they experienced or observed within the confines of purity culture. Twenty years after the publication of *I Kissed Dating Goodbye*, Josh Harris acknowledged that he hadn't really known what he was talking about. He asked his publisher for the book to be withdrawn. "When we try to overly control our own lives or overly control other people's lives, I think we end up harming people," he conceded.[15]

For others, it was coming face to face with sexual abuse within evangelical churches, organizations, or families that prompted them to walk away from the movement as a whole. And for some, it was a growing awareness of the militarism that pervaded evangelicalism. For Don Jacobson, whose Multnomah Press published Dobson, Weber, Farrar, Piper, Holton, and Evans, a growing discomfort with Christian nationalism led him to distance himself from the movement he helped foster. After studying more closely the history of Native Americans and accounts of imperial conquest, he could no longer sustain the idea of America as an anointed nation. If you believe that America is God's chosen nation, you need to fight for it and against others, he realized. But once you abandon that notion, other values begin to shift as well. Without Christian nationalism, evangelical militarism makes little sense. "Jesus makes it really clear in John 13," Jacobson reflected. "People will know you're my disciples if you love me"—but too many evangelicals have forgotten "where our true citizenship is."[16]

And for other evangelicals, it was the election of Donald Trump that prompted them to abandon evangelicalism entirely. Some attempted to use Trump to summon fellow believers to greater faithfulness. Michael Gerson sought to lead evangelicals out of "temptation," warning that President Trump's "tribalism and hatred for 'the other' stand in direct opposition to Jesus's radical ethic of neighbor love." Quoting Matthew 6, columnist Cal Thomas reminded evangelicals that "No one can serve two masters," and he challenged Christians to choose their true master, Jesus or Trump: "They can't serve both." But, for evangelicals who have transformed the Jesus of the Gospels into a model of militant masculinity, the conflict is not apparent.[17]

Although the evangelical cult of masculinity stretches back decades, its emergence was never inevitable. Over the years it has been embraced, amplified, challenged, and resisted. Evangelical men themselves have promoted alternative models, elevating gentleness and self-control, a commitment to peace, and a divestment of power as expressions of authentic Christian manhood. Yet, understanding the catalyzing role militant Christian masculinity has played over the past half century is critical to understanding American evangelicalism today, and the nation's fractured political landscape. Appreciating how this ideology developed over time is also essential for those who wish to dismantle it. What was once done might also be undone.

ACKNOWLEDGMENTS

MORE THAN FIFTEEN YEARS AGO, my students introduced me to the material at the center of this story. In subsequent years, friends, fellow scholars, church members, acquaintances, and, increasingly, perfect strangers have shared their experiences with me and helped me make sense of things.

I am profoundly grateful to the many conversation partners along the way who have told me what I needed to know, where I needed to look, who I needed to talk to, and what I was getting wrong. These include: Tim Gloege, David Henreckson, Daniel Rück, Tami Parks, Josh Drake, Jessica Ann Hughes, Kate VanNoord Kooyman, Kris Van Engen, Amy Sullivan, Kevin den Dulk, Scott Culpepper, David Hollinger, Michael Lackey, Neil Carlson, Dale Williams, Kerry Pimblott, T. Ashton Reynolds, Nate Pyle, Mark Mulder, Sarah Walsh, John Hawthorne, Darren Dochuk, John Haas, Bill Svelmoe, Tommy Kidd, Christy Lubbers Berghoef, James Schaap, Heath Carter, Joel Carpenter, George Marsden, Michael Hamilton, Patricia Bouma, Kevin Timpe, Debra Rienstra, Tim Ellens, Joe Stubenrauch, Sonya Jongsma Knauss, Dan Knauss, Jamie Skillen, Mark Bjellend, Daniel José Camacho, James Vanden Bosch, Janine Giordano Drake, Christina Edmondsen, Mika Edmondsen, John Turner, Melissa Borja, Jonathan Hiskes, Janel Kragt Bakker, Brandon Blakeslee, Caleb Lagerway, Paul Verhoef, John Contant, Anne Contant, Sarah Van Timmeren, Corrie Bakker, Jenna Hunt, Karin DeLapp, Nevada DeLapp, Garrett Strpko, Ruth Everhart, Diana Butler

Bass, Rich Mouw, Wes Granberg-Michaelson, Don Jacobson, Danae Jacobson, Gail Bederman, Lauren Kerby, Lisa Cockrel, Sally Steenland, Doug Koopman, David Malone, Greg Jones, Jemar Tisby, Fred Appel, David Bratt, Malcolm Foley, David Swartz, Jared Burkholder, Devin Manzullo-Thomas, Karie Cross Riddle, Will Katerberg, James Bratt, Bruce Berglund, Bob Schoone-Jongen, Frans van Liere, Kate van Liere, Eric Washington, Bill Van Vugt, Bert de Vries, Doug Howard, Karin Maag, Steve Staggs, Nick Cunigan, Darrell Rohl, Dan Miller, Dale VanKley, and David Diephouse. I am grateful, too, for all who have contributed to this project who prefer to remain unnamed, including those who have entrusted me with their stories. Thank you.

I am deeply indebted to scholars and participant-observers who read all or parts of this manuscript: Elesha Coffman, George Marsden, Daniel Silliman, James Bratt, Will Katerberg, Lauren Turek, Greg Jones, Devin Manzullo-Thomas, Nevada DeLapp, Doug Koopman, David Malone, David Henreckson, Josh Parks, and Darren Dochuk. And especially to Tim Gloege, who slogged through early drafts and prodded me forward at key moments along the way. Thanks, too, to Alan Bean, Hunter Hampton, and Daniel Silliman for their scholarly generosity. This endeavor has always been part of a larger academic conversation, and it has been a distinct privilege to engage with such brilliant colleagues, critics, and coconspirators.

Throughout this project I've been the beneficiary of the prompt and able assistance of librarians and archivists, including Calvin University's David Malone and the Hekman Library staff, Melissa Nykanen of Pepperdine's Special Collections and University Archives, Katherine Graber and Keith Call of Wheaton College's Billy Graham Center Archives, and also Bill Lindsay of the Hamblen Music Company.

Without the generous support of the Louisville Institute and their investment in scholarship serving the church and society, this book could not have been written; special thanks to Don Richter for wholeheartedly endorsing this undertaking. Calvin University also provided essential research support. The Calvin Research Fellowship, Civitas Program, McGregor Scholars Program, Calvin Center for Christian Scholarship, Dean for Research and Scholarship, and Provost's office have all facilitated this work in indispensable ways. I am especially grateful to Cheryl Brandsen, Matt Walhout, and Susan Felch for their support in seeing this project through to completion. Thanks also to Todd Buchta and Beth Dykstra for help in securing additional support, to Jenna Hunt for expert assistance, and to John Hwang for working to ensure that this research finds a larger public.

Perhaps most critically, Calvin University has enabled me to work with an exceptional team of research assistants. Austin Hakes helped launch this study with his keen interest and dedication, and along the way Kate Guichelaar and Isaac LaGrand provided additional expertise and assistance. More recently, Josh Parks, Kathryn Post, and Kelly Looman signed on, devoting countless hours to reading bad novels, collecting disturbing internet missives, and going down rabbit holes wherever they might lead, always with meticulous care, perceptive insight, and sparkling wit. Your camaraderie brought light to an otherwise somber study. There would be no book without you three, but you already know that.

Opportunities to present this research in a variety of public settings have enriched and expanded the project. Harvard Divinity School's Religious Literacy and the Professions Initiative provided a remarkable setting for interdisciplinary conversation that generated new friendships and intellectual partnerships; I am especially grateful for the guidance and encouragement offered by Stephen Prothero and David Hempton. I had the honor, too, of returning to the University of Notre Dame's CORAH seminar and to Notre Dame's Enduring Trends and New Directions conference to engage in lively discussions around themes in this book; special thanks to Jonathan Riddle and Darren Dochuk for extending these invitations. Thanks also to the University of Iowa's Geneva Lecture series and to Tom Wolthuis and Dawn Wolthuis for their generous hospitality, and to Calvin University's Festival of Faith and Writing, Just Citizenship series, and the Henry Institute for the Study of Christianity and Politics for additional opportunities to share portions of this research. Talks at local churches, the National Women's

Studies Association, the American Historical Association, the Conference on Faith and History, and the American Society of Church History also provided spaces for illuminating exchanges. At each of these venues, I benefited from thoughtful audience engagement; I am especially appreciative of the many white evangelical men who responded with such interest and investment in this project.

Earlier forays into this research have appeared in print, sparking further constructive conversation. I am grateful to Marie Griffith and Tiffany Stanley at the John C. Danforth Center on Religion and Politics for publishing my initial exploration into evangelical masculinity and militarism at *Religion & Politics*. I am grateful, too, to Wendy McDowell and the *Harvard Divinity Bulletin* and Bob Smietana and the Religion News Service for publishing further iterations of this work.

In recent years, I've had the privilege of being part of a wonderful group of historians writing at Patheos's *Anxious Bench*. Thanks especially to Chris Gehrz for leading this team, and to Beth Allison Barr for bringing me on board and for being both friend and accomplice. It seems appropriate, too, to offer a word of thanks to the many religion journalists whose careful reporting has been essential to my own research, and whose work will no doubt prove indispensable to future historians.

Over the course of this project I've benefited immensely from the guidance of my agent Giles Anderson, who shepherded this book from its inception and ensured that it ended up in the right hands. It has been an honor to work with the Liveright team, from Katie Adams, who first loved this project and helped give it shape, to Robert Weil who tended it along the way, and, finally, to my editor Dan Gerstle, who has the uncanny ability to be right about everything. Thank you, too, to Gina Iaquinta for efficient and cheerful production assistance, to Nancy Palmquist for copyediting with such care, and to Peter Miller, Jessica R. Friedman, Haley Bracken, and all those who have worked to bring this book into the world.

My family, near and far, have supported me in ways that are difficult to capture in words, not least by providing a beautiful reminder on a daily basis that there are things more important than politics, and that love extends across political divides. My early stages of writing coincided with my mom's diagnosis with ALS, and although she did not live to see this book's completion, she remains a part of who I am and what I do.

As this book cut into family vacations and time with my kids, their aunts, uncles, cousins, and grandparents stepped in to pick up the slack, taking them camping, fishing, on trips, and out for donuts. This made all the difference. My children, in turn, also contributed to this project, each in their own way. Zak made sure that my long stretches of writing were filled with just the right sort of distractions in the form of assorted fish, a cockatiel, chickens, and unexpectedly also two roosters. Eva, who has been an enthusiastic supporter of all my scholarly endeavors, contributed to an early paper on this topic by sharing with me her expertise on the house of Slytherin. For far too long she also took care of things on the home front so that I could write. I couldn't have finished this book without your help, Eva. And, of course, Lulu, who provided welcome interruptions at very regular intervals to ask for hugs, smiles, and snacks.

Finally, to Jack, my most long-suffering conversation partner who never flagged in his support for this project, who believed this book needed to be written even when I had my own doubts, who stepped in to offer technical assistance and help securing images for publication, and who took the kids away for weeks at a time in the project's final stages. Thank you.

Although it probably goes without saying, I'll say it anyway. The analysis and conclusions found in these pages do not necessarily represent the views of many who contributed to this project and provided essential support along the way, including friends, family, and my place of employment. I am grateful for the grace that so many have shown, and for the mutual investment we share in engaging in civil conversation about things that matter.

NOTES

INTRODUCTION

1. "Trump Hosted a Campaign Event at Dordt College," filmed January 23, 2016, YouTube, posted November 5, 2016, https://www.youtube.com/watch?v=JGjpIUFNXyQ.
2. Lauren Markoe, "Trump gets official and unofficial endorsements from two leading evangelicals," *Washington Post*, January 26, 2016; New York Times/CBS News Poll, *New York Times*, January 7–10, 2016.
3. "2016 Iowa Presidential Election Results," *Politico*, updated December 13, 2016; Jessica Martínez and Gregory A. Smith, "How the faithful voted: A preliminary 2016 analysis," Pew Research Center, November 9, 2016.
4. Jim Lobe, "Politics—U.S.: Conservative Christians Biggest Backers of Iraq War," Inter Press Service, October 9, 2002; "The Religious Dimensions of the Torture Debate," Pew Research Center, May 7, 2009; Dan Cox, "Young White Evangelicals: Less Republican, Still Conservative," Pew Research Center, September 28, 2007; Kate Shellnutt, "Packing in the Pews: The Connection Between God and Guns," *Christianity Today*, November 8, 2017; Betsy Cooper et al., "How Americans View Immigrants, and What They Want from Immigration Reform: Findings from the 2015 American Values Atlas," PRRI, March 29, 2016; "Data Shows How Passionate and Partisan Americans Are About the Border Wall," PRRI, January 8, 2019; Hannah Hartig, "Republicans turn more negative toward refugees as number admitted to U.S. plummets," Pew Research Center, May 24, 2018; Alexander Vandermaas-Peeter et al., "American Democracy in Crisis: The Challenges of Voter, Knowledge, Participation, and Polarization," PRRI, July 7, 2018; "How the U.S. general public views Muslims and Islam," Pew Research Center, July 26, 2017; German Lopez, "Survey: white evangelicals think Christians face more discrimination than Muslims," Vox, March 10, 2017; Brian Kennedy, "Most Americans trust the military and scientists to act in the public's interests," Pew Research Center, October 18, 2016.
5. For an overview of ways in which religion can shape "overarching attitude structures" linking domestic and foreign policy, see James L. Guth, "Religion and Ameri-

can Public Opinion: Foreign Policy Issues," in *The Oxford Handbook of Religion and American Politics*, ed. Corwin E. Smidt, Lyman A. Kellstedt, and James L. Guth (Oxford: Oxford University Press, 2009), 243–65. Here, too, Guth identifies evangelical support for militant internationalism. See also Corey Rubin, *The Reactionary Mind: Conservatism from Edmund Burke to Sarah Palin* (Oxford: Oxford University Press, 2011). On the politics of Christian nationalism, see Andrew L. Whitehead, Landon Schnable, and Samuel L. Perry, "Gun Control in the Crosshairs: Christian Nationalism and Opposition to Stricter Gun Laws," *American Sociological Association* 4, 2018, 1–13; Andrew L. Whitehead and Samuel L. Perry, "Is a 'Christian America' a More Patriarchal America? Religion, Politics, and Traditionalist Gender Ideology," *Canadian Review of Sociology*, April 30, 2019; Samuel L. Perry, Andrew L. Whitehead, and Joshua T. Davis, "God's Country in Black and Blue: How Christian Nationalism Shapes Americans' Views about Police (Mis)treatment of Blacks," *Sociology of Race and Ethnicity*, August 2, 2018; Robin, *The Reactionary Mind*, 16.

6. James L. Guth, "Are Evangelicals Populists? The View from the 2016 American National Election Study," paper presented at the Henry Symposium on Religion and Public Life, Calvin College, April 27, 2019.

7. "What is an Evangelical," National Association of Evangelicals, accessed March 15, 2018, https://www.nae.net/what-is-an-evangelical/. This definition draws on David Bebbington's classic "quadrilateral," introduced in his *Evangelicalism in Modern Britain: A History from the 1730s to the 1980s* (London: Routledge, 1989).

8. Thomas S. Kidd, "Polls show evangelicals support Trump. But the term 'evangelical' has become meaningless," *Washington Post*, July 22, 2016; Jeremy Weber, "Christian, What Do You Believe? Probably a Heresy About Jesus, Says Survey," *Christianity Today*, October 16, 2018; Bob Smietana, "What Is an Evangelical? Four Questions Offer New Definition," *Christianity Today*, November 19, 2015.

9. Ed Stetzer, "No, Evangelical Does Not Mean 'White Republican Who Supports Trump,'" *Christianity Today*, November 10, 2016; Anthea Butler, "The History of Black Evangelicals and American Evangelicalism," Anthea Butler, accessed February 23, 2018, http://antheabutler.com/the-history-of-black-evangelicals-and-american-evangelicalism/; Jemar Tisby, "How Ferguson widened an enormous rift between black Christians and white evangelicals," *Washington Post*, August 9, 2019; Deidra Riggs, panelist, "Still Evangelical in the Age of #MeToo?", Calvin College Festival of Faith and Writing, April 13, 2018.

10. Like earlier fundamentalism, evangelicalism can be seen as "a web of mutually legitimating relationships." See Molly Worthen, *Apostles of Reason: The Crisis of Authority in American Evangelicalism* (Oxford: Oxford University Press, 2014), 103.

11. Garry Wills, *John Wayne's America* (New York: Simon & Schuster, 1998), 149.

12. Sara Moslener, *Virgin Nation: Sexual Purity and American Adolescence* (New York: Oxford University Press, 2015), 78.

13. Emma Green, "Why White Evangelicals Are Feeling Hopeful About Trump," *The Atlantic*, December 1, 2016.

14. Robert P. Jones, "The Evangelicals and the Great Trump Hope," *New York Times*, July 11, 2016.

Chapter 1: SADDLING UP

1. Sarah Watts, *Rough Rider in the White House: Theodore Roosevelt and the Politics of Desire* (Chicago, IL: University of Chicago Press, 2006), 6–7.

2. Gail Bederman, *Manliness and Civilization: A Cultural History of Gender and Race in the United States, 1880–1917* (Chicago, IL: University of Chicago Press, 1996), 170, 178, 186.

3. Watts, *Rough Rider*, 2.

4. Gail Bederman, " 'The Women Have Had Charge of the Church Work Long Enough': The Men and Religion Forward Movement of 1911–1912 and the Masculinization of Middle-Class Protestantism," *American Quarterly* 41, no. 3 (Sept. 1989): 432–65; Fred B. Smith, *A Man's Religion* (New York: Association Press, 1913), 70; Joe Creech, "The Price of Eternal Honor: Independent White Christian Manhood in the Late Nineteenth-Century South," in Craig Thompson Friend, *Southern Masculinity: Perspectives on Manhood in the South since Reconstruction* (Athens: University of Georgia Press, 2009), 25, 34–35.

5. Charles E. Hesselgrave, "Billy Sunday," *The Independent*, February 1, 1915, 161; "40,000 Cheer for War and Religion Mixed by Sunday," *New York Times*, April 9, 1917, 1.

6. Timothy E. W. Gloege, *Guaranteed Pure: The Moody Bible Institute, Business, and the Making of Modern Evangelicalism* (Chapel Hill: University of North Carolina Press, 2015), 2–11.

7. Gloege, *Guaranteed Pure*, 203.

8. "Has Christianity Failed, or Has Civilization Failed, or Has Man Failed?" *Kings Business* (November 1914), 595, quoted in Matthew Sutton, *American Apocalypse: A History of Modern Evangelicalism* (Cambridge, MA: Belknap Press, 2014), 52, 58, 275; George M. Marsden, *Fundamentalism and American Culture* (New York: Oxford University Press, 1980), 146.

9. Owen Wister, *Roosevelt: The Story of a Friendship, 1880–1919* (New York: Macmillan, 1930), 339; excerpt from Sherwood Eddy, "The Case Against War," in *The Messenger of Peace*, vol. XLIX, no. 11, November 1924, 173.

10. Bruce Barton, *The Man Nobody Knows* (Chicago, IL: Ivan R. Dee Publishing, 1925), 4.

11. Marsden, *Fundamentalism and American Culture*, 149.

12. Clifford Putney, *Muscular Christianity: Manhood and Sports in Protestant America, 1880–1920* (Cambridge: Harvard University Press, 2001), 205; National Association of Evangelicals for United Action Executive Committee, *Evangelical Action! A Report of the Organization of the National Association of Evangelicals for United Action* (Boston, MA: United Action Press, 1942), Foreword.

13. Harold John Ockenga, "Unvoiced Multitudes," in *Evangelical Action!*, 20, 24–25, 36–37, 39.

14. Robert Wuthnow, *Inventing American Religion: Polls, Surveys, and the Tenuous Quest for A Nation's Faith* (New York: Oxford University Press, 2015), 95.

15. Ockenga, "Unvoiced Multitudes," 36–37, 39.

16. George M. Marsden, *Understanding Fundamentalism and Evangelicalism* (Grand Rapids, MI: Eerdmans, 1991), 6; Grant Wacker, *America's Pastor: Billy Graham and the Shaping of a Nation* (Cambridge, MA: Belknap Press, 2014), 81.

17. Wacker, *America's Pastor*, 81; Graham, "Youth's Hero," in *Calling Youth to Christ* (Grand Rapids, MI: Zondervan, 1947), 91, quoted in Moslener, *Virgin Nation*, 56; Billy Graham, "Don't Be Like Samson" (sermon, New York City, August 11, 1957), Folder 130, Box 10, Collection 285, Billy Graham Papers, Billy Graham Center Archives, Wheaton College, Wheaton, IL, quoted in Hunter Hampton, "Man Up: Muscular Christianity and the Making of 20th-Century American Religion," University of Missouri, 2017, 195–96; Billy Graham, *The Chance of a Lifetime: Helps for Servicemen* (Grand Rapids, MI: Zondervan, 1952), 38, 44.

18. Harold J. Ockenga, "Letters to the Times," *New York Times*, March 9, 1944, quoted in Sutton, *American Apocalypse*, 277–78.

19. Anne C. Loveland, *American Evangelicals and the U.S. Military 1942–1993* (Baton Rouge: Louisiana State University Press, 1997), 1; Michael L. Weinstein and Davin Seay, *With God on Our Side: One Man's War Against an Evangelical Coup in America's Military* (New York: Thomas Dunne Books, 2006), 41–42.

20. Loveland, *American Evangelicals*, 2.

21. Moslener, *Virgin Nation*, 52.

22. Joel A. Carpenter, *Revive Us Again: The Reawakening of American Fundamentalism* (New York: Oxford University Press, 1999), 223.

23. William Martin, *With God on Our Side: The Rise of the Religious Right in America* (New York: Broadway Books, 1996), 29; Carpenter, *Revive Us Again*, 223; Moslener, *Virgin Nation*, 60–61.

24. Billy Graham, "The Home God Honors," in *Revival in Our Time* (Wheaton, IL: Van Kampen Press, 1950), 65, 67–71.

25. Cynthia Enloe, *The Morning After: Sexual Politics at the End of the Cold War* (Oakland: University of California Press, 1993), 15.

26. Darren Dochuk, *From Bible Belt to Sunbelt: Plain-Folk Religion, Grassroots Politics, and the Rise of Evangelical Conservatism* (New York: W. W. Norton, 2012), 142.

27. Dochuk, *From Bible Belt to Sunbelt*, xvi–xvii.

28. Mike Wyma, "After 80 Years, Stuart Hamblen's Luck Is Still Holding," *Los Angeles Times*, December 30, 1988.

29. Dochuk, *From Bible Belt to Sunbelt*, 181–82.

30. Dochuk, *From Bible Belt to Sunbelt*, 180; Michael S. Hamilton, "How a Humble Evangelist Changed Christianity As We Know It," *Christianity Today*, Billy Graham special issue, April 2018.

31. Daniel Silliman, "Sex-and-marriage manuals and the making of an evangelical market," paper presented at the American Historical Association, Chicago, IL, January 7, 2019.

32. Silliman, "Sex-and-marriage manuals."

33. Rumors persist to this day that Wayne gave his life to Christ after receiving a letter from Robert Schuller's teenage daughter, but there is no evidence to support this; Wayne did apparently convert to Catholicism shortly before his death.

34. Stanley Corkin, *Cowboys as Cold Warriors: The Western and U.S. History* (Philadelphia, PA: Temple University Press, 2004), 2.

35. Wills, *John Wayne's America*, 149.

Chapter 2: JOHN WAYNE
WILL SAVE YOUR ASS

1. Billy Graham, *Just As I Am* (New York: HarperCollins, 1997), xvii–xxi.

2. Graham, *Just As I Am*, 189; Kevin M. Kruse, *One Nation Under God: How Corporate America Invented Christian America* (New York: Basic Books, 2015), 57–64; Daniel K. Williams, *God's Own Party: The Making of the Christian Right* (New York: Oxford University Press, 2010), 25.

3. Williams, *God's Own Party*, 27–28; Kruse, *One Nation Under God*, 60, 81–83, 95–125; Jeff Sharlet, *The Family: The Secret Fundamentalism at the Heart of American Power* (New York: Harper Perennial, 2008), 195.

4. Raymond J. Haberski, *God and War: American Civil Religion Since 1945* (New Brunswick, NJ: Rutgers University Press, 2012), 23; Jonathan P. Herzog, *The Spiritual-Industrial Complex: America's Religious Battle against Communism in the Early Cold War* (New York: Oxford University Press, 2011); Graham, *Just As I Am*, 381.

5. Haberski, *God and War*, 52–53; Loveland, *American Evangelicals*, 2.

6. Williams, *God's Own Party*, 31; Robert O. Self, *All in the Family: The Realignment of American Democracy Since the 1960s* (New York: Hill and Wang, 2012), 332.

7. Charles Reagan Wilson, *Baptized in Blood: The Religion of the Lost Cause, 1865–1920* (Athens: University of Georgia Press, 2009); Jemar Tisby, *The Color of Compromise: The Truth about the American Church's Complicity in Racism* (Grand Rapids, MI: Zondervan, 2019), 149.

8. Williams, *God's Own Party*, 29–31.

9. Williams, *God's Own Party*, 69.

10. Matthew Avery Sutton, "Billy Graham was on the wrong side of history," *Guardian*, February 21, 2018.

11. Randall Balmer, "The Real Origins of the Religious Right," *Politico*, May 27, 2014.

12. Williams, *God's Own Party*, 57.

13. Corkin, *Cowboys as Cold Warriors*, 198; Dochuk, *From Bible Belt to Sunbelt*, 219–22.

14. Dochuk, *From Bible Belt to Sunbelt*, 224.

15. Dochuk, *From Bible Belt to Sunbelt*, 235–36.

16. Dochuk, *From Bible Belt to Sunbelt*, 238.

17. Dochuk, *From Bible Belt to Sunbelt*, 206–9.

18. Dochuk, *From Bible Belt to Sunbelt*, 187, 247.

19. Dochuk, *From Bible Belt to Sunbelt*, 253; "Ronald Reagan: A Time for Choosing," *American Rhetoric*, October 27, 1964, http://www.americanrhetoric.com/speeches/ronaldreaganatimeforchoosing.htm.

20. Williams, *God's Own Party*, 76–78; Steven P. Miller, *Billy Graham and the Rise of the Republican South* (Philadelphia: University of Pennsylvania Press, 2009), 102–6.

21. Miller, *Billy Graham*, 82.

22. Williams, *God's Own Party*, 91–93.

23. Miller, *Billy Graham*, 74; Loveland, *American Evangelicals*, 131; Dochuk, *From Bible Belt to Sunbelt*, 333. On Nixon's embrace of born-again language, see Graham to Nixon, July 14, 1956, Nixon Notebook 10, Collection 685, Billy Graham Archives,

and the November 1962 issue of *Decision* magazine; I am indebted to Daniel Silliman for directing me to these sources.

24. Williams, *God's Own Party*, 95–96.

25. Mark Lempke, *My Brother's Keeper: George McGovern and Progressive Christianity* (Amherst: University of Massachusetts Press, 2017); George McGovern, "Address Accepting the Presidential Nomination at the Democratic National Convention in Miami Beach, Florida, July 14, 1972, The American Presidency Project, https://www .presidency.ucsb.edu/documents/address-accepting-the-presidential-nomination-the -democratic-national-convention-miami; "George McGovern and Wheaton College," Buswell Library Special Collections, Wheaton College, https://recollections.wheaton .edu/2012/10/george-mcgovern-and-wheaton-college/.

26. Dochuk, *From Bible Belt to Sunbelt*, 334.

27. John G. Turner, *Bill Bright & Campus Crusade for Christ: The Renewal of Evangelicalism in Postwar America* (Chapel Hill: University of North Carolina Press, 2008), 144; Dochuk, *From Bible Belt to Sunbelt*, 236.

28. Williams, *God's Own Party*, 102.

29. Loveland, *American Evangelicals*, 155, 161–62.

30. Graham, *Just As I Am*, 197; Loveland, *American Evangelicals*, 121–22.

31. Loveland, *American Evangelicals*, 161–62.

32. Billy Graham, "Billy Graham: On Calley," *New York Times*, April 9, 1971, 31.

33. Wacker, *America's Pastor*, 236; "Are Churchmen Failing Servicemen in Viet Nam?" *Christianity Today*, August 18, 1967, 31.

34. Andrew J. Bacevich, *The New American Militarism: How Americans Are Seduced by War* (New York: Oxford University Press, 2005), 70, 123; Andrew Preston, *Sword of the Spirit, Shield of Faith: Religion in American War and Diplomacy* (New York: Anchor Books, 2012), 533.

35. Loveland, *American Evangelicals*, 164; Bacevich, *New American Militarism*, 140.

36. "Chicago Declaration of Evangelical Social Concern (1973)," Evangelicals for Social Action, November 25, 1973, https://www.evangelicalsforsocialaction.org/about-esa/ history/chicago-declaration-evangelical-social-concern/.

37. Self, *All in the Family*, 302.

38. Bacevich, *New American Militarism*, 123.

39. Bryan Smith, "Let Us Prey: Big Trouble at First Baptist Church," *Chicago Magazine*, December 11, 2012.

40. Jack Hyles, *How to Rear Children* (Hammond, IN: Hyles-Anderson Publishers, 1972), 172.

41. Smith, "Let Us Prey"; Hyles, *How to Rear Children*, 97, 158.

42. Chris Enss and Howard Kazanjian, *The Young Duke: The Early Life of John Wayne* (Guilford, CT: Globe Pequot Press, 2007), 142, 144; Wills, *John Wayne's America*, 13, 202.

43. Wills, *John Wayne's America*, 228, 233; George Fowler, "John Wayne at 70: The Meaning of an American Man," *Human Events*, May 28, 1977. Representative Jack Kemp entered Fowler's article into the *Congressional Record* the week of Wayne's seventieth birthday (*Congressional Record: Extensions of Remarks*, May 24, 1977, https:// www.govinfo.gov/content/pkg/GPO-CRECB-1977-pt13/pdf/GPO-CRECB-1977 -pt13-5-3.pdf).

44. Bill McCloud, *What Should We Tell Our Children About Vietnam?* (Norman: University of Oklahoma Press, 1989), 87; Wills, *John Wayne's America*, 12, 110, 150.

45. Wills, *John Wayne's America*, 13.

46. Wills, *John Wayne's America*, 13, 156.

47. Fowler, "Meaning of an American Man"; "Playboy Interview: John Wayne," *Playboy*, May 1971, 80–82.

48. "Playboy Interview," 80, 84.

49. "Playboy Interview," 82, 84; Fowler, "Meaning of an American Man."

50. "Playboy Interview," 76, 78.

51. Fowler, "Meaning of an American Man."

52. Alan Bean, "Jesus and John Wayne: Must we choose?" Baptist News Global, October 31, 2016.

Chapter 3: GOD'S GIFT TO MAN

1. Jean Marbella, "Totally Marabel," *Sun Sentinel*, September 11, 1985; Marabel Morgan, *The Total Woman* (Old Tappan, NJ: Fleming Revell, 1973); Silliman, "Sex-and-marriage manuals."

2. Morgan, *Total Woman*, 39, 61, 65, 84.

3. Morgan, *Total Woman*, 69, 92–95; Marbella, "Totally Marabel."

4. Morgan, *Total Woman*, 99, 109–10, 112, 127, 183.

5. Morgan, *Total Woman*, 148, 184.

6. Morgan, *Total Woman*, 188; Marbella, "Totally Marabel"; Silliman, "Sex-and-Marriage Manuals."

7. Elisabeth Elliot, *Let Me Be a Woman* (Wheaton, IL: Tyndale House, 1976), 27, 62, 107, 141, 178, 180.

8. Elliot, *Let Me Be a Woman*, 60, 121, 124.

9. Elliot, *Let Me Be a Woman*, 81–83, 158.

10. Carol Felsenthal, *The Sweetheart of the Silent Majority: The Biography of Phyllis Schlafly* (New York: Doubleday, 1981).

11. Douglas Martin, "Phyllis Schlafly, 'First Lady' of a Political March to the Right, Dies at 92," *New York Times*, September 5, 2016.

12. Mark DePue, Interview with Phyllis Schlafly, Interview Session 03 (Audio), Abraham Lincoln Presidential Library and Museum, January 14, 2011, https://multimedia.illinois.gov/hpa/Oral_History/Statecraft/ERA/Schlafly_Phy_03.mp3; Carol Felsenthal, "The Phyllis Schlafly I Knew," *Chicago Magazine*, September 7, 2016.

13. Phyllis Schlafly, "What's Wrong with 'Equal Rights' for Women?" *Phyllis Schlafly Report*, February 1972.

14. Schlafly, "What's Wrong with 'Equal Rights.'"

15. Williams, *God's Own Party*, 111–20; Neil J. Young, *We Gather Together: The Religious Right and the Problem of Interfaith Politics* (New York: Oxford University Press, 2016), 103.

16. Schlafly, "What's Wrong with 'Equal Rights.'"

17. Donald G. Mathews and Jane Sherron De Hart, *Sex, Gender, and the Politics of ERA: A State and the Nation* (New York: Oxford University Press, 1990), 164–65.

18. Phyllis Schlafly, *The Power of the Positive Woman* (New Rochelle, NY: Arlington House, 1977), 11.

19. Schlafly, *Power of the Positive Woman*, 166–72.

20. Mathews and De Hart, *Sex, Gender, and the Politics of ERA*, 174.

21. Mathews and De Hart, *Sex, Gender, and the Politics of ERA*, 165, 174.

22. Danielle McGuire, *At the Dark End of the Street: Black Women, Rape and Resistance* (New York: Vintage, 2010); Mathews and De Hart, *Sex, Gender, and the Politics of ERA*, 165.

23. Felsenthal, *Sweetheart of the Silent Majority*, 4–5.

24. Felsenthal, *Sweetheart of the Silent Majority*, 52–53.

25. Alan Wolfe, "Mrs. America," *New Republic*, October 3, 2005.

Chapter 4: DISCIPLINE AND COMMAND

1. Julie J. Ingersoll, *Building God's Kingdom: Inside the World of Christian Reconstruction* (New York: Oxford University Press, 2015), 17–18, 42, 218–27; Michael J. McVicar, *Christian Reconstructionism: R. J. Rushdoony and American Religious Conservatism* (Chapel Hill: University of North Carolina Press, 2015), 137.

2. Rousas John Rushdoony, *The Institutes of Biblical Law* (Philadelphia: Presbyterian and Reformed Publishing, 1973), 200–203, quoted in Ingersoll, *Building God's Kingdom*, 43–44.

3. Bryan Smith, "The Cult Next Door," *Chicago Magazine*, June 20, 2016.

4. Don Veinot, Joy Veinot, and Ron Henzel, *A Matter of Basic Principles: Bill Gothard and the Christian Life* (Lombard, IL: Midwest Christian Outreach, 2003), 53–54.

5. Ingersoll, *Building God's Kingdom*, 110.

6. McVicar, *Christian Reconstructionism*, 197–98; Ingersoll, *Building God's Kingdom*, 1.

7. Dan Gilgoff, *The Jesus Machine: How James Dobson, Focus on the Family, and Evangelical America Are Winning the Culture War* (New York: St. Martin's Press, 2007), 21, 23; James Dobson, *Dare to Discipline* (Wheaton, IL: Tyndale House, 1970), 23.

8. Seth Dowland, *Family Values and the Rise of the Christian Right* (Philadelphia: University of Pennsylvania Press, 2015), 87.

9. Tim Stafford, "His Father's Son: The Drive Behind James Dobson, Jr.," *Christianity Today*, April 22, 1988, 16.

10. Dale Buss, *Family Man: The Biography of Dr. James Dobson* (Wheaton, IL: Tyndale House, 2005), 18, 33; Gilgoff, *Jesus Machine*, 20.

11. Dobson, *Dare to Discipline*, 6, 81–82; Buss, *Family Man*, 44.

12. Gilgoff, *Jesus Machine*, 20–23.

13. Susan B. Ridgely, *Practicing What the Doctor Preached: At Home with Focus on the Family* (New York: Oxford University Press, 2017), 29; Gilgoff, *Jesus Machine*, 24.

14. Self, *All in the Family*, 314–15.

15. Gail Collins, *When Everything Changed: The Amazing Journey of American Women from 1960 to the Present* (New York: Little, Brown, 2009), 288; Self, *All in the Family*, 310, 338; W. Bradford Wilcox, *Soft Patriarchs, New Men: How Christianity Shapes Fathers and Husbands* (Chicago, IL: University of Chicago Press, 2004), 202.

16. James Dobson, *What Wives Wish Their Husbands Knew about Women* (Wheaton, IL:

Tyndale House, 1975), 62, 64, 114; James Dobson, *Straight Talk to Men and Their Wives* (Waco, TX: Word Books, 1980), 168.

17. Dobson, *Straight Talk*, 22–23, 69, 155, 157, 159; *What Wives Wish*, 35, 140.

18. Dobson, *Straight Talk*, 23, 157, 168.

19. Gilgoff, *Jesus Machine*, 9.

20. Dowland, *Family Values*, 88; Ridgely, *Practicing What the Doctor Preached*, 4–5, 28, 32–34; Corwin E. Smidt, *American Evangelicals Today* (New York: Rowan & Littlefield, 2013), 4.

21. Ridgely, *Practicing What the Doctor Preached*, 34–35; Gilgoff, *Jesus Machine*, 26–28; Dowland, *Family Values*, 86.

22. Stafford, "His Father's Son"; Gilgoff, *Jesus Machine*, 7.

23. Colleen McDannell, "Women, Girls, and Focus on the Family," in *Women and Twentieth-Century Protestantism*, ed. Margaret Lamberts Bendroth and Virginia Lieson Brereton (Urbana: University of Illinois Press, 2002), 115; George Lakoff, *Moral Politics: How Liberals and Conservatives Think* (Chicago: University of Chicago, 1996); John C. Green et al., *Religion and the Culture Wars: Dispatches from the Front* (New York: Rowman & Littlefield, 1996), 81.

Chapter 5: **SLAVES AND SOLDIERS**

1. Jason C. Bivins, *Religion of Fear: The Politics of Horror in Conservative Evangelicalism* (Oxford: Oxford University Press, 2008), 194–95; Tim LaHaye and Jerry B. Jenkins, *Glorious Appearing: The End of Days* (Wheaton, IL: Tyndale House, 2004), 204, 225–26, quoted in Bivins, *Religion of Fear*, 207–8; Jennie Chapman, *Plotting Apocalypse: Reading, Agency, and Identity in the Left Behind Series* (Jackson: University Press of Mississippi, 2013), 4.

2. Tim LaHaye, *How to Be Happy Though Married* (Wheaton, IL: Tyndale House Publishers, 1968).

3. "The Morals Revolution on the U.S. Campus," *Newsweek*, April 6, 1964, quoted in R. Marie Griffith, *Moral Combat: How Sex Divided American Christians and Fractured American Politics* (New York: Basic Books, 2017), 155–56.

4. Griffith, *Moral Combat*, 172–73, 177, 198–99; "The Sins of Billy James," *Time*, February 16, 1976, 68.

5. Tim and Beverly LaHaye, *The Act of Marriage: The Beauty of Sexual Love* (Grand Rapids, MI: Zondervan, 1976), 97.

6. LaHaye and LaHaye, *Act of Marriage*, 22–25, 36.

7. LaHaye and LaHaye, *Act of Marriage*, 234–91.

8. LaHaye and LaHaye, *Act of Marriage*, 38, 133.

9. Green et al., *Religion and the Culture Wars*, 81.

10. Tim LaHaye, *The Battle for the Mind* (Old Tappan, NJ: Fleming H. Revell, 1980), 142.

11. LaHaye, *Battle for the Mind*, 154; Tim LaHaye, *The Battle for the Family* (Old Tappan, NJ: Fleming H. Revell, 1982), 108–9, 127–31.

12. Ingersoll, *Building God's Kingdom*, 22–23, 26–38.

13. David D. Kirkpatrick, "The 2004 Campaign: The Conservatives; Club of the Most Powerful Gathers in Strictest Privacy," *New York Times*, August 28, 2014; Larry

Eskridge, "And, the Most Influential American Evangelical of the last 25 Years Is . . ." *Evangelical Studies Bulletin*, Winter 2001, 3.

14. Williams, *God's Own Party*, 43–45.

15. Michelle Goldberg, *Kingdom Coming: The Rise of Christian Nationalism* (New York: W. W. Norton, 2006), 11; Peter Steinfels, "Moral Majority to Dissolve; Says Mission Accomplished," *New York Times*, June 12, 1989; Frances FitzGerald, "A Disciplined Charging Army," *The New Yorker*, May 18, 1981.

16. Jerry Falwell, *Listen, America!* (New York: Doubleday, 1980), Author's Note; 72, 130–31.

17. Falwell, *Listen, America!*, 19, 123, 132.

18. Falwell, *Listen, America!*, 16–17, 98.

19. FitzGerald, "A Disciplined Charging Army."

20. Jerry Falwell, "Segregation or Integration—Which?" quoted in Williams, *God's Own Party*, 46; FitzGerald, "A Disciplined Charging Army."

21. FitzGerald, "A Disciplined Charging Army."

22. FitzGerald, "A Disciplined Charging Army."

23. FitzGerald, "A Disciplined Charging Army."

24. Self, *All in the Family*, 336–37.

25. Gilgoff, *Jesus Machine*, 31.

26. Jackson Katz, *Man Enough? Donald Trump, Hillary Clinton, and the Politics of Presidential Masculinity* (Northampton, MA: Olive Branch Press, 2016), 75–76.

Chapter 6: GOING FOR THE JUGULAR

1. Dochuk, *From Bible Belt to Sunbelt*, 392.

2. Dochuk, *From Bible Belt to Sunbelt*, 393; Ronald Reagan, "Address by the Honorable Ronald Reagan," Institute for Civic Leadership, August 5, 1980, https://uindy .historyit.com/item.php?id=795341.

3. Green et al., *Religion and the Culture Wars*, 20; Dowland, *Family Values*, 151; Williams, *God's Own Party*, 191; Reagan, "Address by the Honorable Ronald Reagan."

4. Bacevich, *New American Militarism*, 135.

5. Ronald Reagan, "Election Eve Address, 'A Vision for America,'" The American Presidency Project, November 3, 1980, http://www.presidency.ucsb.edu/ws/?pid=85199.

6. Katz, *Man Enough*, 83–84; "Playboy Interview," 84.

7. Katz, *Man Enough*, 109–10; 83.

8. Katz, *Man Enough*, 77; Dowland, *Family Values*, 177.

9. Self, *All in the Family*, 359; Williams, *God's Own Party*, 193.

10. Frances FitzGerald, *The Evangelicals: The Struggle to Shape America* (New York: Simon & Schuster, 2018), 312.

11. Miller, *Billy Graham*, 124–54; James L. Guth, "Southern Baptist Clergy, the Christian Right, and Political Activism in the South," in *Politics and Religion in the White South*, ed. Glenn Feldman (Lexington: University Press of Kentucky, 2005), 192; FitzGerald, *Evangelicals*, 332.

12. Seth Dowland, "A New Kind of Patriarchy: Inerrancy and Masculinity in the Southern Baptist Convention, 1879–2000," in Friend, *Southern Masculinity*, 247.

13. Dowland, "New Kind of Patriarchy," 248–50; Paul D. Simmons, "A Theological Response to Fundamentalism on the Abortion Issue," quoted in Barry Hankins, *Uneasy in Babylon: Southern Baptist Conservatives and American Culture* (Tuscaloosa: University of Alabama Press, 2002), 177.

14. Dowland, "New Kind of Patriarchy," 252–53.

15. Elizabeth H. Flowers, *Into the Pulpit: Southern Baptist Women and Power Since World War II* (Chapel Hill: University of North Carolina Press, 2012), 5, 73–81.

16. Dowland, "New Kind of Patriarchy," 255; Flowers, *Into the Pulpit*, 9–10.

17. Williams, *God's Own Party*, 188, 192.

18. Dochuk, *From Bible Belt to Sunbelt*, 396; Williams, *God's Own Party*, 194.

19. Williams, *God's Own Party*, 188, 197; Self, *All in the Family*, 360.

20. Bacevich, *New American Militarism*, 136.

21. Loveland, *American Evangelicals*, 214–15; Bacevich, *New American Militarism*, 135; John Price, *America at the Crossroads: Repentance or Repression?* (Indianapolis, IN: Christian House Publishing, 1976), 202; Jerry Falwell, *Listen, America!*, 9–10; Hal Lindsey, *The 1980s: Countdown to Armageddon* (King of Prussia, PA: Westgate Press, 1980), 165; Bacevich, *New American Militarism*, 135.

22. Loveland, *American Evangelicals*, 222–23.

23. Dowland, *Family Values*, 191–92; "SALT II: The Only Alternative to Annihilation?" *Christianity Today*, March 27, 1981, 15; Loveland, *American Evangelicals*, 223.

24. Ronald Reagan, "Evil Empire Speech," Voices of Democracy, March 8, 1983, http://voicesofdemocracy.umd.edu/reagan-evil-empire-speech-text/.

25. Bacevich, *New American Militarism*, 137; Dowland, *Family Values*, 195–97; Young, *We Gather Together*, 238.

26. Lauren Frances Turek, "Ambassadors for the Kingdom of God or for America? Christian Nationalism, the Christian Right, and the Contra War," *Religions* 7 (12), 2016, http://www.mdpi.com/2077-1444/7/12/151/htm.

27. Turek, "Ambassadors for the Kingdom."

28. Turek, "Ambassadors for the Kingdom"; Bacevich, *New American Militarism*, 137.

29. Turek, "Ambassadors for the Kingdom."

30. David E. Rosenbaum, "Iran-Contra Hearings: Tension and High Drama; North Insists His Superiors Backed Iran-Contra Deals; Assumes Reagan Approved," *New York Times*, July 8, 1987; "North on the 'Neat Idea' of the Diversion," "North on His Family's Safety and Meeting Abu Nidal," "North on Getting Fired and Covering Up the Diversion," *Understanding the Iran-Contra Affairs*, July 8–9, 1987, https://www.brown.edu/Research/Understanding_the_Iran_Contra_Affair/v-on13.php.

Chapter 7: THE GREATEST AMERICAN HERO

1. David Bauder, "'Olliemania' Fades Away," AP News, September 4, 1987.

2. Donald P. Baker, "Falwell Defends North, Compares Him to 'Savior,'" *Washington Post*, May 3, 1988.

3. Baker, "Falwell Defends North."

4. "Religious Right Drums Up Support for North," *Los Angeles Times*, September 3, 1988.

5.   Highlights of North's Testimony," *Washington Post*, July 14, 1987; Ben Bradlee Jr., *Guts and Glory: The Rise and Fall of Oliver North* (New York: Donald I. Fine, 1988), 21–23, 27, 33.

6.   Bradlee, *Guts and Glory*, 64–65.

7.   Bradlee, *Guts and Glory*, 62, 65, 86, 96–97.

8.   Bradlee, *Guts and Glory*, 101–2, 87, 99.

9.   Bradlee, *Guts and Glory*, 115, 418–19; "Religious Right Drums Up Support for North"; "North spreads religious word," GoUpstate.com, May 3, 1993.

10.   Bradlee, *Guts and Glory*, 413–15, 420–21.

11.   Walter Pincus and Dan Morgan, "Reagan 'Never' Briefed on Funds," *Washington Post*, July 14, 1987; "North Talks to Hall After Resigning," *Understanding the Iran-Contra Affairs*, June 9, 1987; "Iran-Contra Hearings; The Committee's Turn: Speeches to North," *New York Times*, July 14, 1987.

12.   "Southern Baptists Salute 'Patriot'—Ollie North," *Deseret News*, June 4, 1991.

13.   Oliver North, with William Novak, *Under Fire: An American Story* (New York: HarperCollins, 1991); "North spreads religious word"; John F. Persinos, "Ollie, Inc.: how Oliver North raised over $20 million in a losing U.S. Senate race," *Campaigns & Elections*, June 1, 1995.

14.   Kent Jenkins Jr., "The Good, the Bad and the Ollie," *Washington Post*, March 20, 1994.

15.   Edwin Louis Cole, *Maximized Manhood: A Guide to Family Survival* (Springdale, PA: Whitaker House, 1982), 129; Ari L. Goldman, obituary of Edwin Louis Cole, *New York Times*, August 31, 2002.

16.   Cole, *Maximized Manhood*, 63, 176.

17.   Cole, *Maximized Manhood*, 35, 61, 69, 72, 77, 134, 166.

18.   Cole, *Maximized Manhood*, 127, 129.

19.   Cole, *Maximized Manhood*, 132.

20.   Travis M. Andrews, "The Rev. Marvin Gorman, who prompted Jimmy Swaggart's downfall in the '80s, dies at 83," *Washington Post*, January 9, 2017; Frances Frank Marcus, "Swaggart Found Liable for Defaming Minister," *New York Times*, September 13, 1991.

21.   FitzGerald, *Evangelicals*, 374, 399; John Wigger, *PTL: The Rise and Fall of Jim and Tammy Faye Bakker's Evangelical Empire* (New York: Oxford University Press, 2017), 127.

22.   "Jessica Hahn Tells All," *Washington Post*, September 23, 1987; Tim Funk, "Jessica Hahn, woman at center of televangelist's fall 30 years ago, confronts her past," *Charlotte Observer*, December 16, 2017; Andrews, "The Rev. Marvin Gorman."

23.   Joanne Kaufman, "The Fall of Jimmy Swaggart," *People*, March 7, 1988; "Scandals: No Apologies This Time," *Time*, October 28, 1991.

24.   "Religious Right Drums Up Support."

25.   Loveland, *American Evangelicals*, 283–87; "Interview with Army Chief of Staff, General Wickham, with *Decision Magazine*, Washington, D.C., September 27, 1984," quoted in Loveland, *American Evangelicals*, 275; "All Active-duty U.S. Soldiers Are Expected to See Dobson Film," *Christianity Today*, October 5, 1984, 100.

26.   *Where's Dad?* (Army videotape) (Waco, TX), 1981, quoted in Loveland, *American Evangelicals*, 288.

27. Loveland, *American Evangelicals*, 289, 291.

28. John Grinalds, "Evangelism in Command," *Command*, Spring 1985, 37–40, quoted in Loveland, *American Evangelicals*, 319–20.

29. Rus Walton, *One Nation Under God* (Nashville, TN: Thomas Nelson, rev. ed., 1987), 7, 170, 181; Bacevich, *New American Militarism*, 131n29.

30. Michael Lienesch, *Redeeming America: Piety and Politics in the New Christian Right* (Chapel Hill: University of North Carolina Press, 1993), 216; Bacevich, *New American Militarism*, 146.

Chapter 8: WAR FOR THE SOUL

1. Loveland, *American Evangelicals*, 224, 283–85; Kirkpatrick, "The 2004 Campaign." The 2014 Membership Directory of the Council for National Policy was released on the website of the Southern Poverty Law Center, https://www.splcenter.org/sites/default/files/cnp_redacted_final.pdf, accessed April 26, 2018.

2. Katz, *Man Enough*, 83; FitzGerald, *Evangelicals*, 326–27; Andrew Hartman, *A War for the Soul of America: A History of the Culture Wars*, 2nd ed. (Chicago: University of Chicago, 2019), 156.

3. FitzGerald, *Evangelicals*, 327–28.

4. FitzGerald, *Evangelicals*, 382.

5. FitzGerald, *Evangelicals*, 384–90.

6. Green et al., *Religion and the Culture Wars*, 46.

7. Katz, *Man Enough*, 115; Green et al., *Religion and the Culture Wars*, 271.

8. Bacevich, *New American Militarism*, 143.

9. FitzGerald, *Evangelicals*, 412–18; Neil J. Young, "How George H. W. Bush enabled the rise of the religious right," *Washington Post*, December 5, 2018.

10. FitzGerald, *Evangelicals*, 419.

11. Daniel White, "A Brief History of the Clinton Family's Chocolate-Chip Cookies," *Time*, August 19, 2016.

12. Christian Smith, *American Evangelicalism: Embattled and Thriving* (Chicago: University of Chicago Press, 1998); FitzGerald, *Evangelicals*, 420–22.

13. Phyllis Schlafly, "The New World Order Wants Your Children," *Phyllis Schlafly Report*, March 1993; Phyllis Schlafly, "Are All Our Children 'At Risk'?" *Phyllis Schlafly Report*, October 1995.

14. Bacevich, *New American Militarism*, 144; Loveland, *American Evangelicals*, 325–26, 340.

15. Phyllis Schlafly, "The Kelly Flinn Flim-Flam," Eagle Forum, June 4, 1997; Bacevich, *New American Militarism*, 144; Phyllis Schlafly, "The United Nations—An Enemy in Our Midst," *Phyllis Schlafly Report*, November 1995; Phyllis Schlafly, "U.S. Armed Services under Global Control," *Phyllis Schlafly Report*, October 1997.

16. Enloe, *Morning After*, 30, 33, 199.

17. Schlafly, "Will We Allow Clinton to Redefine the Presidency?" Eagle Forum, February 11, 1998.

18. James Dobson, "An Evangelical Response to Bill Clinton," 1998, in *The Columbia*

Documentary History of Religion in America Since 1945, ed. Paul Harvey and Philip Goff (New York: Columbia University Press, 2007), 303–7.

19. Thomas B. Edsall, "Resignation 'Too Easy,' Robertson Tells Christian Coalition," *Washington Post*, September 19, 1998; Laurie Goodstein, "The Testing of a President: The Conservatives; Christian Coalition Moans Lack of Anger at Clinton," *New York Times*, September, 20, 1998; Tom Strode, "Religious leaders differ on impeachment stands," *Baptist Press*, December 29, 1998; Jonathan Merritt, "Trump-Loving Christians Owe Bill Clinton an Apology," *The Atlantic*, August 10, 2016.

20. Stephen J. Ducat, *The Wimp Factor: Gender Gaps, Holy Wars, & the Politics of Anxious Masculinity* (Boston, MA: Beacon Press, 2004), 10–11.

21. James Dobson, *Love Must Be Tough* (Waco, TX: Word Books, 1983), 149–50; Kathryn Joyce, *Quiverfull: Inside the Christian Patriarchy Movement* (Boston, MA: Beacon Press, 2009), 84.

22. Griffith, *Moral Combat*, 245–50.

23. Charles Colson, "The Thomas Hearings and the New Gender Wars," *Christianity Today*, November 25, 1991, 72.

24. Phyllis Schlafly, "Anita Hill Plays Phony Role—'Damsel in Distress'—But Isn't Convincing," *Sun Sentinel*, October 17, 1991.

25. Phyllis Schlafly, "Supreme Court Upholds Constitution in VAWA Decision," *Phyllis Schlafly Eagles*, May 31, 2000; Phyllis Schlafly, "Feminist Assault on Reasonableness," *Phyllis Schlafly Report*, December 1996; Griffith, *Moral Combat*, 250–56.

26. Katz, *Man Enough*, 124–26.

27. Katz, *Man Enough*, 136.

28. Amy Sullivan, "America's New Religion: Fox Evangelicalism," *New York Times*, December 15, 2017.

29. Elisabeth Bumiller, "Evangelicals Sway White House on Human Rights Issues Abroad," *New York Times*, October 26, 2003; Bacevich, *New American Militarism*, 143.

30. FitzGerald, *Evangelicals*, 421, 424.

Chapter 9: **TENDER WARRIORS**

1. Michael Kimmel, "Patriarchy's Second Coming as Masculine Renewal," in Dane S. Claussen, ed., *Standing on the Promises: The Promise Keepers and the Revival of Manhood* (Cleveland: Pilgrim Press, 1999), 111–12.

2. Patricia Ireland, "A Look at . . . Promise Keepers," *Washington Post*, September 7, 1997; Laurie Goodstein, "Women and the Promise Keepers; Good for the Gander, but the Goose Isn't So Sure," *New York Times*, October 5, 1997.

3. Kimmel, "Patriarchy's Second Coming," 113, 117; Bill Bright, *The Coming Revival* (Orlando, FL: New Life Publications, 1995), 49–58; David S. Gutterman, "Exodus and the Chosen Men of God," in Claussen, *Standing on the Promises*, 143; John Stoltenberg, "Christianity, Feminism, and the Manhood Crisis," in Claussen, *Standing on the Promises*, 102.

4. Stoltenberg, "Christianity, Feminism, and the Manhood Crisis"; John D. Keeler, Ben Fraser, and William J. Brown, "How Promise Keepers See Themselves as Men Behav-

ing Goodly," in Claussen, *Standing on the Promises*, 79; Dane S. Claussen, "What the Media Missed about the Promise Keepers," in Claussen, *Standing on the Promises*, 29.

5. Gary Oliver, *Real Men Have Feelings, Too* (Chicago: Moody, 1993); John P. Bartkowski, *The Promise Keepers: Servants, Soldiers, and Godly Men* (New Brunswick, NJ: Rutgers University Press, 2004), 50–52.

6. Bartkowski, *The Promise Keepers*, 53–56.

7. Wilcox, *Soft Patriarchs*, 4; Bethany Moreton, *To Serve God and Wal-Mart: The Making of Christian Free Enterprise* (Cambridge, MA: Harvard University Press, 2009), 101–2, 143; Self, *All in the Family*, 324.

8. Wilcox, *Soft Patriarchs*, 143–50; Elizabeth Brusco, *The Reformation of Machismo: Evangelical Conversion and Gender in Colombia* (Austin: University of Texas Press, 1995).

9. Kimmel, "Patriarchy's Second Coming," 115–16; Gutterman, "Exodus and the Chosen Men of God," 143; Jeff Sharlet, *C Street: The Fundamentalist Threat to American Democracy* (New York: Back Bay Books, 2010), 66; Moreton, *To Serve God and Wal-Mart*, 102.

10. Kimmel, "Patriarchy's Second Coming," 117–18; Don McClanen, "Fellowship of Christian Athletes Founder," *Fellowship of Christian Athletes*, https://www.fca.org/aboutus/who-we-are/don-mcclanen, accessed June 7, 2018; Paul Putz, "The Role of Sports Ministries in the NFL Protests," *Religion & Politics*, October 17, 2017.

11. FitzGerald, "A Disciplined Charging Army."

12. Randall Balmer, *Evangelicalism in America* (Waco, TX: Baylor University Press, 2016), 134–35; Randall Balmer, "Keep the Faith and Go the Distance," in Claussen, *Standing on the Promises*, 201.

13. Kimmel, "Patriarchy's Second Coming," 116, 118; Judith L. Newton, "A Reaction to Declining Market and Religious Influence," in Claussen, *Standing on the Promises*, 40; Marcia Slacum Greene and Hamil R. Harris, "Preaching a Promise of Inclusiveness," *Washington Post*, September 25, 1997.

14. John Trent, ed., *Go the Distance: The Making of a Promise Keeper* (Colorado Springs, CO: Focus on the Family Publishing, 1996); Keeler et al., "How Promise Keepers," 82; Claussen, "What the Media Missed," 18.

15. Claussen, "What the Media Missed," 18–19.

16. Claussen, "What the Media Missed," 28–29.

17. Steve Rabey, "Where Is the Christian Men's Movement Headed?" *Christianity Today*, April 29, 1996, 60; Kimmel, "Patriarchy's Second Coming," 113.

18. Leanne Payne, *Crisis in Masculinity* (Westchester, IL: Crossway Books, 1985); Gordon Dalbey, *Healing the Masculine Soul: God's Restoration of Men to Real Manhood*, rev. ed. (Nashville, TN: Thomas Nelson, 2003), x.

19. Dalbey, *Healing the Masculine Soul* (2003), x.

20. Gordon Dalbey, *Healing the Masculine Soul: An Affirming Message for Men and the Women Who Love Them* (Nashville, TN: Thomas Nelson, 1988), 118–19.

21. Dalbey, *Healing the Masculine Soul* (1988), 9, 21, 120.

22. Dalbey, *Healing the Masculine Soul* (1988), 9–10, 43–46, 61, 75, 120–21, 123.

23. Dalbey, *Healing the Masculine Soul* (1988), 76, 128–29.

24. Dalbey, *Healing the Masculine Soul* (1988), 132–33.

25. Steve Farrar, *Point Man: How a Man Can Lead His Family* (Sisters, OR: Multnomah, 1990), 16–17, 24, 183.

26. Farrar, *Point Man*, 13, 24, 201–3, 205, 207–8; Dobson, *Straight Talk*, 21, quoted in Farrar, *Point Man*, 13.

27. Stu Weber, *Tender Warrior: Every Man's Purpose, Every Woman's Dream, Every Child's Hope* (Sisters, OR: Multnomah, 2006), 18.

28. Weber, *Tender Warrior*, 18, 45, 92, 100–101, 104, 114, 120.

29. Weber, *Tender Warrior*, 34–43, 74–75, 207–9.

30. Weber, *Tender Warrior*, 69–71.

31. Weber, *Tender Warrior*, 172, 176.

32. Farrar, *Point Man*, 56–57.

33. "Our History," CBMW.org, https://cbmw.org/about/history/, accessed February 17, 2019.

34. Council on Biblical Manhood and Womanhood, "Danvers Statement," CBMW.org, https://cbmw.org/about/danvers-statement, accessed February 17, 2019.

35. John Piper, "A Vision of Biblical Complementarity: Manhood and Womanhood Defined According to the Bible," in John Piper and Wayne Grudem, ed., *Recovering Biblical Manhood and Womanhood: A Response to Evangelical Feminism* (Wheaton, IL: Crossway Books, 1991), 48, 53.

36. Bob Miller, "Resolution on Women in Combat," CBMW News, 6, http://cbmw.org/wp-content/uploads/2013/05/2-2.pdf#page=5, accessed June 8, 2018.

37. Dowland, "New Kind of Patriarchy," 254, 260; Flowers, *Into the Pulpit*, 129.

38. Dowland, *Family Values*, 140; Flowers, *Into the Pulpit*, 145.

39. Herb Hollinger, "Biblical manhood, womanhood conference makes note of Southern Baptists' stance," *Baptist Press*, March 23, 2000; Kevin Giles, *The Rise and Fall of the Complementarian Doctrine of the Trinity* (Eugene, OR: Cascade Books, 2017), 60.

40. Jared Burkholder, "Before 'true love waits' there was Josh McDowell and Petra," Patheos, January 8, 2019, https://www.patheos.com/blogs/anxiousbench/2019/01/before-true-love-waits-there-was-josh-mcdowell-and-petra/.

41. Burkholder, "Before 'true love waits.'"

42. Moslener, *Virgin Nation*, 109, 113–16.

Chapter 10: NO MORE CHRISTIAN NICE GUY

1. Douglas Leblanc, "Wildheart," *Christianity Today*, August 1, 2004, 33; John Eldredge, *Wild at Heart: Discovering the Secret of a Man's Soul* (Nashville, TN: Thomas Nelson, 2001); Jonathan Merritt, "The book that revolutionized 'Christian manhood': 15 years after 'Wild at Heart,'" Religion News Service, April 22, 2016.

2. Eldredge, *Wild at Heart*, 9, 83.

3. Eldredge, *Wild at Heart*, 6–9, 68, 79–80, 84, 175.

4. Eldredge, *Wild at Heart*, Introduction, 11–12.

5. Eldredge, *Wild at Heart*, 15–16, 36, 51, 180–82; Sharlet, *The Family*, 332–33.

6. Randy L. Stinson, "Is God Wild at Heart? A Review of John Eldredge's Wild at Heart," *Journal for Biblical Manhood and Womanhood* 08:2 (Fall 2003), 55.

7.   Mark Mulder and James K. A. Smith, "Are Men Really Wild at Heart?" *Perspectives: A Journal of Reformed Thought*, October 16, 2004.

8.   James C. Dobson, *Bringing Up Boys* (Wheaton, IL: Tyndale House, 2001), 19, 26, 39.

9.   Dobson, *Bringing Up Boys*, 23, 27, 68, 148.

10.   Dobson, *Bringing Up Boys*, 13–15, 76, 120, 151, 161–62, 165, 179, 194–95, 228.

11.   Dobson, *Bringing Up Boys*, back cover, front matter.

12.   Molly Worthen, "The Controversialist," *Christianity Today*, April 17, 2009, 42–49.

13.   Douglas Wilson, *Future Men: Raising Boys to Fight Giants* (Moscow, ID: Canon Press, 2012), 10–16, 125, 130–31.

14.   Douglas Wilson, *Federal Husband* (Moscow, ID: Canon Press, 1999), 63, 80–82; Douglas Wilson, *Reforming Marriage* (Moscow, ID: Canon Press, 1995), 16, 19; Douglas Wilson, *Fidelity* (Moscow, ID: Canon Press, 1999), 45–46, 64, 75–76; Douglas Wilson, *Her Hand in Marriage: Biblical Courtship in the Modern World* (Moscow, ID: Canon Press, 1997), 74–75.

15.   Wilson, *Reforming Marriage*, 22–23, 28, 139; Wilson, *Federal Husband*, 36; Wilson, *Fidelity*, 76.

16.   Katz, *Man Enough*, 170.

17.   Phyllis Schlafly, "Feminism Meets Terrorism," *Phyllis Schlafly Report*, July 2002; Phyllis Schlafly, "The Premier American Hero—George Washington," *Phyllis Schlafly Report*, May 2002.

18.   Steve Farrar, *King Me: What Every Son Wants and Needs from His Father* (Chicago, IL: Moody Publishers, 2005), 116, 120, 124–28.

19.   Dalbey, *Healing the Masculine Soul* (1988), 176; Dalbey, *Healing the Masculine Soul* (2003), 188, 120.

20.   Paul Coughlin, *No More Christian Nice Guy: When Being Nice—Instead of Good—Hurts Men, Women and Children* (Bloomington, MN: Bethany House Publishers, 2007), 26–27, 49, 51, 149–51.

21.   David Murrow, *Why Men Hate Going to Church* (Nashville, TN: Thomas Nelson, 2011), 21, 27, 97, 135, 143–44, 149; Amazon author biography, https://www.amazon.com/Why-Men-Hate-Going-Church/dp/B0086KHTOQ/ref=pd_lpo_sbs_14_t_0?_encoding=UTF8&psc=1&refRID=9SAB0J9MX3FNSYNXGTD8, accessed November 18, 2018.

22.   Robert Lewis, *Raising a Modern-Day Knight: A Father's Role in Guiding His Son to Authentic Manhood* (Colorado Springs, CO: Focus on the Family, 1997), 121, 123, 135; Jenny Jarvie and Stephanie Simon, "Manliness is next to godliness," *Los Angeles Times*, December 7, 2006. On the "Braveheart games," see Lyndon Christian School Home Bulletin, December 2006/January 2007, 14; Jeff Sharlet, "Teenage Holy War," *Rolling Stone*, April 19, 2007.

23.   Bartkowski, *The Promise Keepers*, 6; David Murrow, *Why Men*, 229; Jarvie and Simon, "Manliness is next to godliness"; Charles Honey, "United Against Evil: Promise Keepers says its Ministry is Needed now More Than Ever," *Grand Rapids Press*, 2005, reposted at Men's Resource Center of West Michigan, https://menscenter.org/promise-keepers/, accessed July 24, 2019.

24.   David W. Moore, "Eight of 10 Americans Support Ground War in Afghanistan," Gallup.com, November 1, 2001; NPR, "Profile: Silent Evangelical Support of Bush's Proposed War Against Iraq," *Morning Edition*, February 26, 2003.

25. Richard Land, "The so-called 'Land Letter,'" Dr. Richard Land, October 3, 2002, http://www.drrichardland.com/press/entry/the-so-called-land-letter; NPR, "Profile: Silent Evangelical."

26. Jim Lobe, "Politics—U.S.: Conservative Christians Biggest Backers of Iraq War," Inter Press Service, October 9, 2002; "War Concerns Grow, But Support Remains Steadfast," Pew Research Center, April 3, 2003; NPR, "Profile: Silent Evangelical."

27. Jerry Falwell, "God is Pro-War," WND, January 31, 2004, http://www.wnd.com/2004/01/23022/.

28. "Michael W. Smith—There She Stands—2004 RNC," YouTube, https://www.youtube.com/watch?v=zlRrtY2QEK0, accessed July 25, 2019.

Chapter 11: **HOLY BALLS**

1. Jarvie and Simon, "Manliness is next to godliness"; John Donvan, "Christian Men . . . Too Wimpy?" ABC News, March 15, 2007; Lillian Daniel, "Missing Men," *Christian Century*, April 2, 2007, 20.

2. R. M. Schneiderman, "Flock Is Now a Fight Team in Some Ministries," *New York Times*, February 1, 2010.

3. Gilgoff, *Jesus Machine*, 34–35; "U.S. Department of Education, 1.5 Million Home-schooled Students in the United States in 2007" (NCES 2009-030), 2008, https://nces.ed.gov/pubs2009/2009030.pdf; Jaweed Kaleem, "Homeschooling Without God," *The Atlantic*, March 30, 2016.

4. Smith, "The Cult Next Door."

5. Ingersoll, *Building God's Kingdom*, 140–41, 144; Doug Phillips, *The Little Boy Down the Road: Short Stories & Essays on the Beauty of Family Life* (San Antonio, TX: Vision Forum, 2008), 183–85; Doug Phillips, *Poems for Patriarchs* (San Antonio, TX: Vision Forum 2002), front panel, 3–4, 14, 59–60, 103–4.

6. Joyce, *Quiverfull*, 5; Ingersoll, *Building God's Kingdom*, 143; "The All-American Boy's Adventure Catalog," Vision Forum, March 20, 2009, https://web.archive.org/web/20090320183141/http://www.visionforum.com/boysadventure; "Beautiful Girlhood Collection," Vision Forum, April 1, 2009, https://web.archive.org/web/20090401013608/http://www.visionforum.com/beautifulgirlhood; Julie Ingersoll, "Doug Phillips: The Big Scandal You Didn't Hear About and Why It Matters," *Huffpost*, November 6, 2013; Libby Anne, "Kirk Cameron's Insidious Christian Patriarchy Connections," Patheos, March 8, 2012, https://www.patheos.com/blogs/lovejoyfeminism/2012/03/kirk-cameron-seriously-why-are-we-surprised.html.

7. Joyce, *Quiverfull*, 134, 172.

8. Goldberg, *Kingdom Coming*, 4.

9. Sharlet, *The Family*, 233–36, 322–35, 345–56.

10. Jessica Johnson, *Biblical Porn: Affect, Labor, and Pastor Mark Driscoll's Evangelical Empire* (Durham, NC: Duke University Press, 2018), 23–25, 28.

11. Brandon O'Brien, "A Jesus for Real Men," *Christianity Today*, April 18, 2008, 49; Mark Driscoll and G. Breshears, *Vintage Jesus: Timeless Answers to Timely Questions* (Wheaton, IL: Crossway Books, 2008), 11, 31, 43, 150.

12. Johnson, *Biblical Porn*, 30–33; Driscoll, *Vintage Jesus*, 127–29; Mark Driscoll, "Men

and Masculinity: Proverbs," YouTube, filmed 2009, https://www.youtube.com/watch?v=o-X5ajR206E.

13. Mark Driscoll, "Sex: A study of the Good Bits of Song of Solomon," YouTube, published March 13, 2014, https://www.youtube.com/watch?v=J8sNVDyW-ws&has_verified=1.

14. Matthew Paul Turner, "Mark Driscoll's Pussified Nation," Matthew Paul Turner, July 29, 2014, http://matthewpaulturner.com/2014/07/29/mark-driscolls-pussified-nation/.

15. Turner, "Mark Driscoll's Pussified Nation"; Johnson, *Biblical Porn*, 52; Jason Molinet, "Seattle-based Mars Hill Church reeling after founding pastor calls women 'homes' for God's penis," *New York Daily News*, September 10, 2014.

16. Mark Driscoll, *Confessions of a Reformission Reverend: Hard Lessons from an Emerging Missional Church* (Grand Rapids, MI: Zondervan, 2006), 129–32, quoted in Johnson, *Biblical Porn*, 58–59.

17. Johnson, *Biblical Porn*, 46–47, 53.

18. Johnson, *Biblical Porn*, 65–69.

19. Turner, "Mark Driscoll's Pussified Nation"; Al Mohler Q&A in David Murray, "Al Mohler on Mark Driscoll," HeadHeartHand, October 7, 2011, http://headhearthand.org/blog/2011/10/07/al-mohler-on-mark-driscoll/.

20. Name withheld, email correspondence with the author, February 25, 2019.

21. Zach Hoag, "Smokin' Hot Wives and Water to the Soul," *Huffington Post*, April 25, 2013, updated June 25, 2013; 2019; Mary DeMeuth, "The Sexy Wife I Can't Be," A Deeper Story, February 26, 2013, http://deeperstory.com/the-sexy-wife-i-cant-be/, accessed June 20, 2019.

22. Collin Hansen, "Young, Restless, Reformed," *Christianity Today*, September 22, 2006, 32–38.

23. Steve Chalke and Alan Mann, *The Lost Message of Jesus* (Grand Rapids, MI: Zondervan, 2004), 182–83; Colin Hansen, *Young, Restless, Reformed: A Journalist's Journey with the New Calvinists* (Wheaton, IL: Crossway Books, 2008), 44; John Piper, " 'The Frank and Manly Mr. Ryle'—The Value of a Masculine Ministry," Desiring God 2012 Conference for Pastors, January 31, 2012, https://www.desiringgod.org/messages/the-frank-and-manly-mr-ryle-the-value-of-a-masculine-ministry.

24. Roger E. Olson, "What Attracts People Into the Young, Restless, Reformed Movement?" Patheos, March 14, 2014, http://www.patheos.com/blogs/rogereolson/2014/03/what-attracts-people-into-the-young-restless-reformed-movement/.

25. Yoshito Noguchi, "Celebrate our 600th Church," Acts 29, August 2, 2016, accessed June 21, 2018, http://www.acts29.com/celebrate-600th-church/; "About," Acts 29, accessed June 21, 2018, http://www.acts29.com/about/; Jonathan Merritt, "The Gospel Coalition and how (not) to engage culture," Religion News Service, June 6, 2016.

26. Hansen, *Young, Restless, Reformed*, 19, 32, 133, 136; Matt Smethurst, "Where Did All These Calvinists Come From?" The Gospel Coalition, October 23, 2013, https://www.thegospelcoalition.org/article/where-did-all-these-calvinists-come-from/.

27. Hansen, *Young, Restless, Reformed*, 107; David Van Bierma, "The New Calvinism," *Time*, March 12, 2009.

28. Hansen, *Young, Restless, Reformed*, 103.

29. Wilson, *Federal Husband*, 22–23, 27, 44–45, 98; Wilson, *Fidelity*, 107; Douglas Wilson, *For Kirk & Covenant* (Nashville, TN: Cumberland House Publishing, 2000), 183.

30. Douglas Wilson, *Southern Slavery as It Was* (Moscow, ID: Canon Press, 1996), 13, 22–25, 38; Wilson, *Black & Tan: A Collection of Essays and Excursions on Slavery, Culture War, and Scripture in America* (Moscow, ID: Canon Press, 2005), 19, 52.

31. Keith Throop, "Disappointed in John Piper's Judgment About Doug Wilson," Reformed Baptist Blog, June 26, 2009, https://reformedbaptistblog.com/2009/06/26/disappointed-in-john-pipers-judgment-about-doug-wilson/; Tony Reinke, "The Church and the World: Homosexuality, Abortion, and Race with John Piper and Douglas Wilson," Desiring God, October 4, 2013, http://www.desiringgod.org/articles/the-church-and-the-world-homosexuality-abortion-and-race-with-john-piper-and-douglas-wilson.

32. Davey Henreckson, interview with the author, September 15, 2017; Douglas Wilson, *Evangellyfish* (Moscow, ID: Canon Press, 2011).

33. Hansen, *Young, Restless, Reformed*, 139; Rachel Marie Stone, "John Piper and the Rise of Biblical Masculinity," *Christianity Today*, February 9, 2012.

Chapter 12: **PILGRIM'S PROGRESS IN CAMO**

1. Jeff Sharlet, "Soldiers of Christ," *Harper's*, May 2005, 42.

2. Suzanne Goldenberg, "Evangelicals start soul-searching as prospect of Obama win risks Christian gains in politics," *Guardian*, October 20, 2008; Weinstein and Seay, *With God on Our Side*, 8–9.

3. Weinstein and Seay, *With God on Our Side*, 9; Gilgoff, *Jesus Machine*, 32–35.

4. Gilgoff, *Jesus Machine*, 2, 5; Ridgely, *Practicing What the Doctor Preached*, 41.

5. Gilgoff, *Jesus Machine*, 6–7.

6. Gilgoff, *Jesus Machine*, 36; Balmer, *Evangelicalism in America*, 148.

7. Sharlet, "Soldiers," 42; Weinstein and Seay, *With God on Our Side*, 9.

8. Sharlet, "Soldiers," 43–45; Elizabeth Bernstein, "All the Candidates' Clergy," *Wall Street Journal*, updated August 13, 2004.

9. Sharlet, "Soldiers," 46–47.

10. Sharlet, "Soldiers," 42, 47; Burkholder, "Before 'true love waits.'"

11. Laurie Goodstein, "Air Force Academy Staff Found Promoting Religion," *New York Times*, June 23, 2005.

12. Peter Biskind, "The Rude Warrior," *Vanity Fair*, March 2011.

13. Weinstein and Seay, *With God on Our Side*, 136–39.

14. Bobby Welch, *You, the Warrior Leader: Applying Military Strategy for Victorious Spiritual Warfare* (Nashville, TN: B&H Publishing, 2004), 1, 19, 22, 24, 139–40, 150.

15. Weinstein and Seay, *With God on Our Side*, 137–38.

16. Weinstein and Seay, *With God on Our Side*, 81–82; Goodstein, "Air Force Academy."

17. Jeff Brady, "Evangelical Chaplains Test Bounds of Faith in Military," NPR, *All Things Considered*, July 27, 2005; Laurie Goodstein, "Evangelicals Are a Growing Force in the Military Chaplain Corps," *New York Times*, July 12, 2005.

18. Weinstein and Seay, *With God on Our Side*, 19.

19. Philip Shenon, "Oliver North Tells a Tall Tale of White House Intrigue," *New York Times*, August 27, 2002; Todd Starnes, "Oliver North tour promotes novel 'Mission Compromised,'" *Baptist Press*, September 11, 2002.

20. Oliver North and Chuck Holton, *American Heroes: In the Fight Against Radical Islam* (Nashville, TN: B&H Publishing, 2009), 10, 20, 139, 229.

21. North and Holton, *American Heroes*, 57, 68.

22. North and Holton, *American Heroes*, 150–51, 163, 221, 271.

23. Chuck Holton, "Boots on the Ground," *Making Men*, http://makingmenbook.com/bio/, accessed August 8, 2018; Chuck Holton, *A More Elite Soldier: Pursuing a Life of Purpose* (Sisters, OR: Multnomah, 2003), 12, 47, 55–56, 61, 119, 152, 183.

24. Alice Gray and Chuck Holton, *Stories from a Soldier's Heart: For the Patriotic Soul* (Sisters, OR: Multnomah, 2003), 25–26, 218, 236.

25. Chuck Holton and Gayle Roper, *Allah's Fire* (Sisters, OR: Multnomah, 2006), 17; Chuck Holton, *Island Inferno* (Colorado Springs, CO: Multnomah, 2007), 186–88; Chuck Holton, *Meltdown* (Colorado Springs, CO: Multnomah, 2009), 33–34, 229.

Chapter 13: WHY WE WANT TO KILL YOU

1. Laurie Goodstein, "Seeing Islam as 'Evil' Faith, Evangelicals Seek Converts," *New York Times*, May 27, 2003; Melani McAlister, *The Kingdom of God Has No Borders: A Global History of American Evangelicals* (Oxford: Oxford University Press, 2018), 159–65; Peter Waldman and Hugh Pope, "'Crusade' Reference Reinforces Fears War on Terrorism Is Against Muslims," *Wall Street Journal*, September 21, 2001.

2. Goodstein, "Seeing Islam"; NPR, "Profile: Silent Evangelical"; James Dobson, "Family in Crisis," Focus on the Family *Newsletter*, http://www.focusonthefamily.com/docstudy/newsletters/A000000639.cfm, accessed July 12, 2007; Sharlet, "Soldiers of Christ," 48; "Evangelical Views of Islam," Ethics & Public Policy and Beliefnet, https://www.beliefnet.com/news/politics/2003/04/evangelical-views-of-islam.aspx. Results of this poll were released April 7, 2003.

3. *New Man*, May/June 2007; Joyce, *Quiverfull*, 134, 183.

4. Christopher Cameron Smith, "'Ex-Muslims,' Bible Prophecy, and Islamophobia: Rhetoric and Reality in the Narratives of Walid Shoebat, Kamal Saleem, Ergun and Emir Caner," *Islamophobia Studies Journal*, vol. 2, no. 2 (Fall 2014), 84.

5. Bob Lowry, "Former Muslim now heads Falwell's university," *Deseret Morning News*, April 30, 2005; "Former Muslims Attack Islam in New Book," IslamOnline.net, September 29, 2002, https://web.archive.org/web/20070317005052/http://www.islamonline.net/servlet/Satellite?c=Article_C&cid=1158658281186&pagename=Zone-English-ArtCulture%2FACELayout, accessed January 26, 2019.

6. Alan Cooperman, "Anti-Muslim Remarks Stir Tempest," *Washington Post*, June 20, 2002; "Falwell 'sorry' for Mohammed remark," BBC News, October 13, 2002.

7. Lowry, "Former Muslim"; Nathan Lean, *The Islamophobia Industry: How the Right Manufactures Fear of Muslims* (New York: Pluto Press, 2012), 85–87; William Wan and Michelle Boorstein, "Liberty U. removing Ergun Caner as seminary dean over contradictory statements," *Washington Post*, June 30, 2010; John W. Kennedy, "Bloggers Target Seminary President," *Christianity Today*, May 3, 2010.

8. Wan and Boorstein, "Liberty U"; Lean, *Islamophobia Industry*, 89; Kennedy, "Bloggers Target Seminary President"; Jennifer Riley, "Liberty Univ. Demotes Ergun Caner After Investigation," *Christian Post*, June 29, 2010.

9. Chris Rodda, "CNN to Air Report on Taxpayer Funded Fake Former Terrorist," *Huffpost*, July 13, 2011, updated September 12, 2011; Katie Ward, "Cedar Hill Baptist to host Zachariah Anani Aug. 7," *Times Free Press*, August 3, 2011; Mary Sanchez, "Tales of terror don't jibe," *Kansas City Star*, November 16, 2011; Aaron M. Little, "Kamal Saleem: A Muslim Cries Out to Jesus," CBN, http://www1.cbn.com/700club/kamal-saleem-muslim-cries-out-jesus; Doug Howard, "Mixed Message," *Books and Culture*, May/June 2010.

10. Tim Murphy, "I Was a Terrorist . . . Seriously," *Mother Jones*, March/April 2012; Gary Schneeberger, "Craze be to Allah," Focus on the Family *Citizen*, November 2006, 10–11; Doug Howard, phone interview with the author, June 28, 2018.

11. Reza Aslan, "Apparently, terrorism pays. It pays very well," CNN, February 27, 2008; Jorg Luyken, "The Palestinian 'Terrorist' Turned Zionist," *Jerusalem Post*, March 30, 2008; Howard, "Mixed Message."

12. Aslan, "Apparently, terrorism pays"; Luyken, "The Palestinian 'Terrorist'"; MacFarquhar, "Speakers at Academy."

13. Ward, "Cedar Hill Baptist"; Murphy, "I Was a Terrorist."

14. Howard, "Mixed Message."

15. "'A Common Word' Christian Response," Yale Center for Faith & Culture, accessed August 8, 2018, https://faith.yale.edu/common-word/common-word-christian-response.

16. "Mohler: Evangelical-Muslim Letter Troubling," A Common Word, January 11, 2008, https://www.acommonword.com/mohler-evangelical-muslim-letter-troubling/; Stephen Adams, "Common Ground?" Focus on the Family *Citizen*, March 2008, 18–23; "NPR comments force out NAE's Cizik," Baptist News Global, December 17, 2008.

17. "Public Expressed Mixed Views of Islam, Mormonism," Pew Research Center, September 25, 2007; "The Religious Dimensions of the Torture Debate," Pew Research Center, April 29, 2009, updated May 7, 2009.

18. Seymour M. Hersh, "The Coming Wars," *The New Yorker*, January 24, 2005.

19. Hersh, "Coming Wars."

20. Sidney Blumenthal, "The religious warrior of Abu Ghraib," *Guardian*, May 19, 2004; Seymour M. Hersh, "Moving Targets," *The New Yorker*, December 15, 2003; Seymour M. Hersh, "Who's In Charge Here?" *New York Times*, November 22, 1987.

21. R. Jeffrey Smith and Josh White, "General's Speeches Broke Rules," *Washington Post*, August 19, 2004; Blumenthal, "Religious Warrior."

22. Smith and White, "General's Speeches"; Holton, *Meltdown*, 229.

23. Blumenthal, "Religious Warrior"; Seymour M. Hersh, "The Gray Zone," *The New Yorker*, May 24, 2004.

24. Dan Lamothe, "Exclusive: Lt. Gen. William Boykin, past Delta Force commander, hit with Army reprimand," *Washington Post*, May 22, 2014; "*The Watchman*: Lt. Gen. Jerry Boykin and Kamal Saleem Discuss 'The Coalition,'" https://www1.cbn.com/video/the-watchman/2015/12/22/the-watchman-lt-gen-jerry-boykin-and-kamal-saleem-discuss-the-coalition, accessed August 9, 2019; "The Coalition:

What Happens When Islam Rules?" November 11, 2014, https://www.frc.org/familypolicylecture/the-coalition-what-happens-when-islam-rules, accessed August 9, 2019.

25. Haberski, *God and War*, 190–92.
26. Bacevich, *New American Militarism*, 31.
27. Bacevich, *New American Militarism*, 14–15, 23–24, 63; Thomas E. Ricks, "The Widening Gap Between the Military and Society," *Atlantic Monthly*, July 1997, quoted in Bacevich, *New American Militarism*, 24.
28. Ed Stoddard, "U.S. evangelical support for Iraq war slipping," Reuters, January 19, 2007; "Thompson Demonstrates Broad Potential Appeal," Pew Research Center, June 4, 2007.
29. Dan Cox, "Young White Evangelicals: Less Republican, Still Conservative," Pew Research Center, September 28, 2007.

Chapter 14: SPIRITUAL BADASSES

1. "Religion and Politics '08: John McCain," Pew Research Center, November 4, 2008; Doug Gross, "Focus on the Family's James Dobson steps down," CNN, February 28, 2009.
2. "Michelle Obama Takes Heat," Fox News, February 19, 2008.
3. The Daily Dish, "The Wright Post 9/11 Sermon," *The Atlantic*, March 22, 2008; "(2003) Rev. Jeremiah Wright, 'Confusing God and Government,'" Blackpast, May 6, 2008.
4. "Barack Obama's Speech on Race," *New York Times*, March 18, 2008.
5. Peter Wehner, "Dobson vs. Obama," *Washington Post*, June 28, 2008.
6. Amy Sullivan, "Is Dobson's Obama Hit Backfiring?" *Time*, June 26, 2008; Gross, "Focus on the Family's James Dobson steps down"; "McCain picks Alaska Gov. Sarah Palin for VP," *Christianity Today*, August 29, 2008.
7. John Piper, "Why a Woman Shouldn't Run for Vice President, but Wise People May Still Vote For Her," Desiring God, November 2, 2008, http://www.desiringgod.org/articles/why-a-woman-shouldnt-run-for-vice-president-but-wise-people-may-still-vote-for-her.
8. "Is Palin an evangelical?" *Christianity Today*, August 30, 2008; Slavoj Zizek, *Living in the End Times* (London: Verso, 2011), 270, quoted in Katz, *Man Enough*, 218; Barbara Bradly Hagerty, "How McCain Shed Pariah Status Among Evangelicals," NPR, *All Things Considered*, October 23, 2008.
9. Martínez and Smith, "How the faithful voted"; Laurie Goodstein, "Obama Made Gains Among Younger Evangelical Voters, Data Show," *New York Times*, Nov. 6, 2008.
10. Goldenberg, "Evangelicals start soul-searching."
11. Bradley Blackburn, "The Rev. Franklin Graham Says President Obama was 'Born a Muslim,'" ABC News, August 20, 2010; Frank Schaeffer, "Franklin Graham Is Big Time Religion's 'Donald Trump,'" *Huffington Post*, April 28, 2011.
12. Jane C. Timm, "Amid call for religious freedom, Values Voter speakers slam Islam,"

MSNBC, September 26, 2014; David Brody and Scott Lamb, *The Faith of Donald J. Trump: A Spiritual Biography* (Northampton, MA: Broadside Books, 2018), 293; "Growing Number of Americans Say Obama is a Muslim," Pew Research Center, August 18, 2010.

13. Brian Montopoli, "Conservatives Fight 'Homosexual Extremist Movement,'" CBS News, September 28, 2009, updated September 29, 2009; Dana Priest and William M. Arkin, "Monitoring America," *Washington Post*, https://web.archive.org/web/20101222221143/http://projects.washingtonpost.com/top-secret-america/articles/monitoring-america/6/.

14. Wayne A. Grudem, *Politics—According to the Bible: A Comprehensive Resource for Understanding Modern Political Issues in Light of Scripture* (Grand Rapids, MI: Zondervan, 2010), 150–51, 388–89, 392, 396, 409–10, 472–73, 527.

15. Martínez and Smith, "How the faithful voted"; Mark Driscoll, Twitter post, January 21, 2013, 8:17 a.m., https://twitter.com/PastorMark/status/293391878949335043.

16. John Fea, *Believe Me: The Evangelical Road to Donald Trump* (Grand Rapids, MI: Eerdmans, 2018), 25.

17. John Piper, "The Folly of Men Arming Women for Combat," Desiring God, January 6, 2014, https://www.desiringgod.org/articles/the-folly-of-men-arming-women-for-combat, accessed January 28, 2019; James Dobson, "Protect Your Kids from Tyrant Obama," WND, May 30, 2016, http://www.wnd.com/2016/05/protect-your-kids-from-tyrant-obama/; Anugrah Kumar, "College Reverses Decision to Fire Lt. Gen Boykin Over Transgender Bathroom Comments," *Christian Post*, May 21, 2016.

18. Mark Joseph, "The President & The Prophet: Obama's Unusual Encounter with Eric Metaxas," *National Review*, February 7, 2012.

19. Eric Metaxas, *Seven Men: And the Secret of Their Greatness* (Nashville, TN: Thomas Nelson, 2016), 47; Jon Ward, "Author Eric Metaxas, evangelical intellectual, chose Trump, and he's sticking with him," Yahoo! News, February 23, 2018.

20. Metaxas, *Seven Men*, xiii.

21. Metaxas, *Seven Men*, xv–xvi.

22. Metaxas, *Seven Men*, xvii–xviii.

23. Sarah Pulliam Bailey, "'Duck Dynasty' success thrives on Christian stereotypes," Religion News Service, August 21, 2013.

24. Pulliam Bailey, "'Duck Dynasty'"; Drew Magary, "What the Duck," *GQ*, December 17, 2013.

25. Moreton, *To Serve God and Wal-Mart*, 90–91.

26. Thomas Kidd, "Duck Dynasty's Cultural Christianity," Patheos, August 27, 2013, http://www.patheos.com/blogs/anxiousbench/2013/08/duck-dynastys-cultural-christianity/.

27. John McDougall, *Jesus Was an Airborne Ranger: Find Your Purpose Following the Warrior Christ* (Colorado Springs, CO: Multnomah, 2015), 11, 101, 114, 119.

28. Jerry Boykin and Stu Weber, *The Warrior Soul: 5 Powerful Principles to Make You a Stronger Man of God* (Lake Mary, FL: Charisma House, 2015), 18, 31–32.

29. Boykin and Weber, *The Warrior Soul*, 45, 86.

30. Boykin and Weber, *The Warrior Soul*, 107–8, 183, 198.

31. Betsy Cooper and Harmeet Kamboj, "Ahead of Farewell Address, Obama's Favora-

bility Across the Country," PRRI, January 9, 2017; Robert P. Jones, *The End of White Christian America* (New York: Simon & Schuster, 2016).

Chapter 15: A NEW HIGH PRIEST

1.   C. Eugene Emery Jr., "Hillary Clinton's approval ratings as secretary of state were high, but they're not now," Politifact, May 22, 2016.
2.   Aaron Blake, "The Final Trump-Clinton Debate Transcript Annotated," *Washington Post*, August 19, 2006; Kevin den Dulk, "What Do We Know about Hillary Clinton and Religious Freedom?" Religious Freedom Institute, October 20, 2016.
3.   Fea, *Believe Me*, 25, 27.
4.   Fea, *Believe Me*, 30–32.
5.   Eric Garcia, "Can Marco Rubio Appeal to Evangelicals?" *Roll Call*, January 8, 2016; Samuel Smith, "Rubio Not Only Candidate With 'Billy Graham' Evangelicals, Cruz Campaign Says," *Christian Post*, January 25, 2016; Brody and Lamb, *Faith of Donald J. Trump*, 179.
6.   Brody and Lamb, *Faith of Donald J. Trump*, 260.
7.   "Full text: Donald Trump announces a presidential bid," *Washington Post*, June 16, 2015.
8.   Jonathan Merritt, "Why Do Evangelicals Support Donald Trump?" *The Atlantic*, September 3, 2015; Sarah Pulliam Bailey, "Which Presidential Candidate Leads among Evangelicals? Right now, it's Donald Trump," *Washington Post*, August 6, 2015; Washington Post-ABC News National Poll, July 16–19, 2015.
9.   Michelle Boorstein, "Why Donald Trump is tearing evangelicals apart," *Washington Post*, March 15, 2016.
10. Robert Costa and Jenna Johnson, "Evangelical leader Jerry Falwell Jr. endorses Trump," *Washington Post*, January 26, 2016.
11. "Donald Trump Speech at Liberty University," CNN Transcripts, January 18, 2016.
12. "Donald Trump Speech at Liberty University."
13. Mitzi Bible, "Donald Trump addresses largest Convocation crowd, praises Liberty's growth," Liberty University, *Liberty News*, September 24, 2012; Karen Swallow Prior, "The Fake 'Holy War' Over Donald Trump's 'Get Even' Advice," *Christianity Today*, October 3, 2012.
14. Robin, *Reactionary Mind*, 29–30.
15. Kelley Smith, "Trump holds campaign rally at Dordt College," KSFY News, January 23, 2016; Boorstein, "Why Donald Trump is tearing evangelicals apart"; Eliza Collins, "Christian leaders balk at Falwell's Trump endorsement," *Politico*, January 26, 2016.
16. Frances Robles and Jim Rutenberg, "The Evangelical, the 'Pool Boy,' the Comedian and Michael Cohen," *New York Times*, June 18, 2019; Nick Gass, "Poll: Evangelicals flocking to Trump," *Politico*, January 26, 2016.
17. Ruth Graham, "The Pundit Pastor," *Slate*, May 14, 2018; Ian Schwartz, "Pastor Jeffress: Without Trump We Will Have Most Pro-Abortion President in History," Real

Clear Politics, February 26, 2016; Bob Allen, "'Evangelical elite' just doesn't get it, claims pastor and Trump supporter," Baptist News Global, March 16, 2016.

18. Bean, "Jesus and John Wayne: Must we choose?"

19. Tessa Berenson, "John Wayne's Daughter Endorses Donald Trump," *Time*, updated January 19, 2016.

20. Russell Moore, "Have Evangelicals Who Support Trump Lost Their Values?" *New York Times*, September 17, 2015; Trip Gabriel, "Donald Trump, Despite Impieties, Wins Hearts of Evangelical Voters," *New York Times*, February 27, 2016; Russell Moore, "Why this election makes me hate the word 'evangelical,'" *Washington Post*, February 29, 2016; Russell Moore, "A White Church No More," *New York Times*, May 6, 2016; Elizabeth Dias, "Donald Trump's Feud With Evangelical Leader Reveals Fault Lines," *Time*, May 9, 2016.

21. Denny Burk, "#NeverTrump has only just started," *Denny Burk* (blog), May 4, 2016, http://www.dennyburk.com/nevertrump-has-only-just-started/; Michael Gerson, "Evangelicals must not bear the mark of Trump," *Washington Post*, June 2, 2016.

22. Gabriel, "Donald Trump, Despite Impieties."

23. Boorstein, "Why Donald Trump"; Trip Gabriel and Michael Luo, "A Born-Again Donald Trump? Believe It, Evangelical Leader Says," *New York Times*, June 25, 2016.

24. Wayne Grudem, "Why Voting for Donald Trump Is a Morally Good Choice," *Townhall*, July 28, 2016.

25. Jonathan Chait, "Mike Pence Strongly Believes Donald Trump's Shoulder Width Guarantees His Foreign-Policy Acumen," *Intelligencer*, August 22, 2017; Chris Cillizza, "Mike Pence compared Donald Trump to Teddy Roosevelt. About that . . ." CNN, August 18, 2017.

26. Ward, "Author Eric Metaxas"; Eric Metaxas, Twitter post, May 22, 2016, 4:57 a.m., https://twitter.com/ericmetaxas/status/734352577710657536; Casey Harper, "Leading Evangelical Makes the Case for Christian Support of Trump," Daily Caller, July 18, 2016.

27. "Evangelicals Rally to Trump, Religious 'Nones' Back Clinton," Pew Research Center, July 13, 2016.

28. Phyllis Schlafly, "The Stupidity of Feminists," Self-Educated American, May 21, 2012, accessed October 19, 2018, https://selfeducatedamerican.com/2012/05/21/the-stupidity-of-feminists/; Brody and Lamb, *Faith of Donald J. Trump*, 241; Rebecca Morin, "Trump honors 'true patriot' Phyllis Schlafly at her funeral," *Politico*, September 10, 2016.

29. "Transcript: Donald Trump's Taped Comments About Women," *New York Times*, October 8, 2016.

30. Wayne Grudem, "Trump's Moral Character and the Election," *Townhall*, October 9, 2016.

31. Sarah Pulliam Bailey, "'Still the best candidate': Some evangelicals still back Trump despite lewd video," *Washington Post*, October 8, 2016.

32. Russell Moore, Twitter post, October 7, 2016, 6:54 p.m., https://twitter.com/drmoore/status/784572768922791936; John Piper, "Christian, You are Free Not to Vote," Desiring God, November 3, 2016, https://www.desiringgod.org/messages/sons-of-freedom-and-joy/excerpts/christian-you-are-free-not-to-vote; Ed Stetzer,

"Evangelicals: This Is What It Looks Like When You Sell Your Soul For a Bowl of Trump," *Christianity Today*, November 2, 2016.

33. Caitlin Moscatello, "Our Bodies, Their God," *The Cut*, November 17, 2016; Anne Helen Petersen, "The New Evangelical Woman Vs. Trump," BuzzFeed News, November 7, 2016; Tiffany Stanley, "This Evangelical Leader Denounced Trump. Then the Death Threats Started," *Politico*, December 17, 2017.

34. Smith and Martínez, "How the faithful voted."

35. "For GOP Voters, a Winding Path to a Trump Nomination," Pew Research Center, July 18, 2016; Gregory A. Smith, "Churchgoing Republicans, once skeptical of Trump, now support him," Pew Research Center, July 21, 2018; Timothy Gloege, "#Itsnotus: Being Evangelical Means Never Having To Say You're Sorry," *Religion Dispatches*, January 3, 2018; Gregory A. Smith, "Among white evangelicals, regular churchgoers are the most supportive of Trump," Pew Research Center, April 26, 2017.

36. Daniel Cox, Rachel Lienesch, and Robert P. Jones, "Beyond Economics: Fears of Cultural Displacement Pushed the White Working Class to Trump," PRRI, May 9, 2017; Janelle S. Wong, *Immigrants, Evangelicals, and Politics in an Era of Demographic Change* (New York: Russell Sage Foundation, 2018); Diana C. Mutz, "Status threat, not economic hardship, explains the 2016 presidential vote," *PNAS*, May 8, 2018, first published April 23, 2018; Green et al., *Religion and the Culture Wars*, 268.

37. Chris Moody, "The Survival of a Southern Baptist Who Dared to Oppose Trump," CNN Politics, July 2017.

38. Sarah Pulliam Bailey, "The Trump effect? A stunning number of evangelicals will now accept politicians' 'immoral' acts," *Washington Post*, October 19, 2016; Tom Gjelten, "White Evangelicals Conflicted by Accusations Against Roy Moore," NPR, November 14, 2017.

39. Brody and Lamb, *Faith of Donald J. Trump*, 260.

40. Brody and Lamb, *Faith of Donald J. Trump*, 19–21.

41. Brody and Lamb, *Faith of Donald J. Trump*, 72.

42. Brody and Lamb, *Faith of Donald J. Trump*, 76–77.

43. Brody and Lamb, *Faith of Donald J. Trump*, 75–76.

44. Betsy Cooper et al., "The Divide Over America's Future: 1950 or 2050?" PRRI, October 25, 2016.

Chapter 16: EVANGELICAL MULLIGANS: A HISTORY

1. Smith, "Among white evangelicals."

2. Michael Paulsen, "A Brash Style That Filled Pews, Until Followers Had Their Fill," *New York Times*, August 22, 2014; Warren Cole Smith, "Unreal sales for Driscoll's *Real Marriage*," *World*, March 5, 2014.

3. Douglas Wilson, "Ten Notes on the Driscoll Dogpile," *Blog & Mablog*, August 25, 2014, https://dougwils.com/the-church/ten-notes-on-the-driscoll-dogpile.html; Douglas Wilson, "Ask Doug: What Are Your Thoughts on the Mark Driscoll Situation," *Canon Wired*, October 20, 2014, http://www.canonwired.com/featured/

thoughts-on-the-mark-driscoll-situation/; John Piper, "Do You Regret Partnering with Mark Driscoll?" Desiring God, November 13, 2014, http://www.desiringgod .org/interviews/do-you-regret-partnering-with-mark-driscoll; "Reflections on Mark Driscoll and the Church," John Piper interviewed by Norm Funk, July 31, 2015, YouTube, https://www.youtube.com/watch?v=4Yhn_4mmowU, accessed August 8, 2018; Sarah Pulliam Bailey, "Mark Driscoll charged with abusive behavior by 21 former Mars Hill pastors," *Washington Post*, August 22, 2014.

4.   T. F. Charlton, "A Church Group, A Lawsuit, and a Culture of Abuse," *Religion Dispatches*, March 6, 2013.

5.   Kate Shellnutt, "Darrin Patrick Removed from Acts 29 Megachurch for 'Historical Pattern of Sin,'" *Christianity Today*, April 13, 2016; Eric Kelderman, "Accreditor Cites Leadership Problems in Keeping Master's U. on Probation," *Chronicle of Higher Education*, March 8, 2019; Samuel Smith, "John MacArthur's Master's University Put on Probation by Accrediting Agency," *Christian Post*, August 22, 2018; Julie Roys, "Hard times at Harvest," *World Magazine*, December 13, 2018; Emily McFarlan Miller, "James MacDonald fired as Harvest Bible Chapel pastor," Religion News Service, February 13, 2019.

6.   Meghan Keneally, "List of Trump's accusers and their allegations of sexual misconduct," ABC News, June 25, 2019.

7.   Katie Frost, "Dr. James Dobson Endorses Judge Roy Moore," Judge Roy Moore U.S. Senate, https://www.roymoore.org/Press-Releases/38/DR.-JAMES-DOBSON -ENDORSES-JUDGE-ROY-MOORE; Michelle Boorstein, "Alabama state official defends Roy Moore, citing Joseph and Mary; 'They became parents of Jesus,'" *Washington Post*, November 10, 2017; Russell Moore, Twitter post, November 13, 2017, 2:16 p.m., https://twitter.com/drmoore/status/930197784959115264; Carlos Ballesteros, "Alabama Evangelicals More Likely to Support Roy Moore After Sexual Assault Allegations, Poll Shows," *Newsweek*, November 12, 2017; "Exit poll results: How different groups voted in Alabama," *Washington Post*, December 13, 2018; Amy Yurkanin, "Roy Moore had ties to groups that didn't believe in gender equality," AL.com, December 9, 2017, updated March 6, 2018.

8.   Edward-Isaac Dovere, "Tony Perkins: Trump gets 'a Mulligan' on Life, Stormy Daniels," *Politico*, January 23, 2018.

9.   "NPR/PBS News Hour/Marist Poll National Tables September 22nd through September 24th, 2018," NPR, September 22–24, 2018, http://maristpoll.marist.edu/ wp-content/uploads/2018/09/NPR_PBS-NewsHour_Marist-Poll_USA-NOS-and -Tables_1809251359.pdf#page=3.

10.   Kathryn Joyce, "By Grace Alone: The Next Christian Sex-Abuse Scandal," *Kathryn Joyce* (blog), May 5, 2014, http://kathrynjoyce.com/by-grace-alone-the-next-christian -sex-abuse-scandal/, accessed August 12, 2019.

11.   "Evangelical Leader quits, denies male escort's allegations," CNN, November 2, 2006.

12.   "Evangelical leader quits"; David Goldstein, "Who's to blame for Pastor Haggard's fall from grace? His fat, lazy wife," *Huffington Post*, November 4, 2006, updated May 25, 2011.

13.   Randy Turner, "Judge to Kanakuk's Joe White: Stay away from sex abuse victim," *Turner Report*, October 4, 2011, https://rturner229.blogspot.com/2011/10/judge -to-kanakuks-joe-white-stay-away.html; Andrew W. Griffin, "Sandusky-like camp

director arrested in Missouri—what did Kanakuk's 'godlike' Joe White know?" *Red Dirt Report*, August 27, 2012, http://www.reddirtreport.com/red-dirt-news/ sandusky-camp-director-arrested-missouri-what-did-kanakuks-godlike-joe-white -know. ChristianPost.com, "Christian men's conference decried for featuring speakers accused of rape, sex abuse cover-up," *Fox News*, February 18, 2017, updated July 5, 2017, https://www.foxnews.com/us/christian-mens-conference-decried-for-featuring -speakers-accused-of-rape-sex-abuse-cover-up.

14. Tiffany Stanley, "The Sex-Abuse Scandal That Devastated a Suburban Megachurch," *Washingtonian*, February 14, 2016.

15. C. J. Mahaney, *Sex, Romance, and the Glory of God: What Every Christian Husband Needs to Know* (Wheaton, IL: Crossway Books, 2004), 16, 87, 98, 123; Charlton, "A Church Group."

16. Bob Allen, "Mahaney gets support from John Piper," Baptist News Global, February 18, 2103; Sarah Pulliam Bailey, "Evangelical leaders stand by pastor accused of abuse cover-up," *Washington Post*, May 24, 2013; Julie Anne Smith, "Mohler, Dever, and Duncan break their silence and release statement in support of C.J. Mahaney," Spiritual Sounding Board, May 23, 2013, https://spiritualsoundingboard .com/2013/05/23/mohler-dever-and-duncan-issue-statement-in-support-of-c-j -mahaney/, accessed July 1, 2019; Benjamin Sledge, "Together for the Go$pel," *Medium*, January 28, 2019, https://medium.com/s/story/together-for-the-go -pel-26a23116d46b; Don Carson and Justin Taylor, "Why We Have Been Silent about the SGM Lawsuit," The Gospel Coalition, May 24, 2013, https://www .thegospelcoalition.org/article/why-we-have-been-silent-about-the-sgm-lawsuit/.

17. Watchkeep (Amy Smith), "Albert Mohler and CJ Mahaney," (sound recording) 2016, https://soundcloud.com/watchkeep/albert-mohler-and-cj-mahaney, accessed August 13, 2018; Bob Allen, "Al Mohler says he was wrong about C.J. Mahaney," Baptist News Global, February 18, 2019.

18. Sledge, "Together for the Go$pel."

19. Sarah Pulliam Bailey, "New charges allege religious leader, who has ties to the Duggars, sexually abused women," *Washington Post*, January 6, 2016; Bill Gothard, "Wisdom Booklet 36," 1839, quoted in Sara Jones, "An ATI Education, Final Chapter: Guilty Silence," Recovering Grace, January 4, 2016, http:// www.recoveringgrace.org/2016/01/an-ati-education-final-chapter-guilty-silence/, accessed August 7, 2018; "Statement from Recovering Grace regarding the lawsuit against Bill Gothard and IBLP," Recovering Grace, March 28, 2018, http://www .recoveringgrace.org/2018/03/statement-from-recovering-grace-regarding-the -lawsuit-against-bill-gothard-and-iblp/#more, accessed August 7, 2018. See also Libby Anne, "Bill Gothard Explains Road Safety (aka How Not to Get Raped)," Patheos, August 17, 2015, accessed September 6, 2019, https://www.patheos.com/ blogs/lovejoyfeminism/2015/08/bill-gothard-explains-road-safety-aka-how-not-to -get-raped.html.

20. Lourdes Torres-Manteufel v. Douglas Phillips et al., April 15, 2014, https://www.wnd .com/files/2014/04/TorresComplaintFinalwithCoverSheet.pdf, 1–15.

21. Jamie Dean, "What Went Wrong? An In-depth Report on the Vision Forum Scandal," World News Service, March 25, 2014; Douglas Wilson, "Vice, Victims, and Vision Forum," *Blog & Mablog*, Friday, April 18, 2014, https://dougwils.com/s7

-engaging-the-culture/vice-victims-and-vision-forum.html, accessed August 12, 2019.

22. Wilson, *Her Hand in Marriage*, 48, 54, 85; Wilson, *Fidelity*, 62; Doug Wilson, "Mark Driscoll and the Problems of Citation," *Blog & Mablog*, December 9, 2013, accessed June 22, 2017, https://dougwils.com/s7-engaging-the-culture/mark-driscoll -and-problems-of-citation.html#more-105845.

23. Wilson, "Vice, Victims, and Vision Forum"; Wilson, *Fidelity*, 85; "Douglas Wilson to Judge Stegner: "I have been asked to provide a letter on behalf of Steven Sitler, which I am happy to do," Steven Sitler, August 19, 2005, http://sitler .moscowid.net/2005/08/19/douglas-wilson-to-judge-stegner-i-have-been-asked-to -provide-a-letter-on-behalf-of-steven-sitler-which-i-am-happy-to-do/; Rod Dreher, "Scandal in Moscow," *American Conservative*, September 29, 2015, https://www .theamericanconservative.com/dreher/scandal-in-moscow/; Doug Wilson, "An Open Letter from Christ Church on Steven Sitler," *Blog & Mablog*, September 5, 2015, accessed June 1, 2017, https://dougwils.com/books-and-culture/s7-engaging-the -culture/an-open-letter-from-christ-church-on-steven-sitler.html; Doug Wilson, "The High Mountain Air of Public Calumny," *Blog & Mablog*, September 7, 2015, accessed June 1, 2017, https://web.archive.org/web/20150915024225/http:/dougwils.com/s7 -engaging-the-culture/the-high-mountain-air-of-public-calumny.html.

24. F. L. Stollar, "The Jamin C. Wight Story: The Other Child Molester in Doug Wilson's Closet," Homeschoolers Anonymous, September 8, 2015, https:// homeschoolersanonymous.org/2015/09/08/the-jamin-c-wight-story-the-other-child -molester-in-doug-wilsons-closet/. Wilson offers his own version of events with regard to Sitler and Wight in Rod Dreher, "Doug Wilson's 'Reluctant Response,'" *American Conservative*, October 1, 2015.

25. Abby Ohlheiser, "Josh Duggar molested four of his sisters and a babysitter, parents tell Fox news," *Washington Post*, June 4, 2015.

26. Richard Pérez-Peña, "Bob Jones University Blamed Victims of Sexual Assaults, Not Abusers, Report Says," *New York Times*, December 11, 2014; Kiera Feldman, "Sexual Assault at God's Harvard," *New Republic*, February 17, 2014.

27. Smith, "Let Us Prey"; Sarah Smith, "Hundreds of sex abuse allegations found in fundamental Baptist churches across U.S.," *Fort Worth Star-Telegram*, December 9, 2018.

28. Smith, "Hundreds of sex abuse allegations"; Smith, "Let Us Prey."

29. Smith, "Let Us Prey."

30. "I Was Assaulted. He Was Applauded," *New York Times*, March 9, 2018.

31. Laurie Goodstein, "He's a Superstar Pastor," *New York Times*, August 5, 2018.

32. Michelle Boorstein and Sarah Pulliam Bailey, "How women led to the dramatic rise and fall of Southern Baptist leader Paige Patterson," *Washington Post*, June 10, 2014; Bobby Ross Jr., Sarah Pulliam Bailey, and Michelle Boorstein, "Prominent Southern Baptist leader removed as seminary president following controversial remarks about abused women," *Washington Post*, May 23, 2018; Robert Downen, "More men accuse former Texas judge, Baptist leader of sexual misconduct," *Houston Chronicle*, April 13, 2018. Robert Downen, "The women are hurting," *Houston Chronicle*, August 22, 2019.

33. Smith, "Hundreds of Sex Abuse Allegations."

34. Robert Downen, Lise Olsen, and John Tedesco, "Abuse of Faith," *Houston Chronicle*,

February 10, 2019; Kate Shellnutt, "Report: How Southern Baptists Failed to Care About Abuse," *Christianity Today*, June 10, 2019; Michael Gryboski, "Southern Baptist Convention Sever Ties With Kentucky Churches Over Female Pastors," *Christian Post*, December 17, 2015.

35. Rachael Denhollander and Morgan Lee, "My Larry Nassar Testimony Went Viral. But There's More to the Gospel Than Forgiveness," *Christianity Today*, January 31, 2018.

36. Denhollander and Lee, "My Larry Nassar Testimony Went Viral."

37. Al Mohler, "The Humiliation of the Southern Baptist Convention," *Christianity Today*, May 23, 2018.

38. Mohler, "The Humiliation of the Southern Baptist Convention"; Russell Moore, "Will Complementarianism Survive After the #MeToo Movement?" Russell Moore, August 3, 2018, https://www.russellmoore.com/2018/08/03/will -complementarianism-survive-after-metoo/, accessed August 15, 2018.

39. John Piper, "Sex-Abuse Allegations and the Egalitarian Myth," Desiring God, March 16, 2018, https://www.desiringgod.org/interviews/sex-abuse-allegations-and-the -egalitarian-myth; John Piper, "Does a woman submit to abuse?" *Ask Pastor John*, September 1, 2009, YouTube, https://www.youtube.com/watch?v=3OkUPc2NLrM.

40. Nathan A. Finn, "Complementarian Caricature," *Journal of Biblical Manhood and Womanhood*, Fall 2010, 48–49.

CONCLUSION

1. Gaither Vocal Band, "Jesus And John Wayne," track 3 on *Lovin' Life*, Spring House, 2008, compact disc.

2. Niraj Chokshi, "Oliver North Is Named N.R.A. President," *New York Times*, May 7, 2018; Bobby Ross Jr., " 'Jesus loves me and my guns': Faith and firearms touted at the NRA's prayer breakfast," *Washington Post*, May 7, 2018; Shellnut, "Packing in the Pews."

3. Nancy LeTourneau, "How Identity Politics Fuels the NRA and White Evangelicals," *Washington Monthly*, March 5, 2018; Peter Beinart, "Conservatives Are Losing the Culture War Over Guns," *The Atlantic*, March 1, 2018.

4. Cooper et al., "How Americans View Immigrants"; Hannah Hartig, "Republicans turn more negative toward refugees as number admitted to U.S. plummets," Pew Research Center, May 24, 2018; "Data Shows How Passionate and Partisan Americans are About the Border Wall," PRRI, January 8, 2019; "Evangelical Views on Immigration," LifeWay Research, February 2015.

5. Bob Allen, " 'Evangelical elite' just doesn't get it, claims pastor and Trump supporter," *Baptist News*, March 16, 2016; Kristin Kobes Du Mez, "Understanding White Evangelical Views on Immigration," *Harvard Divinity Bulletin* 46, nos. 1 & 2 (Spring/ Summer 2018).

6. Caleb Lindgren, "Gender and the Trinity: From Proxy War to Civil War," *Christianity Today*, June 16, 2016; Giles, *Rise and Fall of the Complementarian Doctrine*.

7. I am indebted to Corrin Van Bemden, Corrie Bakker, Steve McMullen, Laura McMullen, Jenna Hunt, Brooklyn Walker, Rhonda Mejeur, Jonathan Harwell, Bryan

Berghoef, Tami Parks, Joe Stubenrauch, Katherine Swart, and Tim Krueger for sharing these examples.

8. I am grateful to Rachel Maxson and Mandy McMichael for bringing these to my
    attention.

9. Kristin Kobes Du Mez, "Hobby Lobby Evangelicalism," Patheos, September 6,
    2018, https://www.patheos.com/blogs/anxiousbench/2018/09/hobby-lobby
    -evangelicalism/.

10. Don Jacobson, phone interview with the author, February 13, 2019.

11. Carlos Maza, "This Right-Wing Legal Powerhouse Wants To Make Gay Sex Illegal,"
    Media Matters, November 19, 2014; Claire Provost and Marty Fitzgerald, "Revealed:
    Trump-linked US Christian 'fundamentalists' pour millions of 'dark money' into
    Europe, boosting the far right," openDemocracy, March 27, 2019; Jack Jenkins,
    "When Franklin Graham Met Putin," Religion News Service, August 7, 2018; Eliza
    Griswold, "Franklin Graham's Uneasy Alliance with Donald Trump," The New
    Yorker, September 11, 2018; Jack Jenkins, "The emerging alliance between Putin and
    Trump's God squad," ThinkProgress, July 12, 2017.

12. Daniel Rück, FB message, February 6, 2018.

13. Name withheld, FB message, January 10, 2019; Name withheld, email correspon-
    dence, February 25, 2019.

14. Name withheld, email correspondence, February 25, 2019.

15. Sara Moslener, "Sexual Purity, #ChurchToo, and the Crisis of Male Evangelical Lead-
    ership," Religion & Politics, June 12, 2018; "Former Evangelical Pastor Rethinks His
    Approach to Courtship," Weekend Edition Sunday, NPR, July 10, 2016.

16. Don Jacobson, phone interview with the author, February 13, 2019. In later e-mail
    correspondence (June 20, 2019), Jacobsen added that he still agrees with many of the
    teachings of those writers, but that many of the new strains have gone too far: "Jesus
    said to make disciples of all men, not to make Americans of all men."

17. Michael Gerson, "The Last Temptation," The Atlantic, April 2018; Cal Thomas,
    "Are today's Evangelicals following Jesus or following Trump?" Fox News "Opin-
    ion," April 24, 2018, https://www.foxnews.com/opinion/cal-thomas-are-todays
    -evangelicals-following-jesus-or-following-trump.

INDEX

Note: Page numbers in *italics* refer to illustrations.